MW01480270

Spinoza's Revelation
Religion, Democracy, and Reason

Nancy Levene reinterprets a major early modern philosopher, Benedict de Spinoza – a Jew who was rejected by the Jewish community of his day but whose thought contains, and critiques, both Jewish and Christian ideas. It foregrounds the connection of religion, democracy, and reason, showing that Spinoza's theories of the Bible, the theologico-political, and the philosophical all involve the concepts of equality and sovereignty. Professor Levene argues that Spinoza's concept of revelation is the key to this connection, and above all to Spinoza's view of human power. This is to shift the emphasis in Spinoza's thought from the language of *amor Dei* (love of God) to the language of *libertas humana* (human freedom) without losing either the dialectic of his most striking claim – that man is God to man – or the Jewish and Christian elements in his thought. Original and thoughtfully argued, this book offers new insights into Spinoza's thought and should have wide appeal.

NANCY K. LEVENE is Associate Professor of Religious Studies at Indiana University, Bloomington, Indiana. She is coeditor, with Peter Ochs, of *Textual Reasonings: Jewish Philosophy and Text Study at the End of the Twentieth Century* (2002).

Spinoza's Revelation

Religion, Democracy, and Reason

Nancy K. Levene

CAMBRIDGE
UNIVERSITY PRESS

PUBLISHED BY THE PRESS SYNDICATE OF THE UNIVERSITY OF CAMBRIDGE
The Pitt Building, Trumpington Street, Cambridge, United Kingdom

CAMBRIDGE UNIVERSITY PRESS
The Edinburgh Building, Cambridge, CB2 2RU, UK
40 West 20th Street, New York, NY 10011-4211, USA
477 Williamstown Road, Port Melbourne, VIC 3207, Australia
Ruiz de Alarcón 13, 28014 Madrid, Spain
Dock House, The Waterfront, Cape Town 8001, South Africa

http://www.cambridge.org

© Nancy K. Levene 2004

This book is in copyright. Subject to statutory exception
and to the provisions of relevant collective licensing agreements,
no reproduction of any part may take place without
the written permission of Cambridge University Press.

First published 2004

Printed in the United Kingdom at the University Press, Cambridge

Typeface Plantin 10/12 pt.   *System* LaTeX 2$_\varepsilon$ [TB]

A catalogue record for this book is available from the British Library

ISBN 0 521 83070 2 hardback

The publisher has used its best endeavours to ensure that the URLs for external websites
referred to in this book are correct and active at the time of going to press. However, the
publisher has no responsibility for the websites and can make no guarantee that a site will
remain live or that the content is or will remain appropriate.

For my parents, Aasta and Sam Levene
with love and gratitude

[H]e who practices justice and charity in accordance with God's command is fulfilling God's law, from which justice and charity have the force of law and command. And here I acknowledge no distinction whether it is by the natural light of reason or by revelation that God teaches and commands the true practice of justice and charity, for it matters not how the practice of these virtues is revealed to us as long as it holds the place of supreme authority and is the supreme law for men. So that if I now show that justice and charity can acquire the force of law and command only through the right of the state, I can readily draw the conclusion – since the state's right is vested in the sovereign alone – that religion can acquire the force of law only from the decree of those who have the right to command, and that God has no special sovereignty over men save through the medium of those who hold sovereignty.

(TTP, 219–220)

Contents

Preface

In this book I argue that what is most at stake in Spinoza's thought, *libertas humana* (human freedom), can only be understood as the labor of human beings to become increasingly like God, a labor fraught with philosophical, theological, and political peril. Philosophically, the challenge is to understand God as neither internal nor external to human striving – neither transcendent of nor immanent in human existence – but as the continually revealed difference between human beings in bondage and human beings in freedom. This is to see, on the one hand, that human beings are most empowered in their relations with each other: "Man is God to man," Spinoza tells us (E IV p35s). But it is also to see that the obstacles to realizing (enacting, creating) this truth are profound – rooted in nature and culture alike. Unlike traditional theistic pictures, Spinoza's view does not rule out the attainment of *libertas* from the outset – God is not forever beyond human grasp. But it becomes clear that placing God between human beings serves precisely to reveal how difficult (*because* possible) this life's work is – how unattainable God (freedom) can truly seem once human beings can no longer console themselves with the "humility" that they will never attain it.

Theologically and politically, it is to tackle several related issues. Religion, for Spinoza, means at least two things. It refers most basically to the divine law, "the knowledge and love of God" that is "our supreme good and blessedness" (TTP, 51). The divine law is rational, universal, and true, and is the foundation of enlightenment in all senses. Yet religion also refers to human laws, to those laws that are enacted in particular times and places as interpretations of the divine law, or as manipulations of it. This second notion of religion is at once rooted in political life and also a dire threat to it. For those laws that claim divine authority will be most effective at galvanizing the majority, for good and for ill, and they will also, inevitably, attempt to set themselves up as an autonomous power, a "dominion within a dominion" (E III pref), in competition with legitimate sovereign political power. That the divine law taken in itself is rational does not prevent its turbulent involvement in human conflicts, and indeed, more strongly, this involvement is part and parcel of the divine law itself, for, as Spinoza puts it, "religion can acquire the force of law only from the decree of those who have the right to command, and . . . God has no special sovereignty over men save through the medium of those who hold sovereignty" (TTP, 220). This key statement reveals Spinoza's dual commitments to truth and interpretation, religion and law, the divine and the human, the rational and the revealed that are, I show, at the heart of his work. What Spinoza calls true religion is not the divine law taken in its pristine, apolitical form as opposed to its false interpretations by flawed human beings. True religion is the exceedingly delicate and always unstable balance between the commands of God which issue in universal principles of justice and charity and the commands of the political sovereign whose concern is peace and security for its particular realm; false religion is simply the tipping of this balance at the expense of one side or the other. Religion, the divine law, can only be true if it is also political, human. Politics, human law, can only be true if it is also divine, for "I acknowledge no distinction whether it is by the natural light of reason or by revelation that God teaches and commands the true practice of justice and charity, for it matters not how the practice of these virtues is revealed to us as long as it holds the place of supreme authority and is the supreme law for men" (TTP, 219–220).

Theology, in Spinoza's parlance, also has this dual reference. On the one hand, it refers to two kinds of unscrupulous interpreters of the divine law: those who seek to divide the divine from the human as a way to divide the privileged few (who are to have special access to the truth) from the ignorant many (who are denied such access); and those who seek to conflate the divine and the human by claiming that the divine law is only available to one particular people, in one particular human law. To the first, he insists that the few and the many are identically in the position of having to construct a particular polity commensurate with universal commands (a job for ordinary human beings, not for God or his philosophical-theological experts) – that human law cannot be abandoned for the presumed brighter truth of the divine law since the latter does not command without the former. To the second, he insists that no particular polity is the sole repository of divinity and that the mark of chosenness is simply the fact of enacting divine laws and not of possessing some divine origin.

On the other hand, theology refers to the prophetic task of enacting such divine laws, as distinct from the "knowledge and love of God" which the *Ethics* calls *beatitudo*, blessedness. Theology (prophecy) and philosophy (reason) are separate (*separare*), sovereign, equal, Spinoza insists (TTP, 170). The theologian, the prophet, is the one who may not "know" the psychological, emotional, and ontological obstacles to freedom – she may not have read the *Ethics* – but she knows that such knowledge is not the only avenue to what Spinoza calls *salus*, salvation, which is not for philosophers alone. This is emphatically not to say that salvation is a lesser form of enlightenment for Spinoza. Indeed, I argue that the efforts to square Spinoza's notions of blessedness and salvation by placing the latter on a lower level than the former (e.g., blessedness is theoretical, eternal, true; salvation is practical, historical, useful) have missed Spinoza's crucial reason for separating philosophy and theology in the first place, which is to show that they cannot be understood separately outside of the political existence that connects them ("for God has no special sovereignty over men"). While it is possible to speak in a preliminary way of a difference in Spinoza between theoretical and practical truth – between truths that concern rational understanding and truths that concern how to act – this distinction cannot be used to justify the assumption that these truths correspond to two different ways of living in the world, one the individual, philosophical pursuit of the highest good and the other the (less privileged) pursuit of common goods that simply enable societies to function. This distinction – between truth and practice, individual and social, philosophy and theology, truth and power – ultimately does not hold up in Spinoza and falsifies his conclusions.

Spinoza does think there are greater and lesser kinds of knowledge (power), greater and lesser forms of ignorance (disempowerment). He does think the former is directly connected to understanding the causes of things and that this understanding is exceedingly difficult to achieve and will not be pursued by all, or even most. But he also thinks that to construct and live according to laws, dogmas, commands that prioritize love, friendship, justice, and charity is not only just as valuable as "knowing" these things in their philosophical complexity; it is, if realized, the same thing. In other words, justice and charity (leading to *salus*) are no less complex and laborious than the "knowledge and love of God" (leading to *beatitudo*) and thus the few (who pursue philosophy) and the many (who are "merely" capable of justice and charity) will each find that the obstacles are the same, for "all men are born in a state of complete ignorance, and before they can learn the true way of life and acquire a virtuous disposition, even if they have been well brought up, a great part of their life has gone by" (TTP, 180). In Spinoza's mind, if the obstacles to understanding are no less political than they are philosophical, this is because understanding itself is no less political than it is philosophical. If indeed it does not matter "whether it is by the natural light of reason or by revelation that God teaches and commands the true practice of justice and charity," this is because this true practice – both rational and revealed – is the supreme task commanding all human beings equally. It is human beings who conjoin the separation between (God as) reason and (God as) practice, law, command.

Religion is thus a particularly rich concept for Spinoza. On its own it encapsulates the major tension his work enunciates between what is rational and what is faithful; what are "eternal truths" and what are laws and commands (TTP, 247, n. 31); what is universal and what is political. It is also the place in his work where his rhetoric is the most difficult to negotiate. Spinoza's genuine criticisms of religion – his pronounced exasperation at despots, experts, and those seeking to foster hate and contention in religion's name – lead him to suggest in places that this tension is in fact a simple opposition: that ultimately one can have access to "eternal truths" separate from laws and commands; that if human beings were genuinely rational they would have no need of laws at all; and thus that politics, the construction of just laws, is, for the truly chosen, but a prolegomenon to achieving wisdom beyond the law. This suggestion is nowhere in evidence in the *Ethics*, which maintains from beginning to end that genuine rationality is always about lawfulness (both the natural law that binds us and the human and divine laws that command us), and thus that no one escapes its challenges. But it does pop up in several places in the TTP – in the notion that "simple obedience" is a way for the majority to achieve salvation (presumably in distinction to the learned, who can be truly free and thus not obedient) (TTP, 177); in the contention that the wisdom of the prophets was mere "moral certainty" as opposed to the "mathematical certainty" that is far superior (TTP, 24); in the suggestion that the mind, the intellect, is the true site of the handwriting of God as opposed to "carnal man," who seeks only to feed his "appetites" (TTP, 52).

It is not that Spinoza did not *mean* these distinctions. He clearly felt that philosophy was never going to be the desired occupation of more than a tiny minority, that it was enough for the majority to devote themselves to "simple obedience," which he defines as "justice and charity, or love towards one's neighbor" (TTP, 167), for "all men without exception are capable of obedience, while there are only a few – in proportion to the whole of humanity – who acquire a virtuous disposition under the guidance of reason alone" (TTP, 177–178). Such obedience, Spinoza says, is a "dogma of universal faith," and if "faith requires not so much true dogmas as pious dogmas," this nevertheless does not mean the majority are incapable of greater understanding but only that inasmuch as they do not possess it, they can still be saved (TTP, 166). The prophets, Spinoza held, were such ordinary pious people, at once promoters and exemplars of the pious dogmas of faith. They cannot be expected to have known what they knew with mathematical certainty. But, given their authority (and the authority of the Bible), Spinoza felt the need to defend the "mind" against carnal man, truth against prophecy, insofar as the latter unthinkingly prefers miracles designed to impress the senses to what the mind knows without such miracles.

But the rhetoric of separation (between faith and philosophy, prophecy and truth, obedience and understanding) in the TTP easily overwhelms the more subtle point Spinoza is making, which is that separation is the key to relation. To this end, it is not enough to say that the *Ethics* (with its connection of determination and freedom, mathematics and moral- ity, the mind and the appetite) reveals the rhetoric of the hierarchy of one to the other to be utterly spurious according to Spinoza's first prin- ciples. It is that, even as Spinoza periodically indulges in this rhetoric, the TTP is itself a sustained critique of it. Spinoza's language of "reason alone" and "eternal truth" (outside of law) is baffling precisely because what Spinoza shows in the TTP is that the very notion of an "eternal truth" is constituted – politically and hermeneutically – through a pact: between human beings and God, between human being and human be- ing, between text and reader, mind and history, self and other – that God has no special sovereignty over human beings save through the human sovereignty over God. To say, then, that the one who can embrace "divine commandments" as "eternal truths" is the one who can "love God, but not obey him" (i.e., the one whose obedience "passes into love") is to say that the love of God involves obedience not to God but to human beings (to oneself and others), to "those who hold sovereignty" (TTP, 248). It is not obedience that disappears with the appearance of truth; it is the very image of God as a sovereign in competition with human sovereignty, and thus the very notion of an eternal truth that would preexist human efforts to practice it. When Spinoza says (in a footnote to the TTP) that "I have called [the love of God] a law in the same sense as philosophers apply the term 'law' to the universal rules of Nature according to which all things come to pass," he directly contradicts what the TTP otherwise consistently argues, which is that both divine and human laws (unlike natural law) depend "not on Nature's necessity" but on "human will," as law that "men lay down for themselves or for others to some end" (TTP, 49–50).

This is not a matter of deciding which is Spinoza's true view, but of noticing that, in places, he is not careful enough to encapsulate his own conclusions – that obedience "passes into love" (of God) no more than love (of God) passes into obedience (to human beings), and thus that "simple obedience" is never simple. It is a matter of reading Spinoza, as he would have us read the Bible, according to his own standards. For indeed what Spinoza argues is that the "fiction" of covenant (making, originating, revealing) is the only way to make sense of the way in which human beings are themselves not given (the eternal, the good, the truth, the end) in nature but made, makers of the eternal, the good, the truth, the end in nature. It is the labor of relationship – *pactum* – that, in the beginning, makes what is natural also cultural, what is divine also human, what is determining also free.

What the TTP thus shows is that the very notion of an "eternal truth" which preexists covenant – so at odds with his two key notions in the *Ethics*, the *causa sui*, the eternal truth which originates itself, and *conatus*, the work of doing so – is also the grossest tyranny, subjecting minds to something they can never attain and creating political orders divided between those (experts) who know they are ignorant and those who, under this sign, they claim to rule. Whether in his insistence that the sacred can emerge only from the mutual sovereignty of text and mind, or whether in his elaboration of covenant as that which structures both religion and politics, Spinoza is consistent, and even ruthless in demolishing the pretense of human beings to avoid the work of relationship, interpretation, and law – to take refuge in pristine "eternal truths" that are simply there to be discovered. His suggestion that obedience (salvation) is easy and philosophy (blessedness) hard is no more true than the reverse: that philosophy is easy and obedience hard, for philosophy (no less than prophecy) can easily deceive itself that it is extraordinary, miraculous, privileged. Whether by reason or revelation, blessedness and salvation require the same immense effort: "no one enjoys blessedness because he has restrained the affects. Instead, the power to restrain lusts arises from blessedness itself" (E V p42dem). To paraphrase, no one enjoys truth because she obeys; instead the power to obey arises from truth. Neither truth nor obedience is a shortcut for anyone. Spinoza's critique is thus of the subordination of politics to religion, theology to philosophy, faith to reason, multitude to learned (and, in each case, vice versa), and his defense is of human power and its fragility as the pivot that keeps each side of these distinctions sovereign. This critique, this defense, is the heart of what follows.

A word on audience. This book brings together several strands of Spinoza's thought – his views on religion and the Bible, interpretation, democracy, and rationality – showing that each involves the concepts of equality and sovereignty and, above all, revelation (covenant, creation, making). I am indebted to the many close readers of Spinoza whose works have helped me to find my way through his difficulties, and I hope my own work contributes to these efforts. It may cut a rather broader swath through Spinoza's major ideas than suits some, but I have attempted to capture a snapshot, as it were, of the dynamism and creativity of Spinoza's project overall. In places, my account of Spinoza's metaphysical views is quite compressed and I do not seek here to indicate more than a general sense of the complexity and fascination of these views. This also goes for the technical commentaries on Spinoza that animate the world of Spinoza scholarship. I have flagged only those of most pressing relevance to my argument. The book is directed at all readers with an interest in Spinoza's thought, but will have especial interest for those in the philosophy of religion, theology, Jewish studies, and political theory (working on issues in antiquity, modernity, or postmodernity) for whom the question of the relationship between religion, reason, and politics remains urgent. Spinoza's is one voice on this question, but one that is well worth exploring. In Spinoza's day, the biggest threat to equality and sovereignty came from religion itself – from despotic leaders using religion to advance their aims and from squabbling theologians concerned to manipulate the masses. In the modernity that unfolded after him, these threats changed. Reason ascended as the dominant discourse, though one that provoked, at times, no less despotism and squabbling. Spinoza is one of the only thinkers in modernity to make a case for why religion *and* reason are political and what difference – political, philosophical, theological – it makes for one to dominate the other. On this question, we still have much to learn from him.

Acknowledgments

The research and writing of this book were greatly assisted by grants from the Social Sciences and Humanities Research Council of Canada, The Woodrow Wilson Foundation (Charlotte Newcombe Fellowship on Ethical and Religious Values), and the Mellon Foundation. An earlier version of chapter 2 appeared in *Philosophy and Theology* 13 (2001). Thanks to the editor, Andrew Tallon, for permission to use this material here.

My editors at Cambridge University Press, first Kevin Taylor and then Katharina Brett, provided invaluable assistance at every stage of the production of the manuscript. I also want to thank Angela Blackburn, who was an incisive reader and editor of the final draft. I am grateful, too, to the anonymous readers whose critical insights and advice have made this, I hope, a better book. Edwin Curley graciously provided me with a copy of his translation of the TTP in the very final stage of the revising of this book, and I gained enormously from reading through it.

There are many other individuals whose advice and friendship contributed to this effort, and it is a pleasure to thank them. Hilary Putnam and Jay Harris expertly guided me through the process of writing the thesis that constituted the first version of the book. Both were rigorous and critical readers, as well as being wonderfully supportive in crucial moments. I also benefited greatly from Alison Simmons's detailed and sharply observed comments. Other readers who helpfully commented on earlier chapters and papers that went into this project and/or whose conversations were crucial to its unfolding include David Novak, Warren Zev Harvey, Eugene Shepard, Hava Tirosh-Samuelson, Edith Wyschogrod, and Yirmiyahu Yovel. Peter Ochs has been an interlocutor and teacher of uncommon generosity and inspiration. Charles Hallisey has quietly imprinted everything I now think and write. And I am especially grateful to Brayton Polka, whose extraordinary powers of mind and pedagogy first awoke in me the desire to do likewise.

At Williams College, my colleagues and friends in the Department of Religion, Denise Buell, William Darrow, Georges Dreyfus, and James Robson, as well as Matthew Kraus in the Program in Jewish Studies,

Sigma Coran at the Jewish Center, and Bradford Verter at Bennington College, have sustained my thinking and writing for the last few years. My students at New York University and at Williams, as well as friends and students on Fire Island, have been the backbone of working out so many ideas.

Other teachers and friends who have been vital readers, interlocutors, and critics include Jill Abrams, Lisa Alter, Jeannine Amber, William Arnal, Zachary Braiterman, Sarah Coakley, Arthur Egendorf, Marq Frerichs, Stephanie Green, Shai Held, Bouran Irfaeya, Wajda Irfaeya, Martin Kavka, Avron Kulak, Terri Kulak, David Lamberth, Bernard Lightman, Laura Levitt, Sally Matless, Richard R. Niebuhr, Randi Rashkover, Eva Robertson, Francis Schüssler-Fiorenza, Bill Showkowy, and Bernard Zelechow. Special thanks to my sister Julie Levene, interlocutor, critic, and friend from the beginning.

Since meeting at a panel on Spinoza, Shaul Magid and I have had countless conversations about this material, and countless arguments about what it all comes to. Without those conversations, and especially without those arguments, it would have been a much paler book, if it had been completed at all. To Shaul, my lasting thanks and love.

Finally, I dedicate this book to my parents, Aasta and Sam Levene. Long before I read Spinoza, I learned from them, and will eternally learn from them, what he means when he says, "no one has yet determined what the body can do." They have empowered me, supported my independence of mind and body, and imagined the impossible for me for so long that there can be nothing in these pages that is not fully and lovingly dependent on them.

Abbreviations

I have used the following abbreviations in referring to frequently cited texts.

Collected Works	*The Collected Works of Spinoza*, ed. and trans. Edwin Curley
DPP	*Descartes' Principles of Philosophy*, in *Collected Works* (I refer to the Part in roman numerals)
E	*Ethics*, in *Collected Works* (I refer to the Part in roman numerals)
Ep	*The Letters*, trans. Samuel Shirley (except where otherwise indicated)
G	*Spinoza Opera*, ed. Carl Gebhardt (I refer to the volume number with a roman numeral and the page number in arabic numerals. I give the page number only if I am citing more than a single word.
KV	*Short Treatise on God, Man, and His Well-Being*, in *Collected Works*
MT	*Appendix Containing Metaphysical Thoughts* (to DPP), in *Collected Works*
TdIE	*Treatise on the Emendation of the Intellect*, in *Collected Works* (I reference by section)
TP	*Tractatus Politicus*, in *The Political Works*, trans. A. G. Wernham (I quote the section number, followed by the page number)
TTP	*Theological-Political Treatise*, trans. Samuel Shirley

I have used the following abbreviations for Spinoza's terminology. In the interest of clarity I have omitted most of Spinoza's cross-references within the texts. I indicate these by ellipses.

app	appendix
a	axiom

c	corollary
d	definition
Def.Aff.	Definition of the Affects (located at the end of *Ethics* Part III)
dem	demonstration
Exp	Explanation
L	Lemma
p	proposition
pref	preface
s	scholium

Introduction

The focus of this study is Spinoza's revelation, a term that is meant in both its principal senses. In the first place, it refers to what Spinoza incisively reveals, which is the connection of religion, democracy, and reason. What he reveals is that rationality (reason, truth) and religion (morality, piety) depend upon democracy (independence, freedom) – that each depends upon the others, without which "the peace of the commonwealth," as Spinoza puts it, cannot be secure (TTP, 3). To follow out this connection between philosophy, theology, and politics – reason, religion, and democracy – is to trace the effort in Spinoza to secure this peace. In the second place, revelation – equally covenant, pact, prophecy – refers to the substance of this connection between religion, democracy, and reason, and between the divine and the human as Spinoza understands them. What revelation means in this second sense is literally that which is revealed; that which has an origin, originates, is original; that which comes into existence, creates existence; that which causes itself (*causa sui*). God, or Nature.

The contrast is with what perpetually endures, what has always been, what will always be. In this contrast, Spinoza has several complex distinctions at play: between the eternal as something that is uncaused and the eternal as something that causes itself; between nature as something that endures and nature as something that originates; between reason as something that is universal because it has always been in the world and reason as something that is universal because it has a beginning; between creation as something an eternal God does and creation as something God does for eternity. God, or Nature. We keep both, for Spinoza, because of something we are habitually blind to in each taken on its own, namely that God, or Nature, is rational, faithful, and free – human – only insofar as the human, as rational, faithful, free, is divine. As Spinoza always insists, God, or Nature, "exists for the sake of no end" and "acts for the sake of no end." It is human beings, "human appetite," which give God, or Nature, ends and it is these ends that we put before ourselves in striving to be like God, or Nature (E IV pref).

1

Revelation is ordinarily held to occur at the limits of universal reason. Where reason applies in all times and all places, revelation is specific, community-bound, theologico-political. Revelation (religion, piety,
God) is about the particular (*this* people, *this* nation); reason (nature,
truth) about the universal (humankind). A religious standpoint would
be one that sought to hold together both imperatives. A nonreligious
standpoint would be one that simply got rid of revelation – that found
its particularity in a political realm without theology. Spinoza sets up the
contrast differently. God and nature are on the same side, the side of the
universal, the "natural divine law" that rationally holds in all times and
all places. Religion and reason are thus both on the side of God or nature. But so is revelation: "we must concede without qualification that the
[universal] divine law began from the time when men by express covenant
promised to obey God in all things, thereby surrendering, as it were, their
natural freedom and transferring their right to God" (TTP, 188). For
this reason, perhaps, Spinoza tells us in the early pages of the TTP that
"the nature of the mind . . . is the primary cause of divine revelation"
(TTP, 10).

This is a striking claim. What is universally true is enacted in a covenant,
in a certain time and place, with a finite group of people. Who are these
"men"? *All* men? *All* people? Why covenant, then? What is the nature
of this transfer to God? What existed before it? These questions will be
pursued in due course. What is important to note at this stage is that
there no longer seem to be two sides in Spinoza. There is no longer the
difference of what endures and what begins, what holds for everyone and
what only holds for some. The universal divine law, "man's highest happiness and blessedness" belonging to and deduced from "human nature
as such" and thus "of universal application" (TTP, 51–52) – this began
from the time when human beings covenanted. The covenant began when
human beings universalized, when the divine became human and the human divine. But what is the meaning of this elision? What difference does
God, or Nature, make – what is the difference between them and what
is the meaning of their connection? What of the difference between the
realm of the divine and the realm of the human? Between religion and
politics? What can now count as the difference between a religious and a
nonreligious standpoint?

It is Spinoza's abiding claim that no standpoint is free of revelation.
This is not because religion is true (it is just as often false); nor is it
because one must believe in God (one is free not to); nor miracles (one
must not); nor the churches and synagogues (one might prefer not to).
Spinoza thinks that the narrow notion of revelation as the divine gift to
a particular community of law or sacrality has the same significance as a

humanly given law. But there is a wider notion of revelation in Spinoza's thought which can be seen throughout his work. This is the notion that even the most universal, the most eternal, the most natural things – peace, rationality, freedom, morality (God, or Nature) – originate from nothing. That is, peace, rationality, freedom, and morality (God, or Nature) have not always been in the world, are not rights or faculties or insights or endowments or possibilities human beings possess by nature. Or rather, they *are* possessed by nature, Nature or God. Like God (or Nature, for now we see what this might mean), they come into existence – their creation, creativity, making, origination is the ground of, the essence of, existence itself. Like Nature (or God, for now we see what this might mean), they are eternal. Both religion (God) and reason (Nature) are revealed, created, made; both reason (Nature) and religion (God) are sovereign, eternal, true. From a religious standpoint, God is eternal and nature is made; from a nonreligious standpoint, God is made and nature is eternal. Both, to Spinoza, are right.

At the center of Spinoza's metaphysics are two orienting concepts. The first is *causa sui* – that which causes itself, creates itself, brings itself about; that which is thus free, independent, undetermined, eternal: "that whose essence involves existence, or that whose nature cannot be conceived except as existing" (E I d1). The second is *conatus* – what strives, labors, endeavors, perseveres, empowers. Spinoza employs the language of God to describe the first. God is "absolutely infinite" (E I d6), "free" (E I d7), and "eternal," a being who "cannot be explained by duration or time even if the duration is conceived to be without beginning or end" (E I d8Exp). For the second, *conatus*, he employs the language of nature: "each thing [*res*], as far as it can by its own power, strives [*conatur*] to persevere in its being" (E III p6). *Conatus* refers to a capacity or power to act, something that is shared among all natural beings, human and nonhuman. Spinoza continually stresses this continuity between human and other beings – the manifold ways in which human beings are not a "dominion within a dominion" (*imperium in imperio*), a separate category within natural species. Not only do human beings not form a separate *imperium* unto themselves; they do not even command the *imperium*, nature, of which they are a part, for "insofar as [man] is a part of nature, whose laws human nature is compelled to obey . . . [he is] forced to accommodate [himself] in ways nearly infinite" (E IV appVI).

Yet nature is also the principal thing human beings must strive to know, for "our supreme good and perfection depends solely on the knowledge of God," and "since nothing can be or be conceived without God, it is clear that everything in Nature involves and expresses the conception of God in proportion to its essence and perfection; and therefore we acquire a greater and more perfect knowledge of God as we gain more knowledge of natural phenomena" (TTP, 51). Since the knowledge of nature and the knowledge of God are connected, one might assume that the natural sciences are the path of wisdom here. But Spinoza's "Nature" is "infinite": it includes not only what we think of as the natural order (in its parts, principles, or taken together as one thing) but "everything that is conceived even by the divine intellect" (TTP, 74).[1] This clearly qualifies what can be meant by "knowledge of natural phenomena." In calling human beings "natural," Spinoza doesn't just mean that their bodies act like other natural bodies – like trees and rocks and cows. He means the human mind is natural, too, and he therefore means to subject to science (or, if one prefers, to widen science to include) what a human being does and makes over time, human social and political life: "since all men, savage and civilized alike, everywhere enter into social relations and form some sort of civil order, the causes and natural foundations of the state are not to be sought in the precepts of reason, but must be deduced from the common nature of the constitution of men" (TP I: 7).

Given these different standpoints, nature is both an unattainable ideal (considered in itself) and, as united to the mind, all that human beings can, in fact, know. Nature is at once transcendent and immanent, infinite and finite, extraordinary and ordinary. As Spinoza relates in the TdIE, it is the highest good to acquire a nature (and strive that others acquire it) that knows "the union that the mind has with the whole of Nature." But to achieve this knowledge, he continues, it is necessary only to "understand as much of Nature as suffices for acquiring such a nature" (§§13–14).

What is at work here is the concept with which Spinoza begins (and ends) the *Ethics*, the *causa sui*. This concept is not only an account of the origin of God, or Nature. It is an account of human origins, an account of freedom – a freedom that comes into existence as the standard of human power and disempowerment. In the beginning, it is only God who is self-caused, self-created, free, eternal; humans are caused by another, in bondage, singular. But the *causa sui* reveals to human beings what are their origins, and ultimately, with effort, their ends. It is not that human beings ever escape the bondage of limitation. It is that they can, also, be free. The difference is one of *conatus*, creation, power, making. What is revealed from the beginning of Spinoza's works to the end is what it means *to human beings* to assert something like the revelation, the *causa*

---

[1] See also E I p16: "From the necessity of the divine nature there must follow infinitely many things in infinitely many modes (i.e., everything which can fall under an infinite intellect)."

sui, of *God*. What Spinoza shows is that *if* we assert this power of God, we must be prepared to assert something *like* this of human beings, too, for nothing is given in the beginning, including God, especially God. The *causa sui* is only possible because of *conatus*. God is Nature in Spinoza because God possesses the most *conatus*, the most ability, the most power; Nature is God in Spinoza because nature is caused by nothing but itself; nature comes into existence; nature originates. There is no nature that has not been inflected by creation, creativity, making, culture, society, politics, particularity; there is no creation, culture, making that is not part of nature.

This dynamic of nature and culture, divine and human, can readily be seen, first, in Spinoza's claim that the Bible is both natural – a book like other books, written by human beings for a particular audience in a certain time and place; and sacred – a book that contains the word of God, the divine law that commands justice and charity. What the Bible reveals, Spinoza shows, is that human beings don't need the Bible, since the word of God is written preeminently in the book of the human heart and must be expressed in the work of living justly. What the word of God reveals, Spinoza equally shows, is that human beings, at a loss as to how to interpret the book of the heart, at a loss as to the nature of justice, can find no better teacher than the Bible, which grounds both justice and interpretation in faith, obedience, love. What Spinoza shows is that faith and reason – books and minds – are both sovereign. To be sure, each will seek to make itself the standard for the other, to subordinate and disempower the other, to transcend the other; each will claim to be universal over against the particularity of the other. This is only possible, Spinoza reveals, because they have come into existence – they have been revealed, created, made – together. As he says of prophecy, it is a form of natural knowledge (natural knowledge is not inferior to it; it does not add to natural knowledge). Yet natural knowledge, too, is revealed – for, as above, the mind "contains the nature of God within itself in concept" and therefore we may regard "the nature of the mind" itself as "the primary cause of divine revelation" (TTP, 10).

Second, this dynamic of nature and culture, divine and human can be seen in Spinoza's discussion of law in the TTP, in which, unlike natural law, both the *lex divina* and the *lex humana* – divine as well as human laws – are conceived as "manmade." Although the divine law, once made, binds human beings universally and without exception, although this making is such that the divine law must be considered "innate in the human mind and inscribed therein, as it were," it is not a law of nature. What this means is that if we follow Spinoza in understanding politics or human social existence to be original, natural, inevitable – that is, that there is no human nature that preexists some kind of primitive sociality, there is no sociality that is not natural – we must paradoxically see that each has an origin: that nature and politics come into existence together, and thus are always disrupting and complicating each other. For God (or Nature), too, makes a pact with humankind, in "the manner we described in speaking of the civil state" (TTP, 188). God, or Nature, is theologico-political – always someone's and some society's God; theology and politics are natural, eternal – founded on universal principles of self-interest and justice. There can be a natural history of politics just as there can be a political history of nature, since neither exists separate from the other. It does not add anything to this notion to say that politics and nature only exist inseparably *for us* (human creators) while eternal nature (as that which we did not create) extends far beyond us. For insofar as nature is not for us it does not exist (for us); existence is for us; eternity is ontological: "by eternity I understand existence itself" (E I d8).

Third and finally, the dynamic can be seen in Spinoza's discussion of the Hebrew commonwealth and the election of the Hebrews. Spinoza is notorious among Jewish readers for his claim that the election of the Hebrews, and by extension, their covenantal law, *only* refers to "the temporal prosperity of the state" and "therefore could have been of practical value only while their state existed" (TTP, 60–61). As he says of Christian ceremonies as well, although they existed outside of a sovereign state per se, "their only purpose was the unification of a particular society" (TTP, 67). Blessedness is for individuals in pursuit of God or Nature (philosophy); security and health is for communities and nations (theologico-politics); blessedness is universal and rational; security and health are particular and revealed. Therefore, Spinoza notes, "he who lives in solitude is by no means bound by [these ceremonial observances]"; by no means bound by chosenness, by revelation. Yet for Spinoza no one actually *does* live in solitude. Every striving individual must be concerned with security, polity, solidarity. The formation of societies is not only "advantageous," it is "essential" (TTP, 64). And every society must become rational, that is, free, sovereign, *causa sui*. What the Hebrews precisely inaugurate is the connection between the divine and human laws, the connection, namely, between blessedness and security, rationality and the theologico-political, *causa sui* and *conatus*.[2] What they inaugurate, for Spinoza, is democracy as that which itself is both natural (or godly) ("the most natural form of state, approaching most closely to that freedom which nature grants to

---

[2] For the opposite view, that blessedness and human law have nothing whatsoever to do with each other, see Douglas Den Uyl, "Power, Politics, and Religion in Spinoza's Political Thought," in *Piety, Peace, and the Freedom to Philosophize*, ed. Paul Bagley (Dordrecht: Kluwer Academic Publishers, 1999), 133–158, esp. 140.

every man" [TTP, 185]) and social (originating from when human beings gave up the "unrestricted right naturally possessed by each individual" and put it "into common ownership" [TTP, 181]). Like the Bible, then, the Hebrews are both unique and ordinary. They are like all other nations in insisting that they are chosen. This, Spinoza knows, is what a nation (like a book considered sacred) does. They are unlike all other nations in showing that chosenness is original – that nations, including the nation that is humankind, originate, come into existence, are revealed. The Hebrews are chosen in showing what chosenness can only ever mean: that a society "freely" and "equally" pledges to live according to the divine law of justice, the law, namely, of democracy (TTP, 195).

For Spinoza, then, the task of every particular polity, every human law, is to strive as much as possible to conform to the divine law ("charity and love towards one's fellow-citizen"), something that depends on ensuring that access to religious and political knowledge – to law – is public, communal, accessible (TTP, 206). As Spinoza observes of the ancient Hebrew commonwealth, although in his day it can no longer be imitated "in all respects" (TTP, 212), it has one distinctive feature from which we might learn: "as in a democracy," the Hebrews transferred their natural rights "on equal terms," not "to any other man," who might very well take power for himself, but to God. "It follows," Spinoza says, "that this covenant left them all completely equal, and they all had equal right to consult God, to receive and interpret his laws; in short, they all shared equally in the government of the state" (TTP, 196). Of course, this is as unlike a democracy as it is like one, since God is not ordinarily understood as playing any role in a democratic government. Yet the case of the Hebrews teaches us precisely why the dissimilarity is as relevant as the similarity, and by extension the complexity of religion and politics as they play out in any given regime.

By the same logic, it is the task of every reader (of the Bible) to strive to be holy as the text is holy – to secure the holiness of the text by becoming holy oneself, or as Spinoza puts it, to lead a "better life" in light of what one reads (TTP, 70). This is something that also depends on ensuring clarity and accessibility – in this case of a particular text. For "Scripture was written and disseminated not just for the learned but for all men of every time and race" (TTP, 164), and since "obedience to God consists solely in loving one's neighbor . . . it follows that Scripture commands no other kind of knowledge than that which is necessary for all men" (TTP, 158).

In both cases, Spinoza considers the human labor involved to have been misplaced. In the political realm, immense efforts have been expended to control and manipulate the multitude, "and with the specious title of religion to cloak the fear by which they must be held in check" (TTP, 3). In the hermeneutical realm, it is "imagine[d] that the most profound mysteries [whether philosophical or theological] lie hidden in the Bible, and [interpreters] exhaust themselves in unraveling these absurdities while ignoring other things of value" (TTP, 89). Spinoza's claim is that these activities not only obscure the real work of political justice – the "set disposition to render to every man what is his by civil right" (TTP, 186) – and the real work of transforming oneself and others into persons of *pietas*. They intentionally obstruct these goals. Thus, given the manipulation of religion in the public sphere, defending *vera religio*, true religion, is a profoundly hermeneutic act. Given the weight of the Bible, reading it anew is a profoundly political act. As he puts it, since the approach to Scripture that finds in it "mysteries of the deepest kind" has led "to gross superstition and other pernicious ills . . . I feel I must not abandon my task, and all the more so because religion stands in no need of the trappings of superstition. On the contrary, its glory is diminished when it is embellished with such fancies" (TTP, 149).

What connects religion and politics in Spinoza's work is thus a third way of construing revelation: as a defense of the accessible, the clear, the plain, the ordinary – a critique, in other words, of the tyranny of legal, theological, metaphysical, and hermeneutic esotericism. The work – the labor, the effort of interpretation and lawmaking – is something common to the social order as a whole – it is something that individuals have in common with one another and it is, or should be, something that is common knowledge.

This notion of revelation as the expression of the common and the ordinary, then, has two sides. On the one side, it defends against the claims of elites that religious truth is something mysterious, supernatural, or esoteric, requiring "ecclesiastical authority" for its interpretation and dissemination, whether philosophical or theological. As Spinoza says of prophecy, what is distinctive about it does *not* rest on its exclusion of what is "common to all men," for what is common may properly be termed divine.[3] On the other side, it directs the attention of individuals to a conception of lawfulness as justice and charity that, while perfectly ordinary to understand, is nevertheless very difficult to achieve. What Spinoza is suggesting is that all of the zeal expended on the quest for vaporous and "extraordinary" religious and philosophical ideals has precisely distracted and subverted what actually does require enormous

---

[3] "Cognitio naturalis omnibus hominibus communibus est, dependet enim a fundamentis omnibus hominibus communibus . . . aequali jure, ac alia, quaecunque illa sit, divina vocari potest" (G III: 15).

effort, namely the struggle to bring about a political order that is truly democratic and truly just, an order that he thinks would be truly and rightly extraordinary.

What is at stake in Spinoza's revelation, therefore, is the dialectical relationship between the human and the divine. What the term *dialectic* captures is a relationship of identity and difference, continuity and separation, between terms that are in tension with one another, and whose tension is part of their richness. Spinoza's tendency is to dwell on the negative consequences of subordinating one side of an opposition to the other, for example by allowing a desire for the divine as extraordinary (God as a miracle worker, God as that which utterly transcends what we know) to subordinate what we know to be naturally or ordinarily the case. Spinoza calls this alternately superstition and anthropomorphism, for it involves both spurning the natural for the supernatural (as the "masses" do), and taking the familiar and the ordinary and making it all-powerful, extraordinary (as despotic leaders do). Superstition and despotism are two sides of the same coin for Spinoza, for, as he observes, power-hungry political leaders often seek to advance themselves by virtue of the credulity of the masses; but this very credulity guarantees that such advancement will be temporary, for it will precisely exacerbate the volatility (caused by superstition) that is difficult to control.

The key to understanding Spinoza's critique in the broadest sense – his critique of both philosophy and theology and his critique of the social and political status quo – is that it is focused on the ability to see oppositions like those between reason and revelation, freedom and obedience, and independence and dependence as part of the same project of *libertas humana*, human freedom. That is, freedom is impossible, illusory, or tyrannical unless it is also understood to be about obedience to laws (both human and divine), and vice versa: obedience, or dependence on others, is simply *summum arcanum*, superstition and ignorance, without the achievement, however hard won, of freedom, of acting independently.

The dialectic of the human and the divine is repeated at every level and in various ways throughout the *Ethics* and the TTP: if one aims for God (as opposed to Nature) one will find neither; if one seeks to live according to the divine law (with no appreciation of how it is instantiated in particular human laws), one will achieve nothing but religio-political disaster; if one strives to understand the terms of theology (in opposition to those of reason and logic), one will have debased both discourses; if one seeks the truth of a text without regard to its multiple meanings and contexts of authorship, one will grasp neither. The priority of terms in these formulations can also be reversed (if one aims for Nature as opposed to God, human law as opposed to divine law, philosophy as opposed to theology, contexts as opposed to truths), and more importantly, the error can be cast through the mode of conflation as well (if one simply identifies these terms, one will understand neither). As he says of the proper relationship between theology and philosophy, we must discern "what is the essential nature of each, and [show that] neither of them is subordinate to the other, each of them holding its own domain without contradicting the other." The problem, he says, is not only making one the standard of the other (subordination), but "the absurdities, the damage and the harm that have resulted from the fact that men have thoroughly confused these two faculties, failing to make an accurate distinction between them and to separate one from the other" (TTP, 177).

Spinoza's revelation of the connection between reason, religion, and democracy has not been sufficiently unraveled. This is partly due to the absorption of so many readers in the critical posture Spinoza takes toward religion and the popular mentality to which it gives rise, and partly due to Spinoza's own rhetorical context in the TTP especially – his need, socially and politically, to separate (theology and philosophy) rather than connect (God and nature). To see that Spinoza makes his argument for democracy on the grounds that it most fully expresses both the theologico-political and the philosophical is to confront one of the dominant stereotypes that have been promulgated about Spinoza over the last fifty years or so: that while his political project is overtly democratic, his philosophical project, and indeed his ultimate aim, is an elitist or undemocratic one. That is, Spinoza is a democrat in his politics and an elitist in his philosophy, and thus in some sense, even Spinoza's political thought is ultimately undemocratic. Founded on principles that divide societies between elites and masses, its democratic character is ultimately the exoteric dimension of a fundamentally hierarchical world view, one that is contemptuous of the majority, and politically interested only in securing enough stability so that philosophy can, esoterically, go on unmolested. Spinoza's democracy, on this reading, however radical and important for its time, is ultimately only a necessary means to enable the philosophical enlightenment of a privileged few.

This portrait, most sharply articulated by Leo Strauss, significantly distorts Spinoza's project by forcing him into the medieval rubric of a "persecuted" author (a complex Strauss first develops in reading Maimonides and Halevi).[4] As a work avowedly addressed to the

---

[4] Leo Strauss, *Persecution and the Art of Writing* (Chicago: University of Chicago Press, 1952).

philosophic or learned reader (*philosophe lector*) (TTP, 8), the meaning
of the TTP, Strauss contends, cannot but conceal an esoteric heart. For,
according to Strauss, truth is never something which is available to the
multitude – it is always "merely and purely theoretical," and thus always hidden, even from the philosophers, who only demonstrate their
philosophical aptitude by deciphering it.[5] This argument directly recalls Maimonides' *Guide of the Perplexed* and its readers (including especially Strauss himself).[6] The chief difference between Spinoza and
Maimonides, for Strauss, is that Maimonides affirms and Spinoza denies that the Bible is doing what the *Tractatus* and the *Guide* are identically doing – presenting the truth in esoteric form. The very orthodoxy
of Spinoza's text – its repeated implication that the "literal meaning of
the Bible hides a deeper, mysterious meaning" – in fact testifies to its
thoroughgoing heterodoxy – that the Bible and theology are founded on
"untruth."[7] It is the TTP that has a hidden truth, and it is that the Bible
contains no truth, hidden or otherwise.[8]

Strauss himself learned much from Harry Wolfson's portrait of Spinoza
as a late medieval (Maimonidean) proponent of "rational religion" directed to the elite few. As Wolfson saw it, "[Spinoza's] religion of reason . . . is nothing but a modified form of the philosophic conception of
Judaism as described by Maimonides."[9] What Strauss and Wolfson share
(which is picked up by their many inheritors) is a sense that the problems faced by Maimonides in his effort to square Judaism and Greek
philosophy are identical to what Spinoza faced. Unable to articulate their
philosophical first principles without risking a hostile religious response,
both thinkers couched their systems in a marriage between reason and
revelation that ultimately could not hold. On this reading, the language
of revelation in Spinoza is at best, in Yirmiyahu Yovel's words, about the

---

[5] Strauss, *Persecution*, 36.

[6] In the standard English translation of the *Guide*, Strauss provides a long explanatory essay detailing Maimonides' hermeneutics. *The Guide of the Perplexed*, trans. Shlomo Pines,
2 vols. (Chicago: University of Chicago Press, 1963), vol. I, xi–lvi. For a more recent argument along these lines, see Warren Zev Harvey, "A Portrait of Spinoza as a Maimonidean,"
Journal of the History of Philosophy 19 (1981): 151–172. See also Shlomo Pines, "Spinoza's
Tractatus Theologico-Politicus, Maimonides, and Kant," in *Further Studies in Philosophy*, ed.
Ora Segal, Scripta Hierosolymitana, vol. XX (Jerusalem: Magnes Press, 1968), 3–54.

[7] Strauss, *Persecution*, 170.

[8] Strauss, *Persecution*, 179. Strauss's thought on the relationship between Athens (philoso-
phy, reason) and Jerusalem (religion, revelation) is subjected to a recent appraisal in David
Novak, ed., *Leo Strauss and Judaism: Jerusalem and Athens Critically Revisited* (Lanham,
Md.: Rowman & Littlefield, 1996).

[9] Harry Austryn Wolfson, *The Philosophy of Spinoza*, 2 vols. (Cambridge, Mass.: Harvard
University Press, 1934), vol. II, 328.

construction of an "imaginary, semirational bridge where a genuinely rational one could not have been erected":[10] something that encourages the masses to conform to rational precepts as a substitute for understanding them in themselves, and at worst, a tool to distract the majority while the minority get on with the dangerous business of truth.[11] In other words, the opposition between reason and revelation – between what is universal and what is particular – ironically constitutes the opposition between the few who can discern what is universally true and the many who are left with what can be true only for them.[12]

But Spinoza's revelation – and thus Spinoza's reason – begins from entirely different premises.[13] The crucial issue is that since Spinoza's God is no more transcendent than immanent – since revelation itself is no more faithful than rational – all human beings are equally in

[10] Yirmiyahu Yovel, *Spinoza and Other Heretics, vol. I: The Marrano of Reason* (Princeton: Princeton University Press, 1989), 144. Yovel also argues for this position in "Bible Interpretation as Philosophical Praxis: A Study of Spinoza and Kant," *Journal of the History of Philosophy* 11 (1973): 189–212, and "Spinoza: The Psychology of the Multitude and the Uses of Language," *Studia Spinozana* 1 (1985): 305–333. This is also the thesis of Steven B. Smith, *Spinoza, Liberalism, and the Question of Jewish Identity* (New Haven, Conn.: Yale University Press, 1997). Smith is a careful reader of Spinoza's political thought, and argues persuasively for Spinoza's importance in the articulation of "a new kind of liberal citizen" (20). But he assumes that Spinoza's "purpose" in the TTP is "the liberation of philosophy from religion" (20), and thus that Spinoza's defense of true religion is insincere and manipulative.

[11] For Strauss, Spinoza conceals his meaning not only in order to avoid persecution but also because he regards the masses as incapable of understanding him and because those who can understand him need further instruction. Such strategies as "obscurity of plan, contradictions, pseudonyms, inexact repetitions of earlier statements . . . do not disturb the slumber of those who cannot see the wood for the trees, but act as awakening stumbling blocks for those who can" (*Persecution*, 36).

[12] Confronting the difficulties of Spinoza's view of religion needn't take the view that religion is entirely contradictory or external to rationality. For treatments of religion as a useful and indeed integral dimension of political life, see Heidi Ravven, "Spinoza's Rupture with Tradition: His Hints of a Jewish Modernity," in *Jewish Themes in Spinoza's Philosophy*, ed. Heidi M. Ravven and Lenn E. Goodman (Albany: State University of New York Press, 2002), 187–223; Michael Rosenthal, "Why Spinoza Chose the Hebrews: The Exemplary Function of Prophecy in the *Theologico-Political Treatise*," in *Jewish Themes in Spinoza's Philosophy*, ed. Ravven and Goodman, 225–260; Douglas Den Uyl, "Power, Politics, and Religion in Spinoza's Political Thought," and Richard Mason, "Faith Set Apart from Philosophy? Spinoza and Pascal," in *Piety, Peace, and the Freedom to Philosophize*," ed. Paul Bagley (Dordrecht: Kluwer Academic Publishers, 1999), 133–158 and 1–23 respectively; and Alan Donagan, "Spinoza's Theology," in *The Cambridge Companion to Spinoza*, ed. Don Garrett (Cambridge: Cambridge University Press, 1996), 343–382. My own argument is closest to Mason and Donagan insofar as both make clear that faith (theology, piety) is not unrelated to blessedness. I part with both, however, insofar as they conclude that the relationship between the two is hierarchical.

[13] For a more extensive treatment of Strauss and his legacy in the interpretation of the TTP, see Nancy Levene, "Ethics and Interpretation, or How to Study Spinoza's *Tractatus Theologico-Politicus* without Strauss," *Journal of Jewish Thought and Philosophy* 10 (2000): 57–110.

possession (and equally dispossessed) of the way to salvation. Both reason and revelation come into existence, both are revealed – as natural, sovereign, universal. Understanding God or Nature is necessary to
Spinoza because it is above all in our views of these entities, as transcendent or immanent, that we are most likely to enslave ourselves, that is,
enslave ourselves to false ideals, enslave one another by claiming divine
authority (*summum arcanum*), and enslave ourselves to a natural world
which will have all that much more power over us the less we understand
how it works (and the ways in which *we* are natural). The two false alterna-
tives are to see human beings, as theology traditionally has, as beginning
(through the fall) without a knowledge of God, making God humanity's
transcendent standard, and to see human beings and human reason, as
many other Enlightenment thinkers would, as the measure of all things,
including God. The first position ensures we will never know what it is
that we are seeking, the second that there is nothing to seek.[14] Both, to
Spinoza, eventuate in despotic, or as we would put it today, totalitarian
political regimes. If he was in some ways the archetypal retiring philosopher, it is nevertheless clear to him that the struggle against tyranny is
always the struggle against the ideology that supports it. As he says in
introducing the TTP, "when I saw that the disputes of philosophers are
raging with violent passion in Church and Court and are breeding bitter hatred and faction which readily turn men to sedition, together with
other ills too numerous to recount here, I deliberately resolved to examine
Scripture afresh" (TTP, 5).

In the preliminary pages of the TdIE, Spinoza presents the prereq-
uisites for "emending the intellect and rendering it capable of understanding things in the way the attainment of our end requires." In these
passages, he speaks of "bringing the intellect back to the right path,"
and of adopting in this context "certain rules of living as good." Among
these rules is "to speak according to the power of understanding of ordinary people, and to do whatever does not interfere with our attaining
our purpose . . . For we can gain a considerable advantage, if we yield as
much to their understanding as we can" (TdIE, §17). It is easy to see why
these rules might support the contention that Spinoza's posture vis à vis
"ordinary people" is one of dissimulation, or at the very least condescension, a kind of condescension that could warrant deceptive measures.

---

[14] I borrow this Socratic "pugnacious proposition" from the opening to Kierkegaard's *Philosophical Fragments* (trans. Howard V. Hong and Edna H. Hong [Princeton, N.J.: Princeton University Press, 1985]). Kierkegaard uses the proposition to explore the difference
between Socrates' way out of the dilemma – learning as the recollection of what one once
knew and has forgotten – and his own, which involves the notion that the truth can be
learned even if one is not in possession of it – even if one is, in fact, dispossessed of it.

However, on the previous page Spinoza introduces what the work will show to be the highest good, namely (as I quoted above) "the knowledge of the union that the mind has with the whole of Nature." Spinoza then writes,

This, then, is the end I aim at: to acquire such a nature, and to strive that many acquire it with me. That is, it is part of my happiness to take pains that many others may understand as I understand, so that their intellect and desire agree entirely with my intellect and desire. To do this it is necessary, *first* to understand as much of Nature as suffices for acquiring such a nature; *next*, to form a society of the kind that is desirable, so that as many as possible may attain it as easily and as surely as possible. (TdIE, §14)

In this light, it would seem that for Spinoza, there is not only no reason to deceive the "many" or the vulgar. There are positive philosophical reasons – which, we will see, are equally theological and political – for ensuring their participation in the attainment of what Spinoza considered the highest good.

What Spinoza says in the TdIE is telling, for it depicts Spinoza's philosophical and theologico-political goals as significantly continuous, not simply in the sense that the polity will allow for philosophy to go on unmolested.[15] Rather the continuity is itself at once philosophical, theological, and political. What Spinoza is saying here is that it is precisely *part of* the ends of *conatus*, of human striving, to ensure that an understanding of Nature (or God), the *causa sui*, is attained by "as many as possible"; that God or Nature is at the origins of society, culture, the human multitude. What he clarifies in his later works, in the *Ethics* and the TTP alike, is that the reverse is just as true: that the human multitude is at the origin of God or Nature; that each depends on, constitutes, and is constituted by the other.[16]

The notion of speaking according to the understanding of "ordinary people" must thus be squared with what Spinoza clearly aspires to bring into existence for such people – not simply a life that in its external form resembles his own, but one substantively the same in content, a profoundly radical view, then as now. In this light, speaking according to the

---

[15] Cf. Den Uyl, who claims that "the ends of the state [for Spinoza] are limited; it [the state] makes no contribution to blessedness" ("Power, Politics, and Religion," 138).

[16] I have learned a great deal on the relationship of Spinoza's philosophy and politics from the Continental literature on him, beginning with Alexandre Matheron's *Individu et communauté chez Spinoza* (Paris: Editions de Minuit, 1969), and including Pierre Macherey, *Hegel ou Spinoza* (Paris: François Maspero, 1979); Andre Tosel, *Spinoza ou le crépuscule de la servitude: Essai sur le* Traité Theologico–Politique (Paris: Aubier Montaigne, 1984); Etienne Balibar, *Spinoza and Politics*, trans. Peter Snowdon (London: Verso, 1998); and Antonio Negri, *The Savage Anomaly: The Power of Spinoza's Metaphysics and Politics*, trans. Michael Hardt (Minneapolis: University of Minnesota Press, 1991).

understanding of ordinary people is about pedagogy, not dissimulation. It is a pedagogy directed toward the dissemination of wisdom, but one that sees this task in theologico-political as well as rational terms. For, as he puts it in the *Tractatus Politicus*, "Rebellions, wars, and contemptuous disregard for law must certainly be attributed to the corrupt condition of the commonwealth rather than to the wickedness of its subjects. For citizens are not born, but made" (TP V: 2).

1 *Vera religio*

Whatever we desire and do of which we are the cause insofar as we have the idea of God, *or* insofar as we know God, I relate to Religion.

(E IV p37s)

Just as men are accustomed to call divine the kind of knowledge that surpasses human understanding, so they call divine, or the work of God, any work [*opus*] whose cause is generally unknown. For the common people [*vulgus*] suppose that God's power and providence are most clearly displayed when some unusual event occurs in Nature contrary to their habitual beliefs [*opinionem*] concerning Nature, particularly if such an event is to their profit or advantage.

(TTP, 72)

Superstition

Spinoza uses the term true or universal religion, *vera religio*, in the TTP to distinguish between those precepts that teach "the divine law revealed to all mankind through the Prophets and the Apostles" (TTP, 6) and the teachings of sectarians that "preach only such novel and striking doctrine as might gain the applause of the crowd" (TTP, 4). He distinguishes, in other words, between true and false religion, between religion and superstition, between what is truly divine and what is merely a "relic of man's ancient bondage" (TTP, 3), between the divine light that produces equanimity and fellowship and the "arrogant ravings" that produce strife and persecution (TTP, 5). In this sense the TTP goes further than the *Ethics*, which reserves the term religion only for what Spinoza directly approves, namely, as in the quotation above, the idea and knowledge of God. But both works strive to disentangle true and false ways of understanding God, true and false ways of forming relationships, true and false ways of understanding (and thus attaining) freedom. The question is *how and to what end* are these pairs disentangled? How does one know when one's religion, one's ideas, one's relationships, one's aims are true as opposed to false, adequate as opposed to inadequate, liberating as opposed to enslaving? What both works pursue in detail is that truth and falsity are

16

not simply about error, delusion, or ignorance – they are not simply about being mistaken about one's object or end. Truth and falsity imply states of being, and they imply political and social stances. It may be convenient, Spinoza will show, to attribute truth and falsity to the realm of ideas alone while attributing convention, custom, and what practically works to the theologico-political realm, the realm of law, of polity, of nation. It is much harder to see that not only do ideas have social and political consequences; ideas *are* social and political – they are embodied, they are made. As the case of the ancient Hebrews demonstrates, once "religion [begins] to acquire the force of law . . . governments are the guardians and interpreters of religious law as well as civil law, and they alone have the right to decide what is just and unjust, what is pious and impious" (TTP, 8). But then, again, what becomes of the difference between truth and falsity? What becomes of true religion if the difference is not between the universal divine law and the law of chosen others but between two kinds of chosenness, two kinds of revelation – between the Word of God "as revealed to the prophets" (TTP, 6) and the divine law of any given regime, any given "bible"? What makes religion true (or false), and what are the obstacles to differentiating them?

In this chapter, I set the stage for my reading of Spinoza's Bible and his theologico-politics by introducing his concepts of reason and religion, and specifically, his conception of human inadequacy and disempowerment. By exploring Spinoza's notion of the pervasiveness of superstition (and also its amelioration) I show that Spinoza's critique of credulous masses, theologians, and despots is fundamentally connected to his critique of philosophical and intellectual concepts of God (the "God of the philosophers"). The masses anthropomorphize God and the philosophers, theologians and despots deify God (and, by implication, themselves), but what Spinoza shows is that both are versions of the same inadequacy – the same mistaken judgment that what will most enable human power is the denigration of oneself (in relation to God) or others (in relation to oneself). What Spinoza insists on is that "man is God to man"[1] – that this principle of human liberation (at once self-interested and virtuous)

---

[1] For the most part I use the gender-inclusive "human being" to translate *homo*, which is faithful to Spinoza's philosophy as I understand it, notwithstanding his occasional disparaging views of women (TP XI: 4, TTP, 49 and 100, and E IV p37s1). He uses the more specific *vir* and *virtus* to mean manliness, power, and virility. But in the case of the proverb *hominem homini Deum esse*, none of the gender-inclusive terms work well – the singular "human being" needs an article, and the plural "humanity" doesn't capture the power of the singular. The proverb can be translated either as man is a God to man, or man is God to man (i.e., equally, God is man to man). The indefinite article in English does not add anything to the concept. Thanks to Brayton Polka for pointing this out to me.

is as common and ordinary as it is difficult; that in this one case "all things excellent are as difficult as they are" ordinary (not rare), and that this very ordinariness is part and parcel of the difficulty.[2] It is far easier, Spinoza suggests, to conceive of truth as other than where we begin; far more difficult (intellectually, psychically, and politically) to conceive of it as present in the beginning as that which we continually fail to realize and bring to fruition. Spinoza's God is about this power, striving, and self-causation that are our origins and ultimately, with great effort, our end. It is these features of God – known to human beings primarily in the breach – that enable the understanding and solidarity that are the keys to human liberation.

Part IV of Spinoza's *Ethics* is entitled "On Human Bondage, or the Power of the Affects."[3] The word "bondage," *servitus,* captures a key dimension of Spinoza's concern throughout his work, which is to demonstrate the ways in which human beings are not free, either in the terms of the inherited vocabularies with which Spinoza was confronted, wherein freedom originates in the individual will, or in the terms of ordinary experience (as Spinoza understands it), wherein freedom denotes simply the ability to bring about whatever we desire. In neither of these cases is freedom seen as perfectly realizable, since for most free will theorists, the will itself is ever corruptible by "sensual impulses," while for Spinoza's modern contemporaries, the ones who "think themselves free" because "they are conscious of their own actions, and ignorant of the causes by which they are determined," there is always plenty to frustrate any given desired outcome (E I app).[4] But both cases nevertheless express a single basic premise, which is that the human being can be liberated only if these

---

[2] This is in contrast to Spinoza's famous statement at the end of the *Ethics* that "all things excellent are as difficult as they are rare" (E V p42s). But the contrast is not as radical as might be assumed. What Spinoza shows is that what is ordinary and common – what is known to all, learned and ignorant – may be, in fact, the most difficult thing to enact – may be, in fact, the most rare thing of all.

[3] *The Collected Works of Spinoza,* ed. and trans. Edwin Curley, vol. I (Princeton, N.J.: Princeton University Press, 1985), is now the standard English translation of the *Ethics.*

[4] Thomas is exemplary of the free will position (St. Thomas Aquinas, *On Law, Morality, and Politics,* ed. William P. Baumgarth and Richard J. Regan, S.J. [Indianapolis: Hackett, 1988). His view is that, on the one hand, human beings are endowed by God with a law of reason which "has its power of moving the will" in accordance with some end (13). On the other hand, "when man turned his back on God, he fell under the influence of his sensual impulses" which is a "deviation from the laws of reason" (28). Spinoza's contemporaries seem to him to hold the opposite, namely that "they are free to the extent that they are permitted to yield to their lust, and that they give up their right to the extent that they are bound to live according to the rule of the divine law" (E V p41s). Neither are correct, to Spinoza.

obstacles to freedom are overcome, whether by grace, or the judicious use of reason, or by sheer human strength.[5]

By contrast, when Spinoza uses the term *servitus*, he means to set the question of freedom on an entirely different basis. *Servitus*, he insists, is entirely natural. It is not something that happened as a result of a "fall" nor is it something temporary from which one could be liberated through effort or the intervention of a divine being.[6] Rather, *servitus* describes something about the human condition that will always be true, namely that "there is no singular thing in nature than which there is not another more powerful and stronger" (E IV a1). As he puts it more bluntly in the TTP, "fish are determined by nature to swim, and the big ones to eat the smaller ones." This fact is a fish's "sovereign natural right," and the same is true for human beings insofar as they are "considered as living under the rule of Nature alone" (TTP, 179). Spinoza's point, at least initially, is *not* to discriminate between "singular" human beings and the other beings that comprise the natural order, "nor between men endowed with reason and others to whom true reason is unknown, nor between fools, madmen, and the sane" (TTP, 179). If escaping this condition shared by all singular things is what one would count as freedom, Spinoza says, it doesn't exist.

Bondage, then, refers to the fact that human beings are part of the natural order, and a comparatively fragile part at that. As Spinoza puts it, "the force by which a man perseveres in existing is . . . infinitely surpassed by the power of external causes" (E IV p3). But the term has the advantage of connoting not simply a static state of unfreedom, in the way one might speak about a tree or a rock, but a state of disempowerment at least partly exacerbated by human beings.[7] To Spinoza, it is crucial to understand the degree to which (and the ways in which) we are at the mercy of other natural things, for failing to do so precisely compounds, indeed constitutes, our bondage. Understanding, for Spinoza, is power;

---

[5] Descartes is a frequent target. His theory of the will, especially as articulated in "Passions of the Soul" (*The Philosophical Writings of Descartes*, trans. John Cottingham, Robert Stoothoff, and Dugald Murdoch [Cambridge: Cambridge University Press, 1985], vol. I, 348) leads Spinoza to accuse him of holding that "that there is no Soul so weak that it cannot – when it is well directed – acquire an absolute power over its Passions" (E V pref).

[6] Wolfson unaccountably translates *servitus* as vice or sin (*Philosophy of Spinoza*, vol. II, 184).

[7] As Spinoza retorts to Willem Van Blyenbergh: "When you say that by making men so dependent on God I reduce them to the level of the elements, plants and stones, this is enough to show that you have completely misunderstood my views and are confusing the field of intellect with that of the imagination . . . This dependence on God and necessity of action through God's decrees can best be understood when we have regard, not to logs and plants, but to created things of the highest degree of intelligibility and perfection" (Ep 21, 156).

understanding the nature of disempowerment, unfreedom, bondage, is part and parcel of liberation. Thus the thrust of the language of *servitus* is to ask: What exactly is the nature of human power and disempowerment? How do we avoid being eaten by bigger fish or alternatively worsen our vulnerability? Given our bondage, to what can we aspire – what *is* human power, relative to the power of fish? If on the one hand it is true that we did not put ourselves in bondage (through sin, for example), it is nevertheless legitimate to ask: What is our role in keeping ourselves in this state? If the point is not freedom *from* bondage, what *is* the meaning of freedom, the *libertas humana* that forms the title of the climactic portion of the *Ethics* and that structures the TTP throughout? Spinoza's first response is to say what unfreedom is; what restricts and inhibits freedom. To this end, superstition – a term that covers both what we might normally think of as religious beliefs and also other beliefs and actions that are disempowering – is the principal obstacle. To this, then, let us turn.

The pervasiveness of superstition is the problem with which Spinoza begins the TTP:

> If men were able to exercise complete control [*certo consilio*] over all their circumstances, or if continuous good fortune were always their lot, they would never be prey to superstition. But since they are often reduced to such straits as to be without any resources, and their immoderate greed for fortune's fickle favours often makes them the wretched victims of alternating hopes and fears, the result is that, for the most part, their credulity knows no bounds. In critical times, they are swayed this way or that by the slightest impulse, especially so when they are wavering between the emotions of hope and fear; yet at other times they are overconfident, boastful and arrogant. (TTP, 1)

Superstition above has two sources. First, there is the misery that results from being "without any resources," and second, there is the "immoderate greed [*cupiditas*] for fortune's fickle favours." The first is a kind of sadness, which Spinoza defines in the *Ethics* as "the idea of any thing that . . . diminishes [or] restrains our Body's power of acting" (E III p11). This use of the word *sadness* to denote everything that diminishes or restrains us gives an affective character even to such seemingly indifferent or habitual experiences as, for example, being unable to see at night. But the language of sadness has a sharper valence in the TTP where its connection to "being without resource" is closer to a conventional use of the term. The second source of superstition, greed, is also a form of sadness through its connection to hope and fear, which are species of joy and sadness conditioned by uncertainty. Hope is "nothing but an inconstant Joy which has arisen from the image of a future or past thing whose outcome we doubt," and fear is "an inconstant Sadness, which has also arisen from the image of a doubtful thing" (E III p18s2). Hope and fear can easily become overconfidence and pride since, if the doubtful thing is given, we will tend to overcompensate for our experience of inconstancy by veering into a dogmatic certainty all the stronger for being unwarranted. Greed is simply to place the bulk of one's energy in what is only ever inconstant, and thus to exacerbate a vulnerability that is already pervasive.

One might assume that Spinoza is holding individuals responsible only for the second source of superstition, "immoderate greed," since being without resources is surely not something that is as easily controlled. Spinoza spells out in the *Ethics* that "to be preserved, the human Body requires a great many other bodies" (E IV p39dem), and insists in the TP that "it is hardly possible for men to maintain life and cultivate the mind without mutual help" (II: 15). Thus "the case of the poor falls upon society as a whole, and concerns . . . the general advantage" (E IV appXVII). But it is precisely this partial lack of control that *both* features of superstition share, for as Spinoza notes, even features of temperament like a "tranquil and friendly disposition" are possible "only in a state," only in a setting in which one's basic needs are taken care of (TP II: 21). This is not to say there is an inevitable correspondence between being "reduced to such straits as to be without any resources" and "immoderate greed," as if only the poor are greedy or as if greed by definition signals poverty. Spinoza very clearly distinguishes them, and undoubtedly intends the language of "greed" to have precisely the connotation of culpability that being "reduced to such straits" does not. Yet Spinoza's deployment of the experience of scarcity in the TTP recalls what in the *Ethics* he identifies as the feeling of being overpowered in a more inclusive sense. It is this feeling, he holds, that accompanies the "passions," that is, the ways we are affected by things of which we are not the cause:

It is impossible that a man should not be part of Nature, and that he should be able to undergo no changes except those which can be understood through his own nature alone, and of which he is the adequate cause . . . From this it follows that man is necessarily always subject to the passions, that he follows and obeys the common order of Nature, and accommodates himself to it as much as the nature of things requires. (E IV p4)

Spinoza speaks drily of human beings "accommodating" themselves to nature as much as is required. But experientially, this fact is a source of continual anxiety. By nature we strive to preserve our being, but we cannot do so alone, and therefore we can never be certain *that* we will be able to do so, nor by virtue of whom or what. Our lack of power over against nature is equally a lack of power over, and a fundamental uncertainty about, others. Taken together, human vulnerability and the dependence on others is termed "fortune" (*fortuna*), for "anything whatever can be the accidental cause of Hope or Fear . . . and we are so constituted by nature that we easily believe the things we hope for, but believe only with difficulty those we fear, and we regard them more or less highly than is just" (E III p50 and s). "Human beings," then, "are *necessarily* always subject to the passions," and thus "by nature they pity the unfortunate, but envy the fortunate, and incline more to vengeance than to compassion" (TP I: 4). In other words, we are subject to greed and other "immoderate" desires as inevitably as we are subject to scarcity:

Man's lack of power to moderate and restrain the affects I call Bondage [*servitus*]. For the man who is subject to affects is under the control, not of himself, but of fortune, in whose power he so greatly is that often, though he sees the better for himself, he is still forced to follow the worst. (E IVpref)[8]

This inevitability ("by nature") should not be confused with the claim that we are not responsible to address these things. On the contrary, Spinoza considers greed, envy, vengeance, and pity to be among the greatest obstacles to "true knowledge" (E IV p73s). But there is a tension here in seeking to evaluate what is in our control and what is not. For as Spinoza also observes, "when a greedy man thinks of nothing else but profit, or money, and an ambitious man of esteem, they are not thought to be mad, because they are usually troublesome and are considered worthy of Hate. But Greed, Ambition, and Lust really are species of madness, even though they are not numbered among the diseases" (E IV p44s).

The claim is not that affects per se enslave us. An affect is simply "an idea by which the Mind affirms of its Body a greater or lesser force of existing than before" (E IV p14dem). All knowledge – ideas – are accordingly "nothing but an affect of Joy," if we increase our force of existing, "or Sadness," if we decrease it (E IV p8). Joy and sadness can themselves be constant (a function of understanding) or inconstant (a function of uncertainty, and therefore hope and fear), but all human states, both laudable and lamentable, are "affected," according to Spinoza. Yet he also notes that superstition arises not from "reason [*ratio*] but from emotion [*affectus*]" (TTP, 2, G III: 6). In the terminology of the *Ethics*, this is simply to say that not all affects are equal. Some empower and some occlude reason, and affects like hope and fear are most definitely the latter. Bondage, then, is the "lack of power to moderate and restrain the affects," meaning the lack of power to prevent ourselves from "swaying this way or that by the slightest impulse" (TTP, 1). One could just as correctly say bondage arises from uncertainty. It concerns both something

---

[8] The allusion is to Medea's complaint in book 7 of Ovid's *Metamorphoses: video meliora, proboque, deteriora sequor* (I see and approve the better, but follow the worst). Spinoza gives the full reference in E IV p17s. See Curley's note, *Collected Works*, 554.

we ourselves are doing (or not doing) *and* those things against which we can do nothing.

This lack of control or feeling of being overpowered can torment us for two reasons. First, while understanding something truly or adequately, which Spinoza also connects to the power to act, is augmented by the desire (and joy) that comes from the sense of the increase in power – power is the cause of itself, it increases itself – the desire that "arises from affects by which we are torn is also greater as these affects are more violent. And so their force and growth . . . must be defined by the power of external causes, which, if it were compared with ours, would indefinitely surpass our power" (E IV p15dem). The desire (and thus the power to act) that arises from understanding something truly is significantly less powerful than the desire that arises from understanding things only inadequately.

Spinoza defines an inadequate idea as an idea that it is incomplete, missing information, and therefore one that has completion as a standard. The example Spinoza gives is that of the human body. On the one hand, the human mind doesn't know anything except through the way its body is affected. The mind knows neither itself (E II p23), nor the body (E II p19), nor external bodies (E II p26), except "through the ideas of the affections of its own Body" (E II p26). Knowledge doesn't bypass the body; it is not something that happens irrespective of bodies. This claim is implicated in *conatus* – in striving – and in the self-interest that goes along with it. It is not only that we won't ordinarily care about something unless we have a vested interest in it. What Spinoza is saying is that we *can't* know anything at all except insofar as we are affected by it. We are thus correct in saying that, at the very least, we know "our body," for, in Spinoza's distinctive phrase, the idea of the body is the "first thing that constitutes the actual being of a human Mind" (E II p11). What this means is that "whatever happens in the object of the idea constituting the human Mind must be perceived by the human Mind," and therefore "if the object of the idea constituting a human Mind is a body, nothing can happen in that body which is not perceived by the Mind" (E II p12).

On the other hand, "the human Mind does not involve adequate knowledge of the parts composing the human Body," i.e., "the parts of the human Body are highly composite Individuals," each of which itself has many parts (E II p24dem). We have only inadequate knowledge of the body taken as something composed of thousands or millions (or more) of parts, most of which we do not even sense, let alone understand ("Nature's power is infinite" [TTP, 74]). But we "perceive" whatever happens in the body (E II p12) according to the logic that "the order and connection of ideas is the same as the order and connection of things" (E II p7). I may not sense, for example, that the blood flow through one of my arteries will soon be blocked; but this inadequacy is also mental, which means, to Spinoza, that I do not discover this fact about my body as I would a fact about a foreign body. It does not mean that my body's frailties *correspond* to mental ones. It means that physical limitation is part of the confusion and vacillation that Spinoza sees as characteristic of superstition and credulity. As one might put it more colloquially, my body does not belong to me; it *is* me. Its power and ability is my power and ability, and conversely its frailties are mine. Thus I experience bondage to the natural order as a limitation on my ability both to reason and to act. But this experience of bondage provides its own standard: bondage, as opposed to freedom. We know, according to Spinoza, not only *that* we are not free, unlimited, all-powerful, all-knowing. We know what it would mean to be free – we know, we sense, what freedom is.

The intensity of the feeling of being aided or restrained in the context of inadequate ideas, as well as the hope for whatever helps us and the fear of what disables us, is relative to the thing in question (the external cause). Indeed, as above, "anything whatever can be the accidental cause of Hope and Fear" (E III p50). This creates a situation where not only do we easily become dependent on the presence of such causes ("greed"), striving to "use them as means to the things we hope for, or to remove them as obstacles or causes of fear" (E III p50). We are also "torn," because hope and fear simply mirror each other – there can be no hope without the fear of not successfully attaining what one desires, and this fear increases the hope itself; by the same token, there can be no fear without the desperate hope that whatever is fearful will be removed, and this hope can easily quicken the feelings of fear.

There is a second reason why we are tormented by bondage, and thus less able to moderate and restrain the affects. Other people can precisely be an "external cause" on which we depend, and this is a tremendous source of ambivalence, or as Spinoza calls it, "vacillation of mind," i.e., a state in which one and the same thing is both a source of joy and sadness, power and weakness (E III p17). For to the extent that we lean on others in pursuit of things we hope for or fear, they are also by definition rivals for those very same things – rivals for limited goods and limited sources of power. This attachment reminds us of our vulnerability, which in turn is exacerbated by the fact that the very desirability of such goods depends on the envy of those same rivals. The rub as Spinoza sees it is that, on the one hand, "if we imagine that someone loves, desires, or hates something we ourselves love, desire, or hate, we shall thereby love, desire, or hate it with greater constancy" (E III p31); yet on the other hand, "if we imagine that someone enjoys some thing that only one can possess, we shall strive to bring it about that he does not possess it" (E III p32). He calls this potent brew by the innocuous name of "love of esteem":

He who exults at being esteemed by the multitude is made anxious daily, strives, sacrifices, and schemes, in order to preserve his reputation. For the multitude is fickle and inconstant; unless one's reputation is guarded, it is quickly destroyed. Indeed, because everyone desires to secure the applause of the multitude, each one willingly puts down the reputation of the other. And since the struggle is over a good thought to be the highest, this gives rise to a monstrous lust of each to crush the other in any way possible. The one who at last emerges as victor exults more in having harmed the other than in having benefited himself. (E IV p58s)

Spinoza moves very rapidly from "the multitude is fickle and inconstant" to "everyone desires to secure the applause of the multitude." As he says of the hope and fear that constitute our vacillation of mind, "this is the source of the Superstitions by which men are everywhere troubled" (E III p50s). He seems to hold both of these positions at once – that the multitude (in the sense excluding himself and others who live according to the guidance of reason) is fickle and inconstant *and* that, in the same breath, "everyone" is implicated in the multitude. The *Ethics* and the TTP both attempt to keep this tension alive: we are necessarily subject to the affects, but there is much we can do to moderate them; we "are naturally inclined to Hate and Envy" others (E III p55s) and we are "God" to each other (E IV p35s); we are infinitely surpassed by things more powerful than us, and yet, the more adequate ideas we possess the more power over fortune we will have. Insofar as we act like the multitude – giving in to our "monstrous lusts" – we can count on very little sympathy from Spinoza. There is thus a real double edge to his invocation of Ovid in the line quoted above on bondage (from the preface to Part IV): "though [man] sees the better for himself, he is still forced to follow the worst." To be sure one is "forced to follow the worst" in many circumstances significant and insignificant; but insofar as we "see the better," Spinoza wants us to see, we have at least some power to choose it.

Although Spinoza thinks human beings do not as a rule know themselves all that well, he considers the turmoil which results from the impact of fortune on reason and prudence obvious:

No one can have lived in this world without realizing that, when fortune smiles at them, the majority of men, even if quite unversed in affairs, are so abounding in wisdom that any advice offered to them is regarded as an affront, whereas in adversity they know not where to turn, begging for advice from any quarter; and then there is no counsel so foolish, absurd, or vain which they will not follow. (TTP, 1)

Everyone realizes this, he says, although this realization doesn't itself solve the problem.[9] The question is, what use is wisdom if it vanishes in adversity when, it would seem, one most needs it? What use is wisdom if we see the better and nevertheless choose the worst? It might be possible to read this as the prelude to an exhortation to seek equanimity in the face of suffering and to disassociate wisdom from the turmoils of personal experience. But personal experience is what is at issue here: Who can have lived in the world and not known that it is easier to be wise when things go well for us than when they do not? Does this mean the wisdom we possess in good times only – the wisdom that vanishes, or chooses the worst when we see the better – isn't wisdom? Or alternatively, does it mean we ought to strive harder to maintain what little wisdom we do possess when we enter more "critical times"?

Where Spinoza focuses his energy in the TTP is on the ways in which, given the close relationship between the insecurity of "material welfare" (TTP, 48) and "an inconstant and irresolute spirit" (TTP, 53), the dissemination of extraordinary and wondrous things is incredibly attractive, all too easily performing the function of a consolation, regardless of whether their contents are silly or reasonable – regardless of whether what is being disseminated is "religion, true or false" (TTP, 3). The "common people," Spinoza observes, usually "take [more] pleasure in the stories and in strange and unexpected happenings [in the Bible] than in the doctrine implicit in the narratives," which might require them actually to address their own conditions, or to live otherwise than they are living (TTP, 69). In this light, whatever its intrinsic merits, the extraordinary or the novel effectively distracts people from turning their efforts to what can actually ameliorate both material and mental hardship, and by the same token prevents them from detaching themselves from those things they genuinely cannot change. There is nothing intrinsically false or disingenuous about novelty.[10] But the origin of superstition is fear, and therefore,

> like all other instances of hallucination and frenzy, [superstition] is bound to assume very varied and instable forms [since] it is sustained only by hope, hatred, anger and deceit. For it arises not from reason but from emotion, and emotion

---

[9] Spinoza's use of knowledge from experience here can be summed up in the paradox that no one ignores the lessons of experience except the fact that, or the extent to which, they themselves are subject to them. Pierre-François Moreau interprets Spinoza's point here more strongly, viz., "the conditions of experience ensure that experience is opaque to its own lessons" ("Fortune and the Theory of History," in *The New Spinoza: Theory Out of Bounds*, ed. Warren Montag and Ted Stolze [Minneapolis: University of Minnesota Press, 1997], 102).

[10] Spinoza grounds his critique of the novel on his critique of miracles, arguing that here more than anywhere, novelty is used in superstitious ways.

of the most powerful kind . . . Indeed, as the multitude remains ever at the same level of wretchedness, so it is never long contented, and is best pleased only with what is new and has not yet proved delusory. (TTP, 2)

Wisdom, then, appears to have something to do not only with *what* one knows but with the effects of knowledge and the condition of those apprehending it. Such information as the multitude is able to glean in the condition of wretchedness cannot properly be considered wisdom, whatever its contents, for their wretchedness prevents them from putting it to use. But what of the sense of resignation in this passage, the claim that "as," i.e., *since* "the multitude remains *ever at the same level* of wretchedness" (*imo quia vulgus semper aeque miserum manet*), it is never long content (G III: 6)? The implication seems mixed: superstition is connected to and at least partly explained by wretchedness, but wretchedness, no less than superstition, is constitutive of the multitude in itself – multitudes will always be wretched (through scarcity and greed equally), and thus the problem to be ameliorated is not wretchedness per se but simply its most egregious symptoms, the hope and fear of superstition or, more generally, the sense that things could be otherwise.

Spinoza gives direct support to such a reading when he counsels in the *Ethics* that "concerning matters of fortune, or things which are not in our power, i.e., concerning things which do not follow from our nature . . . [these] we must expect and bear calmly both good fortune and bad" (E II p49s[IVB]). To the extent that there are things about the human condition that cannot be changed (death being the most dramatic example), it is proper for human beings not to meditate on this at all. Indeed, "a free man thinks of nothing less than death," not because a free man accepts or resigns himself to his death, nor because a free man studiously avoids this recognition, but simply because a free man is not led by fear. His wisdom, Spinoza says, "is a meditation on life" (*vitae meditatio est*), on what he can actually do to preserve his life and advance his own interests (E IV p67, G II: 261). It is fear of fortune (and conversely hope for fortune's favor) that most detracts from wisdom, for it is fear that makes human beings at odds with what is in their own interest, "doing what they are most opposed to doing, taking no account of the usefulness and the necessity of the action to be done, concerned only not to incur capital or other punishment" (TTP, 64).

Fear, then, is most destructive of both the power and the genuine and hard-won equanimity that reason confers. Accordingly "we shall bear calmly those things which happen to us contrary to what the principle of our advantage demands, if we are conscious that we have done our duty, that the power we have could not have extended itself to the point where we could have avoided those things, and that we are a part of the whole of nature, whose order we follow" (E IV appXXXII). But this "if" is not insignificant regarding the multitude and their wretchedness. We (we the multitude *and* we the philosophers) are necessarily fearful, subject to misery, and likely to be carried away by lusts (we are necessarily fearful at least in part *because* we are subject to misery and lust). However, we (we the philosophers *and* we the multitude) can adopt a calm bearing – an attitude of stoicism or dispassion in the face of misery and lust – *only* when "the power we have could not have extended itself to the point where we could have avoided those things." In other words, misery and wretchedness beget themselves (just as tyrannical regimes do). But this is hardly the end of the story.

Spinoza wants to know exactly what disempowers the multitude, what contributes to its servitude, its bondage, its wretchedness, all of which are "facts." But he permits *himself* a calm bearing toward these facts only when he himself has done his duty, has extended his power to the furthest extent possible. As he says in the *Ethics*, "because, among singular things, we know nothing more excellent than a man who is guided by reason, we can show best how much our skill and understanding are worth by educating men so that at last they live according to the command of their own reason" (E IV appIX). "At last" indeed. Educating men so that they live at the command of their own reason is no easy thing given the structural and psychical obstacles. Speaking to enlightened and unenlightened alike (for both are part of nature), Spinoza's point is that there will be things that happen to us over which we are powerless. In this case we should try to be phlegmatic. But it is the very "essence" of human beings, and thus of the multitude, too, to strive to augment their power, and this striving ("the first and only foundation of virtue"[E IV p22c]) is the beginning of the way out of wretchedness:

He who wishes to avenge wrongs by hating in return surely lives miserably. On the other hand, one who is eager to overcome Hate by Love, strives joyously and confidently, resists many men as easily as one, and requires the least help from fortune. Those whom he conquers yield joyously, not from lack of strength, but from an increase in their powers. (E IV p46s)

Those who would have us rise above human misery, or those who think that this misery "depends on our will" alone "and that we can [therefore] command [the affects] absolutely," get it wrong, according to Spinoza. For "experience cries out against this . . . [and] much practice and application are required to restrain and moderate them" (E V pref).[11]

---

[11] As Spinoza puts it in the TTP, "one needs godly and brotherly exhortation, a good upbringing, and most of all, a judgment that is free" (TTP, 106).

Thus it may be ironic but it is thoroughly predictable that those most in the thrall of fortune, "greedily coveting [its] favors," are least successful at procuring its goods. In retaliation for this injustice, what is "merely" ordinary is not only ignored; it is vilified:

reason they call blind, because it cannot reveal a sure way to the vanities that they covet, and human wisdom they call vain, while the delusions of the imagination, dreams, and other childish absurdities are taken to be the oracles of God. Indeed they think that God, spurning the wise, has written his decrees not in man's mind but in the entrails of beasts, or that by divine inspiration and instigation these decrees are foretold by fools, madmen or birds. To such madness are men driven by their fears. (TTP, 2)

Spinoza's account of superstition is intended to emphasize that it does not simply consist in having a "confused idea of the deity" (TTP, 2). He thinks the majority of human beings *do* have confused ideas of the deity, but what also interests him about superstition is where it comes from, and it comes, not from simply being *mistaken* about who and what God really is, due, say, to an insufficient philosophical education, but from the tumult of vacillating between hope and fear. The extraordinary in this sense is a shortcut, a way for human beings to avoid doing the work that is actually before them and a way to surpass by far what any actual, human work could actually accomplish. This is why ordinary reason is seen as so threatening – it denies our fantasies to be gods.

But superstition is clearly only half of the problem; or rather, the superstitious multitude includes both the wretched and the tyrannical. What concerns Spinoza is the relationship between greed and adversity, the promulgation of "novel and striking doctrine" by those "actuated by desire . . . to attract admiration," and the provocation of "great quarrels, envy, and hatred, which no passage of time could assuage" (TTP, 4). Novelty, and the wonder to which it gives rise, are not only problematic from the standpoint of the wretched; they are also usually the sign of a desire for self-aggrandizement. Unlike Descartes, who lumped wonder among the primary affects and considered it fruitful, Spinoza thinks it simply signifies a lack of understanding.[12] To Descartes, wonder is useful in that "it makes us learn and retain in our memory things of which we were previously ignorant," i.e., it is a passion which accompanies the experience of the unusual and provokes us to learn about it.[13] Thus he says, "we see that people who are not naturally inclined to wonder are usually

---

[12] Descartes defines wonder as "a sudden surprise of the soul which brings it to consider with attention the objects that seem to it unusual and extraordinary" ("Passions of the Soul," *Philosophical Writings*, vol. I, 353).
[13] "Passions of the Soul," *Philosophical Writings*, vol. I, 354.

very ignorant."[14] Spinoza defines wonder in a similar way, as the unusual, noting that "when we suppose that we imagine in an object something singular, which we have never seen before, we are only saying that when the Mind considers that object, it has nothing in itself which it is led to consider from considering that." But it is not, for him, a provocation to knowledge, nor is it especially useful in other ways. "If," for example, "[Wonder] is aroused by an object we fear, it is called Consternation, because Wonder at an evil keeps a man so suspended in considering it that he cannot think of other things by which he could avoid that evil" (E III p52dem and s). What is wondered at is simply what doesn't connect up with what we already know. As an emotion, wonder "detains" or "fixes" the mind "until [such a time as] it is determined by other causes to think of other things," that is, until we can connect the novel to the storehouse of things we already know and hence demystify it (E III Def.Aff.IV). It is certainly not in itself either the condition for knowledge (it easily acts as a "distraction" [E III Def.Aff.IV]) or something to be cultivated, for rather than stimulating a desire to understand, it tends to stimulate just the opposite – what is "least comprehensible . . . evokes the greatest wonder" (TTP, 72):

If [those in the grip of fortune's fickle favors] are struck with wonder at some unusual phenomenon, they believe this to be a portent signifying the anger of the gods or of a supreme deity, and they therefore regard it as a pious duty to avert the evil by sacrifice and vows . . . There is no end to the kind of omens that they imagine, and they read extraordinary things into Nature as if the whole of Nature were a partner in their madness. (TTP, 1)

Wonder and mystery are crutches for the ignorant and swords for the impious, for the latter "know that if ignorance is taken away, then foolish wonder, the only means they have of arguing and defending their authority, is also taken away" (E I app).

It is not simply that human beings can be contrary to one another due to their lust for, and pursuit of, goods that cannot be shared ("immoderate greed"). It is that those goods that *can* be shared are made "wondrous," and subjected to "so much quarreling and such bitter feuding" that they become virtually unrecognizable. Even wisdom, which is ostensibly insusceptible of being hoarded, is made to seem as if it is something elite or exclusive. As Spinoza says of theologians who "make no attempt whatsoever to live according to the Bible's teachings," the "blind and passionate desire to interpret Scripture and to introduce innovations in religion" is substituted for what is "most clearly taught by Scripture itself" (TTP,

---

[14] "Passions of the Soul," *Philosophical Writings*, vol. I, 355.

88). What is in actuality least dependent on fortune, least relative to circumstance or to goods like wealth and honor that people naturally covet and fight about, but rather is "the greatest good . . . common to all, and . . . enjoyed by all equally," namely "to know God" – *this* can become something enviable, private, exclusive (E IV p36 and dem). For Spinoza this attitude toward what can be common to all is much more than simply losing something in translation. It is perverting and upending the very meaning and import of the "thing" in question – it is burying "the divine light" with the tools (avarice) used for wealth and honor, and calling this burial faith (TTP, 5).

Spinoza's arguments with theologians were directed toward many of his contemporaries, both friend (Ludwig Meyer) and foe (Calvinist establishment, rabbis).[15] This immediacy is undoubtedly what accounts for both the anger Spinoza shows in places in the TTP and some of the anger with which so many of his readers were afflicted. It is Spinoza who teaches (though this would likely be among the things he felt common experience amply shows) that "hate is increased by being returned" (E III p43). One could also attribute the anger to Spinoza's refusal to "bear calmly" things (wretchedness, superstition, bondage) that did not overreach his own powers. But, more importantly, Spinoza's arguments are first and foremost directed toward the medieval opponents he actually names. Meyer was no match for a thinker of Spinoza's stature; surely not worthy of an entire book, least of all in a corpus where only one other book was actually published in his lifetime. In fact none of Spinoza's theologico-political opponents in contemporary Holland was a serious interlocutor.[16] To be sure there were serious *opponents*, and it must be true to say that it was easier to criticize Maimonides (not only long dead but Jewish!) than to criticize Meyer. But Spinoza has an argument with Maimonides (and his conceptual twin, Alpakhar) in particular – with the God of wonder – and it is this argument to which he devotes all of his intellectual energy. It is therefore absolutely crucial to ask what exactly is Spinoza's argument with this God – the most extraordinary, most novel, idea with which theologians enthrall the multitude, the God of transcendence, creator of heaven and earth? Spinoza's claim is that the God who is transcendent – perfect – not only emerges out of impotence

[15] J. Samuel Preus has written extensively on Spinoza's contemporary interlocutors. See most recently, *Spinoza and the Irrelevance of Biblical Authority* (Cambridge: Cambridge University Press, 2001. See also Lee C. Rice, "Meyer as Precursor to Spinoza on the Interpretation of Scripture," *Philosophy and Theology* 13.1 (2001): 159–180.
[16] On Spinoza's interlocutors, friend and foe, see the introduction by Steven Barbone, Lee Rice, and Jacob Adler to *Spinoza: The Letters*, trans. Samuel Shirley (Indianapolis: Hackett,1995), 1–58.

(superstition). It perversely constructs impotence as the only possible human state.

The God of the philosophers

Spinoza begins his treatment of the God of the philosophers by denying the word perfection its classical and medieval connotations.[17] "Perfection and imperfection [like good and evil] are only modes of thinking, i.e., notions we are accustomed to feign because we compare individuals of the same species or genus to one another" (E IV pref). We imagine that this comparison is simply a reflection of nature, he thinks, because of what is the most elementary error we can make, which is to assume that nature is created for our benefit, and that what is perfect are those things in nature that most correspond to what *we* happen to desire or find useful, while what is imperfect are those things that inhibit, horrify, or repel us. As Spinoza flatly puts it, while this line of thinking seeks "to show that nature does nothing in vain (i.e., nothing which is not of use to men), [it] seems to have shown only that nature and the Gods are as mad as men." For "daily experience" vividly confirms otherwise in the simple fact that nature just as often thwarts as supports human flourishing (E I app, 441).[18] Rather than concluding that terms like good and evil or perfect and imperfect are modes of human valuation that have little to do with the way the world is taken in itself, "it was easier . . . to put [the reasons for nature's inconveniences or imperfections] among the other unknown things whose use they were ignorant of, and so remain in the state of ignorance in which they had been born, than to destroy that whole construction, and think up a new one" (E I app, 441). To Spinoza, God's unknowable "perfection," along with the elaborate theodicies that come out of it, are simply a "sanctuary of ignorance" (E I app, 443).

Spinoza thinks there *is* a valid way to use the word *perfection*, but he thinks we would do well to notice first, that human beings do so on the basis of their desires and experiences, and second, that they tend immediately to alienate themselves from their own judgments. Thus, for example, when they "see the structure of the human body, they are struck

---

[17] The term "God of the philosophers" comes from Pascal (*Pensées*, trans. A. J. Krailsheimer [New York: Penguin Books, 1966]), who distinguishes between the God of the philosophers (the deists, and heathens, and the Epicureans), "who is the author of mathematical truths and the order of the elements," and "the God of Abraham, Isaac, Jacob, the God of the Christians," who is a "God of love and consolation" (§449, 141). I use the term sharply to distinguish Spinoza's God from the God of the medieval philosophers (Jewish and Christian). For another recent view, see Richard Mason, *The God of Spinoza: A Philosophical Study* (Cambridge: Cambridge University Press, 1997).

[18] I provide page numbers here since the appendix is seven pages long.

by foolish wonder, and because they do not know the causes of so great an art, they infer that it is constructed, not by mechanical, but by divine, or supernatural art, and constituted in such a way that one part does not injure another" (E I app, 443). Although we may be dimly aware that "infinitely many things are found which far surpass our imagination," and thus far surpass in complexity our conception of what is "ordered" or "disordered," we nevertheless assume that our notions of harmony are God's, and that he has "created all things in order" (E I app, 445, 444).

Spinoza holds, by contrast, that *everything* in nature can be seen as "perfect," not because he claims to understand its true purpose, but because everything strives in its own way to preserve its being and to flourish on its own terms, even when in doing so it causes grief or suffering for us:

> many are accustomed to arguing in this way: if all things have followed from the necessity of God's most perfect nature, why are there so many imperfections in nature? why are things corrupt to the point where they stink? so ugly that they produce nausea? why is there confusion, evil, and sin? [But] those who argue in this way are easily answered. For the perfection of things is to be judged solely from their nature and power; things are not more or less perfect because they please or offend men's sense, or because they are of use to, or are incompatible with, human nature. (E I app, 446)

This is not to deny that we should see the world in the terms that most matter to us. Indeed, this is the only thing we *can* actually do, that is, judge things on the basis of whether they are useful or repellent, pleasing or offensive, life-enhancing or life-denying to us (there is no world taken in itself). Spinoza's view is precisely that "from the laws of his own nature, everyone necessarily wants, or is repelled by, what he judges to be good or evil . . . [for] knowledge of good and evil is itself an affect of Joy or Sadness, insofar as we are conscious of it . . . [and] this appetite is nothing but the very essence, *or* nature of man" (E IV p19). The error is in assuming that in doing so we are simply conforming ourselves to the way things actually are, or to the way God has made things.

The problem with the model of a perfect God guiding nature providentially is not simply that it is false, i.e., it is not simply that this view of God fails to agree with its object, as a true idea must (E I a6). The problem is that the view is not adequate. Spinoza distinguishes between a "true idea" (agreement between idea and object) and an adequate idea, an idea "which, insofar as it is considered in itself, without relation to an object, has all the properties, *or* intrinsic denominations of a true idea" (E II d4), such as clarity and distinctness. One faces here a potentially fatal conflict between what we would call a correspondence theory of truth and a coherence theory of truth. Adequate ideas can be considered apart from their relation to an object because, considered in themselves, they are truth-bearing; they are productive of truth, one might say, constrained only by their fit with other adequate ideas. True ideas, by contrast, connect up with a particular object, and are relative thereto. Spinoza intends these two "theories" to fit together, for he claims that all adequate ideas are also true: "Every idea that in us is absolute, or adequate and perfect, is true" (E II p34), which presumably means that, although correspondence with an object is not what makes an idea adequate, there still could be some kind of test whereby such an idea was shown not to conflict with the world.[19] It is more difficult to reverse the situation, however, by asking whether all true ideas are adequate, that is, meaningful within a particular system, since what makes an idea true is its correspondence with something, not its coherence relative to other ideas.

   This difficulty is partly due to the poverty, or at least the anachronism, of this contemporary philosophical distinction.[20] Once Spinoza gets to Part II, he introduces a second conception of truth, holding that "an idea true in us is that which is adequate in God insofar as he is explained through the nature of the human Mind" (E II p43dem). Since God is not external to the mind (though nor is he internal to it), our ideas cannot be said to correspond to him or his ideas. Therefore, Spinoza tells us, "to have a true idea means nothing other than knowing a thing perfectly, *or* in the best way. And of course no one can doubt this," he continues, "unless he thinks that an idea is something mute, like a picture on a tablet, and not a mode of thinking, viz. the very [act of] of understanding" (E II p42s). The continued advantage of the first meaning of truth is that it emphasizes Spinoza's conception of reality as *real*, i.e., not constructed by the mind or language. The notion of agreement continues to make sense in a Spinozian universe in a common sense way (i.e., with reference to objects other than God). But at the same time, adequacy (with the second meaning of truth) becomes the stronger term for him because it makes reference to the ways in which, even though the world does not take our wishes into account, the world *we value* is not a different world. Thus,

---

[19] In the demonstration to this proposition, Spinoza simply reiterates the conditions of adequacy, noting that "when we say that there is in us an adequate and perfect idea, we are saying nothing but that . . . there is an adequate and perfect idea in God insofar as he constitutes the essence of our Mind, and consequently . . . we are saying nothing but that such an idea is true" (E II p34dem).

[20] Dan Nesher solves this problem by way of Peirce, arguing that Spinoza no more suffers a contradiction here than other "pragmaticists" ("Spinoza's Theory of Truth," in *Spinoza: The Enduring Questions*, ed. Graeme Hunter [Toronto: University of Toronto Press, 1994]), 140–177.

Spinoza writes a few lines after having introduced adequacy, "by reality and perfection I understand the same thing" (E II d6).[21]

Truth is something we perceive (knowledge). Adequacy is something we do (power). The difference between truth/falsity and adequacy/inadequacy is one of emphasis. As Spinoza puts it, "there is nothing positive in ideas on account of which they are called false" (E II p33). Rather (as so many medievals had similarly expressed it), "falsity consists in the privation of knowledge" (E II p34). However, once this privation is related to adequacy and inadequacy, it becomes clear that falsity is not simply a lack of knowledge. We cannot be said to err insofar as we are ignorant of something. Rather, falsity consists in "mutilated and confused" ideas, and this comes, he thinks, from the fact that we are not autonomous relative to nature, from the fact that we are disempowered, in a condition of *servitus*, and, as above, from the fact that we worsen these things through our misery, our greed, our preference for consolatory illusions. Therefore on one level, "inadequate and confused ideas follow with the same necessity as adequate, *or* clear and distinct ideas," for inadequacy is just limitation (E II p36). Yet at the same time this is what the *Ethics* is explicitly seeking to remedy, that is, to "lead us, by the hand, as it were, to the knowledge of the human Mind and its highest blessedness" (E II pref).

Falsity/inadequacy, then, also signifies a misdirection of energy and constitutes a decrease of power (including both cognitive and physical power). By contrast, true/adequate ideas act in the opposite way, constituting an increase of power. Both indicate modifications (increases and decreases) of perfection rightly understood, that is, a model of flourishing which explicitly *does* take human grief and suffering into account, and against which we can judge as "good what we know certainly is a means by which we may approach nearer and nearer to [this] model of human nature we set before ourselves" (E IV pref, 545).

The two crucial things to see here are first, perfection is something that can be augmented or diminished, and second, perfection is both a model *we* put before ourselves and one against which we may be measured. The paradox is that it is we who determine what perfection amounts to, but insofar as we don't live up to it, the degree of perfection in/of the world as a whole is diminished – in other words, our making (*factum*) has reality. Perfection itself (God itself) is both finite and infinite. On this view, perfection is at once essentially human and humanly essential (essential

---

[21] The literature on Spinoza's notion of truth is vast, and needless to say I cannot do justice to it here. A good place to begin is Thomas Carson Mark, *Spinoza's Theory of Truth* (New York: Columbia University Press, 1972), and the essays in Yirmiyahu Yovel, ed., *Spinoza on Knowledge and the Human Mind* (Leiden: E. J. Brill, 1994).

for human beings), in contrast to some essence or quality human beings lack: "the main thing to note is that when I say that someone passes from a lesser to a greater perfection, and the opposite, I do not understand that he is changed from one essence, *or* form, to another . . . Rather we conceive that his power of acting, insofar as it is understood through his nature, is increased or diminished" (E IV pref).

According to Spinoza's notion of falsity, the judgment that perfection and imperfection simply describe something about the world (independently of human valuation) is a major source of the diminution of human power because it leads to two assumptions that confuse us and thus make us more vulnerable to being "acted on" (disempowered) by things external to us: first, that, as human beings, we are by definition imperfect and are striving more and more to perfect ourselves according to a transcendent standard that functions as our telos; and/or second, that as human beings we originate in some kind of lost perfect state that we are striving more and more to recover. While both of these assumptions clearly have a place in the religions of Judaism and Christianity, Spinoza's philosophical interlocutors here are Aristotle and Plato and their "followers" (KV, 86–87). As Spinoza puts it in the preface to the TTP, the enormous and convoluted effort to find Greek philosophical teachings in the Bible is utterly inconsistent with the "divine light" that is properly there:

I grant that they have expressed boundless wonder at Scripture's profound mysteries, yet I do not see that they have taught anything more than the speculations of Aristotelians or Platonists, and they have made Scripture conform to these so as to avoid appearing to be the followers of heathens. It was not enough for them to share in the delusions of the Greeks: they have sought to represent the prophets as sharing in these same delusions. This surely shows quite clearly that they do not even glimpse the divine nature of Scripture, and the more enthusiastic their admiration of these mysteries, the more clearly they reveal that their attitude to Scripture is one of abject servility rather than belief. (TTP, 5)

With respect to Aristotle, the "delusions" Spinoza has in mind concern the structure of potentiality and actuality, whereby movement and change are always signs of imperfection and where one's "end" is always figured in opposition to (that is, absolutely transcendent of) where one begins. For Aristotle, the absolute good against which all partial, practical goods are measured is that intellectual contemplation of the eternal, substantial, first principle of all existence, and the attainment of a self-sufficient life.[22] In a similar vein, in Plato's structure of being and becoming, becoming

---

[22] Aristotle, *Nicomachean Ethics*, in *The Complete Works of Aristotle*, ed. Jonathan Barnes (Princeton, N.J.: Princeton University Press, 1984), vol. II, 1860–1862 (bk. VII).

is always the sign that being proper has been lost. As Socrates puts it in the *Phaedo*, we must strive in life to recollect the truth that we once knew before birth but which is lost by virtue of coming into existence;[23] and as the end of the *Republic* similarly displays, to be born is to be separated from this truth (true being) by the waters of the stream of Oblivion.[24] The philosophical life, to be sure, is that life that can most closely approximate this original knowledge, for "it is only those who practise philosophy in the right way, we say, who always most want to free the soul; and this release and separation of the soul from the body is the preoccupation of philosophers."[25] But as Socrates also tells us, the philosopher simply knows more than others that he is and forever in life must be in ignorance of what he seeks, since what he seeks is the end of life, the end of change, the end of existence:

Philosophy then persuades the soul to withdraw from the senses in so far as it is not compelled to use them and bids the soul to gather itself together by itself, to trust only itself and whatever reality, existing by itself, the soul by itself understands, and not to consider as true whatever it examines by other means, for this is different in different circumstances and is sensible and visible, whereas what the soul itself [in its pure state apart from the body] sees is intelligible and invisible . . . it [ideally] has no willing association with the body in life but avoid[s] it and gather[s] itself together by itself and always practise[s] this, which is no other than practising philosophy in the right way, in fact, training to die easily . . . Therefore, as I said at the beginning, it would be ridiculous for a man to train himself in life to live in a state as close to death as possible, and to resent it when it comes? In fact, Simmias [Socrates] said, those who practise philosophy in the right way are in training for dying and they fear death least of all men.[26]

While Spinoza would agree that the "enlightened" fear death least of all, the notion that one is to train oneself in life to live in a state close to death contrasts sharply with his insistence that "a free man thinks of nothing less than death . . . instead his wisdom is a meditation on life" (E IV p67). "Withdrawing from the senses" equally doesn't make sense to Spinoza because all modes of thinking involve the affections of the body. In order to engage in reasoning or to form "common notions and the adequate ideas of the properties of things," we have to engage with "singular things which have been represented to us through the senses." On its own, this knowledge is "mutilated, confused, and without order for the intellect" – Spinoza calls it "knowledge from random experience" (E II p40s2). But

---

[23] Plato, *Phaedo*, in *Five Dialogues*, trans. G. M. A. Grube (Indianapolis: Hackett, 1981), 114.
[24] Plato, *Republic*, trans. G. M. A. Grube (Indianapolis: Hackett, 1974), 263.
[25] Plato, *Phaedo*, 104.   [26] Plato, *Phaedo*, 122, 119–120, 104.

this random experience is not "mute" – it, too, is a mode of thinking, and what's more, it is the very source of the "imaginary object" Plato calls the "soul" above, as it is of Aristotle's notion of a rational human essence. For "since we are accustomed to depict in our fantasy also images of whatever we understand, it happens that we *imagine* nonentities positively, as beings" (MT, 300).

According to Spinoza, we can see both Greek models at work in the medieval philosophical commentaries on the story of the Garden of Eden. As he notes, "I am . . . astonished at the ingenuity displayed by those . . . who find in Scripture mysteries so profound as not to be open to explanation in any human language, and who have then imported into religion so many matters of a philosophic nature that the Church seems like an academy, and religion like a science, or rather, a subject for debate" (TTP, 157). Spinoza's target is Maimonides here, whom he accuses of holding both "that every passage of Scripture admits of various – and even contrary – meanings" and that the only way we can secure the (single) true meaning is by ascertaining whether it is "in agreement with reason, or is contrary to reason" (TTP, 103). Thus Maimonides' claim is that Scripture's meaning cannot be plain, but that reason – conceived as that which constitutes human beings most essentially – is sufficient to unravel its profundities. In this claim Maimonides is representative not only of Greek philosophy but also of Paul, who Spinoza claims did "more philosophising" than all the other Apostles, most of whom "taught a religious doctrine free from all speculation." "Happy indeed," Spinoza says, "would be our age, if we were to see religion freed again from all superstition" (TTP, 148), i.e., "speculation" is no less superstitious than the embrace of miracles; it, too, is about "boundless wonder."

In chapter 2 of the first part of Maimonides' *Guide*, the movement that Adam undergoes by virtue of his sin is one of descent: from the perfected state of the knowledge of truth and falsity to the imperfect state whereby this knowledge is no longer available to him and is replaced with the relative concepts of good and evil. For Maimonides, as for Plato and Aristotle, the philosophical life – the life of the perfection of the intellect – is that endeavor that human beings can undertake in recognition of this loss. Thus on the one hand we begin, post-Eden, without the knowledge that we seek, for as Maimonides says,

when man was in his most perfect and excellent state, in accordance with his inborn disposition and possessed of his intellectual cognitions – because of which it is said of him: *Thou hast made him but little lower than Elohim* [Ps. 8: 6] – he had no faculty that was engaged in any way in the consideration of generally accepted things [good and evil], and he did not apprehend them . . . However, when he disobeyed and inclined towards his desires of the imagination and the pleasures of his corporeal senses – inasmuch as it is said: *that the tree was good for food and that it was a delight to the eyes* [Gen. 3: 6] – he was punished by being deprived of that intellectual apprehension.[27]

Yet on the other hand, this deprivation that results from human disobedience does not prevent a person from seeking this lost knowledge, and indeed this very lack drives such a quest, for, having become "absorbed in judging things to be bad or fine . . . [Adam] knew how great his loss was, what he had been deprived of, and upon what a state he had entered."[28] To be sure, for Maimonides human beings do not know the content of the loss, i.e., they have lost access to the truth entirely, but they know *that* they have lost something of absolute value and they thus seek to remedy it in diverse ways.

On Maimonides' model, the best way to seek what has been lost is to pursue a life whereby one increasingly pares away the superfluities of worldly knowledge (the knowledge that stems from pursuing pleasure and imaginings)[29] in order to arrive finally (or perhaps only ever approximately) at the telos that structures the quest from the beginning and indeed constitutes the essence of humanity per se (what Aristotle called a final cause).[30] Whether this telos for Maimonides also includes *halakhah* (Jewish law) or not, i.e., whether once we get there the "there" is something both philosophic and practical or even political, is immaterial on this point.[31] The point is simply that the path is one of ascent, from the lower perfections of wealth, health, and virtue, to the ultimate perfection of the knowledge of God. As in the stepping stones Socrates speaks of

[27] Maimonides, *Guide*, vol. I, ch. 2, 25. The conceptual difficulties involved in this passage (from perfection to imperfection) – and exactly what it means to be "deprived" of intellectual apprehension – have been much commented upon. See Lawrence V. Berman, "Maimonides on the Fall of Man," *AJS Review* 5 (1980): 1–15, and Warren Zev Harvey, "Maimonides' Commentary on Genesis 3: 22," *Daat* 12 (1984): 15–22. For a resolution of this question in the final chapters of the *Guide*, see Menachem Kellner, *Maimonides on Human Perfection* (Atlanta, Ga.: Scholars Press, 1990). What is significant in comparison to Spinoza is that while the latter denies that the first state is one of perfection (in Maimonides' sense), he does not think that the imperfect state is "devoid of intellectual apprehension." In other words, Spinoza's human being is in some sense both less and more exalted than Maimonides'. For an alternative account that contends Spinoza's is a Maimonidean reading of the fall, see Heidi M. Ravven, "The Garden of Eden: Spinoza's Maimonidean Account of the Genealogy of Morals and the Origin of Society," *Philosophy and Theology* 13.1 (2001): 3–51.

[28] Maimonides, *Guide*, vol. I, ch. 2, 25.   [29] Maimonides, *Guide*, vol. I, ch. 2, 26.

[30] Aristotle, *Metaphysics*, in *Complete Works*, vol. II, 1600 (bk. II).

[31] This is a subject of heated debate in Maimonides scholarship, i.e., whether the end of the *Guide* counsels a kind of purified intellectual perfection beyond law or whether this perfection is only possible in the context of the Jewish commandments (*mitzvot*), which are never suspended. For a good discussion of the terms of the debate, see Kellner, *Maimonides on Human Perfection*.

in the *Republic* on the way towards such a goal, these lower perfections are but shadows, entirely defined with reference to what they are not and ultimately outside of or external to what they are to culminate in. As Socrates explains, in seeking to understand the Forms, the soul must proceed from hypotheses (comprised of visible figures, images, mathematical examples) "not to a first principle but to a conclusion." In the case of students of geometry, for example,

they use visible figures and talk about them, but they are not thinking about them but about the models of which these are likenesses . . . These figures which they fashion and draw, of which shadows and reflections in the water are images, they now in turn use as images, in seeking to understand those others in themselves, which one cannot see except in thought . . . This is what I called the intelligible class [Forms], and said that the soul is forced to use hypotheses in its search for it, not travelling up to a first principle, since it cannot reach beyond its hypotheses, but it uses as images those very things which at a lower level were models and which, in comparison with their images were thought to be clear and honoured as such . . . Understand also that [reason] does not consider its hypotheses as first principles, but as hypotheses in the true sense of stepping stones and starting points, in order to reach that which is beyond hypothesis, the first principle of all that exists.[32]

Likewise for Maimonides wealth is a stepping stone to health, and health a stepping stone to virtue. But the difference *between* these three is unlike the difference between all of them and the highest perfection, since the latter involves the knowledge of God, and God, for Maimonides, cannot be known (in the same way as anything else). As he puts it in the final chapter of the *Guide*,

if you consider each of the three perfections mentioned before, you will find that they pertain to others than you, not to you, even though, according to the generally accepted opinion, they inevitably pertain to you and to others. This ultimate perfection, however, pertains to you alone . . . the prophets too have explained to us and interpreted to us the self-same notions . . . clearly stating to us that neither the perfection of possession nor the perfection of health nor the perfection of moral habits is a perfection of which one should be proud or that one should desire; the perfection of which one should be proud and that one should desire is knowledge of Him, may He be exalted, which is the true science.[33]

"All men by nature desire to know," says Aristotle in the opening lines of the *Metaphysics*.[34] But this originary desire only ever shows us that we "must in a sense end in something which is the opposite of our original

[32] Plato, *Republic*, 165.   [33] Maimonides, *Guide*, vol. III, ch. 54, 635–636.
[34] Aristotle, *Metaphysics*, *Complete Works*, vol. II, 1552 (bk. I).

inquiries," for desire exists only in the realm of perishable life, and perishable life is the opposite of eternal life.[35] As Maimonides asks:

what then should be the state of our intellects when they aspire to apprehend Him who is without matter and is simple to the utmost degree of simplicity, Him whose existence is necessary, Him who has no cause and to whom no notion attaches that is superadded to His essence, which is perfection – the meaning of its perfection being, as we have made clear, that all deficiencies are negated with respect to it – we who only apprehend the fact that He is?

His response is unequivocal. We desire to know God. But we cannot do so:

when the intellects contemplate His essence, their apprehension turns into incapacity; and when they contemplate the proceedings of His actions from His will, their knowledge turns into ignorance; and when the tongues aspire to magnify Him by means of attributive qualifications, all eloquence turns into weariness and incapacity![36]

Here, then, the model is one of the individual positioned between two transcendents, one might say: her origin and her end. Between these two markers, life in all its chaos takes place as the striving to overcome what stands between the achievement – the recovery – of what is finally true. Spinoza begins his critique of transcendence here, i.e., not with the God of the Bible but with the particular transcendence of origins and ends whereby one cannot simultaneously be in possession as well as in quest of what is being sought. The notion of God's transcendence falls into two errors, equally generated by what is commonly called the "Euthyphro" problem.[37] As Socrates states the question to Euthyphro, either something is good because God (or the gods) loves it or God loves something because it is good – either God is the absolute arbiter of value to which everything is subject or God himself is subject to the value-creating standard of the good.[38] At Socrates' prompting, Euthyphro is cajoled into opting for the latter, the sovereignty and independence of the good. But Spinoza's claim is that these are versions of the same error,

---

[35] Aristotle, *Metaphysics*, *Complete Works*, vol. II, 1555 (bk. II).

[36] Maimonides, *Guide*, vol. I, 58, 137.

[37] David Novak employs the Euthyphro problem to good effect in his discussion of the validity of the notion of natural law in Judaism. In fact, while he makes Spinoza something of a scapegoat in his discussion, his conception of "God's wisdom" as both rationally available beyond its articulation and inseparable from its historical and theological context and source is not altogether unlike what I argue Spinoza is saying about the relation of divine and human laws. Novak, *Natural Law in Judaism* (Cambridge: Cambridge University Press, 1998), 16–26.

[38] Plato, *Euthyphro*, in *Five Dialogues*. As Socrates asks Euthyphro, "Consider this: Is the pious loved by the gods because it is pious, or is it pious because it is loved by the gods?" (14).

for either way what is of value is transcendent, i.e., constituted independently of human beings. In Spinoza's terms, both conceptions of God – the one making God the sole measure of value (the position attributed to R. Alpakhar in the TTP) and the other utterly subjecting God to some higher standard (the position attributed to Maimonides) – are anthropomorphic displacements that deprive human beings of understanding the nature of both *servitus* and freedom. Euthyphro's either-or is, for Spinoza, a both-and: both positions subject the human being to something outside of her (the biblical text, for Alpakhar) or inside of her (reason, for Maimonides), and thus both imprison her in a world of ignorance.

Spinoza thinks there are good reasons for anthropomorphisms of both varieties, for when we experience the ways in which the satisfaction of our appetites is limited by nature, we immediately imagine "nothing less" than an "all-powerful" God who, stronger than us but with identical human interests, can rectify these limitations; and when we then contemplate the expansiveness of the divine in this light, "we can think of nothing less than of [these] first fictions," that God, as simply a stronger version of humankind, is subject to limitation, too (E II p10s).

The connection between the imagination and impotence is likely responsible for the idea that the masses as a whole (as opposed to the philosopher) live solely under the guidance of the imagination – that this is Spinoza's "theologico-political" problem.[39] Certainly, if it were possible to live solely under the guidance of the imagination, the masses would be especially likely to do so since, in the main, poverty is more prevalent than wealth, and laziness is more prevalent than zeal for self-knowledge. But the imagination is never found alone. Or as Spinoza puts it, "I grant that no one is deceived insofar as he perceives, i.e., I grant that the imaginations of the Mind, considered in themselves, involve no error. But I deny that a man affirms nothing insofar as he perceives." All figments of the imagination, then, are modes of thinking involving assent and judgment, and it is at the level of judgment and assent that their actual reality is affirmed or excluded (E II p49s [IIIB(ii)]). Thus the imagination is not simply random, fantastic opinions. Grounded in, and emotionally inflected by, the ways in which the body is affected by other bodies, the imagination, and its inadequate ideas, is just as essential

---

[39] See Yovel, who contends that "Spinoza regards the multitude as a special category in itself. Individuals could rise above the *imaginatio* and attain *ratio*, even *scientia intuitiva*; but the great majority is incapable of doing this – and the concept of the multitude is defined by this majority" ("Spinoza: The Psychology of the Multitude and the Uses of Language," 305).

as reason.[40] It expresses the essential ways in which reasoning (the conception of that which is common in things) is always undertaken in the context of limitation.[41] This emphasis on finitude means for Spinoza that "imaginations do not disappear through the presence of the true insofar as it is true, but because there occur others, stronger than them, which exclude the present existence of the things we imagine" (E IV p1s). It is therefore possible in this light to understand "the Superstitions by which men are everywhere troubled" in terms not only of human impotence (E III p50s). For if the imagination is, through the emotions of hope and fear, the "instrument of fortune,"[42] it is also the faculty whose attention to the fate of the body helps to ward off fortune's power. As Spinoza notes, "if the Mind, while it imagined nonexistent things as present to it, at the same time knew that those things did not exist, it would, of course, attribute this power of imagining to a virtue of its nature, not to a vice" (E II p19s).

Even a qualified version of this thesis – that the masses live mainly under the guidance of the imagination – is predicated on the assumption that Spinoza's model of enlightenment involves a passage from one form of knowledge to another, from the imagination to reason to intuitive knowledge (the highest kind of knowledge, for Spinoza), from inadequate and confused knowledge (imagination) to adequate knowledge (second and third kinds of knowledge). Yet, as above, Spinoza thinks that "inadequate and confused ideas follow with the same necessity as adequate, or clear and distinct ideas" (E II p36). He thinks, in other words, that because the mind can have only an inadequate knowledge of its own body, even knowledge "from the common order of nature," not to mention the flights of the imagination, is "confused and mutilated," that is, incomplete, inadequate, and a source of limitation (E II p29c). One could say negatively, then, that this inadequacy is never transcended. Or one could

---

[40] On this see F. Mignini, "Theology as the Work and Instrument of Fortune," in *Spinoza's Political and Theological Thought*, ed. C. De Deugd (Amsterdam: North-Holland, 1984), 130ff.

[41] While Spinoza defines reason partly as knowledge of "common notions," he thinks that reasoning on the basis of "the common order of nature" alone is a source of confusion (E II p29c). He therefore includes in his definition of reason both "common notions" and "adequate ideas of the properties of things," by which he means ideas "common to all men" (E II p38c). While both involve commonality, the former can include those things by which we are all "externally" determined "from fortuitous encounters with things," while the latter imply being "determined internally," that is, understanding "a number of things at once . . . their agreements, differences, and oppositions" (E II p29c).

[42] The locution is Mignini's, "Theology."

say positively that, in the passage from a lesser to a greater knowledge, all modes of knowing make the passage.[43]

We will see that, as Spinoza discusses in the case of the prophets, and to some degree in the case of the Mosaic polity, the imagination can under some conditions be a very profound gift. The imagination *can* dominate in some more than others, and this will be either a cause for celebration or a cause for lament, depending on the proportion of inadequate to adequate ideas: For "the Mind acts most, of which adequate ideas constitute the greatest part, so that though it may have as many inadequate ideas as the other, it is still distinguished more by those which are attributed to human virtue than by those which betray man's lack of power" (E V p20s). This is a crucial passage in comprehending Spinoza's conception of the imagination in relation to prophecy, for he insists that the prophets did not excel in anything other than virtue, and yet virtue here, and *not* the absence of the imagination, is the one thing that signifies the dominance of adequacy over inadequacy. At the very least, the imagination is something that no one really transcends, for the imagination gives us a basic or primary involvement with singular things, and his view is most emphatically that "the more we understand singular things, the more we understand God" (E V p24).[44]

So how to figure these metaphysical dead-ends differently? In part the crucial point is Spinoza's claim that the mind is the idea of the body, i.e., that this relation is not a union between two things but an identity. The mind is the idea of which the body is the ideatum, and they therefore have the same power. Positively, this means that "in proportion as a Body is more capable than others of doing many things at once, or being acted on in many ways at once, so its Mind is more capable than others of perceiving many things at once" (E II p13s). Negatively, it means that "the idea that constitutes the nature of the human Mind is not, considered in itself alone, clear and distinct" (E II p28s), i.e., much goes on in the human body, and its encounters with other bodies, of which we cannot be aware (E II p24).

The most common way to overcome the constitutive limitations of one's body (the simple fact that there will always be other stronger bodies),

[43] As Mignini usefully puts it, "the imagining mind does not . . . surpass itself by resolving itself in reason, that is, transmuting itself from a representation into a concept" ("Theology," 131). This point is not deducible solely from Spinoza's introduction of the imagination in Part II, where he claims that knowledge of common notions and intuition are the only sources of adequate knowledge. In Part V, however, Spinoza's elaboration of the knowledge of the third kind via the knowledge of singular things resolves this apparent gap between the singularizing imagination and the connecting reason.

[44] Or as Spinoza also puts this key notion, "The Mind can bring it about that all the Body's affections, or images of things, are related to the idea of God" (E V p14).

and thus the limitations of one's mind, is to engage in flights of imaginative fancy. This is unproblematic for Spinoza insofar as one is aware that this is what one is doing and that disembodied ideas are really images and not truths. But insofar as such images are taken for a power the mind possesses apart from the body, e.g., insofar as one conjures the incorporeality of a divine being and assumes thereby to have understood something about God, there will be a diminution of understanding and power. For insofar as we do not see the ways in which we are *in fact* limited – including being unable to think that which contradicts our thinking as it is embodied in the world – the world will have that much more power over us (*fortuna*). By the same token, insofar as we do not appreciate the ways in which we are *not* limited, we will fail to understand that all true ideas involve and express God, and therefore that we have a say in who God is. This appreciation is not one that Spinoza thinks we accept without struggle, for he acknowledges that it can be much more gratifying to feel that one is conforming oneself to a preexisting standard, one that we can tangibly grasp and make immediately present for ourselves. He acknowledges, in other words, that

the true knowledge of good and evil arouses disturbances of the mind, and of-ten yields to lust of every kind. Hence the verse of the Poet [Ovid]: video me-liora, proboque, deteriora sequor [I see and approve the better but follow the worst] . . . Ecclesiastes also seems to have had the same thing in mind he said: "He who increases knowledge increases sorrow." (E IV p17s)

But while knowledge may increase sorrow, it is absolutely crucial not to wallow in melancholy, for melancholy "is always evil." It is "that which consists in this, that the Body's power of acting is absolutely diminished":[45]

I do not say these things in order to infer that it is better to be ignorant than to know, or that there is no difference between the fool and the man who understands when it comes to moderating the affects. My reason, rather, is that it is necessary to come to know both our nature's power and its lack of power, so that we can determine what reason can do in moderating the affects, and what it cannot do. (E IV p17s)

There is something here of the flavor of negative theology in reverse: it is not that we constitutively can't think God, but that by nature we *can* and nevertheless ignore this fact in quest of something illusory. If hubris according to Maimonides is to think we can identify God correctly, hubris

---

[45] Cheerfulness, on the other hand, "is always good, and cannot be excessive" (E IV p42dem).

according to Spinoza is to deny that we are in fact always doing this in one way or another.

The tension between the human ability to act powerfully and the natural disempowerment that we seek vainly to surmount is encapsulated for Spinoza in the confusions surrounding the story of the fall "of our first ancestor" (TP II: 6). The fact that Adam's actions are called "sinful" assumes first, that he was "so completely independent of every other thing that [he] had an absolute power to determine himself and to use reason correctly," and second, that he chose not to, having been overcome by his appetites. Spinoza finds this incoherent, not only because these two propositions are in contradiction, but because he holds that human beings are by nature dependent on things around them, and thus by definition subject to appetites that can easily multiply, rather than relieve, this dependence. As he puts it,

since everything does all it *can* do to preserve its own being, we cannot have the slightest doubt that, if it *were* as much in our power to live by the precept of reason as it is to be led by blind desire, all men *would* be guided by reason, and *would* order their lives wisely; which is very far from being the case. For everyone is captivated by his own pleasure. (TP II: 6)

What does it mean, Spinoza asks, to attribute an ahistorical origin to this fact, namely, to suggest, as many theologians do, that this pursuit of pleasure stems from a first disobedience which disturbed the connection between the human mind or soul and God? It is not the story's fanciful quality that bothers him – he is perfectly comfortable with assessing the philosophical significance of many other passages in the Bible that he also considers mythic or fictive. Rather, what disturbs him is the perverse attempt to cast human existence in some ideal form, from which actual human beings diverge in every way, and thus to misconstrue (misplace) the actual challenges that human beings face. For "if the first man himself was sound in mind and master of his own will, how could he possibly have allowed himself to be seduced and tricked?" This has always been a terrifying question for theologians, who have sometimes responded with the seductiveness of the "devil." To Spinoza this simply begs the question. For the devil, like everyone else, must have striven only to preserve his own being, and hence the question remains as to who seduced the devil, and so on ad infinitum (TP II: 6). Spinoza's point is not only to claim that "the first man" was "subject to passions like ourselves," but to show that the implications of asserting otherwise – the postulate of a pristine state – paralyzes understanding, "for there is no end to the questions which can be asked . . . and so they will not stop asking for the causes of causes until you take refuge in the [mysterious] will of God" (E I app 443), or in other words, the sanctuary of ignorance:

> Since, then, error is nothing, in relation to man, but a privation of the perfect, or right, use of freedom, it follows that it is not placed in any faculty which man has from God, nor in any operation of faculties insofar as it depends on God. Nor can we say that God has deprived us of a greater intellect than he could have given us, and so has brought it about that we can fall into error. For nothing is such that its nature can require anything of God, nor does anything pertain to anything except what the will of God has willed to bestow on it . . . So God has no more deprived us of a greater intellect, or a more perfect faculty of understanding, than he has deprived a circle of the properties of a spherical surface. (DPP I p15s)

It should not be concluded that the views that are erroneous for Spinoza – that we are entirely imprisoned within a sinful world (paradise lost) or that we can entirely escape or surmount such a world (paradise regained) – are caused by the failure to bear fortune's accidents calmly. The failure, rather, is an exorbitant dependence on fortune, and specifically *bona fortunae* – the goods nature or fortune can yield. In moderation, these goods are "inevitable, useful and necessary," but in excess they produce an obsessive hope for fortune's favors (and fear of their withdrawal).[46] As Spinoza puts it, "the more we strive to live according to the guidance of reason, the more we strive to depend less on Hope, to free ourselves from Fear, to conquer fortune as much as we can, and to direct our actions by the certain counsel of reason" (E IV p47s). In other words, the more human beings live according to the guidance of reason, which to Spinoza means categorically rejecting the notion that something was lost in Eden, the more power over fortune we will possess. By the same token, the more human beings have power, the more rational they will be. For "in proportion as the actions of a body depend more on itself alone, and as other bodies concur with it less in acting, so its mind is more capable of understanding distinctly" (E II p13s), and the more we will choose good over evil (i.e., whatever contributes to human flourishing over what doesn't). As he puts it in the *Tractatus Politicus*,

> it is quite impossible to call a man free because he can fail to exist, or fail to use reason; he can be called free only in so far as he has the power to exist and act in accordance with the laws of human nature. So the more free we conceive a man to be, the less we can say that he can fail to use reason, and choose evil in preference to good. (TP II: 7)

Spinoza's critique doesn't by any means cover all of medieval theology and philosophy (there is no evidence that he intended it to). One can

---

[46] Mignini, "Theology," 128.

see Anselm's definition of God as "that than which nothing greater can be thought" in quite Spinozian terms.[47] Anselm, too, argued that when we try to fill in the content of this greatness with total disregard for what thinking can and can't do, we are no longer thinking of God but of something of our own imagining. As he says to Gaunilo's objections on behalf of the fool, it is not that thought posits existence, e.g., because I can think of a "lost island" it must therefore exist, the fool's reductio ad absurdum (or just as absurdly, that existence can be predicated of a "concept of pure reason," as Kant would later point out).[48] It is rather that we form an idea of that "than which nothing greater can be thought" by reflecting on what *can* be thought, and then we magnify what is most valuable to us as much as we can. Anselm doesn't take this as far as Spinoza – he does not presume that what is great (and therefore greatest) is arbitrary, that is, dependent on desire. Anselm, for example, holds that it is self-evident that "that which has neither beginning nor end" is greater than that which has a beginning and no end, or a beginning and an end; and thinks "that which is not forced to change or move" is greater than that which changes and moves.[49] But the investment in reasoning from thought and experience (and thought *as* experience) – and the refusal to accept either (what we would call) reductive idealism/projectionism or reductive materialism – is resonant, and this investment is what remains valuable to Spinoza about the ontological argument.

"By reality and perfection I understand the same thing." The claim is that human ideals must begin on a premise other than the formulation of "oughts" and the denigration of what "is." Our task is not to make what is imperfect perfect, what is finite infinite. This is functionally impossible and a phantasm of the imagination. Our task, rather, is to bring about more perfection, by which he means more knowledge of the world as it is, and thus more that we can do and realize and bring about according to the good as we understand it. There is no guarantee that this good as we understand it is actually life-enhancing rather than life-denying. But it is a human standard predicated on human flourishing, and this is the only test of its adequacy. To the extent that one can use this language, this is what Spinoza would mean by conforming oneself to the perfection of God. This perfection is not an image of something we have taken

---

[47] Anselm, *Proslogion*, trans. M. J. Charlesworth (Notre Dame, Ind.: University of Notre Dame Press, 1965), 117.

[48] See Immanuel Kant, "The Impossibility of an Ontological Proof of the Existence of God," *Critique of Pure Reason*, trans. Norman Kemp Smith (New York: Macmillan, 1929), 500–507. I don't think that Kant's critique is valid against Anselm, but I cannot, of course, make a case for this view here, except indirectly, by connecting Anselm to Spinoza.

[49] Anselm, *Proslogion*, 187.

from the world and superimposed on the heavens, nor is it an absent and indefinable object of transcendental ignorance. God's perfection is, rather, the continual transfiguration of the profane and chaotic world within which God's existence is intrinsically realized, and continually realizable, by us.

Spinoza's God

It remains to ask just who or what is Spinoza's God? It is one of the most striking things about the *Ethics* that it begins with a set of very stark distinctions. Despite Spinoza's investment of the ancient and medieval concept of substance with more power and plenitude than it arguably ever possessed, these distinctions qualify a common assessment of the Spinozistic universe as serenely monistic, self-identical, or infused with the divine.[50] One of the anchors of Spinoza's monism is the claim that "Whatever is, is in God, and nothing can be or be conceived without God" (E I p15), although even this proposition can be interpreted in a theologically conventional way (especially if one doesn't pay too much attention to the locution "in God") according to which all finite objects are dependent for their existence on a creator God. Taken together with the claim that "a substance [God] which is absolutely infinite is indivisible" (E I p13), the reading (popularized by Hegel) which finds in Spinoza no determinate finite or concrete objects at all is prima facie plausible. If everything is in God, and God is indivisible, then there is really only one thing, metaphysically speaking.

Yet Spinoza spends a great deal of time in Part I distinguishing God from other things, and these distinctions play a crucial role in comprehending his concept of substance and the kind of finitude, or as Spinoza also calls it, singularity, to which it gives rise. They include, first, the distinction between substance, i.e., "what is in itself and is conceived through itself," and its modes, i.e., "that which is in another through which it is also conceived" (E I d3 and d5); second, between an infinite thing, i.e., what is "absolutely infinite . . . consisting of an infinity of attributes," and a finite thing, i.e., what "can be limited by another of the same nature" (E I d6 and d2); third, between something that is free, i.e., that "which exists from the necessity of its nature alone, and is determined to act by itself

---

[50] Before Hegel, it was Pierre Bayle, in his *Historical and Critical Dictionary* (1697), who insisted on this reductive monism, along with so many other clichés about Spinoza (Indianapolis: Hackett, 1991). Hegel's reading can be found in *Lectures on the Philosophy of Religion*, ed. P. C. Hodgson, trans. R. F. Brown, P. C. Hodgson, and J. M. Stewart (Berkeley: University of California Press, 1984), vol. I, 377. For a critique of Hegel's reading of Spinoza, see Macherey, *Hegel ou Spinoza*.

alone," and something that is determined, i.e., that "which is determined by another to exist and to produce an effect in a certain and determinate manner" (E I d7); and fourth, between eternity, i.e., "Existence itself, insofar as it is conceived to follow necessarily from the definition alone of the eternal thing," and duration, i.e., existence insofar as it involves the definition of something else, "even if the duration is conceived to be without beginning or end" (E I d8). While each of these distinctions is making a different metaphysical point, they are of a piece in delineating from the beginning the key differences for Spinoza between God (or substance) and "singular things" (including human beings), by which he means "things that are finite and have a determinate existence" (E II d7).

God, then, is an eternal being, a being "in itself and conceived through itself," "which exists from the necessity of its nature alone, and is determined to act by itself alone." Such a being, he tells us, possesses infinite attributes (E I d6). Only two of God's attributes are accessible to human beings: thought and extension. However, this difference between God's ontological makeup and human epistemological limitation is not itself the key to Spinoza's distinction between God and human beings, for when he defines God's attributes, he does so precisely with reference to human knowledge: the attributes per se are "what the intellect perceives of a substance, as constituting its essence" (E I d4). The attributes simply are what the intellect perceives of God. The question then is, if an attribute is already, *by definition*, that which is perceived by the intellect, how can there be *any* that the intellect does not know, much less an infinity of attributes (or put negatively, why can we know only two)?

Spinoza does not explicitly tell us in these first definitions that by intellect he means human intellect, leaving open the possibility that the ontological and the epistemological can be held together by the postulate of a divine intellect. On this reading, the human intellect would perceive only two attributes, but the divine intellect could perceive infinitely many (i.e., all) of its own attributes. However, Spinoza for the most part avoids the language of the divine intellect, since he does not conceive of God as a being that thinks. It is "man" that "thinks" (E I a1), and indeed the notion that God has an intellect gives rise to many of the errors above. One key place where he uses the notion of the divine intellect in an illuminating way is in chapter 6 of the TTP, where he asserts that "since the virtue and power of Nature is the very virtue and power of God, and the laws and rules of Nature are God's very decrees, there can be no doubt that Nature's power is infinite, and her laws sufficiently wide to extend to everything that is conceived even by the divine intellect" (TTP, 74). The point there is that the power of nature far exceeds human power, and natural laws are more extensive than what the human intellect could conceive. But there is a similar paradox to that in the *Ethics*, namely, that while these laws may outstrip what human intellects conceive, they are still "laws," and thus in principle humanly cognizable. By the same token, human power is vastly limited, yet it is not of a different *kind* than divine power.[51]

What is clear is that Spinoza means God qua substance to be "absolutely infinite," i.e., limited by no other being. This is God in itself, *Natura naturans*, as he puts it a little further on: "what is in itself and conceived through itself." This is in contrast to what "follows from the necessity of God's nature," what is "in another," which he calls *Natura naturata*. What is interesting about the distinction between *Natura naturans* and *Natura naturata* is that the attributes are part of *Natura naturans* – they are part of what is conceived through itself. Thus, Spinoza notes, *Natura naturans* is "what is in itself and is conceived through itself, or such attributes of substance as express an eternal and infinite essence" (E I p29s). By contrast the "modes," which Spinoza defines as "the affections of a substance, or that which is in another through which it is also conceived" (E II d5), and which constitute the world of singular things, "follow from the necessity of God's nature, or from any of God's attributes" (E I p29s). The modes are part of *Natura naturata*. The distinction at stake, then, is not between God (a being absolutely infinite) and his attributes (what the intellect perceives of this infinity), but between God and the attributes (*Natura naturans*), on the one hand, and the modes of God (God's affections), on the other, i.e., what follows from God's attributes, what are "in another." Thus even if what the intellect perceives of a substance as constituting its essence is not all there is to perceive, what *is* perceived is essentially God. To be sure, Spinoza doesn't think any given intellect – a particular intellect, the "actual intellect" – is anything other than *Natura naturata*, for "by intellect we understand not absolute thought, but only a certain mode of thinking," i.e., by thinking we mean thinking about this or that, not things in themselves (E I p31dem). Rather the point is, first, that the attributes *are* substance, i.e., substance is differentiated. As Spinoza puts it, "by God's attributes are to be understood what . . . expresses an essence of the Divine substance . . . The attributes themselves, I say, must involve it itself" (E I p19dem). Second, the attributes do not exist as things to be known (or not known), but are the condition of knowing

---

[51] See also E I p16, where Spinoza refers to an "infinite intellect": "From the necessity of the divine nature there must follow infinitely many things in infinitely many modes, (i.e., everything which can fall under an infinite intellect)." The point here is the same as TTP, chapter 6 – not that God "knows" many more things than the human intellect but that God's intellect, which is the same as his will and his very existence, is infinitely various.

anything in particular: "singular thoughts, or this or that thought, are modes that express God's nature in a certain and determinate way. Therefore . . . there belongs to God an attribute whose concept all singular thoughts involve and through which they are also conceived" (E II p1dem). It is not that the human mind can be understood through *Natura naturata* as "opposed" to *Natura naturans*. For these categories are themselves not opposed to each other. The former is simply what follows from the latter.[52]

Human beings, then, are those beings that "perceive" substance through its attributes. "Man thinks" (E II a1) and "consists of a Mind and a Body" (E II p13c). In this Spinoza agrees with Descartes, who also held that human beings are dual, comprised of thought and extension, although it is only thought, for Descartes, which expresses the essence of God.[53] Spinoza, as above, also finds the notion that God or substance is divisible inconsistent with God's nature, but he has no trouble attributing extension to God. "Extension [like thought] is an attribute of God," he says, and the "demonstration" of this fact proceeds the same way as the demonstration to the proposition that "Thought is an attribute of God," namely that singular things (like singular thoughts) are modes of God's attributes (E II p1 and 2). The scholium tells us that on the basis of the fact that we can conceive an infinite thinking (or extended) being (again, one differentiated in an infinite numbers of ways), it must follow that each singular thought (or thing) is part of this infinity.

The distinctiveness of Spinoza's position is expressed in his proposition that "the order and connection of ideas is the same as the order and connection of things" (E II p7). In relation to God, what this means is that "God's power of thinking is equal to his actual power of acting. I.e., whatever follows formally from God's infinite nature follows objectively in God from his idea in the same order and with the same connection"

---

[52] For a clear discussion of the more technical, metaphysical dilemmas here, see Edwin Curley, *Behind the Geometrical Method* (Princeton, N.J.: Princeton University Press, 1988), especially "On God," 3–50. Curley also cites all the main commentaries and more technical disagreements in his own footnotes, and one can thus get a good sense of the philosophical parameters of the debates. His main interlocutor is Jonathan Bennett. On this issue see also Bennett's discussion, "Are there more than two attributes," in *A Study of Spinoza's "Ethics"* (Indianapolis: Hackett, 1984), 75–79.

[53] Descartes' view is that the mind and the body can both be considered substances, each having one principal attribute: "in the case of mind, this is thought, and in the case of body, it is extension." We "thus can easily have two clear and distinct notions or ideas, one of created thinking substance, and the other of corporeal substance, provided we are careful to distinguish all the attributes of thought from the attributes of extension." Both Descartes and Spinoza hold that we know God by virtue of thought or ideas. But to Descartes, God is "an uncreated and independent thinking substance," whereas for Spinoza thought is only one of God's two attributes ("Principles of Philosophy," in *Philosophical Writings*, vol. I, 211).

(E II p7c). We know that "from the necessity of the divine nature there must follow infinitely many things in infinitely many modes, (i.e., everything which can fall under an infinite intellect)" (E I p16). But the point here seems simply to be that whatever *could* follow from God *does* follow. What the corollary tries to make clear is that Spinoza's identification of extension with God does not consist in predication, i.e., Spinoza does not really assert what Descartes denies. He agrees that God doesn't "have" a body in the way that human beings do: "everyone who has to any extent contemplated the divine nature denies that God is corporeal" (E I p15sI).[54] According to the proposition that singular things are "things that are finite and have a determinate existence" (E II d7), God "himself" is not a singular thing (though God *is* singular, i.e., one [E I p14]). While Descartes assumed that the material order was corruptible in the way individual bodies are, Spinoza contends that extended substance is simply another way of talking about reality. "For example," he says, "a circle existing in nature and the idea of the existing circle, which is also in God, are one and the same thing, which is explained through different attributes" (E II p7s). Extension should be imagined to be like water, he says:

we conceive that water is divided and its parts separated from one another – insofar as it is water, but not insofar as it is corporeal substance. For insofar as it is substance, it is neither separated nor divided. Again, water, insofar as it is water, is generated and corrupted, but insofar as it is substance, it is neither generated nor corrupted. (E I p15sV)

This proposition and its demonstration, corollary, and scholium encapsulate what is both so fascinating and so vexing about Spinoza's metaphysical picture, namely, its simultaneous commitments to unity and to distinction. Spinoza does not say ideas and things are one (whether by reducing ideas *to* things, as a materialist might, or by reducing things *to* ideas, as might an idealist). Rather, there are two attributes (known to the human intellect), but they are "the same as" each other in that they follow the same "order and connection." In conceiving the world in the way that he does, Spinoza hopes at the very least to have avoided the problem Descartes faced of accounting for how causation occurs between two orders of reality that, logically at least, have nothing to do with each other, i.e., that could logically exist independently of each other. Descartes's hypothesis that "the Soul, or Mind, was especially united to a certain

---

[54] As Spinoza notes in the TTP, the attribution to God of corporeal features is due both to the vivid imaginations of the prophets and to the fact that "in concession to the frailty of the multitude, [Scripture] is wont to depict God in the likeness of man and to attribute to him mind, heart, emotions, and even body and breath" (TTP, 18).

part of the brain, called the pineal gland, by whose aid the Mind is aware of all the motions aroused in the body and of external objects, and which the Mind can move in various ways simply by willing it" is to Spinoza "more occult than any occult quality" (E V pref). But while he doesn't agree with Descartes's division of the kinds of things there are into two, he does hold a version of "property dualism," as Jonathan Bennett puts it. His aversion to soul/body dualism and his preference for naturalistic explanations of things does not, in other words, commit him to the view that "human beings are fully describable in physical terms – that mental terminology may be brought in through definitions but is not needed on the ground floor."[55] Spinoza very clearly does think the ground floor is, as it were, doubled.

There are two kinds of dualisms, if one can call them that, with which the reader of Parts I and II of the *Ethics* is confronted: the initial distinctions Spinoza makes in the first definitions and axioms, distinctions that are clearly about establishing the difference between God and human beings; and the second distinction he makes between the two dimensions of reality (ideas and things, thought and extension). In the first case, when Spinoza distinguishes between what is "in itself" and what is "in another" (E I a1) he means to privilege the former, i.e., substance as opposed to mode, what is free as opposed to what is determined to exist by another, and so on. Part I of the *Ethics* is "On God," and these divisions seek to establish God's primacy by distinguishing God from everything else. For Spinoza, in other words, saying that everything else other than God is *in* God is not at all to say that everything is God. On the contrary, the distinction between God and finite things establishes an essential hierarchy that the rest of the book is directed toward unpacking. In the second case, however, there is no priority to either thought or extension. They have exactly the same value. Each is an attribute of God and therefore, by E I d6, each one "expresses [God's] eternal and infinite essence." In the case of both dualisms, the identity or continuity between two things is no less important than their absolute distinction. As dimensions of the same reality, they need to be distinguished so that they will not be related (or conflated) in the wrong ways.

The human being is the pivot between the two kinds of dualisms, for it is the one kind of singular thing that can "bring it about that all the Body's affections . . . are related to the idea of God," thus modifying the distinction between what is in itself and what is in another with which Spinoza begins the *Ethics* (V p14):

---

[55] Bennett, *Study*, 41.

we . . . cannot deny that ideas differ among themselves, as the objects themselves do, and that one is more excellent than the other, and contains more reality, just as the object of the one is more excellent than the object of the other and contains more reality. And so to determine what is the difference between the human Mind and the others, and how it surpasses them, it is necessary for us . . . to know the nature of its object, i.e., of the human Body . . . I say this in general, that in proportion as a Body is more capable than others of doing many things at once, or being acted on in many ways at once, so its Mind is more capable than others of perceiving many things at once. And in proportion as the actions of a body depend more on itself alone, and as other bodies concur with it less in acting, so its mind is more capable of understanding distinctly. And from these [truths] we can know the excellence of one mind over the others, and also see the cause why we have only a completely confused knowledge of our Body. (E II p13s)

The human being is the one kind of thing, Spinoza holds, that can connect singularity to eternity, coming to see the ways in which God's absolute infinity is qualitative, so to speak, i.e., expressive in a single thing, or body, or mind: "the more we understand singular things, the more we understand God" (E V p24). We do so, he holds, not only by perfecting our intellect, but also by bringing it about that our actions depend as much as possible on ourselves alone. It is not the case, then, that human beings share a finite body with other natural things while excelling them by virtue of their intellect. What distinguishes human beings from other natural things is the complexity of their body – their ability to do many things at once and to be affected by many things at once – and their ability to achieve a greater degree of independence vis à vis others. "For indeed," Spinoza notes, "no one has yet determined what the Body can do, i.e., experience has not yet taught anyone what the Body can do from the laws of nature alone," not because we haven't yet determined how the mind can move the body, but because "no one has yet come to know the structure of the Body so accurately that he could explain all its functions" (E II p2). For all that philosophers have perennially cast human beings as a "dominion within a dominion" (E III pref), e.g., the only rational beings, the only beings capable of intellection or the knowledge of the absolute, the only beings capable of asking the question concerning the meaning of their own existence – for all that these statements have oriented philosophical thinking, no one has yet "determined what a Body can do" – no one has yet determined what human power, and therefore, for Spinoza, human virtue, can be.

The single difference between God and everything else (including human beings) is that God is the one thing "in" nature that is self-caused (*causa sui*), and therefore (his effect) can be conceived entirely through his cause. What does it mean for something to be conceived through itself or self-caused? What Spinoza does not do in responding to this question is peel back every apparently contingent attribute of things in order to get to what is most primordial, nor does he seek the first cause from finite or secondary causes. Such a tactic, he holds, simply leads to an infinite series of finite causes:

Every singular thing, or any thing which is finite and has a determinate existence, can neither exist nor be determined to produce an effect unless it is determined to exist and produce an effect by another cause, which is also finite and has a determinate existence; and again, this cause also can neither exist nor be determined to produce an effect unless it is determined to exist and produce an effect by another, which is also finite and has a determinate existence, and so on, to infinity. (E I p28)

His question is, is there something that is not dependent on other things, something not caused by anything? He answers yes to the first part of the question. There is something not dependent on other things, and we can conceive of this simply because the things in the world as a whole can be taken as one (independent and determinate) thing, just as we take the body as one thing even though it is millions of things. As Spinoza tells us in Part II, "By singular things I understand things that are finite and have a determinate existence. And if a number of Individuals so concur in one action that together they are all the cause of one effect, I consider them all, to that extent, as one singular thing" (E II d7).

However, his response to the second part of the question (is there something not caused by anything?) is no. Everything has a cause. By this he does *not* mean (i) that everything has a cause except God, who is not a thing, or (ii) everything has a cause, including God, and so God is caused by some thing, or (iii) God just is the fact that everything has a cause (i.e., God is eternal causation). The first is ruled out by E I p28 above. There is no way to get from finite causation to the so-called cause of causes, without an incoherent leap from the finite to the infinite. At the same time, (ii) can't be right, because that would mean that God was "in another" rather than "in itself." And (iii) is not right either, because Spinoza thinks God himself has a cause. Rather, everything (the world taken as one thing) has a cause, namely itself: "God is a cause through himself" (E I p16c2). In this light, God doesn't produce other things. God produces himself (all things), i.e., "God must be called the cause of all things in the same sense in which he is called the cause of himself" (E I p25s), and this entails that "God is absolutely the first cause" (E I p16c3).

This is the claim that is the crux of Spinoza's doctrine of creation such as it is, the claim that God's creation is simultaneously of himself and the world – that God's creation of the world is simultaneously of himself.

All the other apparent denials of creation – the doctrine that God could have created no other world than the one he did create, the denials of free will, of miracles, and of teleology – can be found condensed in this single scholium, which holds the position that the only thing creation *ex nihilo* can mean is that God, too, came into existence with (as) the world. It follows that to become like God is to bring oneself into existence (to become independent, self-causing, adequate), an impossible task according to most theologies (both Christian and Jewish) because God has already created human beings. One can be *creative*, having already come into existence, but this creativity is, at best, only a very pale shadow of what God does. In Spinoza's formulation, however, God does not (only) create human beings; he creates himself – to create is to be independent of any (other) cause. It is not be uncaused but to cause oneself.

The problem of creation (causation) is the problem of the *Ethics* as a whole, from the first proposition, on the *causa sui*, to the last, on human blessedness. How could it be otherwise? In reunderstanding what creation – origin – is and can be, Spinoza is rethinking ends. In beginning with God he is rethinking where human beings came from and where they are going. In moving from an uncaused God to one that is self-caused, Spinoza is revising the human project, from what is metaphysically impossible, to become like an uncaused God, to what is suggestively possible, to become *causa sui*, independent, original. In its own way, Spinoza's is a biblical concept of creation insofar as it maintains an absolute distinction between God and humankind while insisting that humankind transform itself into (because it is made from) the divine image.[56] The crucial thing to see is that God's nonseparation from the world – a sore point for most theological readers – is at the center of Spinoza's understanding of the most valuable and most difficult human project, which, as the Bible would put, is to become holy as God is holy (Lev. 19: 2) – to become, in the words of Genesis, "like" God (Gen. 3: 22). What Spinoza relentlessly shows is that this *human* project is what is at stake in the doctrine of creation – not the meaning or existence of God so much as the meaning and existence of human beings. Or rather, he shows that to understand God is necessarily to understand what a human being is and can be, and we are far more opaque to ourselves and to each other than we are accustomed to think. Our inability to understand God just is

---

[56] For a list of the ways in which Spinoza's concept of creation is different from the biblical views, see Sylvain Zac, "On the Idea of Creation in Spinoza's Philosophy," in *God and Nature: Spinoza's Metaphysics*, ed. Y. Yovel (Leiden: E. J. Brill, 1991), 231–233. But Zac also contends that Spinoza's "philosophy is not only an account of natural origins, but also a spiritual path." In short, says Zac, "It is a path which starts off from God and leads back to God" (238).

our inability to understand human beings – our inability to understand God just is our human inability.

The claim is that to deprive ourselves of the knowledge of God (whether through negative theology or its opposite, anthropomorphism; whether through atheism or classical theism) is to condemn ourselves to live in absolute ignorance and disempowerment. Were God to exist utterly separate from human beings, the human project of achieving holiness would be over before it had begun. Were God to be solely identified with human beings, there would be nothing to achieve. In so arguing, Spinoza does not collapse the divine and the human, because he holds that there is nothing between them – "nothing can be or be conceived without God" (E I p15); but he equally refuses their identity because a human being is precisely a being with nothing so much before her as the distance which separates her from holiness, salvation, *beatitudo*. The distance, in short, is *not* between humans and God, as theologians have so often seen the matter. The distance, as Martin Buber would put it three hundred years later, is "between man and man" – between self and neighbor, between what I am and what I can become, between idolatry and holiness, unfreedom and freedom.[57] The distance and transcendence of God is the distance and transcendence of human being.

This dialectic of the human and the divine is what begins the *Ethics*, from the first definition, E I d1: "By cause of itself I understand that whose essence involves existence, or that whose nature cannot be conceived except as existing." Here, the conjunction of essence and existence, which Spinoza holds to denote eternity, is held together with self-causation; bringing oneself about; the reflexive of "to cause." This is already to enter extraordinary territory. God, the eternal, has a cause, in contrast to the picture that has God with no beginning or end, something, namely, that subsists always (in Spinoza's language, something with duration). Eternity, for Spinoza, is "existence itself, insofar as it is conceived to follow necessarily from the definition alone of the eternal thing" (E I d8). Spinoza thereby follows Anselm in holding that God (or substance, here) cannot but be conceived to exist – that God is a concept of existence. But he makes more explicit than Anselm that what "cannot be conceived except as existing" *comes into existence*. This is the move that, until he gets to finite causation (E I p28), is only implicit: that God has an origin, God is original, God originates, as opposed to finite things, whose cause is always something other than themselves. These latter may be traced back "ad infinitum." But this tracing back is not an eternal one.

57 Martin Buber, *Between Man and Man*, trans. Ronald Gregor Smith (New York: Collier Books, 1965).

To be sure, Spinoza denies that God "has a beginning" in the way that natural things do (E I p8s2I). Substance is not "created," he says, that is, it is absurd to think that "a substance which was not, now begins to be," for this is simply to apply finite causation to God.[58] Indeed, the postulate that God is created (as natural things are) and the postulate that God creates (natural things) are identically false, to Spinoza. Both conceive of God and God's actions in finite terms. His claim, rather, is that the cause "on account of which a thing exists, either must be contained in the very nature and definition of the existing thing *(viz. that it pertains to its nature to exist)* or it must be outside it" (E I p8s2IV). God, or substance, then, is the cause of itself – its cause is "contained in the very nature and definition" of it; it "pertains to its nature to exist" because it contains its own cause, because it has no cause outside itself.

Spinoza's first move, then, before he gets any further than E I d1, is to contest the concept of God's eternity which denies it an origin (or, equally, which understands that origin in finite terms, according to the logic of E I p28). To say, he contends, that human beings are caused by something that itself has no cause is simply to say that God's cause is unknown to us. It is simply to push back into the mists of the primordium the circumstances of God's own origin. In Spinoza's formulation, God's power is immense relative to the standard theological view that posits God as preexisting matter. Surely it is easy enough, if one can put it this way, for an infinite, all-powerful God to create a world that is not infinite or all-powerful, even if this raises further questions about how this could happen without impugning his mastery. Spinoza deftly circumvents this conundrum. God causes himself; the infinite is infinite in power, as well as everything else, for only something infinitely powerful (eternal) could bring itself about. This is the first claim of the *Ethics*, and one that shapes everything that is to come. The second claim is that there is something else other than God that exists, and this second kind of thing may be characterized most basically in contrast to God, i.e., it does not cause itself. A finite thing, he tells us, is what "can be limited by another of the same nature" (E I d2), what can be compelled or overpowered by other things. This distinction is then what is elaborated in these first eight definitions. We find out, for example, that what causes itself is also free; what does not cause itself is bound, determined, unfree. We learn that what is the cause of itself and free is also eternal, and we learn that what does not cause itself and is unfree is also not eternal. And finally, we

---

[58] This location is quoted from *De Negelate Schriften van B.D.S.*, the Dutch translation of Spinoza's works that appeared, along with the *Opera Postuma*, in 1677. See Curley's preface in *Collected Works*, ix–x.

learn that what is the cause of itself and free and eternal also possesses infinite attributes, whereas what is caused by another, unfree, and not eternal is a mode of these attributes.

It is not until the first axiom, however, and its connection to the later propositions (especially E I p15) that Spinoza's revision of the picture of God and human beings – and the implications of E I d1 – become clear. Until E I a1, Spinoza has given us his version of God and he has given us his version of human beings. He can be seen to have tinkered here and there with both concepts, but the portrait of a universe divided between the infinite and the finite – with this distinction between them the primary one – can be read as fundamentally untouched. God causes himself, and – would it not follow? – God also causes the world. This would leave Spinoza with a standard creation account, except for the *causa sui*. But it would still be possible to hold, first, that God brings himself into being, and then, second, creates the world. Nothing in the second act would theoretically be impugned by the first, and indeed it would seem to be necessitated by it. If God is *causa sui*, and there are things that are not *causa sui*, they must have been brought about by God. However, E I a1 tells us more than E I d1–d8 both about the *causa sui*, and about what follows from it: "Whatever is, is either in itself or in another." The meaning of this axiom, while it can be provisionally deduced from the several that follow, is best expressed in E I p15: "Whatever is, is in God and nothing can be or be conceived without God." E I a1 tells us that, in all that exists, things are in themselves or in another. E I p15 tells us that by things being "in another" Spinoza means they are *in* what is "in itself." It is also the case that finite things can be "in another" that is not "in itself." They can be caused by, indebted to, other finite things. However, all of finite causation is itself in the "in itself." What is "in another" (dependent on another) finite thing is also in the "in itself" (by E I p15).

What does this mean? Between E I a1 and E I p15, Spinoza gives his argument for the singularity of substance. Substance is infinite, eternal, free, independent, real (perfect) – there is only one thing that can be all of these, because (in brief) if there were two, then one would have to cause the other, and it would thus not be self-caused. One can of course imagine all kinds of hypothetical counterscenarios here, some of which Spinoza claims to vanquish in these propositions. His argument, however, simply wants to establish that there is *something* that is self-caused. He does this not by theoretical speculation concerning the world's origins and not by reasoning backwards from the fact of everything having a cause. He does it by ontology: "since being finite is really, in part, a negation, and being infinite is an absolute affirmation of the existence of some nature, it follows . . . that every substance must be infinite" (E I p8s1). There is something that is independent because human beings deploy this as their standard – human beings desire freedom as the good, that is, "the model of human nature that we set before ourselves" (E IV pref). There is something that is eternal because this is a concept that the mind thinks. Human beings may be compelled to exist by others, but insofar as we think, we think of something that is not compelled. What follows for Spinoza is something that can not have been plain in E I d1 alone. The proposition that God causes himself is the same proposition that God causes the world. There is no lag between these; no relationship of entailment, given the other distinctions he has made. In causing himself, God causes the world. God causes the world by causing himself. The world is God. God is the world. Hence: "Whatever is, is in God, and nothing can be or be conceived without God" (E I p15).

What has happened to the distinctions from the first definitions? What happened to the infinite and the finite; the free and the compelled; the eternal and the noneternal? What happened to the distinction between God and human beings? Who disappeared: God or human beings? Who is the book now about: human beings or God? In laying out those first definitions, Spinoza suggested that he was dealing with two kinds of things: those that were infinite and those that were finite. It is unsurprising to learn that it follows that there can only be one infinite thing and many finite things (E I p14: "except God, no substance can be or be conceived"). But then what? How does one relate those two kinds of things?

It might be tempting to pinpoint this as the place where Spinoza denies creation. Everything is in God, therefore God is not separate, therefore there are not really two kinds of things but one kind of thing, and therefore creation cannot possibly have occurred. To be sure, this kind of reading cannot make sense of Spinoza's insistence on every page of the *Ethics* that finite, or as he comes to call them, singular, things are not God – his distinction between *Natura naturans* and *Natura naturata* (E I p29s). But it certainly is a possible reading of E I p15 taken on its own. It also makes explicit an intuition one might have in reading E I d1. The sense that God causes himself (creates himself, one could say) is unorthodox from every angle. It may not prima facie rule out God's creation of the world (that is, one may not know that it does so until later on), but it certainly is puzzling. Why would the *causa sui* be necessary to hold? Why wouldn't it just be cleaner to have God (or Nature) be eternal in the sense of having no beginning and end? What is one thereby signing onto when one accepts the *causa sui*?

It is instructive once again to turn to Aristotle for comparison. In Aristotle, and the corpus of post-biblical theology that gains its conceptual apparatus from Aristotle, the universe is caused by something that cannot itself be caused. In Aristotle's case, the "change" that manifests itself in the first cause of the universe (and continually manifests itself in all change) is a change "from something to something."[59] The first cause does not distinguish itself by its eternity, for there are other things that are eternal, such as the heavens, time, movement.[60] But such things do not contain the principle of their own movement: "matter will surely not move itself – the carpenter's art must act on it; nor will the menstrual fluids nor the earth set themselves in motion, but the seeds and the semen must act on them."[61] Motion, time, the heavens, matter itself – these things were not conjured into existence from nothing (as the "mythologists" see it, who "generate the world from night"), nor are they simply random natural events with no origin (as the "natural philosophers who say that all things were together" assume). For Aristotle, there can be no movement "if there is no actual cause."[62] What moves cannot move itself, even if it is eternal. Indeed, that the first heavens are eternal entails that "there is also something that moves them."[63] This something can not itself be moved, since, again, what is moved cannot have moved itself and thus must need a further cause. It must not only be eternal. It must also, and primarily, be unchanging. As Aristotle puts it, although the heavens, matter, time, movement are eternal, they are "capable of being otherwise" because they are moved by another. The first cause is the one thing that cannot have been otherwise:

> But since there is something which moves while itself unmoved, existing actually, this can in no way be otherwise than as it is. For motion in space is the first of the kinds of change, and motion in a circle the first kind of spatial motion; and this the first mover *produces*. The first mover, then, of necessity exists; and in so far as it is necessary, it is good, and in this sense a first principle.[64]

The language of necessity and the picture of an eternal universe have thrown off many a theological and philosophical reader. Aristotle explicitly denies creation from nothing and he claims that the existing universe necessarily exists. God is confined to getting things that exist necessarily (if not unchangingly) moving and then keeping them so. There is no room for miracle, no room for the will of God, no room for destiny, providence, mercy, love, and all the other attributes that the biblical traditions impute to God. But Aristotle has also been a very intimate interlocutor

---

[59] Aristotle, *Metaphysics*, in *Complete Works*, vol. II, 1599 (bk. IV).
[60] Aristotle, *Metaphysics*, in *Complete Works*, vol. II, 1693 (bk. VI).
[61] Aristotle, *Metaphysics*, in *Complete Works*, vol. II, 1693 (bk. VI).
[62] Aristotle, *Metaphysics*, in *Complete Works*, vol. II, 1693 (bk. VI).
[63] Aristotle, *Metaphysics*, in *Complete Works*, vol. II, 1694 (bk. VII).
[64] Aristotle, *Metaphysics*, in *Complete Works*, vol. II, 1694 (bk. VII).

for theology. What he preserves that has been of such use is the distinction he makes between what moves and what is moved – what moves only another and what is also moved by another. This is the distinction that is conserved in a post-biblical theology like that of Maimonides, and this is the distinction that Spinoza contests. While it may seem that it is Spinoza who picks up the Aristotelian language of necessity and eternity, and Maimonides who defends the biblical (miraculous) creation against Aristotle and (by implication), Spinoza, it is in fact Spinoza who shows that Aristotle and Maimonides, mutatis mutandis, share the same position.[65] In the one case, the movement "from something to something" is necessary, lawful, inexorable; in the other case, the movement from nothing to something is spontaneous, miraculous, incomprehensible. In both cases, however, there is something (if not some thing) that preexists movement, generation, creation – God and matter, for Aristotle; God alone, for Maimonides. In both cases, the movement is onesided. That which originates is not itself originated; that which is originated cannot originate. The difference – between God and change, between God and nature – is that of opposition. What moves cannot itself be moved; what is moved cannot move itself.

Spinoza changes all this: what moves can move itself. What moves must come to be able to move itself. What are estranged in Aristotle are conjoined in Spinoza. Movement, change, becoming, increasing, multiplying – all are signs of power and fecundity for Spinoza. Indeed, the greatest actor in Spinoza's metaphysics is not the one who remains changeless but the one who enacts the greatest change there is – the change that brings change into existence. Movement is not the opposite of eternity, but its signature. Change is good; the good changes, and God most of all. The standard theological pieties concerning God's unmoving preeminence are certainly turned on their heads in Spinoza. But it is not, as some of his opponents would like to think, in order to abandon religion for naturalism or science or atheism. For Spinoza, true religion involves a critique of both theology and philosophy, both anthropomorphism and the deification of the human being.

---

[65] Wolfson points out that the language of *causa sui* had been employed by medieval philosophers to mean necessary existence, i.e., "causelessness" (*The Philosophy of Spinoza*, vol. I, 127). He concludes that, since Spinoza also thinks God's existence is necessary, he must therefore have used *causa sui* in the same way, i.e., to mean that which has no cause. However, Spinoza's position is articulated in opposition to this view; not in the sense that he holds God has a cause (other than himself), but rather that causation is intrinsic to God's very being, and this is what both connects God to the world ("God is the efficient cause of all things which can fall under an infinite intellect") and distances God from the world ("God is absolutely the first cause") (E I p16c1, 3).

The difference (opposition) between the realm of God or the Prime Mover and the universe attempts to account for why the world is so full of corruption, disease, and death, while also holding out the hope that things could be otherwise, through the notion of the final cause, toward which everything is moving. But it has also created a great deal of anxiety. If God and world are so different, *how* could one produce the other? And *why* would a perfect and immutable being produce something that was neither? While there are many answers given to these two questions, from a single creation we cannot understand to an emanationism that seeks to delay this nonunderstanding as long as possible, nothing satisfactorily responds to these questions without having recourse to what some call faith or tradition, and Spinoza bluntly calls ignorance. However impolitic his language, the point is one that even his theological and philosophical opponents would have to grant: from the infinite to the finite (even if both are conceived as eternal, in Aristotle's sense), there can be no metaphysical bridge.

The paradox is that the very thing that Spinoza gets accused of – failing to maintain a distinction between God and world – is much truer of the Aristotelian position he rejects than it is of his own putative monistic view. For the postulate of the Prime Mover emerges for Aristotle in asking the question of how causation arises. That is, he wonders, can one look at the world we live in, where everything has a cause, and avoid falling into infinite regress, unable to pinpoint a beginning or first cause, and stuck with a conception of everlasting change in which nothing is permanent? What Aristotle says is that the very fact of matter in motion (cause and effect) implies that there is something that causes without itself being caused; there is a first cause that gets everything moving but is not itself subject to its own principle. How do we know this? Because of causation itself. The Prime Mover is part of the system of causation *as* its master: "since that which is moved and moves is intermediate, there is a mover which moves without being moved, being eternal, substance, and actuality."[66] Metaphysically, what this means is that there is no bridge to cross between the infinite and the finite, for two reasons. First, because the Prime Mover is absolutely opposed to what it moves, since what moves will never stop moving and the Prime Mover will never itself move (move itself); and second because, *pace* Aristotle, the Prime Mover is absolutely identical to what moves, since both move something other than themselves; both cause another. Neither can contain both movement and origination. This is the Aristotelian trap, in Spinoza's terms. The difference in the system

---

[66] Aristotle, *Metaphysics*, in *Complete Works*, vol. II, 1694 (bk. VII).

(between the infinite and the finite) can be conceived only in terms of opposition, and this means that the opposition, at any time, can become a simple identity. Only what is finite can be opposed. As Aristotle puts it, trying to avoid this conclusion, what is "eternal and unmovable and separate from sensible things" is neither finite nor infinite. The only thing clear is that "it is impassive and unalterable," that is, self-identical in its opposition to what is "posterior" to it.[67]

This paradox can be seen in Maimonides' attempt to distinguish his view of the world's origin from that of Aristotle.[68] As Spinoza presents it in the TTP, Maimonides falls into one of the two hermeneutical errors, making Scripture say whatever reason dictates (as opposed to making reason say whatever Scripture dictates), and thus abandoning both reason and Scripture. While, to Spinoza, the Scriptural texts clearly assert the world's creation (not eternity), this is not the reason Maimonides gives for his own assent to Scripture. Rather, he establishes this assent on extra-Scriptural grounds, arguing that "the eternity of the world has not been demonstrated" by reason and therefore we have no grounds for overturning Scripture's literal sense in this case. (In the case of God being depicted as corporeal in the Bible, we *do* have such grounds, i.e., these passages must be figurative.) Indeed, since reason is undecided, we have no way of establishing what Scripture means to teach on this score unless we see that deciding that Scripture teaches the eternity of the world is fatal to the Mosaic Law and cannot therefore be Scripture's true teaching:

[67] Aristotle, *Metaphysics*, in *Complete Works*, vol. II, 1695 (bk. VII).
[68] Maimonides gives his account of Aristotle's position on creation in *Guide*, vol. II, ch. 13, 284 and vol. II, ch. 14. He gives his own view, or rather, that of the Law of Moses in vol. II, ch. 13, 281–282 and vol. II, chs. 25 and 26. As with my treatment of Maimonides on the Garden of Eden, I cannot display the complexity of the issues in Maimonides himself, much less the secondary literature. On Maimonides and creation, see Herbert Davidson, "Maimonides' Secret Position on Creation," and Shlomo Pines, "The Limitations of Human Knowledge According to Al Farabi, Ibn Bajja, and Maimonides," both in *Studies in Medieval Jewish History and Literature*, ed. Isadore Twersky (Cambridge, Mass.: Harvard University Press, 1979); Sara Klein-Braslavy, "The Creation of the World and Maimonides' Interpretation of Genesis I–V," in *Maimonides and Philosophy*, eds. Shlomo Pines and Yirmiyahu Yovel (Dordrecht: M. Nijhoff, 1986); Harry A. Wolfson, "The Platonic, Aristotelian, and Stoic Theories of Creation in Halevi and Maimonides," in *Studies in the History of Philosophy and Religion*, ed. Isadore Twersky and George H. Williams, vol. I (Cambridge, Mass.: Harvard University Press, 1973); and Alfred Ivry, "Maimonides on Possibility," in *Mystics, Philosophers, and Politicians: Essays in Jewish Intellectual History in Honor of Alexander Altmann*, ed. Judah Reinharz and Daniel Swetschinski (Durham, N.C.: Duke University Press, 1982).

Our belief that the deity is not a body destroys for us none of the foundations of the Law and does not give the lie to the claims of any prophet. The only objection to it is constituted by the fact that the ignorant think that this belief is contrary to the text; yet it is not contrary to it, as we have explained, but is intended by the text. On the other hand, belief in eternity the way Aristotle sees it – that is, the belief according to which the world exists by virtue of necessity, that no nature changes at all, and that the customary course of events cannot be modified with regard to anything – destroys the Law in its principle, necessarily gives the lie to every miracle, and reduces to inanity all the hopes and threats that the Law has held out, unless – by God! – one interprets the miracles figuratively also, as was done by the Islamic internalists; this, however, would result in some sort of crazy imaginings.[69]

In short, since reason doesn't know, and the Law does, that the world is created, the Bible in this case must accord with the Law, even as what the Law teaches – miracles, hopes, threats – is, at least in part, given in the Bible itself.

In the TTP, Spinoza simply wants to point out that Maimonides is not a faithful reader, that is, that he neither reads the actual text faithfully nor does he do so with faith (morality), being concerned to set up a philosophical *ecclesia* that would exclude the audience for whom the Bible was intended (TTP, 104). But Spinoza's point in the TTP has a crucial metaphysical component. While Maimonides makes a great deal of his rejection of Aristotle on this question of "Law," they are, to Spinoza, identical, both hermeneutically and ontologically. Both hold reason to be the highest court of approval in all matters, and thus both subordinate what appears contingent and changeable to what is unchanging and eternal. It could never be the case that reason would itself change in relation to something that changes, for reason never changes, and therefore never learns anything it doesn't already know. This makes for a curious circularity in reading and interpretation, with Maimonides, the philosopher, reading his mind alone without the text and Alpakhar, the theologian, reading the text alone without his mind. But Spinoza also has in mind that on the actual metaphysical problem at hand, creation, Maimonides and Aristotle are also saying the same thing – that, despite the language of miracles versus necessity, both thinkers construe the relationship between God and the world (and thus God and human beings) to be one of opposition. God is immutable and unchangeable; the world is corruption and change. God originates movement (God creates the world), the world cannot (create God). What matters, in Spinoza's terms, is not the nature of the relationship between the two opposing sides – creation (i.e., we are ignorant as to how the world came about from God) or causation

---

[69] Maimonides, *Guide*, vol. II, ch. 25, 328.

(i.e., we know that it came about, mutatis mutandis, the way other forms of causation occur). What matters is the opposition itself.

To Maimonides, clearly, it is of utmost importance to affirm the Law over against Aristotle, to affirm our unknowing over against the ironclad transparency of causation:

> Thus it might be said: Why did God give prophetic revelation to this one and not to that? . . . Why did He legislate at this particular time . . .? Why did He impose these commandments and these prohibitions? . . . What was God's aim in giving this Law? . . . If this were said, the answer to all these questions would be that it would be said: He wanted it this way; or His wisdom required it this way. And just as He brought the world into existence, having the form it has, when He wanted to, without our knowing His will with regard to this or in what respect there was wisdom in His particularizing the forms of the world and the time of its creation – in the same way we do not know His will or the exigency of His wisdom that caused all the matters, about which questions have been posed above.[70]

To Aristotle, clearly, it is of utmost importance to affirm the deductive inevitability of the cause of causes, the foundation of causation itself, the mover that moves everything else, over against the "mythologists," who cloak their speculations in "night." It is Spinoza who provides a way out of the opposition – which is equally an identity – between reason and faith; between what is eternal and what changes; between spontaneity and necessity; between minds and texts, between clarity and interpretation. It is Spinoza who shows that what is eternal is also what originates, and thus Spinoza who does not fatally divide the human from the divine (or fatally identify them) – who makes it possible both to separate God and human beings and to connect them. God creates (himself), and this creation is the very power for human beings to do so. In Aristotle no less than Maimonides, the highest value in the system – what is eternal, unchanging, immutable – is by definition that which human beings can never know.

With the *causa sui*, Spinoza moves the gaze from the question of how God and world cohere to the nature of God himself and his human image makers. What is it, he wonders, that has led human beings to posit a God whose judgments "far surpass man's grasp" even as these judgments contain the blueprint for human existence (E I app, 441)? Why conceive of a being one can never understand and then hold oneself subject to him, whether God or reason itself? One answer, from TTP and TP, is that this is the principal posture of despotism, namely that religious authorities solidify their power over the masses precisely by mystifying

---

[70] Maimonides, *Guide*, vol. II, ch. 25, 329.

and concealing their God's identity. Another is that, as a detour around the labor involved in attaining adequate knowledge, it is all too tempting to fill in the gap in knowledge, not with what we do know, but with what we don't know. In the case of the Aristotelian/Maimonidean God, the lethal conjunction of an absolute power that is absolutely unknowable produces exactly what one would predict: a posture of submission and servility. For Spinoza, this is to take what is fundamentally to be combated – human weakness and disempowerment – and, under the guise of humility, make it the highest virtue.

To Spinoza, such humility is a terrible waste. Far better to be humble about something you can do something about than about something you can't; far better to hold yourself to the highest human model (the model "we set before ourselves" [E IV pref]), than to hold yourself to the model of something that is the very opposite of what you are. In truth, this latter is not really humility at all, but, given an already fundamental *servitus*, sheer masochism. What Spinoza rejects is the position of classical theists that, if God were to be knowable, he wouldn't be God anymore – the mystery, the difference would be gone. For Spinoza, ignorance is powerlessness. One begins not in ignorance of the truth, but in ignorance as disempowerment. The effort to know is the effort to achieve freedom and independence, and the movement, therefore, is from the partial or inadequate experience of these things to a full achievement of them (blessedness). There is no need for mystery because this journey is the most difficult one imaginable; difficult, not impossible (what is impossible cannot be even remotely difficult). For classical theists, to accept the opening of Genesis is to accept the transcendent God of Maimonides.[71] For Spinoza, it is this God above all that must be rejected.

Man is God to man

When each man most seeks his own advantage for himself, then men are most useful to one another. For the more each one seeks his own advantage, and strives to preserve himself, the more he is endowed with virtue . . . *or* what is the same . . . the greater is his power of acting according to the laws of his own nature, i.e., . . . of living from the guidance of reason. But men most agree in nature, when they live according to the guidance of reason . . . Therefore . . . men will be most useful to one another, when each one most seeks his own advantage, q.e.d. What we have just shown is also confirmed by daily experience, which provides so much and such clear evidence that this saying is in almost everyone's mouth: man is a God to man [*hominem homini deum esse*]. (*Ethics*, Part IV, p35c2 and s)

[71] This is Kenneth Seeskin's conclusion in "Maimonides, Spinoza, and the Problem of Creation," in *Jewish Themes in Spinoza's Philosophy*, ed. Heidi M. Ravven and Lenn E. Goodman (Albany: State University of New York Press, 2002), 126–127.

One might well ask, since Spinoza's is a critique of theism (and equally atheism), what his own position has to do with the God of the Bible. Is Spinoza's rejection of the conflation of Aristotle and the Bible – his defense of their difference – in the interest of defending the Bible itself or of proposing a third alternative? Does Spinoza ultimately agree with Maimonides that to demonstrate the eternity of God or Nature is to "void" the whole Law?[72] Who exactly is Spinoza's God if not either the God of the Philosophers or, in any obvious way, the God of Abraham, Isaac, and Jacob? This question will be taken up in the following chapters. But I want to take this notion of the *causa sui* and return to the question of bondage and true religion with which this chapter began. We have seen that the difference between true and false religion depends on human effort and desire – on confronting the ways in which we are limited and disempowered, both in body and in mind; we have seen that, if hope and fear are inevitable results of human fragility, they are strongly exacerbated by tyrannical theologies and philosophies that place human beings outside of or external to what they most desire; and we have seen that to envisage human beings as the authors of what they most desire is not to get rid of the difference between human beings and God but rather to magnify this difference exponentially: what human beings most desire is to be their own authors and this, in experience, seems the most formidably difficult thing of all.

But this stress on the *causa sui* as a principle of self-determination neglects what is for Spinoza the most important part of seeing the human project through the lens of *conatus*: the relationship between desire, striving, power – self-interest – and the "agreement" with others. The word *servitus* does of course mean bondage. But the English is also inadequate in one important respect. For the richness of *servitus* is its connotation of servitude, enslavement, and subjection on the one hand, and duty, obedience, and devotion on the other.[73] The infinitive *servire* connotes to be in service to someone or something, as a servant or slave might be (or even as military personnel might be to a public authority), but it can also be used in the sense of "to work for, to help, to perform ministry for."[74] These connotations are obscured by the word *bondage*, which

---

[72] Maimonides, *Guide*, vol. II, ch. 25, 330.

[73] In medieval Latin, the noun *servitus* has the following meanings: 1. "Personal subserviency, with reference to other kinds of dependants than serfs," 2. "Vassalage, the subordinate status of a vassal with respect to his lord," 3. "Service rendered, serviceability," 4. "Service to which 'ministeriales' are liable," 5. "'tribute,'" 6. "Treat, extra food allowance," 7. "Divine worship," 8. "Divine ministry." J. F. Niermeyer, *Mediae Latinitatis Lexicon Minus* (Leiden: E. J. Brill, 1984), *s.v.*

[74] Niermeyer, *Mediae Latinitatis Lexicon Minus*, *s.v. servire.*

signifies something done to me, or that I do to myself, or, as Spinoza usually means it, something I find myself in.[75] In English it does not signify something I do for the benefit of someone else or something I take on for the sake of someone else. There is theological imagery (both Jewish and Christian) in the notion of service that needn't be overemphasized. Yet Spinoza clearly chose his words carefully on this score, and this dimension of *servitus* as a kind of discipline or work is pivotal for how to read both the *Ethics* and the *Tractatus Theologico-Politicus*, with its deployment of a related term, *obedientia*.[76]

In the quotation at the start of this section, the term *servitus* can be used to draw attention to one of Spinoza's most striking claims.[77] The passage contains many of Spinoza's most critical metaphysical claims: that desire and self-interest are not incompatible with virtue; that to seek one's own advantage is also to seek the advantage of others; that seeking one's own advantage is the most empowering thing one can possibly do, something that puts one in harmony with one's nature, cultivates rationality, and enables us to be useful to one another; that these truths are not remote from ordinary experience but are rather "daily confirmed." These are all controversial, important positions that the *Ethics* advances. But the most striking thing that Spinoza says here is that this concordance of self-interest, power, rationality, and virtue – the notion that "man is God to man" – is "in almost everyone's mouth." To be sure, there have always been philosophers who have sought to show that self-interest could be aligned with the good. What is striking is the claim that the true nature of the relationship between human beings is so commonplace and universal

---

[75] In his glossary, Curley does include "service" as a possible translation of *servitus*, and of course a translator has to choose one or the other meaning to emphasize. He lists the meanings of *servitus*, *servus*, *servire* as "bondage, service; slave; to serve, be a slave," Spinoza, *Collected Works*, 697.

[76] For this term, translated "obedience" in English (with all the negative connotations this word implies), Niermeyer has 1. "Discipline," 2. "Monastic obedience," 3. "Vow of obedience," 4. "Task imposed upon a monk or canon on account of monastic obedience," 5. "a monastic or canonial ministry," 6. "Ministry of a monk or canon charged with the care of outer concerns and especially of manorial management," 7. "Estate of land belonging to a religious house," 8. "District administered by a state official," 9. "Spiritual power." *Mediae Latinitatis Lexicon Minus*, *s.v.*

[77] Warren Montag points out (citing also Macherey and Giancotti) that Spinoza employs the term *servitus* only rarely, using it just seven times in the entire *Ethics* and just as infrequently in the TTP and TP. In the TTP it occurs in a key passage in the preface, where Spinoza notes that in a despotic regime (*regiminis Monarchici*) human beings will "fight for their servitude as if for salvation" (*ut pro Servitio, tanquam pro Salute pugnent*) (TTP, 51, G III: 7). For this reason, given Spinoza's association of it with unfreedom in *Ethics* Part IV, it has made sense simply to read it as enslavement. But Montag is right to insist that this association between "inner" servitude (we are part of nature) and political servitude has a productive role to play in Spinoza's notion of freedom. Montag, *Bodies, Masses, Power* (London: Verso, 1999), 30.

as barely to merit mention. It is Spinoza himself, one wants to protest, who shows us that, in fact, human beings have everywhere and always been the same, i.e., desire and self-interest abound and "in every age virtue has been exceedingly rare" (TTP, 150).[78]

There is, Spinoza well knows, nothing prima facie obvious about the claim that man is God to man. Provisionally taking the statement to be an assertion of the power of human rationality in concert with others, Spinoza tells us in the very next line that "it rarely happens that men live according to the guidance of reason. Instead, their lives are so constituted that they are usually envious and burdensome to one another." We have, therefore, a claim that it is obviously true in the experience of almost everyone that human beings achieve some kind of preeminent good in relation to one another alongside the claim that, nevertheless, this is not sufficiently obvious to most people, since what they experience most frequently is that they are burdensome to one another. Is the notion that man is God to man (the image of human beings harmoniously relating to each other) intended as an ideal, something that is commonly understood to be in our best interests (like the golden rule, for example) but whose motivating power is relatively weak? In this light, one would have two kinds of commonplaces, one that merely seems obvious – that human beings are God to one another – and one that is obvious – that they are burdensome to one another.

This reading, however, has the immediate disadvantage of ignoring Spinoza's insistence that the fact that man is God to man is "confirmed by daily experience [*experientia quotidie*], which provides so much and such clear evidence [*tamque luculentis testimoniis testatur*] that this saying is in almost everyone's mouth [*ut omnibus fere in ore sit*] (G II: 234). This appeal to experience and clear evidence does not square well with the postulate of an ideal. The locution "in almost everyone's mouth" seems to point especially strongly in the direction of a reading that employs the language of intuition in addition to deduction. Spinoza seems to be speaking about something that seems right or basic to us, however difficult it is to bring to full fruition, and even something whose very ordinariness is part of the challenge of comprehending it. For what could possibly be ordinary about even the grammar of relating God (in the accusative) to man (in the dative) in this way?

---

[78] See also E IV appXII and XIII: "It is especially useful to men to form associations, to bind themselves by those bonds most apt to make one people of them, and absolutely, to do those things which serve to strengthen friendships. But skill and alertness are required for this. For men vary – there being few who live according to the rule of reason – and yet generally they are envious, and more inclined to vengeance than to Compassion. So it requires a singular power of mind to bear with each one according to his understanding, to restrain oneself from imitating their affects."

This key statement (with its cluster of associated claims) is among the most difficult ideas to understand in Spinoza's corpus at least in part because it is presented as at once rare and ordinary. As Spinoza observes of virtue at the end of Part V, "of course, what is found so rarely must be hard. For if salvation [*Salus*] were at hand, and could be found without great effort [*magno labore*], how could nearly everyone neglect it?" (E V p42s, G II: 308). And yet, he says, in the same scholium in Part IV in which he tells us that men are ordinarily burdensome to one another, "surely we do derive, from the society of our fellow men, many more advantages than disadvantages" (E IV p35s). In other words, he continues, "men still find from experience that by helping one another they can provide themselves much more easily with the things they require, and that only by joining forces can they avoid the dangers that threaten on all sides," viz., the infinite number of things that surpass us in strength. It is of course possible to see these two statements as referring to two different kinds of values, one having to do with morality (which is uncommon and requires *magnum laborem*) and the other having to do with self-interest (which is simply about common utility). But these are precisely what Spinoza identifies in this proposition with the claim that "the more each one seeks his own advantage, and strives to preserve himself, the more he is endowed with virtue" (E IV p35c2).

Highlighting this tension is not to suggest that Spinoza's thought is internally contradictory. It is to take seriously the rigorous multivalence of his conceptual vocabulary, a multivalence which takes the form of making theologically and philosophically inflected values like goodness and morality immanent to ordinary human experience without losing their power, complexity, or extraordinariness, as well as using a single term in both a positive and a negative sense. Thus the word *servitus*, for example, for all that it makes reference to human inadequacy, appears in the portion of the *Ethics* in which Spinoza begins to move from the vastness and perfection of God in the earlier parts to the perfectibility of human beings, culminating in the achievement of virtue, or the love of God, in Part V. Part IV is also where the reader begins to see the fruit of her own labor, both her labor through what Spinoza himself acknowledges are the conceptual thickets of the earlier parts and her labor through the unsentimental catalogue of human finitude and inadequacy that constitute Parts II and III.[79] Part IV is indeed on "bondage," but it is precisely at this point in the text that Spinoza begins to demonstrate what it is that

[79] There are two places in the *Ethics* where Spinoza makes explicit reference to the difficulty of his book. In Part II, when introducing the mind-body relation in connection with God (from which it follows, he holds, that "the human Mind is a part of the infinite intellect of God"), he writes: "Here, no doubt, my readers will come to a halt, and think of many

human beings can do, make, create in light of what they are "by nature," the climax of which is IV p35s: man is God to man. If we see the *servitus* of Part IV in both its senses, this proverb might read: in service or devotion to one another human beings can, with great effort (*magno labore*), transform the bondage of human existence into the freedom that, at the beginning of Part I, seems to be God's alone.

Spinoza locates the source of this great effort in reason: "men most agree in nature, when they live according to the guidance of reason." What is clear about reason, as well as the related terms of intellection and cognition, is that it is the most important faculty that human beings possess, the sine qua non of blessedness, of freedom. It is by virtue of reason, Spinoza tells us, that we can limit the sway that passions like hate and jealousy have over us, and limit the extent to which we are overpowered by things outside of us; and it is by virtue of reason that we can come to see one another not as obstacles to be conquered or indifferent inhabitants of the same polity, but as partners and neighbors with whom each of us is far stronger and freer than any of us on our own; it is by virtue of reason that we can achieve independence, by depending upon other rational beings. All of these desiderata are conditioned by reason and rationality, for Spinoza.

We have seen that, for Spinoza, what is crucial about reason is that the mental dimension of reality holds no more of a privileged place in the "life of the Mind" than what he calls *extensio* – the body, matter, extended substance in its most general formulation (E IV appV).[80] On this view, rationality is still first and foremost about thinking ("man thinks" [E II a2]); but the claim is that when we think, we are thinking not simply *about* bodies but in and through them – ours and others'. The mind cannot be free unless the body is also free – not simply free from molestation but free in Spinoza's sense: self-caused, self-determined. Yet all bodies are always at every instant affected by other bodies, and so, then, are minds. Thinking, freedom, is thus both individual and social.

---

things which will give them pause. For this reason I ask them to continue on with me slowly, step by step, and to make no judgment on these matters until they have read through them all" (E II p11s). Then again, in Part IV, at the moment when he turns from "the causes of man's lack of power and inconstancy" to "what reason prescribes to us," he notes: "but before I begin to demonstrate these things in our cumbersome [*prolixus*] Geometric order, I should like first of all to show briefly here the dictates of reason themselves, so that everyone may more easily perceive what I think" (E IV p18s). This allusion to the difficulty of his work comes when the stakes are highest, namely, at the moment when the focus of analysis changes from bondage to freedom.

[80] See Bennett, "Eight Questions about Spinoza," for an account of the "privilege" of thought in light of Spinoza's resolute desire to make mind and body equivalent (in *Spinoza on Knowledge and the Human Mind*, ed. Yirmiyahu Yovel [Leiden: E. J. Brill, 1994], 11–26).

In this light, the task of becoming free hinges on the task of taking an always basic dependence and transforming it from something that is solely about bondage to something that is also about liberation. Indeed, this relationship between dependence and independence speaks to the larger complex of issues at stake in Spinoza's concept of reason, for becoming more independent in solidarity with others is dependent on the task of attaining political as well as individual freedom, democracy as well as (or as a form of) blessedness; and the task of democracy is itself dependent on an understanding of "true religion," which is about making, creating, empowering, revealing, in distinction from superstition, which is bondage to the given. God is the *causa sui* – the one who makes himself, reveals himself, the one who empowers himself, from nothing given. Thus as Spinoza says "whatever we desire and do of which we are the cause insofar as we have the idea of God, *or* insofar as we know God, I relate to [true] Religion" (E IV p37s). Man (as a being that strives for independence) is God (creative, empowering) to man (the other, the origin of political life, the site of *servitus*).

Spinoza's philosophical gaze in the *Ethics* – no less than his political gaze in the TTP and TP – is trained *not* on those who live according to the dictates of reason alone but on those whose passions and vacillations of mind (*servitus*) prevent them from seizing the foundations of their own freedom. In fact, Spinoza feels the need to remind his readers in the *Ethics* that, while it might seem that his only purpose is "to tell about men's vices and their absurd deeds," this is not his intention at all, which is simply to "demonstrate the nature and properties of things" (E IV p57dem).[81] In the final proposition of the *Ethics*, Spinoza reflects on the fact that his entire book has been about discerning the "way" to move from ignorance (for "all men are born in a state of complete ignorance" [TTP, 180]) to wisdom: "if the way I have shown to lead to these things [the consciousness of oneself, of God, and of things 'by a certain eternal necessity'] now seems very hard, still, it can be found" (E V p42s). This rather poignant ending to Spinoza's masterwork echoes his sentiment in the TTP that "before [all men] can learn the true way of life and acquire a virtuous disposition, even if they have been well brought up, a great part of their life has gone by" (TTP, 180). Both statements imply that it is the task of all to make this movement, however difficult and from wherever one happens (by birth, ability, social class, and so on) to begin.

The tension in Spinoza is between the ordinary and the extraordinary: between ordinary knowledge (what "no one can have lived in the world

---

[81] This doesn't mean Spinoza is a completely dispassionate observer of "the nature and properties of things." He allows himself irony, humor, disapproval, and occasionally approbation, in both philosophical and political works.

without realizing" [TTP, 1]) and extraordinary knowledge (what can be known only with effort, e.g., that the "the human mind contains the nature of God within itself in concept" [TTP, 10]); between ordinary texts (the Bible as a text that "teaches only very simple doctrines, and inculcates nothing but obedience" [TTP, 157]) and extraordinary texts (the Bible as the "Word of God" [TTP, 149]); between ordinary human law (which concerns only "security and good health" [TTP, 38]) and extraordinary divine law (which concerns "our supreme good and blessedness" [TTP, 51]); between ordinary existence (based on what "men commonly [and inadequately] suppose" [E I app]) and extraordinary or enlightened existence (based on what is "common to all . . . [and] can only be conceived adequately . . . and which [is] the foundation of our reasoning" [E II p38, p40s). In other words, I am interested in the philosophical and theological nature of Spinoza's democracy but also in the ways in which he moves back and forth between the claim that what he is extolling is common and ordinary, available to all, and the claim that "all things excellent are as difficult as they are rare" (E V p42s).

This tension is perfectly exemplified in the statement that "man is God to man" even as "daily experience," no less than Spinoza's books, testifies rather to the fact that "man" is utterly at odds with "man." This move of Spinoza's – to make what is most exalted, rare, and difficult (according to *him*) the thing that is (also) the most ordinary and commonplace – has rarely been commented upon. Far from simply contending that the difference between the ordinary and the extraordinary is not homologous with the distinction between (ignorant) masses and (learned) elites, Spinoza's claim is that the ordinary is the most elite thing of all, something the philosophers and theologians would do well to strive to attain alongside the "common people" they like to revile (TTP, 104). For as he caustically notes, it is precisely the "superstitious," in whatever guise, who "know how to reproach people for their vice better than they know how to teach them virtue, [striving] not to guide men by reason, but to restrain them by Fear, so that they flee the evil rather than love virtues. Such people aim only to make others as wretched as they themselves are" (E IV p63s). In repeating this sentiment in his more concise appendix to Part IV, Spinoza adds a remarkable footnote to this idea that superstition afflicts the powerful and the disempowered alike, illuminating the heart of this notion of the ordinary (as both mistaken and enlightened) and the extraordinary (as both enlightened and mistaken):

That is why many, from too great an impatience of mind, and a false zeal for religion, have preferred to live among the lower animals rather than among men. They are like boys or young men who cannot bear calmly the scolding of their parents, and take refuge in the army. They choose the inconveniences of war and the discipline of an absolute commander in preference to the conveniences of home and the admonitions of a father; and while they take vengeance on their parents, they allow all sorts of burdens to be placed on them. (E IV appXIII)

The ordinary, Spinoza seems to say here, i.e., ordinary struggles, ordinary conflicts, are the hardest of all to bear. We would rather take on the extraordinarily difficult than face the quotidian difficulties that are immediately and pressingly at hand. Indeed, then, it is one of the stranger truths of human nature that while "natural knowledge is common to all men . . . rest[ing as it does] on foundations common to all men," superstition is nevertheless the rule among "nearly all men," "teach[ing them] to despise reason and Nature, and to admire and venerate only that which is opposed to both" (TTP, 9, 88).

The question is, though, given God's absolute and unparalleled infinity and humanity's essential and irredeemable *servitus*, *how* can man be God to man? For Spinoza, what holds together the *causa sui* (freedom) with *conatus* (striving) is *servitus* in both senses: as the ordinary demands that human beings face as part of nature and as the extraordinary solidarity that can transform what is merely disabling into what is also empowering. *Servitus* as bondage and *servitus* as duty, obedience, devotion, labor. In the difference between these two – or rather in their likeness – lies true religion, the religion that is "in everyone's mouth," the religion that is available to all. It is this religion that Spinoza thinks the Bible teaches.

2   Spinoza's Bible
Concerning how it is that "Scripture, insofar as it contains the word of God, has come down to us uncorrupted"

If we read a book relating events which are incredible or incomprehensible, or which is written in a very obscure style, and if we do not know the author or the time or the occasion of its composition, it will be vain for us to try to achieve a greater understanding of its true meaning (TTP, 100) . . . I call comprehensible those narratives, whether of future or past events, that do not exceed human belief, and likewise laws, institutions and customs, although they cannot be proved with mathematical certainty. But mysterious symbols, and narratives that exceed all human belief, I call incomprehensible. Yet even among these there are many that yield to examination by our method, so that we can perceive the author's meaning.   (TTP, 241)

If a man reads the narratives of Holy Scripture and has complete faith in them, and yet pays no heed to the lesson that Scripture thereby aims to convey, and leads no better life, he might just as well have read the Koran or a poetic drama or at any rate ordinary history.   (TTP, 69–70)

[S]ince reason cannot demonstrate the truth or falsity of this fundamental principle of theology, that men may be saved by obedience alone, we may also be asked why it is that we believe it? If we accept this principle without reason, blindly, then we too are acting foolishly without judgment; if on the other hand we assert that this fundamental principle can be proved by reason, then theology becomes a part of philosophy, and inseparable from it. To this I reply that I maintain absolutely that this fundamental dogma of theology cannot be investigated by the natural light of reason, or at least that nobody has been successful in proving it, and that therefore it was essential that there should be revelation.
(TTP, 174–175)

Why the Bible?

Spinoza's critique of the God of the philosophers goes to the heart of what he thinks the Bible teaches, and how he thinks the Bible must be read. The Bible is not "philosophical" in that it does not teach truths of pure reason (the Bible does not need to conform to the mind). Neither is the Bible "theological" in that it does not display an unknowable God (the mind does not need to conform to the Bible). Rather, for Spinoza, the Bible separates philosophy and theology, minds and books, keeping both sovereign. The Bible teaches us something we wouldn't know by reason alone, which is that there is no reason alone. Minds must be interpreted; books must be subjected to judgment, philosophy and theology are on separate footings because they come into existence together and therefore neither is the cause or the standard or the ultimate judge of the other. For Spinoza, then, the Bible *is* special, or sacred, in some fundamental respects. But discerning exactly in what its sacrality consists will depend on showing the ways in which the Bible is profane, the ways in which it is not only not sacred but actually a source of impiety, a source of bondage. In fact, Spinoza will show, the Bible's sacrality consists precisely in its claim that sacrality is relative to the "end" or the liberation of its readers, and *not* in its divine origins.

This chapter will follow the connection between Spinoza's conception of prophecy and his theory of biblical interpretation, linking the two through what he calls "moral certainty." The question of what prophecy conveys is connected to the question of how to read Scripture because readers are in a similar position to both the prophets, who attain sure knowledge of some matter revealed by God, and the audience of prophecy, who have access to this knowledge only through faith. Like prophets, readers are interpreters of something that cannot be known by reason alone; hence the effort to secure certainty involves factors other than purely rational ones (the history of the text, for readers; a vivid imagination, signs, and virtue for the prophet). But like the prophet's audience, the knowledge of texts that we can attain is not always "sure," since texts "transcend" us in a certain sense. That is, they introduce novelties – laws, customs, histories – that we wouldn't know without reading them, and therefore we have to take their authors (prophets, in this case) at their word – as it were, on faith. Ultimately, then, if readers are like prophets, prophets are like readers, who themselves "transcend" us in a certain sense. For readers, no less than texts, do not present their truths transparently; for readers, no less than texts, require interpretation. They require bondage (to the letter) and devotion (to the spirit).

Man is (God, Bible, text, prophet) to man. The sacred both depends on and teaches the value of revelation as the work of interpretation and solidarity. Like the notion of chosenness, the difficulty lies in misplacing the imperative of the sacred, in assuming that it resides in a certain set of laws rather than others, or a certain number of books rather than others, or with a certain author more than others. Ultimately, Spinoza argues, the Bible is rightly called a sacred book, just as, we will see, the Hebrews are rightly called chosen. The question is how and why.

In the course of arguing that the narrative discrepancies, repetitions, and other textual oddities in the biblical books can be attributed to the diversity of authorship and human error, not to divine mystery, Spinoza departs from his case momentarily to survey his efforts. "If anyone thinks that my criticism here is of too sweeping a nature and lacking sufficient foundation," they are invited to "show us in these narratives a definite plan such as might legitimately be imitated by historians in their chronicles" (TTP, 124). The question of in what respects the Bible can be compared to other historical chronicles is one of the things at issue in the TTP. As the second quotation above indicates, the Bible is not, in Spinoza's view, entirely identical to "ordinary history," for reasons beyond the fact that it doesn't always make narrative sense. At stake here, though, are not the analogies and disanalogies between the Bible and other books, but the methods of interpretation to which the Bible has traditionally given rise. Even if, he admits, the Bible is different in at least some respects from such chronicles, the effort to interpret its narratives with the assumption that they can all be harmonized has strayed so far from "the actual diction and . . . manner of exposition, arrangements and organisation of the texts" that it simply fails to help us to understand the book(s) before us in all its (their) wealth of detail (TTP, 124–125).

Spinoza was aware of both Christian and Jewish attempts at such harmonization. Spinoza's friend, Ludwig Meyer, had published his *Philosophy the Interpreter of Sacred Scripture* in 1666, which argued that "true Philosophy is the infallible norm for interpreting the Sacred Letters," and that, by its aid, we may resolve all apparent inconsistencies.[1] It was certainly no less important for post-Reformation Christians than for early modern Jews that the Bible make sense as a single narrative.[2] But when Spinoza's focus in the TTP is biblical interpretation (as opposed to theology), including what he calls skeptical and dogmatic forms of reading, it is the Jews who are his targets:

The Rabbis run quite wild, and such commentators as I have read indulge in dreams, fantasies, and in the end corrupt the language altogether. For example, in the second book of Chronicles where we read that "Forty and two years old

[1] Quoted in J. Samuel Preus, "The Bible and Religion in the Century of Genius": Part III: "The Hidden Dialogue in Spinoza's *Tractatus*," *Religion* 28 (1998), 113.

[2] Perhaps the most heroic effort on the Jewish side in this period was the *Conciliador* by Spinoza's (possible) teacher Menassah ben Israel. On the nature of his effort, as well as the particular Jewish challenge to reconcile oral and written traditions in this period, see Jay M. Harris, *How Do We Know This? Midrash and the Fragmentation of Modern Judaism* (Albany: State University of New York Press, 1995), 103–136. On both Christian and Jewish responses to the new philosophy in this period, see Richard H. Popkin, "The Religious Background of Seventeenth-Century Philosophy," *Journal of the History of Philosophy* 25 (1987): 35–50.

was Ahaziah when he began to reign," some of them pretend that these years are reckoned from the reign of Omri, not from the birth of Ahaziah. If they could prove this to be the real meaning of the author of the book of Chronicles, I should not hesitate to declare that he did not know how to speak. They indulge in many other fancies of this sort; and if these were true, I should declare outright that the ancient Hebrews knew neither their own language nor how a narrative should be arranged, I should acknowledge no method or rule for the interpretation of Scripture, and there would be no restrictions whatsoever on the imagination. (TTP, 124)

This portrait of the rabbis of the Talmuds had a great deal of staying power, eventually becoming the signature of the post-Enlightened Jew uncomfortable with the ostensible irrationalism of midrashic forms of reading, and the Talmudic heritage in general. For Spinoza, as for many of those whom he influenced, rabbinic reading represents a failed attempt to defend against the difficulties of the biblical text, which challenges readers enough, he claims, without the importation of alien schema.[3] But unlike many of his reform-minded descendants, Spinoza is equally critical of philosophical readings, which he defines as those that cannot admit the certainty "of the true meaning of any passage unless we know that, as we interpret it, there is nothing in that passage that is not in agreement with reason, or is contrary to reason" (TTP, 103). This view has the curious consequence that, while reason is employed as the standard of comprehending the Bible, reason on its own ("true beliefs and a true way of life") is thought to "contribute nothing to blessedness" unless it can be shown to have originated in "prophetic inspiration." Spinoza attributes this view to Maimonides, though he identifies it with "the Jews" per se, i.e., Maimonides is the exemplary Jew in this case (as opposed to Moses, to whom he usually refers when he wants to commend the Jews [TTP, 70]).

Spinoza acknowledges that there are good reasons for the failure to understand the Bible, including the fact that there are many passages whose meaning we simply haven't the information to determine with precision, whether because we are unable to reconstruct the ancient Hebrew language (TTP, 96–97), are in doubt as to its ambiguities (TTP, 97–98), or simply because we are deprived of sufficient information concerning the author or audience (TTP, 99). But he also thinks there are more lamentable reasons for this failure, including first and foremost the belief that "God by some singular act of providence has preserved all the Sacred

---

[3] On the defenses readers have employed to deal with the "alien schema" of the oral Torah, see Harris (*How Do We Know This?*), who vividly underscores both that what is "alien" depends on where you are standing and that the anxiety about what scheme is the right one goes back to the Talmuds themselves.

Books uncorrupted," and that they are therefore divine in every line and word. On this premise, ambiguities, seemingly inexplicable repetitions, and chronological disjunctions are signs of "mysteries most profound," and are a spur, not a hindrance, to interpretation (TTP, 125).[4]

To Spinoza, this focus on the text's "mysterious symbols, and narratives that exceed all human belief" leaches effort away from what he sees as the more vexing task of understanding (and understanding the difference between) the meanings of the text and its significance. Cognizant, however, of the extent to which many numbers of people, learned and unlearned, have been committed to the belief that the Bible propounds mysteries, Spinoza assures us that he, too, has not arrived at his skepticism lightly or hastily. "Indeed," he says, "I may add that I write nothing here that is not the fruit of lengthy reflection; and although I have been educated from boyhood in the accepted beliefs concerning Scripture, I have felt bound in the end to embrace the views I here express" (TTP, 125).

This admission would be noteworthy simply for its autobiographical allusion. Readers of the TTP have often speculated on the effect of Spinoza's early education on his subsequent philosophical work, in particular the effect of having learned the Bible and its traditional commentaries on his eventual views of its literal or plain sense and historical character.[5] Here, though, Spinoza gives us no real insight into this question except to assure us that he once did hold accepted beliefs concerning Scripture (a fact that did not go without saying among the largely Christian readership of the TTP) and that he did not abandon them without a preponderance of evidence, which fact evidently entitles him to the confidence with which he expresses his alternate views. What is remarkable nevertheless is that, despite Spinoza's lengthy personal reflection, his confidence, and the care with which he presents his findings, it has remained far from obvious just what his views on the Bible amount to, a fact that complicates the determination of whether Spinoza contributes something important to biblical interpretation or whether his principal contribution lies entirely elsewhere.

To begin with, doubts concerning the Mosaic authorship of the Pentateuch hardly begin with Spinoza. He himself cites Ibn Ezra (1092–1167), "a man of enlightened mind and considerable learning, who was

---

[4] See TTP, 214.
[5] On Spinoza's education, see Steven Nadler, *Spinoza: A Life* (Cambridge: Cambridge University Press, 1999), 61–79. Wolfson's two-volume *The Philosophy of Spinoza* is the most extensive account of medieval sources as they appear in Spinoza, including Rashi and Ibn Ezra. For an alternative interpretation of such influences, see Ze'ev Levy, *Baruch or Benedict: On Some Jewish Aspects of Spinoza's Philosophy* (New York: Peter Lang, 1989).

the first, as far as I know, to call attention to [the] misconception" that
Moses wrote the entire Pentateuch (TTP, 108). A medieval Spanish rabbi
and author of a perfectly traditional commentary on the Bible well known
to both Jews and Christians in the mid-seventeenth century, Ibn Ezra had
observed that the verses at the end of Deuteronomy 34 detailing Moses'
death and its aftermath could not have been written by Moses himself.
He draws no radical conclusion from this observation about the rest of
the Pentateuch; indeed he invests these verses with special (secret) significance, though Spinoza, ironically anticipating Strauss's reading of *him*,
assumes that this is because Ibn Ezra "did not venture to explain his meaning openly" (TTP, 108). Whatever truth this assumption may have, it is
deployed to deradicalize Spinoza's own claims, because to Spinoza (as
opposed to Ibn Ezra), the question of the authorship of these few verses
was only the tip of the iceberg (or rather, it was the tip of a different
iceberg). While he seems to be hanging his entire theory of the Bible and
its history on the verses he uses to show that Moses couldn't have written this or that, a "heresy" he tells us he is maintaining with his ally Ibn
Ezra against the "obstinacy" of the "Pharisees" (TTP, 108), the truth is
more complicated (in both cases). The "Pharisees," among whom Ibn
Ezra ought to be counted, had no real problem with the minor matter of
Moses' death at all, while the major claims Spinoza is also making (that
this aporia in the Bible shows that the entire Pentateuch was written by
someone "who lived long after him"), to which Ibn Ezra would not have
assented, were much more genuinely heretical (TTP, 109).

Until Spinoza's period, doubts about the final verses of Deuteronomy
posed few problems for religious believers.[6] Jewish and Christian interpreters dealt with the question differently, with most Christian commentators from the period beginning with the Reformation accepting that
Joshua had likely written the doubtful verses after the fact, while Jewish
readers tended to struggle with whether Joshua could have known about
Moses' death through prophecy.[7] But for neither Jews nor Christians did
these doubts ordinarily impugn the authority of the biblical text, which
was still (as the Old Testament to Christians) understood to be the faithful record of the revelations of God to Moses. The Bible was considered
the true word of God in form as well as content, and the verses at the end

[6] As Popkin notes, even Luther "agreed that this portion of the text had been added by
another hand," though "he held that Moses was the author of the material up to that
point." The point is that Luther didn't think this a serious problem, insisting that "It
does no harm to say that the Pentateuch could not have been written by Moses" (Richard
H. Popkin, "Spinoza and Bible Scholarship," in *The Cambridge Companion to Spinoza*
[Cambridge: Cambridge University Press, 1996], 387). And as Popkin shows, this view
was by no means exceptional.
[7] Popkin, "Spinoza and Bible Scholarship," 387–388.

of Deuteronomy simply reminded readers that the Bible, unlike ordinary histories, often expressed its meanings indirectly.[8]

Spinoza was part of a burgeoning trend in the seventeenth century to push the question of authorship onto much more threatening ground (others to do so were Hobbes, Isaac La Peyrère, and Samuel Fisher).[9] What was threatening about Spinoza's view was his connection of the internal narrative evidence for multiple authors with the historical fate of the biblical manuscripts as a whole, the latter which he considered to be obviously corrupted by scribal interpretations and oversights.[10] "We have to observe," Spinoza declares, "that [the biblical books] were not so preserved by posterity as not to suffer the intrusion of some errors" (TTP, 125). Indeed, much more strongly,

If one merely observes that all the contents of these five books, histories and precepts, are set forth with no distinction or order and with no regard to chronology, and that frequently the same story is repeated, with variations, it will readily be recognized that all these materials were collected indiscriminately and stored together with a view to examining them and arranging them more conveniently at some later time. And not only the contents of these five books but the other histories in the remaining seven books right down to the destruction of the city were compiled in the same way. (TTP, 121)

This connection between the ambiguities of the text and its chaotic transmission leads to the impression that Spinoza's Bible is, from beginning to end, simply a historically specific document relevant only to its time and place. Since Spinoza says that it is "clear beyond a shadow of a doubt" that most of the Bible was written by human authors "who lived many generations after Moses" (TTP, 112), one can safely assume, on this reading, that his view of its contents must be that they are no more than the idiosyncratic views of these men. If Hobbes had sought to soften the blow of

---

[8] For all that the seventeenth century was a time of tremendous anxiety concerning the literal meaning of the Bible, it was also (or it was therefore, perhaps) a time of enormous exegetical creativity as these anxieties gave rise to successive waves of millenarianism – the hope for the messiah or the return of Christ (or both) or some kind of end-time. On the changes in perceptions of the Bible in the seventeenth century, see Preus, "The Bible and Religion in the Century of Genius," Part II: "The Rise and Fall of the Bible"; on the "millennial madness" of the age, see the essays in D. S. Katz and J. Israel, eds., *Sceptics, Millenarians, and Jews* (Leiden: E. J. Brill, 1990).

[9] In these brief observations about Spinoza in his context, I am indebted to Popkin's account in "Spinoza and Bible Scholarship," especially 388ff.

[10] Cf. Thomas Hobbes, *Leviathan*, ed. Richard Tuck (Cambridge: Cambridge University Press, 1998), P. 3, ch. 33, 260–69. Hobbes's view on this score is far milder. He points to internal evidence in the Scriptures for clues as to their antiquity and authorship, but remains fairly conservative in his speculations about these matters. What concerns Hobbes above all is the nature and scope of scriptural authority, which he ties to the legitimacy of the sovereign (268).

historicism by proclaiming the Church of England the rightful authority to confirm the divinity of Scripture, Spinoza had no such guarantee.[11] What this means is that Spinoza's Bible is unauthoritative through and through, for unlike his Protestant friends, Spinoza did not substitute any kind of inner spiritual certainty for the lack of external sanction.[12] "The testimony of the Holy Spirit," if there is such a thing, cannot assure us of anything, Spinoza notes, its only proper concern being "good works" and the "peace of mind" that results from them (TTP, 177). On this reading, as Richard Popkin recently put it, Spinoza's "literalism and contextualism led to a completely secular reading of the Bible," one that excludes not only "any supernatural" dimension but all "divine elements" whatsoever, and whose sole concession to the Bible's sacredness consists in finding those passages that accord with "the voice of reason," the true Word of God or divine law to Spinoza. "In separating the Message," namely "the Word of God, the Divine Law" from "the historical Scriptures," Popkin writes, "Spinoza made the documents themselves of interest only in human terms, and to be explained in human terms."[13]

This view is fairly representative of the overall evaluation of Spinoza's Bible scholarship. Some consider the secularizing thrust of the text to be disseminated in covert ways. Others see Spinoza's contribution as that of showing how socially and politically useful the Bible can be. However, the assertion that for Spinoza "the documents themselves" are devoid of any divine content other than matters we could also derive from reason alone, and the conclusion that therefore readers of the TTP don't need to make much of Spinoza's defense of the sacredness of the Bible (beyond the historical reasons why he did so, or claimed to do so), is a standard view.[14] It is not only the theory of an esoteric TTP that resists taking this defense of the Bible at face value; such a resistance also undergirds most treatments of Spinoza's Bible scholarship from the standpoint of its historical significance. For such approaches focus entirely on Spinoza's destructive project, his explicit and relentless critique of superstition, superstitious

---

[11] Hobbes, *Leviathan*, 268, discussed in Popkin, "Spinoza and Bible Scholarship," 388–389.

[12] For an account of such certainty, and its transformation into rationalism, see Andrew C. Fix, *Prophecy and Reason: The Dutch Collegiants in the Early Enlightenment* (Princeton, NJ: Princeton University Press, 1991), 185–214.

[13] Popkin, "Spinoza and Bible Scholarship," 396, 399, 403.

[14] Other than Popkin and Preus, Christopher Norris's *Spinoza and the Origins of Modern Critical Theory* (Oxford: Blackwell, 1991) is a good example. As much as Norris appreciates the sophistication of Spinoza's biblical hermeneutics, he ends up reasserting the position that "the upshot of Spinoza's researches was to deny any authority to Scripture beyond that of either reiterating truths self-evident to reason, or revealing those blindspots of error and prejudice that resulted historically from the limiting conditions of knowledge *sub specie durationis*" (261).

forms of reading, and the notion of biblical inerrancy, maximizing his contempt for the reigning theological and philosophical justifications for the
sanctity of the Bible, while minimizing his constructive solution to these
dead ends. If proponents of the theory of esotericism consider Spinoza's
defense of the sacredness of the Bible a ploy to escape censure, intellectual historians consider it, in Preus's words, "irrelevant" to the question of
the TTP's importance.[15] After all, Spinoza tells us that the Bible's truths
are moral ones, and these surely can be illuminated better in the *Ethics*.
From the standpoint of intellectual history, the TTP's novelty lies in what
it *doesn't* assert (that the Bible is different from other books) more than
what it does.

Nevertheless, Spinoza insists that there is something sacred about the
Bible, something that is "in agreement with the intellect" but that stands
on its own "footing" (TTP, 6), and his elaboration of this view is neither veiled nor muted. Even if the divine law, which consists in the "love
of God" and constitutes "the final end and aim of all human action,"
is attainable through "philosophic thinking" and not by Scripture alone
(TTP, 51–52), this law is *also* "unreservedly" commended in Scripture
(TTP, 59). The problem can be stated as follows: if, as Spinoza declares,
Scripture doesn't teach metaphysical truths but only moral ones (TTP,
146), and if philosophy teaches both metaphysical and moral truths,
which the *Ethics* amply demonstrates, then why do we need Scripture at
all, except as a poor (if necessary) substitute for something we (learned
readers) would be better off learning in a philosophical academy?[16] Why
indeed. Moreover, if the TTP is simply telling us that Scripture is useful
for the masses, and religion useful in the construction of a democratic
polity, then why should philosophers really need to read it (much less
Scripture itself)?[17]

These are Spinoza's questions, too, not just ours. After his expulsion
from the Jewish community of Amsterdam in 1656, he spent most of his

---

[15] Preus, *Spinoza and the Irrelevance of Biblical Authority*.

[16] Spinoza uses the Latin *pietas* and *obedientia* when speaking about what Scripture teaches,
as when he says at the end of TTP, ch. 14: "The aim of philosophy is, quite simply, truth,
while the aim of faith, as we have abundantly shown, is nothing other than obedience and
piety" (169) (*Philosophiae enim scopus nihil est, praeter veritatem: Fidei autem, ut abunde
ostendimus, nihil praeter obedientiam, & pietatem* [G III: 179]). He occasionally uses the
word *morality* (*mores*), especially when referring to the bearing of the prophets and to the
nature of their certainty (it was only *certitudo moralis*) (TTP, 24, G III: 32). For example,
he says that prophecies differed according to the varied opinions of the prophets, though
all the prophets shared "uprightness and morality" (*bonos mores*) (TTP, 27, G III, 35).
But *pietas* and *obedientia* dominate his discussions of Scripture, along with *justitia* and
charitatis.

[17] This is Bennett's view (*Study*, 7). Ravven ("Spinoza's Rupture with Tradition") and
Rosenthal ("Why Spinoza Chose the Hebrews") come to more sympathetic but ultimately similar conclusions, as does Den Uyl in "Power, Politics, and Religion."

time engaged in working out the most pressing problems of philosophy as he understood them.[18] Some of these naturally involved questions related to Bible interpretation, especially among friends like Meyer, but he mostly concerned himself with Cartesian metaphysics and his own emerging system. When he turned his energies squarely back to the Bible of his youthful studies, Spinoza himself clearly wondered whether there is something sacred about it. If there is, what is it? If not, how should we revise our understanding of the book? These were questions of philosophical magnitude not least because, from postbiblical antiquity up to (and including) Spinoza's day, philosophy was undertaken almost solely against the background assumption that it bore some kind of intrinsic relationship to revelation. Since Spinoza set his sights on rethinking philosophy from the ground up, it made sense to rethink theology; not just ideas of God, which he thought he could resolve in the realm of philosophy alone, but rather the claims of revelation. When he does turn to these, it becomes clear that they trouble Spinoza not because, like Locke, he feels the need to account for the possibility of supernatural truths (he feels, on the contrary, that he needs to account only for their impossibility).[19] Revelation challenges Spinoza because it is, for him, the claim of absolute particularity and privilege: the Bible is sacred in relation to other books, which are not; the Jews are chosen in relation to other people, who are not. Spinoza does not think these claims are a priori illegitimate. He wants to understand them, and he thinks the popular interpretations, and the forms of life to which they have given rise, aren't worth very much.

Popkin's reading follows Spinoza in insisting that, while the Bible is "faulty, mutilated, adulterated and inconsistent," the "Word of God," "divinely inscribed in men's hearts," survives uncorrupted. In this sense, whoever worries unduly about the fate of Scripture itself, or, even worse, insists that its manifest incongruities are precisely the sign of the divine hand, is "beginning to worship likenesses and images, that is paper and ink . . . instead of God's Word." But it is a feature of this line of argument that the analysis is then cut off before it gets to what is positively at issue for Spinoza in reading the Bible in the first place, namely the question "in what respect *Scripture* [as distinct from the heart or mind of human

---

[18] See Nadler, *Spinoza*, 116–154.

[19] Locke's view is that there are truths that reason cannot discover, for example that "the dead shall rise, and live again" (*An Essay Concerning Human Understanding*, ed. Peter Nidditch [Oxford: Clarendon Press, 1975], bk. IV, 694). This is a miracle, to Locke, i.e., something that requires us to give an assent we would normally withhold (bk. IV, 667). This is diametrically opposed to Spinoza's view, which is that miracles are "natural occurrences, and therefore they should be explained in such a way that they seem to be neither 'new' things . . . nor things contrary to Nature" (TTP, 139).

beings] is called holy and the Word of God," or more basically "in what sense the terms sacred and divine should be applied to Scripture and to any inanimate thing" (TTP, 149–150).[20]

If what Spinoza denies is plain enough, namely that God did not "will to confer on men a set number of books" and thus that *these* (biblical) books in particular neither contain the sum of all there is to know about God nor do some of them tell us much about God at all (TTP, 153), his assertion that nevertheless "true religion . . . is taught" in the Bible, and indeed "is commended in the highest degree in both Testaments," is less plain (TTP, 156). How does Spinoza's perspective on *this* question, the question of the sacredness of the Bible, differ from the accepted beliefs he was taught from boyhood? More precisely, how is it hermeneutically possible to disentangle the Bible's divine "message" from the ostensibly false or at least corrupt and confusing manner in which it is conveyed? How *can* the word of God "come down to us uncorrupted" in a corrupted text (TTP, 149)? If not all of the Bible is divine, how is *any* of it divine, and how do we identify its divinity? How does divinity manifest itself in any written work, and how do we read such a work?

It is these more hermeneutical questions that have been almost entirely displaced by the questions concerning Spinoza's historical project, even though the systematically historical portions of the TTP do not dominate (four out of twenty are devoted solely to historical questions). This is all the more regrettable given that Spinoza's significance as a Bible scholar has been reduced almost to nil; an innovator to be sure, along with Hobbes and the theologian (and heretic) Isaac La Peyrère (author of *Prae-Adamitae*, "Men before Adam," published in 1655), but by no means a brilliant historian.[21] This is fair as far as it goes: Spinoza's is at best one early modern example of a critical-historical approach to the Bible, though he is not the most accomplished.[22] If the purport and significance of the TTP's theory of biblical interpretation were either simply to

[20] My emphasis. Preus is right to emphasize that the issue for Spinoza at least in part is the question of why *others* have considered Scripture divine, and that this, too, is an historical question for him. See Preus, "The Bible and Religion in the Century of Genius," Parts III and IV: "The Hidden Dialogue in Spinoza's *Tractatus*" and "Prophecy, Knowledge, and the Study of Religion," *Religion* 28 (1998), 111–138. But Spinoza's discussion of the divinity or sacrality of the Bible is also (and mainly) normative. None of the others to whom he alludes understood the sacred in the way he understands it, i.e., as relative to practice, and this is precisely his argument with Maimonides and Alpakhar.

[21] On La Peyrère, see Richard H. Popkin, *Isaac La Peyrère (1596–1676): His Life, Work, and Influence* (Leiden: E. J. Brill, 1987) and Yovel, *Spinoza and Other Heretics*, vol. I: *Marrano of Reason*, 80–84.

[22] The most accomplished Bible scholar of the period was probably the French priest Richard Simon. His *Histoire critique du Vieux Testament*, published in 1678, pioneered philological and modern critical method (Geneva: Slatkin Reprints, 1971). Others were Elias Levita (d. 1549), responsible for the first printed Massoretic Hebrew Bible (Venice,

read the Bible in a historical way or to "demythologize" it, as later theologians came to characterize this approach – to show, in other words, that its stories and historical narratives are simply mythological representations of more abstract theological or rational truths – this portion of Spinoza's corpus could not have more than a merely antiquarian significance for contemporary readers.[23]

What the TTP means to argue has always been accompanied by the question of why Spinoza wrote it at all, and why he wrote it when he did – why he interrupted his more sustained philosophical reflections to get into seemingly deliberate trouble with the theologians and censors, whose wrath he had good reasons to fear.[24] In this vein, there are many good accounts of the social and political environment in which Spinoza was writing and of his own experiences with religious unfreedom in the Dutch Republic, and many persuasive attempts to make sense of his reasons for stepping into such a loaded field.[25] These attempts strike me as a necessary, if not sufficient, condition for understanding why Spinoza turned to politics and the Bible. The more organic, or internal, continuities that interest me here between the *Ethics* and the TTP do

1524–25), and the French Reformed scholar Louis Cappel (*Critica Sacra*, published in 1650). See Preus, "The Bible and Religion in the Century of Genius," Part II: "The Rise and Fall of the Bible," 15–27. On Simon, see Paul Hazard, *The European Mind 1680–1715*, trans. J. Lewis May (New York: Meridian, 1963), 180–197, and Jean Steinmann, *Richard Simon et les origines de l'exégèse biblique* (Paris: Desclée de Brouwer, 1960).

[23] For an alternative view on Spinoza's legacy for Protestant liberal theology in general and demythologization in particular, see Manfred Walther, "Spinoza's Critique of Miracles: A Miracle of Criticism?" and on Spinoza's contribution to "scientific" biblical hermeneutics see Edwin Curley, "Notes on a Neglected Masterpiece: Spinoza and the Science of Hermeneutics," both in *Spinoza: The Enduring Questions*, ed. Graeme Hunter (Toronto: University of Toronto Press, 1994), 100–112 and 64–99 respectively.

[24] Spinoza had shown himself and his ideas radical enough to undergo an especially harshly worded *cherem* in 1656. After that, the Dutch authorities (secular and clergy) maintained an uneasy relationship with Spinoza, well known to have ties both to Cartesians and to the dissenting Protestant sects that were the periodic subject of persecution and imprisonment. On the conditions in the Dutch Republic surrounding the banning of Spinoza's works after the publication of the TTP, see Jonathan Israel, "The Banning of Spinoza's Works in the Dutch Republic (1670–1678)," in *Disguised and Overt Spinozism around 1700*, ed. Wiep van Bunge and Wim Klever (Leiden: E. J. Brill, 1996), 3–14.

[25] Nadler's *Spinoza* is a superb contribution in this regard, both updating and fine-tuning the earlier treatments of Spinoza's life and context by J. Freudenthal (*Spinoza: Sein Leben und seine Lehre*, vol. I [Stuttgart: Frommann, 1904], vol. II [Heidelberg: Carl Winter, 1927]) and K. O. Meinsma (*Spinoza et son cercle* [1896], ed. Henri Méchoulan and Pierre-François Moreau [Paris: Vrin, 1980]) and giving us the first truly comprehensive portrait of Spinoza in English. On the early reception of Spinoza's philosophy, see H. J. Siebrand, *Spinoza and the Netherlanders: An Inquiry into the Early Reception of his Philosophy of Religion* (Assen: Van Gorcum, 1988). See also Yosef Kaplan's *From Christianity to Judaism: The Story of Isaac Orobio de Castro*, trans. Raphael Loewe (Oxford: Oxford University Press, 1989), 263–307, for a rich rendering of the wider context in Amsterdam.

not take away from the recognition that it is at least partly true that Spinoza was *provoked* into writing the particular work that he did, and therefore his motivation for doing so may be considered a legitimate part of the question of what the text is about. Indeed, one of the things I am suggesting is that those "internal" continuities are just as much political as philosophical, and thus just as much "external," practical, and social, as they are internal, speculative, and intellectual.

The question, then, of why Spinoza turned to the Bible is a good one. The view that he took on this preeminent religious document because it was the most obvious and easily demolished exemplar of a religious regime that he wanted (however covertly) to criticize has some merit. But that this is the *only* reason Spinoza engages with the Bible – that he does so *only* to undermine it – cannot make sense of a great deal of the TTP, except by regarding it cynically and skeptically. What is fascinating about the work is that it is simultaneously a critique of biblical religion as it is propounded by priests, pontiffs, and rabbis, and a commendation of biblical religion as it is – or can be – understood by ordinary people. This is not to suggest Spinoza thinks one can simply disentangle religion and power. As the second half of the TTP shows, he is convinced that the only way religion can be a force for social good is if at least its public dimension is taken out of the hands of individuals (and institutions that function socially like individuals, such as churches) and placed under the auspices of an ideally democratic state. The combination of religion and power is not the problem; it is the configuration of an autonomously constructed religious authority in competition with the authority of the state that is the problem.

The crucial connection Spinoza makes is that the violence of religious power, understood as the privileged access to some transcendent, esoteric truth (to which the many are subjected) can be identified in the violent way in which the Bible is read: "it is clear from our earlier findings that both [sceptics and dogmatists] are utterly mistaken, for whichever view we embrace we are forced to do violence either to reason or to Scripture" (TTP, 170). He is not only undermining the Bible – he is directly and audaciously claiming it for himself, and for the ordinary reader. Why the Bible? The Bible clearly is the single most foundational text for religious power. But it is also the text, for Spinoza, that fundamentally criticizes this power, displaying plainly that the "worship of God and obedience to him consists solely in justice and charity, or love towards one's neighbor" (TTP, 167), not in either "purely philosophic doctrines" or (what is the same) the embrace of "mysteries . . . lurking in Scripture" (TTP, 157–158). To see this dimension of it, one needs, as he says in the preface, to read the Bible anew (TTP, 5).

The point, therefore, is to reclaim Scripture from the priests and pontiffs and return it to the audience for whom he claims it was intended, namely ordinary people. That said, however, it remains to determine what Spinoza thinks ordinary people should do with the Bible: what they should make of it, how they should go about reading it. It is not enough simply to democratize this text by fiat if part of the problem is with readers themselves, not only insofar as they have been vulnerable to the pernicious aims of others, but also insofar as they have been vulnerable to their own misunderstandings of the Bible and the nature of its divinity. It is not enough, in other words, to return the Bible to the populace and to ensure that they are free to interpret it as they choose. For as Spinoza maintains in a political context, freedom of judgment ultimately cannot mean the freedom to pursue every "fleshy desire" that occurs to us (TTP, 64). To put the matter in conventional, Enlightenment terminology (which Spinoza to some extent inaugurates), freedom must consist, rather, in coming to obey the law for the sake of the law itself and thus coming to be able to pair obedience to oneself (independence) with obedience to others (*servitus*) and to the larger social good (man is God to man).

So, too, in the case of biblical interpretation: while all are free to make of this text what they will (including being free not to read it at all), freedom of judgment in reading will ultimately have to do with "obeying," so to speak, the text as an end in itself, and thus coming to be able to pair free thinking with fidelity to the words on the page, their history, their meaning, their practical import.[26] Thus, on the one hand, "as the sovereign right to free opinion belongs to every man even in matters of religion, and it is inconceivable that any man can surrender this right, there also belongs to every man the sovereign right and supreme authority to judge freely with regard to religion, and consequently to explain it and interpret it for himself" (TTP, 106). And on the other hand, in order to "free our minds from the prejudices of theologians and to avoid the hasty acceptance of human fabrications as divine teachings, we must discuss

---

[26] With respect to making of the text what one will, Spinoza bases this on the principle of *ad captum vulgi*, for "just as Scripture was once adapted to the understanding of the people of that time, in the same way anyone may now adapt it to his own beliefs if he feels that this will enable him to obey God with heartier will in those matters that pertain to justice and charity" (TTP, 163). With respect to not reading it at all, Spinoza thinks that "he who is totally unacquainted with the Biblical narratives, but nevertheless holds salutary beliefs and pursues the true way of life, is absolutely blessed and has within him the spirit of Christ" (TTP, 70). On the other hand, "he who is neither acquainted with these Biblical narratives nor has any knowledge from the natural light, if he be not impious or obstinate, is yet hardly human and close to being a beast, possessing none of God's gifts" (TTP, 68).

the true method of Scriptural interpretation and examine it in depth; for unless we understand this we cannot know with any certainty what the Bible or the Holy Spirit intends to teach" (TTP, 89).

Some of this, to be sure, is the task primarily of scholars, who are obviously the class of people with the greatest opportunity to learn the Bible's languages and to devote themselves to historical study. But what matters most of all to Spinoza is the fact that "Scripture was written and disseminated not just for the learned but for all men of every time and race" (TTP, 164). We may now have difficulties establishing the meaning of words and the context of certain utterances, but we should not read these difficulties into Scripture itself, for "the common people of the Jews and Gentiles . . . were familiar with the language of the prophets and apostles" (TTP, 104). Indeed, since it is the learned throughout the ages who have been charged with preserving "books and the meaning of their contents," it is they who are responsible for the "alterations or corruptions" of "rare books . . . in their possession." By contrast, language, including the language of Scripture, "is preserved by the learned and the unlearned alike," and is "customary," not specialized (TTP, 96). In other words, its challenges have to do with understanding the laws and customs of a particular people, not with discerning something available only to initiates.

Spinoza wants to have it both ways: he wants to be able to claim both that the word of God is utterly immune from human desecration – that it subsists incorruptibly in our hearts and is not reducible to any particular set of texts, rituals, or laws – and that it exists historically in Scripture and survives therein, despite the fact that this is otherwise a mutilated text with a checkered history of additions, marginalia, and faulty transmissions:

I am not going to say that Scripture, in so far as it contains the Divine Law, has always preserved the same markings, the same letters and the same words (I leave this to be proved by the Massoretes, who zealously worship the letter), but I will say this, that its meaning [*sensus*] – and only in respect of meaning can any utterance be called divine – has reached us uncorrupted, even if it be supposed that the words by which it was originally expressed have undergone many changes. (TTP, 155)

The divinity of the Bible is dependent on its meaning (*sensus literalis* [G III: 101]), although its words can have undergone many changes. Spinoza wants, then, to be able to take account of the history of Scripture – as an ordinary text that has suffered the fate of other texts – while also commending it as something that is divine, something that "could not have been corrupted in so far as it teaches what is necessary for obedience and salvation" (TTP, 150).

It is tempting, perhaps, to see these projects as essentially onesided, that is, to see Spinoza's distinction between the meaning of the text, which is not only demonstrably corrupted but is also unrecoverable *in toto*, and the truth of the text, which is uncorrupted and fully recoverable, as his attempt to engage in a thoroughgoing historicization of the Bible while leaving its truth as an afterthought, something we could arrive at without the Bible, but to which the Bible minimally testifies. But Scripture, for Spinoza, is not only a single historical instance of moral maxims available to reason by other means. Scripture teaches something that cannot be found in reason alone, namely that "simple obedience is a way to salvation" (*simplex obedientia via ad salutem sit*) (TTP, 177, G III: 188). This is the claim I want to explore here, the claim that the truth of Scripture is dependent on understanding the meaning of this particular text.

Spinoza is not implying that Scripture is the only or even the primary instance of God's word in the world. He is suggesting something different from both Christian and Jewish readers, and different too from the philosophical and historical-critical readings of the Bible that would continue to develop after him. Spinoza's reading of the Bible is intended to establish that the truth of the Bible is a universal and eternal truth of reason precisely *because* it is revealed, that is, available in the text of a particular instance; we only know its content – its "wages," as he puts it – from its appearance in particular histories directed to particular audiences in particular conditions.[27] Despite Spinoza's occasional implication that obedience is simply the way to salvation for the ignorant multitude, it is not that truth abides eternally and is periodically also revealed in certain texts at certain times (which would imply that obedience is a lesser form of salvation than philosophy).[28] Rather, it is that the truths of reason have

---

[27] This is language Spinoza uses in a letter to Blyenbergh (Ep 21) that I discuss below. Shirley translates it as "reward," but the Latin is *merces*, which has the connotation of a financial reward. Thus Curley's "wages" is more appropriate.

[28] On the role of obedience in Spinoza's corpus, there are those, such as Balibar and Negri, who hold that obedience is not only about engaging in semirational (politically instrumental) forms of behavior but is connected to Spinoza's conception of freedom (i.e., blessedness) itself. Others, such as Den Uyl, Rice, Donagan, and Mason argue that, while obedience does not imply, for Spinoza, any kind of crude behaviorism, it cannot be the same as what he considers true enlightenment, for, as Spinoza himself puts it in the TP, "we cannot, without great impropriety call the rational life 'obedience'" (TP II: 20, quoted in Den Uyl, "Power, Politics, and Religion in Spinoza's Political Thought," 140), and in n. 34 of the TTP, that, in the truly rational, "obedience forthwith passes into love" (TTP, 248). I argue below that it is truest to Spinoza's many views on this topic to pay attention to his distinction between theology and philosophy, not in order to discern which was truly and which only partially rational but in order to see what he understood to be the absolutely critical value in seeing neither as the standard for, and thus neither as lesser than, the other. I thus follow Balibar and Negri in holding that obedience is central to Spinoza's concept of *libertas* in the TTP. See Balibar, *Spinoza and Politics*;

themselves not always been in the world. The truths of reason, like the truths of the Bible, are revealed. They are *causa sui*. Therefore, as we will see with the divine and the human laws, and as will ultimately be clear about the mind (reason) itself, there is no truth (or God or nature) without the *conatus* – the labor – of law, obedience, interpretation (we are all the ignorant multitude). As Spinoza tells us, what human beings share is reason, which means that "there is no singular thing in Nature that is more useful to man than a man who lives according to the guidance of reason" (E IV p35c1). Man is to, or for, man. But there is no getting from one to the other, from self to neighbor, from human being to human being except through God (or Nature). Man is God to man. And there is no God, or Nature, separate from mind, text, polity.

The integrity of each – divine and human, minds and texts, reasoning and obeying – depends on their separation. It depends on understanding that philosophy and theology no more express the same truth from different angles than they express different truths seen from the same angle – that philosophy and theology are each sovereign (absolutely independent of each other) only if they are conceived in relationship to each other.[29] The Bible, then, is not divine through and through, in all of its passages – it is an ordinary human text – and the Bible is a text which is "revealed," which shows itself to be extraordinary and divine precisely in surviving as a text which commends *obedientia, pietas, justitia, charitas*. It is neither merely a human text (the human is never "mere") nor unproblematically a divine text. It is this dialectic that Spinoza's conception of revelation and his theory of interpretation are intended to display.

Prophecy, or revelation

The first two chapters of the TTP, "On Prophecy" and "Of the Prophets," form a conceptual unit. The first deals with the question of the nature of prophetic knowledge and the second surveys the question of who counts as a true prophet and for what reasons. Spinoza's argument, in brief, is that the gift of prophecy was bestowed on individuals regardless of their abilities, knowledge, or previous experience. It did not imply that

Negri, *The Savage Anomaly*; Lee C. Rice, "Faith, Obedience, and Salvation," *Lyceum* 6 (1994): 1–20; Donagan, "Spinoza's Theology"; and Richard Maron, "Faith Set Apart from Philosophy? Spinoza and Pascal," in *Piety, Peace, and the Freedom to Philosophise*, ed. Paul Bagley (Dordrecht: Kluwer Academic Publishers, 1999).

[29] On the issue of the separation between theology and philosophy in Spinoza, as well as Spinoza's biblical interpretation overall, I am indebted to Brayton Polka. See his "Spinoza and the Separation between Philosophy and Theology," *Journal of Religious Studies* 16.1–2 (1990): 91–119, and "Spinoza's Concept of Biblical Interpretation," *Journal of Jewish Thought and Philisophy* 2 (1992): 19–44.

they had more "perfect minds," as Maimonides held, for it was "with the aid of the imaginative faculty," not reason, that "the prophets perceived God's revelations" (TTP, 20). The prophets, then, can be distinguished from others primarily in this sense, namely, that they had especially "powerful imaginations" (TTP, 22).[30] It is important to note, Spinoza emphasizes, that prophecy "did not render the prophets more learned, but left them with the beliefs they had previously held" (TTP, 27). We should thus realize, he says, that "revelation . . . varied . . . in the case of each prophet according to his temperament, the nature of his imagination, and the beliefs he previously held" (TTP, 24). This is in contrast to "all [other] commentators," who "have displayed an extraordinary eagerness to convince themselves that the prophets knew everything attainable by the human intellect." To Spinoza, this view ought to lead us to shut our Bibles altogether, for,

> although certain passages in Scripture make it absolutely clear that there were some things the prophets did not know, rather than admit that there was anything the prophets did not know, they prefer to declare that they do not understand those passages, or alternatively they strive to twist the words of Scripture to mean what they plainly do not mean. If either of these options is permissible, we can bid Scripture farewell. If that which is absolutely clear can be accounted obscure and incomprehensible or else interpreted at will, it will be vain for us to try to prove anything from Scripture. (TTP, 27–28)

These chapters can be identified as introducing the central plank in Spinoza's critique of the historical religions of his time. For if the prophets, the recipients of the word of God, are conceived to be ordinary, flawed human beings, able to comprehend and transmit God's revelation only according to their limited learning and intelligence, it would seem to follow that prophetic narratives and their written monument, Scripture, are nothing more extraordinary than the historical record of the ideas and beliefs of certain men in certain times and places. Spinoza claims not only that the prophets spoke *ad captum vulgi*, shaping their prophesies according to the "understanding of the common people" (TTP, 68), but that the prophets themselves were by and large ordinary and uneducated individuals, and therefore God himself must have spoken *ad captum vulgi*, adapting "his revelations to the understanding and beliefs of the prophets" (TTP, 34).

Since for both Jews and Christians the Bible is a foundational source for the knowledge of God, this claim about the prophets' ordinariness presents a potentially intractable problem, for the prophets are the Bible's protagonists. They are human beings who have, however temporarily,

---

[30] See Maimonides, *Guide*, vol. II, ch. 32, 361.

special access to God and through whom God's will can be known on earth. Spinoza's brusque dismissal of the prophets' intellectual excellence was in some ways more threatening than his researches into the compositional history of the biblical text. While, *pace* Spinoza, not "all commentators" held Maimonides' view that the prophets had to be intellectually superior beings, they were by definition considered exemplary in some crucial respects. The skepticism that Spinoza expresses would have cut fairly deeply into any traditional view of the prophets simply because, if the prophets were merely ordinary, then God's word – in the only medium in which we can know it – must be ordinary as well.

Claims of prophecy have always tended to give rise to at least two kinds of doubt. One concerns the doubt experienced by the prophet himself and/or his audience, i.e., the question of whether he has represented his knowledge accurately and whether he is actually communicating something from God rather than from some other source (e.g., from himself or from another person). According to Spinoza, this doubt stems from the fact that "the imagination by itself, unlike every clear and distinct idea, does not of its own nature carry certainty with it." In the case of ordinary knowledge, reasoning, "in addition to imagination," allows us to attain certainty. But prophetic knowledge cannot become certain on its own since "it depends solely on the imagination." Therefore, Spinoza holds, "the prophets were not assured of God's revelation through the revelation itself, but through a sign." For example, Abraham (Gen. 15: 8), Gideon (Jud. 6: 17), and Moses (Deut. 18: 22) ask God for signs to confirm his prophecies to each of them, and Hezekiah asks for a sign confirming Isaiah's prophecy "predicting his recovery from sickness" (TTP, 23). Such a sign cannot, to be sure, retire all possible doubts, since it itself can be doubtful – a prophet can wonder whether the occurrence of a sign is the same sign that he sought, and by the same token, those to whom a prophet is prophesying may very well have cause to wonder whether such an external guarantee is not in fact of the prophet's own making. The Bible recognizes these doubts, Spinoza says, by way of its distinction between true and false prophets.

But while it is indeed a serious problem, i.e., "the certainty afforded by prophecy was not a mathematical certainty," and therefore it might seem that "prophetic revelation is a matter open to much doubt, it nevertheless did possess a considerable degree of certainty," certainty of a moral kind. For, according to Spinoza, in addition to the first two criteria of prophecy, that "the things revealed were most vividly imagined" and were accompanied by a "sign," there is a third, "and most important," criterion that establishes prophetic certainty, namely, that "the minds of the prophets were directed exclusively to what was right and good"

(TTP, 24). This, to Spinoza, is the single most crucial "sign" of prophecy and the single most crucial guarantee that a prophet has heard God's words correctly. While it is not "mathematical certainty," and while otherwise the prophets were a fairly motley crew, virtue is the one thing, he tells us, which all true prophets share (TTP, 27).

The second, and perhaps more fundamental, doubt that one can have in connection with prophecy is the doubt about the very possibility of it at all. It is one thing to wonder about whether a particular prophet is actually a prophet – whether he is telling the truth, whether he is manipulating this truth, whether there is more of him in the message than of God. And it is one thing for the prophet to ask himself whether it is in fact God speaking to him, as opposed to a hallucination. It is quite another to ask: What is prophecy? Is it possible? If so, how is it possible? What does it mean for God to single out a particular person for some kind of special knowledge, and how is one supposed to relate to the specialness of this knowledge if it is precisely mediated through an ordinary person? Is the prophet thus in some respects superhuman, more like God than his audience, but if so, why do we need to believe that a prophet's words come from God? Might it not be good enough simply to take in what the prophet has to say as someone who is superhuman? Does God choose a particular person to prophesy because that person is in some sense extraordinary, or does God's choice *make* an ordinary person extraordinary? More generally, what is it to mediate between the infinite and finite, to be human and to teach humanly comprehensible truths, but at the same time to convey something that other human beings cannot come to on their own? What is this something? These are the problems that any writer on prophecy has to deal with in some way, and this is where Spinoza begins – this is where, I contend, his real interest in prophecy lies. What is it? And more precisely, how does it differ from "natural knowledge," which, as the knowledge and love of God, he considers the highest kind of knowledge?

The nature of prophetic knowledge, or revelation, as he also calls it, is something that occupies Spinoza's attention in most of the early chapters of the TTP. This is unsurprising given the centrality that knowledge has for him throughout his corpus. But it is also this kind of knowledge that challenges him the most, that puts the most pressure on the working ideas of wisdom and cognition that he had been refining in his philosophical labors in the years before writing the TTP. In both *Descartes' Principles of Philosophy* (DPP), published in 1663, and in letters to friends in the mid-1660s, Spinoza had alluded to the question of the nature of revelation and the status of Scripture at regular intervals, sometimes in response to prodding and other times simply in relation to his own arguments about

God and knowledge.[31] What is consistent in these accounts prior to the TTP is, first, Spinoza's conviction that reason and revelation are totally different ways of knowing and cannot be confused with one another, and second, his unwillingness to specify what theology and revelation are, using them only to clarify the parameters of reason.

Thus, for example, Spinoza notes in DPP that "God is the principal cause of motion" (DPP II p12), not in the sense that God sets things in motion but rather that motion and rest are modes of God and therefore "he still preserves them by the same power by which he created them, and indeed, in that same quantity in which he first created them" (DPP II p13). Motion has two kinds of causes: "there is the primary, *or* general, cause, which is the cause of all the motions that there are in the world, and there is the particular cause, by which it comes about that the individual parts of matter acquire motions that they did not have before . . . And what we say here about motion should also be understood to be true of rest" (DPP II p11s). God is the primary cause of motion and rest, and other singular things (through God) are the particular causes.[32] Both kinds of causes contrast with the theological claim that these natural phenomena are among those things "God does . . . from his good pleasure and to show his power to men." Spinoza grants that there are indeed things that depend on God's "good pleasure," but motion is not one of them, and he does not specify any others. He tells us only that such things as do depend on God in this way "do not become known except by divine revelation," and therefore "they are not to be admitted in Philosophy, where we inquire only into what reason tells us, lest Philosophy be confused with Theology" (DPP II p13s).

The *Appendix* [to DPP] *Containing Metaphysical Thoughts* (MT) contains a similar indication of the purview of theology. Spinoza observes that theologians commonly use the word "personality" to describe God, and in particular to distinguish between "God's essence, his intellect, by which he understands himself, and his will, by which he wills to love himself" (MT VIII). In this, he relates, they have clearly engaged in an act of anthropomorphism, since it is a common view (as well as being that of Descartes) that the will and the intellect are distinct faculties in human beings, and we use this distinction to personalize both ourselves (in whom they are unequal) and God (in whom they are simultaneous).[33] To Spinoza, this notion that the will and the intellect are separable is

---

[31] See Ep 14 and 30 to Oldenburg (117–120, 185–186), Ep 19 and 21 to Blyenbergh (132–136, 151–158).

[32] Spinoza's discussion of causation occupies the second half of *Ethics* Part I, propositions 16–36.

[33] See Descartes, "Principles of Philosophy," *Philosophical Writings*, vol. I, 204–5.

incoherent in both cases. In the case of God, it is simply improper language, for God does not have either an intellect or a will.[34] In the case of human beings, by contrast, "the will and the intellect are one and the same" (E II p49c).[35] Spinoza's point is that "though we are familiar with the term [personality], we do not know its meaning [insofar as it implies a separation between the will and the intellect], nor can we form any clear and distinct concept of it." Rather, the notion of God's personality is something God "reveals . . . to his own, in the most blessed vision of God which is promised to the faithful" (MT VIII). Spinoza stops short here of dismissing theology outright, but he clearly uses it to accommodate concepts that are inconsistent with reason and that he himself finds incomprehensible.

He comes closest to directly identifying theology with falsity in his discussion of created substance a little further on, noting that by this kind of substance he will mean human existence and not angels, who are sometimes included under this rubric. Angels, he notes (representing Descartes's view, which is also his own), are "a subject for theology, but not for metaphysics." Even here, however, he maintains a posture of agnosticism (i.e., he refuses either to deny that angels exist or to explain in what manner they do exist), saying simply that "because they are not known by the natural light, they do not concern Metaphysics. For their essence and existence are known only by revelation, and so pertain solely to Theology. Since theological knowledge is altogether other than, *or* completely different in kind from, natural knowledge, it ought not be

---

[34] As he puts in E I p31, God, understood as what is in itself and conceived through itself (*Natura naturans*), cannot be said to be in possession of any faculties at all. Things like "will, desire, love, etc., must be referred to *Natura naturata*," i.e., "whatever follows from the necessity of God's nature, or from God's attributes, i.e., all the modes of God's attributes insofar as they are considered as things which are in God, and can neither be nor be conceived without God" (E I p29s). Insofar as God is understood according to the laws of nature taken as a whole (*Natura naturata*), any "actual intellect" is always some particular intellect, i.e., "a certain mode of thinking, which mode differs from the others, such as desire, love, etc." (E I p31dem).

[35] Spinoza hereby denies Descartes's position that error results from the fact that we have a greater faculty of willing than we do of intellection. Spinoza holds, by contrast, that to think something is simply to affirm or deny it (to will it), unless of course we "look on ideas . . . as mute pictures on a panel." Spinoza grants that "the will extends more widely than the intellect, if by intellect [is understood] only clear and distinct ideas." But this is not what he means by intellection, which includes both adequate and inadequate ideas. Therefore, he says, "I deny that the will extends more widely than perceptions, or the faculty of conceiving. And indeed, I do not see why the faculty of willing should be called infinite, when the faculty of sensing is not. For just as we can affirm infinitely many things by the same faculty of willing (but one after another, for we cannot affirm infinitely many things at once), so also we can sense, or perceive, infinitely many bodies by the same faculty of sensing (viz., one after another)" (E II p49sII).

mixed with it in any way." Therefore, Spinoza concludes, "no one will expect us to say anything about angels" (MT XII).[36]

In all of these examples, Spinoza's reluctance to dismiss theology outright is matched by an equal reluctance to define what it is. His reference to "God's own," i.e., the "faithful," seems to suggest he is trying to constrict theology's purview to particular communities, as opposed to the universal applicability of reason. But he doesn't pursue this in any of these passages, and indeed they stand out for being almost completely unelaborated. What we can discern from them is only that theology is entirely other than natural knowledge and most of the truths of theology are not available to reason. Since Spinoza gives no indication that theology is different from reason in any positive sense, he gives us no clear way to conclude anything other than that theology is effectively and for the most part false or inadequate knowledge.

There are two places in MT where he indicates otherwise. He insists that "Sacred Scripture must also teach the same things [as natural reason]" (MT VIII) and he claims that the doctrine of the immortality of the mind "has been manifested to men not only by revelation, but also by the natural light" [MT XII]). Spinoza provides no argument whatsoever for the first, claiming only that "truth does not contradict truth, nor can Scripture teach such nonsense as is commonly supposed." For if it did, Spinoza flatly states, "we could refute it with the same freedom which we employ when we refute the Koran and the Talmud. But let us not think for a moment that anything could be found in Sacred Scripture that would contradict the natural light" (MT VIII). Curley holds that this must be ironic on Spinoza's part, since this very notion that Scripture must necessarily be true is ridiculed as Maimonides' false view in the TTP.[37] However, given that in the TTP Spinoza also argues for a version of this agreement between reason and Scripture (distinguishing it from Maimonides), I take Spinoza at face value here, allowing only for the exaggeration that *everything* in Scripture must be sacred. With respect to immortality, the second example, he says this is something whose truth philosophy can demonstrate, even though it is usually held to be demonstrable *only* by way of revelation:

---

[36] Cf. Locke, who agreed that the doings of the angels are available to us through revelation, and are therefore a "matter of faith; with which *Reason* has, directly, nothing to do." However, it is still possible, nay necessary, for reason rigorously to subject this kind of claim to its own standards (*Essay*, bk. IV, §§ 7 and 8, 694). The standard medieval view of angels was that they were incorporeal, like God, yet part of the world God created and thus knowable in a way God himself was not. See Maimonides, *Mishneh Torah*, bk. I: "Knowledge," in *A Maimonides Reader*, ed. Isadore Twersky (West Orange, N.J.: Behrman House, 1972), 46.

[37] See Spinoza, *Collected Works*, 331, n. 22.

It follows clearly from the laws of nature that the soul is immortal. But those laws of nature are God's decrees, revealed by the natural light . . . Now we have also already demonstrated that God's decrees are immutable. From all this we infer clearly that God's immutable will concerning the duration of souls has been manifested to men not only by revelation, but also by the natural light. (MTXII)[38]

Spinoza's concern in these passages in DPP and MT is to elaborate his concept of God and to divest it of theological conventions. While some of these conventions are clearly prejudices in his view, he leaves himself an opening to interrogate the relationship between philosophy and theology further. He leaves unanswered the nature of the relationship between these two kinds of knowledge, and seems of mixed mind on how he would respond to the question were he fully to take it on. There is clearly a sense in which he thinks that theology is simply false, i.e., a repository for ignorance, and in this light he is simply humoring his audience when he refers to it as "the most blessed vision of God which is promised to the faithful." On the other hand, there is also the distinct sense that he has not yet fully worked out what he thinks of revelation beyond the fact that it cannot be confused with philosophy. Were it not for writing the TTP, Spinoza might never have had cause to work this out in any positive sense.

In a letter to Willem van Blyenbergh in January of 1665, Spinoza expresses frustration at the tenacity of the view that all knowledge of God must be made to conform to Scripture.[39] A pious grain broker with an interest in theology, Blyenbergh was not an obvious interlocutor for Spinoza, and indeed would go on in 1674 to publish "a defense of the Christian religion and of the authority of Holy Scripture against the arguments of the irreligious – a refutation of that blasphemous book called the *Theologico-Political Treatise*," followed, in 1682, by a refutation of the *Ethics*.[40] But in the mid-1660s, having read the DPP and the MT, he was intrigued, and corresponded quite frequently with Spinoza. In January 1665, Spinoza responded to Blyenbergh's second letter to him, in which Blyenbergh had prefaced his questions and comments on Spinoza's work with a discussion of the "two general rules according to which I always try to philosophize: the clear and distinct conception of my intellect and the revealed word, or will, of God." "According to the one," Blyenbergh

---

[38] Spinoza gives a much-debated argument for immortality toward the end of *Ethics* Part V, distinguishing it both from those who argue that the mind is destroyed with the body – "something of it remains which is eternal" (E V p23) – *and* from those who interpret this to mean that the mind literally remains after death, which is to confuse eternity with duration (E V p34).

[39] On Spinoza's correspondence with Blyenbergh, see Curley, in Spinoza, *Collected Works*, 349–50, and the introduction by Barbone, Adler, and Rice, *Spinoza: The Letters*, 22–25.

[40] Curley in Spinoza, *Collected Works*, 349.

announced, "I strive to be a lover of truth, according to the other, a Christian philosopher." But these two general rules do not always produce harmonious results. Therefore he gives the following account of his procedure at that point:

Whenever it happens, after a long investigation, that my natural knowledge either seems to contradict this word, or is not easily reconciled with it, this word has so much authority with me that I suspect the conceptions I imagine to be clear, rather than put them above and against the truth I think I find prescribed to me in that book [Scripture]. And no wonder, since I want to persist steadfastly in the belief that that word is the word of God, i.e., that it has proceeded from the highest and most perfect God, who contains many more perfections that I can conceive, and who perhaps has willed to predicate of himself and of his works more perfections than I, with my finite intellect, can conceive today. (Ep 20)[41]

Notwithstanding the fact that it is hard to imagine a view of philosophizing more diametrically opposed to Spinoza's own, Blyenbergh insists on connecting his position to Spinoza's claim that (as Blyenbergh glosses it) "even our clearest knowledge still involves some imperfection." The position Blyenbergh is referring to is Spinoza's argument in the demonstration and scholium to DPP I p15: "Error is not something positive," in which he connects the will and the intellect by holding that even confused ideas involve our assent – in other words, we cannot withhold assent or suspend our judgment. To Spinoza, "assenting to things, even to confused things, is a kind of action, and as such a perfection," and thus any presumption that freedom consists in being able to achieve "indifference" to truth, assenting and denying at will, is entirely mistaken. "On the contrary," he holds, "we have established it as certain that the more we are indifferent, the less we are free." Thus from one angle, as actions of the mind, "all modes of thinking we have are perfect, insofar as they are considered in themselves alone." Yet on the other hand, insofar as we assent to "confused things, we make the mind less fit to distinguish between the true and the false, and bring it about that we lack the best liberty." Spinoza's position is not, as Blyenbergh would have it, that "even our clearest knowledge still involves some imperfection," but rather that imperfection – as error, or the deprivation of our freedom – is relative to human flourishing, just as perfection is.

Nevertheless, Blyenbergh connects his own position to DPP I p15. Since you also maintain, he says to Spinoza, that "even our clearest knowledge still involves some imperfection," you will surely understand that "I rather incline toward that word [God's word], even without reason, merely on the ground that it has proceeded from the most perfect

---

[41] I have quoted Ep 20–21 below from Spinoza, *Collected Works*, 361–382.

being . . . and therefore I must accept it" (Ep 20). One can imagine Spinoza's exasperation as Blyenbergh adds that if he should now judge Spinoza's previous letter – the one to which he is responding – by "the guidance of my first rule, excluding the second . . . I would have to grant a great many things (as I do, too) and admire your penetrating Conceptions. But the second rule causes me to differ from you" (Ep 20). The rest of Blyenbergh's long letter consists of investigating some of Spinoza's claims concerning sin, evil, perfection, and imperfection according to the logic of each of these rules, but deferring, in the case of conflicts, to the second.

Spinoza expresses dismay at Blyenbergh's conclusions, noting that "when I received your first Letter, I thought our opinions nearly agreed. But from the second . . . I see that I was quite mistaken, and that we disagree not only about the things ultimately to be derived from first principles, but also about the first principles themselves":

I see that no demonstration, however solid it may be according to the Laws of Demonstration, has any weight with you unless it agrees with that explanation which you, or Theologians known to you, attribute to sacred Scripture. But if you believe that God speaks more clearly and effectively through sacred Scripture than through the light of the natural intellect, which he has also granted us, and which, with his Divine Wisdom, he continually preserves, strong and uncorrupted, then you have powerful reasons for bending your intellect to the opinions you attribute to sacred Scripture. I myself could hardly do otherwise. (Ep 21)

Spinoza's objection is twofold. He objects to the view Blyenbergh attributes to Scripture, i.e., "that explanation which you, or Theologians known to you," claim to deduce therefrom, and he objects to the guiding principle that Scripture is superior to philosophy, i.e., that "God speaks more clearly and effectively through Sacred Scripture than through the light of the natural intellect." Indeed Blyenbergh's opinions concerning *what* Scripture teaches are entirely prejudiced by the fact that he claims to be reading it without also engaging in rational discernment. Spinoza finds this contemptible. As he would later so memorably put it in the TTP,

He who indiscriminately accepts everything in Scripture as being the universal and absolute teaching about God, and does not distinguish precisely what is adapted to the understanding of the masses, is bound to confuse the beliefs of the masses with divine doctrine, to proclaim as God's teaching the figments and arbitrary opinions of men, and to abuse Scriptural authority. Who, I ask, does not see this as the main reason why so many quite contradictory beliefs are taught by different sects as articles of faith, which they confirm with many citations from Scripture, so that in the Netherlands the saying 'Geen ketter sonder letter' [no heretic without a text] has long become a proverb? (TTP, 163)

At best, then, theologians read the Bible as if every line is a divine truth, and as if the meaning of this truth is so readily available to the intellect that it need bring little of its own power to bear. At worst, they "parade their own ideas as God's Word, their chief aim being to compel others to think as they do, while using religion as a pretext." Spinoza decries both ways of reading, claiming that they "extort from Holy Scripture [the] arbitrarily invented ideas [of theologians], for which they claim divine authority," and he never changes his mind on this position (TTP, 88). It is one of the central claims in the TTP that philosophy is not subordinate to theology, and one that he makes with rhetorical relish from the beginning to the end of the book. "Who but a desperate madman," he says, "would be so rash as to turn his back on reason, or to hold the arts and sciences in contempt, while denying the certainty of reason?"

Even so, we cannot entirely absolve them from censure, in that they seek the help of reason in the task of repelling reason, and they try to employ the certainty of reason to disparage reason's certainty. While they are aiming to prove the truth and authority of theology by mathematical demonstrations and to deprive reason and the natural light of its authority, they are simply drawing theology into the domain of reason, and are quite clearly implying that her authority has no brilliance unless it is illuminated by the natural light of reason. (TTP, 176–177)[42]

But it is a mistake to assume this represents the sum total of Spinoza's attitude to theology and the Bible. The "desperate madmen" above include not only those who would subordinate reason to theology, but "those who think that philosophy and theology are mutually contradictory and that therefore one or the other must be deprived of sovereignty and set aside" (TTP, 176). In response to Blyenbergh's claim that "God speaks more clearly and effectively through sacred Scripture than through the light of the natural intellect," Spinoza notoriously counters that "as for myself, I confess, clearly and without circumlocution, that I do not understand Sacred Scripture, though I have spent years on it" (Ep 21). While this admission of Spinoza's might seem to support the thesis that he desires to replace Scripture altogether with philosophy, his perplexity is with Blyenbergh's Scripture – with the notion of Scripture that requires a subordination of the intellect – and with his attempt to cast Spinoza's views as heretical simply because they do not agree with his. As Spinoza puts it a little further on, "I am, sincerely, very grateful to you for revealing to me in time your manner of Philosophizing. But I do not thank you for attributing to me the things you want to draw from my letter." Sounding very much like Darwin defending himself against his critics two

---

[42] This critique applies to *all* efforts to make theology speculative, whether medieval (Maimonidean) or modern (Lockean).

centuries later, Spinoza writes: "What occasion did my letter give you for ascribing these opinions to me: that men are like beasts, that men die and perish as beasts do, that our works are displeasing to God, etc.?" (Ep 21). The "occasion," of course, was Blyenbergh's encounter with those of Spinoza's metaphysical doctrines that he felt contradicted the teachings of the Bible. But it is Blyenbergh's version of those teachings that Spinoza rejects:

If you had read my letter more attentively, you would have seen clearly that our disagreement is located in this alone: whether God as God – i.e., absolutely, ascribing no human attributes to him – communicates to the pious the perfections they receive (which is what I understand), or whether he does this as a judge (which is what you maintain). That is why you defend the impious, because, in accordance with God's decree, they do whatever they can, and serve God as much as the pious do. But according to what I said, that does not follow at all. For I do not introduce God as a judge. And therefore I value works by their quality, and not by the power of the workman, and the wages which follow the work follow it necessarily as from the nature of a triangle it follows that its three angles must equal two right angles . . . But I confess that anyone who confuses the Divine Nature with human nature is quite incapable of understanding this. (Ep 21)

Spinoza accuses Blyenbergh here of anthropomorphism, rejecting the implication that one must forfeit reason to "communicate" with God, to know God. But more importantly, he rejects the notion that God can be found in some particular source or other, whether Scripture *or* reason. Since God is the source of everything, he cannot be said to distinguish between sacred books and profane books; between men and beasts. Hence Spinoza's vivid statement that "I value works by their quality, and not by the power of the workman, and the wages which follow the work follow it necessarily." With reference to ends that we value, things can absolutely be distinguished, and indeed their distinctiveness follows just as necessarily as their original identity in God.

Insofar as Scripture teaches that God is a judge, Spinoza does "not understand" it. Like his reference to angels and to the distinction between God's will and his intellect, the point is clearly that if Scripture teaches these things, it is indeed absurd, i.e., it is adapted to the common prejudices of the multitude. If Blyenbergh were in doubt on this matter – if, in other words, he were tempted to take Spinoza literally that it was simply about a lack of understanding that further clarification might rectify – Spinoza breezily admits that "I am completely satisfied with what the intellect shows me [on these matters], and entertain no suspicion that I have been deceived in that or that Sacred Scripture can contradict it (even though I do not investigate it). For the truth does not contradict the truth." If this were not bald enough, Spinoza adds an even more emphatic postscript, namely that "if even once I found that the fruits which I have already gathered from the natural intellect were false, they would still make me happy, since I enjoy them and seek to pass my life, not in sorrow and sighing, but in peace, joy, and cheerfulness" (Ep 21). The idea that Spinoza could imagine himself peaceful and happy even if the fruits of his intellect turned out to be false is amusing, and Spinoza perhaps meant it to be. It is also making light of truth itself (something Spinoza very rarely does), or at least making it subordinate to (or contingent upon) the virtues of peace, joy, and cheerfulness (by which "I climb a step higher" [Ep 21]), which is how he understands blessedness in the *Ethics*. Truth, too, he seems to be saying, can function in the way that Scripture does, i.e., as something that people can dogmatically point to when they want to say something authoritative. The thrust of all this is that while he doesn't think Blyenbergh's position is completely insubstantial, devoting several pages to arguing with the points he thinks can be productively corrected, he is offended by it nevertheless. It is not that he thinks Scripture is incomprehensible (he admits he is not investigating it). He thinks Blyenbergh is. He doesn't say much about what *he* thinks Scripture is except, again, to insist that it doesn't contradict reason (and insofar he *does* understand it).

With respect to Blyenbergh's second rule of philosophizing, i.e., the rule that one should defer to the "word" of God in cases where natural knowledge is "not easily reconciled with it," Spinoza readily grants that he does not "attribute to Scripture that Truth which you believe to be in it." But he insists that,

nevertheless, I believe that I ascribe as much, if not more, authority to it, and that I take care, far more cautiously than others do, not to attribute to it certain childish and absurd opinions. No one can do this unless he either understands Philosophy well or has Divine revelations. So I am not much moved by those explanations that Ordinary Theologians give of Scripture, especially if they are of the kind that always take Scripture according to the letter and external meaning. (Ep 21)

Spinoza closes the letter with a final preview of his own view of Scripture. Anticipating his argument in defense of the validity of the prophets in TTP chapter 2, Spinoza insists that this view is not achieved by way of mathematical demonstration

and for that reason I said "I believe" – but not "I know in a mathematical way" – that all the things which God has revealed to the Prophets [to be necessary for salvation are written in the manner of laws . . .]. For I firmly believe, but do not know Mathematically, that the Prophets were God's confidential Counselors and trusty Messengers. (Ep 21)

As he would put it in the TTP, "the certainty afforded by prophecy was not a mathematical certainty, but only a moral certainty" – yet a moral certainty with weight, "for God never deceives the good and his chosen ones" (TTP, 23). Although, as Spinoza tells us here, he has already "spent years on Scripture" (Ep 21), although he had "been educated from boyhood in accepted beliefs concerning [it]," he still has something to add that his boyhood education and his confrontation with theologians did not make clear (TTP, 125). Nothing remains, then, he says to Blyenbergh, on the cusp of writing the *Tractatus Theologico-Politicus*, "except that I should demonstrate . . . that Scripture, just as it is, is the true revealed Word of God" (Ep 21).

The first thing Spinoza tells us about prophecy (or revelation) is that it is "the sure knowledge of some matter revealed by God to men" (*Prophetia sive Revelatio est rei alicuius certa cognitio a Deo hominibus revelata*) (TTP, 9, G III: 15).[43] On its face, this statement contains what one might find in any definition of prophecy, namely that it concerns a communication of something from God to human beings and that the nature of the thing itself is less at issue than the means by which, and the source from which, it is apprehended. Whatever the matter is, it is known through and by means of God, and this is an ostensibly supernatural occurrence given that what is normally meant by "God" is, at the very least, a being to whom human beings have no immediate or automatic access. It is assumed, then, Spinoza observes, that prophetic knowledge is something other than natural knowledge, for since natural knowledge (it is assumed) does not need to be revealed to us, it is not thought to have its provenance in God. One consequence of this is that whereas doubt and uncertainty about the contents of what one apprehends are normal features of natural knowledge, they are not considered endemic to prophecy, for God himself (assuming one knows it is God speaking) cannot be doubted.[44] Prophetic utterances often pertain to things natural and ordinary enough, e.g., the downfall of a city or the birth of a child, but the fact of prophesying testifies to the existence of supernatural gifts on the part of the prophet, however temporary, gifts which, as originating in the divine, are thought to override and in some cases contradict what the prophet is capable of by nature.

Spinoza's first approach to the question of the nature of prophetic knowledge is to dispute the assumption that its distinctiveness is marked either by its source or by its "sureness." Sure knowledge, he holds, is something that is attainable through purely natural means. It arises

---

[43] Shirley translates "man" what should be men, i.e., human beings.

[44] Of course, as I noted, a prophet may wonder whether it is actually God speaking as opposed to someone else, something Spinoza addresses in ch. 2.

through understanding the causes of something correctly, and thereby grasping the common properties and laws that structure the natural order as a whole.[45] What is most important about Spinoza's theory of knowledge for his conception of prophecy is his claim in the *Ethics* that to have a true idea (through these natural means) is to be insusceptible of doubt: "He who has a true idea at the same time knows that he has a true idea, and cannot doubt the truth of the thing" (E II p43). What is significant about this claim is the assertion that certainty is established by virtue of truth alone: there is nothing external to an idea that adds to our certainty of it. This is not because a true idea is simply clear and distinct, though Spinoza does follow Descartes in employing this criterion (he denies, e.g., that we can have a clear and distinct idea of a winged horse [E II p49sIII.B.(Iii)]). Nor is it because a true idea simply corresponds with an object. Rather, a true idea for him is something by which one grasps the connections between things and which itself illuminates the borders of uncertainty:

Who can know that he understands some thing unless he first understands it? I.e., who can know that he is certain about some thing unless he is first certain about it? What can there be which is clearer and more certain than a true idea, to serve as a standard of truth? As the light makes both itself and the darkness plain, so truth is the standard both of itself and the false. (E II p43s)

To Spinoza the "test" of the truth of an idea is that what we come to understand has less power over us: "the more the Mind understands things by the second and third kind of knowledge, the less it is acted on by affects which are evil, and the less it fears death" (E V p38). By the same token, "he who has a Body capable of a great many things has a Mind whose greatest part is eternal" (E V p39). It is not that understanding, e.g., the laws of gravity will make us less subject to them if we jump off a tall building. It is simply that understanding how something like gravity works enables us to be less accidentally victimized by it, and the only proof of the adequacy of this understanding is whether or not we actually are. This connection of truth with its "fruits" would seem to suggest that we can never be certain of anything, on Spinoza's model. But for Spinoza truth involves an experience (of empowerment); it is not simply an idea that then issues in some ability. One never, for Spinoza, has a true idea of a single thing (a thing taken in itself, a thing *in* itself): one always has a true idea of a thing plus what caused the thing plus what other things there are to which the thing is connected, or at least as many of them as possible ("the knowledge of an effect depends on, and involves, the knowledge of its cause" [E I a4]). The more such connections we can correctly perceive,

---

[45] See Spinoza's discussion of the laws of nature, i.e., the ways in which "all bodies agree," E II L1–L7 and E II pp37–40.

the more power we actually have ("if an affect [by which we are acted on] is related to more and different causes which the Mind considers together with the affect itself, it is less harmful, we are less acted on by it, and we are affected less toward each cause, than is the case with another, equally great affect, which is related only to one cause, or to fewer causes" [E V p9]). As I have noted, Spinoza's view emphatically is that, unless we think "that an idea is something mute, like a picture on a tablet, and not a mode of thinking, viz. the very [act of] understanding," we shall be forced to recognize that there is no difference between saying "I have a true idea" and "I am certain" of something (E II p43s).

To the extent, then, that God is understood as a being that transcends us, he can play no role in guaranteeing the truth of an idea. But since, according to Spinoza, God is not transcendent of anything, he is, even more strongly than a guarantor, the very ground of natural knowledge: "the knowledge that we acquire by the natural light of reason" depends "solely on knowledge of God and of his eternal decrees" (TTP, 9). It is not that we can't doubt something that comes from God, for everything that can be conceived is conceived through the concept of God, including inadequate, or false, ideas. It is rather that doubt and certainty are functions of the degree to which we understand things adequately or not, and this has nothing to do with anything God himself does or does not do. Insofar as "thought is an attribute of God," all of our singular thoughts of this or that involve the concept of God (E II p1). Therefore, with respect to their provenance, natural knowledge and prophetic knowledge are indistinguishable.

It is what Spinoza draws from his premise concerning natural and prophetic knowledge that would have presented the most trouble for his readers, namely, that if what we mean by prophecy is "sure knowledge" that originates in the divine, then there is nothing special about it. It is on a par with, and is in some respects lesser than, what we know by nature, for natural knowledge, unlike prophecy, apparently gives us something beyond moral certainty:

all that we clearly and distinctly understand [by virtue of natural knowledge] is dictated to us by the idea and nature of God – not indeed in words [as prophecy is] but in a far superior way and one that agrees excellently with the nature of mind, as everyone who has tasted intellectual certainty has doubtless experienced in his own case. (TTP, 10)

Intellectual certainty of this kind is not granted only to the wise; it is perfectly ordinary (though ordinary in the paradoxical sense that man is God to man is ordinary). Considered in this way, prophecy is one form of the natural knowledge that is "common to all men," and therefore "in respect of the certainty involved in natural knowledge and the source from which it derives, i.e., God," natural knowledge is wholly superior, a fact not generally recognized due to people's tendency to "despis[e] their natural gifts," prizing only what they think of as "strange and foreign to their own nature" (TTP, 9). As Spinoza insists (ever vigilant against superstition), "if [anyone] claims for themselves some supra-rational faculty, this is the merest fiction, and far inferior to reason" (TTP, 70–71).

From the outset, then, Spinoza appears to be denying the possibility of prophecy altogether. If prophecy is simply a subspecies of natural knowledge, and an inferior one at that, then it is something of a misnomer. Insofar as theology is the erroneous investment of the natural with supernatural significance, we would be better off describing prophecy in natural terms, effectively getting rid of it as a religious phenomenon altogether. This is certainly the argument that Spinoza makes regarding miracles, arguing that, since

nothing happens in Nature that does not follow from her laws, [and] her laws cover everything that is conceived even by the divine intellect, [and] Nature observes a fixed and immutable order – it follows most clearly that the word miracle can be understood only with respect to men's beliefs, and means simply an event whose natural cause we – or at any rate the writer or narrator of the miracle – cannot explain by comparison with any other normal event. (TTP, 74–75)

When we not only attribute the cause of miracles to God, but also argue that "the clearest possible evidence of God's existence is provided when Nature deviates . . . from her proper order," we have simply taken our own limited knowledge and read it onto the natural order, thereby giving ourselves reason to assume that those for whom God performs such acts are "more beloved of God than others, and are the final cause of God's creation and continuous direction of the world" (TTP, 72–73).

Thus the Jews, he notes, referred whatever they did not understand to God, calling "a storm . . . the chiding of God, thunder and lightning . . . the arrows of God" (TTP, 16). And not only Jews, but Gentiles too: "When Pharaoh heard the interpretation of his dream, he said that Joseph possessed the mind of the gods; and Nebuchadnezzar, too, told Daniel that he possessed the mind of the holy gods. Indeed, this is quite common in Latin literature. Works of art are said to have been 'wrought by a divine hand'," and so on (TTP, 17). To Spinoza, of course, this is erroneous (taken otherwise than metaphorically), and, given his insistence that reason and revelation occupy different spheres or are on different footings, his conclusion is especially noteworthy in this regard. He claims that if this view of miracles as demonstrating God's love were true, "it would surely have to be maintained that God created Nature so ineffective and prescribed for her laws and rules so barren that he is often constrained to come once more to her rescue if he wants her to be preserved, and the course of events to be as he desires." This, Spinoza says, "I consider to be utterly divorced from reason" (TTP, 74). This, he seems to be saying back to Blyenbergh, "I confess, clearly and without circumlocution . . . I do not understand" (Ep 21).

This is not, however, the route that Spinoza takes with prophecy. To be sure, prophecy is not what it has traditionally been taken to be, but it is something nevertheless not "utterly divorced from reason." It does not "exclude" natural knowledge, but it does, he says, "transcend" what can "be accounted for by the laws of human nature considered in themselves" (TTP, 9). This is a pivotal claim. Spinoza has told us that natural knowledge is in no way inferior to prophetic knowledge, and he has told us that prophetic knowledge contains natural knowledge. Yet he is maintaining that there is something about prophecy for which natural knowledge is not solely responsible, something that *transcends* the bounds of the laws of human nature considered in themselves. What can this mean to a thinker for whom natural knowledge is "dictated to us, as it were, by God's nature in so far as we participate therein," and for whom transcendence is usually figured as an error of reason (TTP, 9), i.e., that mode of thinking whereby we imagine that what is least knowable is most worth knowing (and consequently "denounce as impious heretics" those who seek to understand things in a natural way [E I app])? If certainty ("sure knowledge") and source ("God") are not what distinguish prophetic from natural knowledge, what are we left with? One is tempted to wonder whether all that one could be left with is something precisely erroneous. Is this what Spinoza is getting at, that the prophets excel only in their ignorance of the natural causes of things?

There are many respects in which Spinoza thinks the prophets were not an especially enlightened bunch. Joshua, being no "skilled astronomer," did not seem to have known that the earth goes around the sun (TTP, 28). "Similarly, the sign of the shadow going back [in the case of the story of the sun standing still] was revealed to Isaiah according to his understanding, namely, through the retrogression of the sun" (TTP, 28). Noah "thought the world beyond Palestine was uninhabited" (TTP, 29). Abraham "did not know that God is everywhere and has foreknowledge of all things" (TTP, 29). Adam, "to whom God was first revealed, did not know that God is omnipresent and omniscient" (TTP, 29). Jonah "thought to flee from the sight of God, which goes to show that he, too, believed that God had entrusted the care of lands outside Judaea to other powers, who were nevertheless installed by him" (TTP, 33). Samuel "believed that God never repents of any decision he has made," while to Jeremiah "it was revealed . . . that, whether God has decreed good or whether he has decreed evil for any nation, he turns back from his decree provided that men also change for the better or worse from the time of his sentence" (TTP, 33–34). Even Moses "did not completely comprehend that God is omniscient, and that all human actions are governed solely by God's decree" (TTP, 30). On the positive side, "there is no one in the Old Testament who speaks more rationally of God than Solomon, who possessed the natural light of reason beyond all men of this time" (TTP, 33). But Solomon, too, is not without flaws in this regard, for we can see from the measurements of the Temple that such measurements were "revealed to Solomon in accordance with his understanding and beliefs," and since "we are not required to believe that Solomon was a mathematician," these measurements are not in every respect trustworthy (TTP, 28). We see then, Spinoza says, that "prophetic vision and symbolism . . . varied considerably," for the prophets "saw God as they were wont to imagine him" (TTP, 26). Spinoza maintains that such an observation should not be considered impious, for "Solomon, Isaiah, Joshua and the others were indeed prophets: but they were also men, subject to human limitations" (TTP, 29).

So in what respects were they prophets? In what respects did they engage in something that *transcends* the bounds of the laws of human nature? Given the initial statement that "prophecy, or revelation, is the sure knowledge of some matter revealed by God to man," it would seem that we are left only with the distinguishing criterion that prophetic knowledge differs from natural knowledge in being "revealed." Prophecy is a "gift," Spinoza tells us, that did "not remain with the prophets for long, nor did it often occur," being "very rare, manifesting itself in very few men, and infrequently even in them" (TTP, 24). Rationality is also a divine gift, but it is not one that comes and goes. For the purposes of further clarification, Spinoza divides the notion of revelation itself between the natural and the prophetic. Since he has said that prophetic revelations do not make the prophet's mind superior to ordinary minds, he suggests that we regard the "nature of the mind" itself as "the primary cause of divine revelation," that is, the primary locus of the connection between God and human beings: "the human mind contains the nature of God within itself in concept," and this concept is available to human beings as thinking entities (TTP, 10). Outside of this one proviso in the first pages of the TTP, Spinoza doesn't use the word *revelation* to mean what the mind naturally knows, though the concept will return when he deals with the figures of Moses and Christ and with the covenants between God and human beings. But he clearly felt that it was not enough simply to set aside revelation as the distinguishing feature of prophecy without qualification, since this might tempt one to fasten on it as a unique or privileged *kind* of knowledge (i.e., supernatural knowledge). The mind – ordinary knowledge – is also revealed. The distinction between natural and prophetic revelation is intended to underscore that whatever prophecy is, its uniqueness is not epistemological. The implication is also that our first response to revelations that are not ordinary in this sense, i.e., "native" to the mind as such and thus common to all, ought not to be immediate acceptance. The claim is that *neither* natural *nor* prophetic knowledge is innate. The distinction between them is not between what is inborn or natural and what is made, created, or revealed, but between two distinct notions of revelation.

The prophets, then, are those to whom something is revealed, for whom revelation results in sure knowledge, and who promulgate ("interpret") this knowledge to others, who accept it on faith alone. A prophet, in Spinoza's words, is "one who interprets God's revelations to those who cannot attain to certain knowledge of the matters revealed, and can therefore be convinced of them only by simple faith" (*Propheta autem is est, qui Dei revelata iis interpretatur, qui rerum a Deo revelatarum certam cognitionem habere nequent, quique adeo mera fide res revelatas amplecti tantum possunt*) (TTP, 9, G III: 15). Now the prophet, too, attains certain knowledge by way of faith, for, as above, revelation's vehicle, the imagination, cannot alone yield certainty; the prophet needs the additional support of signs and the "testament" of his own virtue, the latter of which Spinoza also calls "faith," or "obedience to God" (TTP, 165). Thus prophets, too, achieve certain knowledge by faith; and prophets, too, "interpret" God's revelations, according to the opinions and beliefs they already hold. What distinguishes the prophets, what they excel in beyond the ordinary, i.e., what may be "faithful" but is by no means "simple," is virtue, which according to Spinoza is "extraordinary" in their case, far "exceeding the normal" (TTP, 20). This they model to a people as the content of what it is to be "chosen" by God. If natural knowledge is "revealed" to all human beings alike, prophetic knowledge is the faith of (for) a nation.

It is crucial to see that the prophets were not possessed of "human bodies but non-human minds" (TTP, 9–10). In other words, it is not that their bodies only were subject to nature while their minds could transcend it, nor that they had some unique mental potency. The prophets were, he tells us, often "countrymen who had no learning whatsoever – indeed, even women of humble station, like Hagar, the handmaid of Abraham – were endowed with the gift of prophecy" (TTP, 22). What matters, then, is not *how* they knew what they knew, but *what* they knew. While prophecy is commonly conceived as special access to something ordinary (like a birth, as above), Spinoza is claiming the opposite, namely that it is an ordinary apprehension of something extraordinary. Indeed, Spinoza confesses his ignorance as to how prophecy actually occurred, i.e., "the particular laws of Nature involved," other than that it was "with the aid of the imaginative faculty" (TTP, 20). Beyond that, and beyond the meaningless fact that it took place through the power of God ("everything takes place through the power of God" [TTP, 20]), Spinoza claims not to know its causes.

Again one recalls Spinoza's statement to Blyenbergh that he does not "understand" Scripture. In conversation with Blyenbergh, this meant he was "ignorant" of all the superstitious things claimed on Scripture's behalf. Similarly, when faced with "the doctrines held by some Churches about Christ," he notes that "I freely confess that I do not understand them" (TTP, 14), i.e., "they are utterly divorced from reason" (TTP, 74). In the case of the laws whereby prophecy occurred, however, Spinoza's "nonunderstanding" is not as much the issue. The issue, he says, is that "our enquiry is here confined to the teachings of Scripture, with a view to drawing our own conclusions from these," and in this light there is no pressing need to understand "the cause of prophetic knowledge" (TTP, 20–21), other than that its occurrence is connected to the imagination. What seems to matter is what were the consequences of prophecy. What did it produce? With what kinds of things did it concern itself? What prophets know does seem to be something worth knowing, even if it is not the miraculous occurrence it is usually taken to be, and even if one perforce comes to "know" what a prophet knows "by simple faith" alone.

Spinoza is clearly committed to connecting reason and understanding with God, and to dismissing the possibility that these gifts are insufficient for blessedness. They may not be granted to all people in the same way and to the same degree, but they do not require a communication between God and human beings at a particular time and in a particular place, nor do they require intermediaries of any kind (except, of course, God himself). The gifts of the natural light, including the virtue in which the prophets are said to excel, are available to all who have the energy and inclination to pursue them.

"However," Spinoza reminds us, he is not writing a treatise on the natural light of reason (TTP, 10), and indeed the problem from the outset is the temptation to pit reason and revelation against one another, as Blyenbergh does. He is writing a book on Scripture precisely because he has noticed that many of those who consider this book preeminently authoritative despise "the light of reason," substitute "human suppositions" and "credulity" for faith, and generate "bitter hatred and faction" (TTP, 5). Does Scripture itself teach these things? Possibly, though Spinoza never really entertains this seriously, focusing instead on why human beings, or rather, readers (as opposed to texts), are so irrational. If not, then what might we find on the topics of faith, reason, and faction if we read Scripture without "admit[ting] [anything] as its teaching which [cannot be] most clearly derive[d] from it" (TTP, 5)? Must Scripture or faith be something that subordinates the divine reason with which we are all endowed (and thus produce hatred and strife), or alternatively must reason demolish the grounds of faith in order to make room for itself, as Spinoza seemed to do in his work on Descartes?

Spinoza's claim that revelation is continuous with natural knowledge rules out the first of these. He responds to the second charge by maintaining that Scripture must be read on its own terms, quite apart from what we might assume it contains (or want it to contain) from a rational perspective: "our discussion must be confined to what is drawn only from Scripture" (TTP, 10). This is not because Spinoza assumes from the beginning that Scripture is unphilosophical, though at a minimum it is not self-evidently so: "I do not go so far as to maintain that nothing whatsoever of a purely philosophic nature is to be found in Scripture's teaching" (TTP, 158). Morality, for example, is something we ordinarily think of as the domain of philosophy. But "it cannot be proved [by philosophical] axioms that Scripture teaches these doctrines" (TTP, 90). Since "we have shown," Spinoza says, "that the chief characteristic which established the certainty of the prophets was that their minds were directed to what was right and good . . . this must be made evident to us, too, before we can have faith in them." In other words, we must be able to show that Scripture in general, and the prophets in particular, actually do "teach true virtue" before we accede to their divinity, their equality with philosophy (TTP, 90).

What Spinoza claims to discover is that the Bible teaches much more than true virtue. Its most distinctive claim is the theological maxim that "men may be saved by obedience alone," obedience as justice and charity; obedience as *pietas*. Since the maxim presumes, and Spinoza repeatedly contends, that human beings may also be saved by knowledge alone, the question is what is the relationship between these two forms of salvation – between reason and obedience, knowledge and piety, or in the language of *Ethics*, salvation (*salus*) and blessedness (*beatitudo*)?[46] Spinoza finds the key to this relationship in the controversies surrounding the interpretation of the Bible, in which theologians, concerned to preserve the sacrality of the book (to obey its letter), and philosophers, concerned to

---

[46] For the claim that salvation is a lower form of blessedness, see Rice, "Faith, Obedience, and Salvation"; Alexandre Matheron, *Le Christ et le salut des ignorants chez Spinoza* (Paris: Aubier, 1971), ch. 3; and Den Uyl, "Power, Politics, and Religion."

preserve the sacrality of the mind (eternal truths), have alike misplaced the Bible's import, which is to display the sovereignty of both philosophy and theology (obedience and truth). We won't know we can be saved by obedience alone except by reading the Bible. We won't understand what we are reading – what obedience comes to – except by consulting the mind and confronting the reality of *servitus*. Just as the prophets can achieve no greater certainty than moral certainty, we cannot by reason alone come to what it is that they especially know: "I maintain absolutely that this fundamental dogma of theology cannot be investigated by the natural light of reason, or at least that nobody has been successful in proving it" (TTP, 175). Without separating theology from philosophy, obedience from knowledge, morality from truth, neither will yield anything but illusion.

Interpretation

Thus, in addition to the question of what transcends the bounds of natural knowledge, there is the question of what kind of a book Scripture *is*. Spinoza informs us in the preface that we won't know the answer to this question if we "assume as a basic principle for the understanding of Scripture and for extracting its true meaning that it is throughout truthful and divine," claiming that this is a "conclusion which ought to be the end result of study and strict examination" (TTP, 5). But by the same token, we won't be able to discern this meaning if we assume the reverse, that it is throughout fallacious or absent truth: if we miss, in other words, the doctrines it clearly does propound, regardless of whether we can adjudge them true by reason alone. Scripture, unlike many books, is a publicly contested document, requiring interpretive caution. And, internal to the text, it is a book about a phenomenon, prophecy and *its* interpretation by those who comprehend it on the basis of "simple faith," that he thinks has been wildly misinterpreted. Thus, he says, the principles by which we interpret Scripture must not be assumed in advance, but must be derived from Scripture itself (TTP, 5). More precisely,

I hold that the method of interpreting Scripture is no different from the method of interpreting Nature, and is in fact in complete accord with it. For the method of interpreting Nature consists essentially in composing a detailed study of Nature from which, as being the source of our assured data, we can deduce the definitions of the things of Nature. Now in exactly the same way the task of Scriptural interpretation requires us to make a straightforward study of Scripture, and from this, as the source of our fixed data and principles, to deduce by logical inference the meaning of the authors of Scripture. In this way – that is, by allowing no other principles or data for the interpretation of Scripture and study of its contents except those that can be gathered only from Scripture itself and from a historical study of Scripture – steady progress can be made without any danger of error, and one can deal with matters that surpass our understanding with no less confidence than those matters which are known to us by the natural light of reason. (TTP, 89)

This principle of interpretation has often been taken to be about an identification of Scripture and Nature, i.e., a naturalization of Scripture, wherein it is taken as an entity susceptible of scientific analysis.[47] But, as valid as this perspective is, it is only part of what Spinoza means to do here. What is more striking is the fact that they are to be linked through *interpretation* – we are to interpret one the way we interpret the other, and this cannot be simply about reading Scripture as a scientific entity, because *nature*, for Spinoza, is not simply a scientific entity.[48] On the one hand, of course, nature, *Natura naturata*, is "knowable" in the sense of being a "fixed and immutable order" (TTP, 77). But on the other hand, nature, *Natura naturans*, is infinite, a view not simply taken over from the *Deus sive Natura* in the *Ethics* but present in the TTP itself, most notably in Spinoza's discussion of miracles in chapter 6. While his argument there is focused on the claim that natural laws are "infinite in their scope," meaning they extend infinitely and therefore nothing that happens can happen outside of or despite them, he also insists that our cognition of the regularity of natural law is by no means the same thing as a cognition of nature as a whole: "the laws themselves give us some in-dication of the infinity, eternity and immutability of God," and they rule out the category of the supernatural as this is understood in theological language (TTP, 77). But they give us only a partial glimpse of nature or God, for, as I have already quoted, "since the virtue and power of Nature is the very virtue and power of God, and the laws and rules of Nature are God's very decrees, there can be no doubt that Nature's power is infinite, and her laws sufficiently wide to extend to everything that is conceived even by the divine intellect" (TTP, 74).

The question is, what is it to naturalize this text (or any text) if by nature something infinite is meant? Conversely, what is it to connect infinity with text, the divine with the human, the eternal with the historical? Spinoza

---

[47] See Curley, "Notes on a Neglected Masterpiece" Alan Donagan, *Spinoza* (Chicago: University of Chicago Press, 1988), 13–34; and Harris, *How Do We Know This?*, 126–27.

[48] Richard Mason's recent study, *The God of Spinoza*, points out that Spinoza's *Deus sive Natura* not only "reduces" God to nature but elevates nature to God (see P. I, ch. 1, "How God Exists," 21–50). For the connections between Scripture and nature in the medieval period as well as the unraveling of this analogy, see Willemien Otten, "Nature and Scripture: Demise of a Medieval Analogy," *Harvard Theological Review* 88.2 (1995): 257–284.

gives us a preliminary response at the opening of chapter 7, namely, that what is the *same* in the interpretation of both nature and Scripture is that in both cases we go wrong only insofar as we attribute to either nature or Scripture purposes that are in fact specific to human interests and human life. Put differently, we go wrong when we fail to acknowledge that both nature and Scripture are indelibly connected to the mind, and so the interest they possess is just as much about minds as it is about laws or texts taken in themselves. In the case of Scripture, the crux of the matter is adequately to distinguish between the meaning of the text and its truth. The former, like natural law, is theoretically inerrant, for according to Spinoza, "while it may occasionally have been in someone's interest to alter the meaning of some passage, it could never have been to anyone's interest to change the meaning of a word. Indeed this is very hard to accomplish" (TTP, 96). The latter, however, like human law, is fundamentally dependent on human actions, understanding, and effort, for "nothing is sacred or profane or impure in an absolute sense apart from the mind, but only in relation to the mind" (TTP, 151). From this angle, words, or rather the value of words, function in exactly the opposite way:

Words acquire a fixed meaning solely from their use; if in accordance with this usage they are so arranged that readers are moved to devotion, then these words will be sacred and likewise the book containing this arrangement of words. But if these words at a later time fall into disuse so as to become meaningless, or if the book falls into utter neglect, whether from malice or because men no longer feel the need of it, then both words and book will be without value and without sanctity. Lastly, if these words are arranged differently, or if by custom they acquire a meaning contrary to their original meaning [*significationem sumenda*], then both words and book will become impure and profane instead of sacred. (G III: 160, TTP, 151)

When Spinoza speaks of words retaining their meaning, he means simply what they denote. It is rarely in someone's interest to change, say, the word *tree* to *log* or *bush*, all other things being equal. Yet the fixity of this meaning is not separate from our relationship to trees and it is this relationship that determines their value. The "original meaning," then, refers to the second sense of fixity – not to what words denote but to how they have been valued. A change in meaning is commensurate with a change in value.

The principle of understanding Scripture from itself alone is not to imply that the text cannot be read in context. Indeed, this is what must be done in order to ascertain both senses of meaning: the denotation and the "original meaning," i.e., the value. In reading, however, we cannot indiscriminately foist things into it that are not there – the truth of the text, which *is* relative to the reader, thus depends on adequately discerning the meaning of the text, which is not relative. Without this distinction between meaning and truth, Spinoza is liable to the accusation that he does not even follow his own principle of Scriptural interpretation, as he has recourse to external matters to assess the meaning of the text. He also admits in the case of miracles that the way he makes out the truth of what is being said is through his own reason, whereas prophecy must be understood from Scripture alone (TTP, 85).[49] Again, miracles (understood as an abrogation of the laws of nature) are false to Spinoza, and he therefore feels warranted adjudging them on the basis of reason (though evidently not enough to avoid also bringing biblical proof texts to make his case), whereas prophecy "is a purely theological question" (TTP, 85).[50]

Spinoza's claim is that one cannot allow "principles or data . . . except those that can be gathered only from Scripture itself and from a historical study of Scripture" (TTP, 89). The "principle" in question is the maxim that the sacred truth of the Bible depends on piety; and the "data" in question are everything that we require for reconstituting the text's meaning, which includes investigating "lingistic usage," cataloging "the pronouncements made in each book," and investigating

the circumstances relevant to all the extant books of the prophets, giving the life, character and pursuits of the author of every book, detailing who he was, on what occasion and at what time and for whom and in what language he wrote . . . [as well as] what happened to each book, how it was first received, into whose hands it fell, how many variant versions there were, by whose decision it was received into the canon, and, finally, how all the books, now universally regarded as sacred, were united into a single book. (TTP, 90–92)

Unlike nature, we find much that has been corrupted on this score (though one could also say that, *like* nature, we find that our knowledge is constitutively inadequate). The Bible's meaning is in fact by no means inerrant, dependent as it has been on human authors and human transmitters. Thus, in a third conception of the significance of words, Spinoza reminds us that "as the old saying goes, nothing can be so accurately stated

---

[49] This is one of Strauss's accusations, *Persecution* 145–7.

[50] While Spinoza holds that miracles are false insofar as they are understood as acts that suspend the laws of nature, they are useful if taken metaphorically. These portions of the Bible relate events that "strike the imagination, employing such method and style as best serves to excite wonder, and consequently to instill piety in the minds of the masses" (TTP, 80). Despite his critique of wonder, to Spinoza this excitation can be perfectly legitimate; indeed, the stirring of the imagination is one of the things that distinguishes Scripture from ordinary "political histor[ies]" (TTP, 81).

as to be incapable of distortion by misrepresentation" (TTP, 150). In this sense the Bible cannot be fully known, not only because its meanings have been corrupted, and not only because its truth is dependent on readers, but because "misrepresentation" is an unexceptional part of any reading. Thus,

in seeking the meaning of Scripture we should take every precaution against the undue influence, not only of our own prejudices, but of our faculty of reason in so far as that is based on the principles of natural cognition. In order to avoid confusion between true meaning and truth of fact, the former must be sought simply from linguistic usage, or from a process of reasoning that looks to no other basis than Scripture. (TTP, 91)

The confusion he is most worried about stems from using philosophy to interpret the meaning of the Bible, for the Bible "is chiefly made up of historical narratives and revelation" which "cannot be deduced from principles known by the natural light" (TTP, 89). Philosophy as an interpretive tool in this case is basically just an illegitimate shortcut for the lazy, a way of not wrestling with the particular difficulties of the text by refusing its historical details and the idiosyncrasies of its authors and principal characters. Spinoza is often accused (by Hegel, for example) of having no real conception of history, or at least no interest in it. On this view, Scripture, insofar as it concerns historical narratives, is not a significant text for Spinoza; it is significant only insofar as it teaches things that are *not* historical, namely that pertain to all people universally and that are true for all time. On this reading, all of the effort Spinoza expends on comprehending the text's meaning is ultimately, from a philosophical standpoint, in order to discard this portion as a relatively useless husk. Again, either he is seen as banishing all truth from the Bible by focusing on the meaning alone, in which case it is not really an interesting text at all to him, or he is seen as culling from its plethora of narratives the core truths that it most fundamentally teaches, in which case it is not really a special text.

Spinoza does not think the text's value lies where it is traditionally thought to lie. The point is to avoid assuming that it is either the biblical histories that make the text sacred or the biblical "truths," such as they are. Spinoza does not think sacrality lies in a philosophical reading of the Bible any more than a historical one. Again, it is the prophets who are the Bible's "voices" (the mind of the text) and, neither philosophers nor historians, it is they with whom readers (the text of the mind) are engaged. For Spinoza, the prophets avoid the opposition of minds and books, theologies and philosophies, which so many theories of interpretation miss.

They do so by way of the structure of interpretation. The question of what prophecy conveys is integrally connected to the question of how we should read Scripture because readers of the Bible are like prophets (prophets are like readers) and readers are also like the prophet's audience. Indeed, Spinoza says, "the authority of the Bible is dependent on the authority of the prophets, and can thus have no stronger arguments to support it than those by which the prophets of old were wont to convince people of their authority" (TTP, 175). Spinoza sets up a dichotomy between the prophet who attains something "sure" and the audience who accepts this on faith, but this dichotomy is not a rigid one, as I argued above, because the prophet, too, is dependent on faith. Like prophets, readers are translators of something (a text) that requires interpretation. Like the prophet's audience, the knowledge of texts that we *can* attain is not mathematical, since texts "transcend" us. As Spinoza asks the reader of Scripture: "what can we say of things transcending the bounds of our intellect except what is transmitted to us by the prophets by word or writing?" (TTP, 10).

Prophets are those from whom we learn things that "transcend" the bounds of natural knowledge because, whatever else it is, prophecy, like Scripture itself, is narrative – it is conveyed in words or writing and it concerns things – experiences, languages, histories, politics – that, while sources of knowledge for and about human beings, cannot be deduced from human nature alone. Prophecy is theologico-political. The point is not that words are unnatural (nor ultimately, we will see, that nature requires no interpretation).[51] It is that words, for Spinoza, are communal, customary, historical: they extend us outward, toward the others that affect us and whom we affect, and they thus at once express our limits (our inability to know others, and indeed ourselves) and our transgression of those limits (our ability to communicate with others and to achieve self-knowledge). That man is God to man, we saw, is a source of both turmoil and power. In reflecting on the revelation of the Decalogue at Sinai, Spinoza considers the interpretation that the Israelites heard only a "noise without distinct words," apprehending the Ten Commandments "by direct intuition." However, he rejects this interpretation, even though the accounts of the content of God's words differ in Exodus and Deuteronomy, because Scripture clearly says that the Israelites heard the voice of God: "for in Deut. ch. 5 v. 4 it expressly says, 'The Lord talked with you face to face.'" As Spinoza says, this is just how "two

---

[51] See also Montag's reading of Spinoza's profound reorientation towards words and writing in *Bodies, Masses, Power*, 5.

men ordinarily exchange thoughts through the medium of their two bodies" (TTP, 12), and though we might find it repugnant to reason to think of God as having a body, we can make perfect sense of the meaning of the passage (that the mind of God, the law, was revealed in this way). The implication is that this is also what the reader faces with the "body" of the biblical text, namely, that we have to converse with it in order to understand its "mind," regardless of the beliefs we bring to any reading.

To learn from words, which Spinoza tells us in the *Ethics* is learning through the first kind of knowledge, "opinion or imagination," we must attend to the idiosyncracies – the singularity – of the speakers or writers themselves. Words are "signs," he says, through which we imagine, recollect, or form ideas of things (E II p40s2). The historical study of a text is at least partly the effort to delineate this singularity, for "as we have a better understanding of a person's character and temperament, so we can more easily explain his words" (TTP, 92). The imagination is an unreliable teacher because it is not limited by "common notions" shared by all people. But it is also an extraordinary and powerful engine for the perception of God's word; it is that faculty in which the prophets especially excelled. And while Spinoza notes that "those who devote themselves to the cultivation of their more powerful intellect, keep their imagination under greater control and restraint" (TTP, 22), it is also the case that "many more ideas can be constructed from words and images than from merely the principles and axioms on which our entire natural knowledge is based" (TTP, 21).

In Spinoza's view, then, "an examination of the Bible will show that everything that God revealed to the prophets was revealed either by words, or by appearances, or by combination of both." Further, he says, "the words and appearances were either real and independent of the imagination of the prophet who heard or saw, or they were imaginary, the prophet's imagination being so disposed, even in waking hours, as to convince him that he heard something or saw something" (TTP, 11). In other words, all words are comprehended by virtue of the imagination, but only some are "imaginary," while others are "real."

What can this possibly mean? The most straightforward dimension of this distinction is Spinoza's claim that, by and large, the words and appearances vouchsafed to the prophets were *not* independent of their imagination, i.e., they were imaginary. As I discussed above, Spinoza precisely defines prophecy as the possession of a "lively imaginative faculty" through which God can, as it were, speak (TTP, 15), which is why "the certainty acquired by the prophets" was of a moral and not a mathematical kind (TTP, 24), and why "prophetic visions and symbolism . . . varied considerably" (TTP, 26). Thus he relates how Abimelech heard God's voice in a dream (TTP, 11); how "God revealed to Joshua that he himself would fight on [his army's] behalf" by causing "to appear to him an angel with a sword as if to lead his army" and by letting him hear the angel tell him this in words (TTP, 13); and how God "displays his anger to David" in an identical way, "through an angel grasping a sword" (TTP, 13). By "imaginary," Spinoza seems to mean the ability to have the visions, dreams, and vivid experiences that allowed the prophets to step outside of what can ordinarily be seen in a given situation. Thus, for example, Isaiah had a vision of

God's providence forsaking the people: he saw God, the thrice Holy, sitting on his throne on high, and the Israelites stained with the filth of their sins, sunk in foulness, and thus removed from God. Thereby he understood the present miserable plight of the people, while its future calamities were revealed to him by words that seemed to issue from God. (TTP, 13)

So, too, Spinoza notes, this "imaginative" dimension belongs not only to the person of a prophet, but to the very words of the Bible. Taking the notoriously multivalent Hebrew word *ruach*, Spinoza identifies seven different ways that the word is used: 1. "breath" in the Psalms; 2. "life" in Samuel; 3. "courage and strength" in Joshua; 4. "virtue or capacity" in Job; 5. "disposition of mind" in Numbers, i.e., "all the passions, and also the gifts, of the mind" from "jealousy," through the desire for "fornication," from "wisdom, counsel, bravery" through "prudence, courage . . . and the spirit of kindness"; 6. "Mind itself, or Soul" as in Ecclesiastes; and 7. "the quarters of the world" (TTP, 15–16). Spinoza's choice of the word *ruach* is not only based on the fact that it is especially multivalent. For *ruach* precisely expresses the nature of prophetic certainty, that is, what distinguishes prophetic flights of fancy from simply the inadequacy that characterizes the ordinary imagination: that it concerns capacities and dispositions, i.e., it is judged by its fruits; that it concerns the "heart," or "mind," or "soul," not as the Protestant inward certainty of the spirit, but as "life," "breath," that which is (by nature) continuous with the "quarters of the world"; that it is not free from desire and inadequacy, which exist alongside "the gifts of the mind"; that, above all, prophecy is a certain "spirit of kindness." Although Spinoza insists that it is not relevant to know how prophecy occurs, he does want to know what it is, i.e., what the Bible means when it describes the prophets as being "filled by the Spirit of God" (TTP, 15). To this end, he points to the word *ruach*. What is a prophet? A prophet is someone with *ruach*.

Although, as I said, he mentions the possibility of false prophecy, he doesn't dwell on it, and even more, insists that we don't need to worry about it since God doesn't deceive his chosen ones (TTP, 23).[52] He mentions no ignominious prophets, though neither does he deny that there were some. Spinoza's point is that a prophet is precisely someone who has a "heart turned to what is right and good" – this is what prophets are, and this is what they do, and this is how *we* can be "sure" of what they say. The prophets are not miracle-workers, even though they see things that prima facie are "mysterious symbols," for these, too, he shows, can "yield to examination by our method, so that we can perceive the author's meaning." In his accounts of the prophets' visionary flights, there is none of the disdain that Spinoza sometimes expresses for things mysterious. More than this, he claims that "the prophets were endowed with an extraordinary virtue" – with an extraordinary *ruach* – "exceeding the normal" (TTP, 20). *They* based their claims to prophecy, Spinoza tells us, "on no other considerations." And so "there are no other considerations by which their authority could be proved either to the people to whom they once spoke face to face, or to us to whom they speak in writing" (TTP, 175).

At the same time that Spinoza is maintaining that the Bible was written by multiple human authors in many different times and places, and that therefore its narratives do not obey the same logic as ordinary history, he is also, subtly, claiming that ordinary history is, in its own way, prophetic. While the Book of Joshua, for example, "can be shown . . . not to be by the hand of Joshua" (TTP, 114), and the book of Judges by a "single historian" and not the judges themselves (TTP, 115), and while the Pentateuch "was not written by Moses, but by someone who lived many generations after Moses" (TTP, 112), they tell the theologico-political history of a particular people – they contain a people's *ruach*. As Spinoza notes, Exodus 24 "gives evidence of another book called the 'the Book of Covenant,' which Moses read before the Israelites when they first entered into a covenant with God." In Exodus 20–24,

---

[52] Cf. Descartes's efforts to secure certainty against the possibility that God is a "malicious demon," viz., the absolute certainty that he is a thing that thinks (*Meditations on First Philosophy*, in *Philosophical Writings*, vol. II, 18). Descartes, too, held that God never deceived people. But he gave a metaphysical reason for this, namely that "in every case of trickery or deception some imperfection is to be found; and although the ability to deceive appears to be an indication of cleverness or power, the will to deceive is undoubtedly evidence of malice or weakness, and so cannot apply to God" (37). Spinoza, by contrast, thinks this is something about which one can have only the same certainty as the prophets, namely, moral certainty; there can be no "proof" that God does not deceive the chosen other than that they display virtue.

we read that as soon as Moses realized the feelings of the people with regard to a covenant with God, he immediately wrote down God's utterances and laws, and in the morning, when certain ceremonies had been performed, he read out the terms of the covenant to the whole congregation. When the terms had been read out and no doubt understood by the entire assembly, the people bound themselves with full consent. (TTP, 112)

According to Deuteronomy 31: 9, "the historian adds that Moses gave it out into the hands of the priests, and that he further ordered them to read it out to the entire people at an appointed time. This indicates that the book in question was much shorter than the Pentateuch, seeing that it could be read through at a single assembly so as to be understood by all" (TTP, 113). This book of the covenant (containing, in his opinion, simply the laws set out in Exodus 20: 22–24) is a piece of history to Spinoza – it accurately represents what Moses presented to the Israelites, and it has been preserved in the Pentateuch basically intact. The books of Joshua and Judges and much of the other material of the Bible are also history, regardless of who wrote them and what has been changed over time. Indeed, says Spinoza, the Bible is "chiefly made up of historical narratives" (TTP, 89). By the same token, one might say, ordinary history, the kind we can ostensibly read without paying any heed to the lesson it contains (by the logic of the second quotation at the start of this chapter), is nevertheless "imaginary" in some sense. It consists of the words and experiences of authors who are trying to speak with us "face to face," and who thus, like Israel and God, like any human being and any other, find that they can do so only "through the medium of their two bodies," that is, through the realm of the imagination (TTP, 12).

What, then, does Spinoza mean by a "real" (as opposed to "imaginary") voice of God? He tells us that only one prophet heard God's real voice:

With a real voice God revealed to Moses the laws which he willed to be enjoined on the Hebrews, as is clear from Exodus ch. 25 v. 22 where God says, "And there I will meet with thee and commune with thee from that part of the cover which is between the two Cherubim." This clearly shows that God employed a real voice, since Moses found God there ready to speak with him whenever he wished . . . this voice whereby the Law was proclaimed was the only instance [among all the prophetic revelations] of a real voice. (TTP, 11)

Now, he also says, as I pointed out, that the Israelites heard God's voice, too, "for which purpose he descended from Heaven to Mount Sinai" (TTP, 12). But as Spinoza spells out in chapter 17, this voice of God precisely terrified them. While the Israelites proclaimed aloud "whatever God shall speak, we shall do," and "approached God on equal terms to hear what he wished to command," when God *did* speak they were "so thunderstruck" that they begged Moses to intervene, saying "go thou near therefore, and hear all that our God shall say" (TTP, 196). It is therefore Moses who can properly be said to have heard God's real voice, for it is Moses who is able to "commune" with him:

> the position here outlined receives even clearer confirmation in Numbers ch. 12 v. 6, 7, "If there be a prophet among you, I the Lord will make myself known unto him in a vision (that is, through figures and symbols, for in the case of Moses' prophecy God declared that there was vision without symbols) and I will speak to him in a dream (that is, not in actual words and a real voice). But not thus (will I reveal myself) to Moses. With him will I speak mouth to mouth, by seeing and not by dark speeches, and the similitude of the Lord shall he behold"; that is to say, beholding me as a friend might do, and not in terror. (TTP, 13–14)

There is both a mythos here and a truth; something imaginary and something real; a vision with symbols and a vision without symbols. It is not God's mind to which Moses has access, but his "body," his speech. The connection is made or spoken, not given. Like the pact God makes with the Israelites at Sinai, Moses' connection to God involves words: God's words, and the law of "whatever God shall speak, we shall do." While only Moses heard the law as it was revealed, the law he heard is addressed to his people eternally: it is that "to which nothing might be added and from which nothing might be taken away" (TTP, 12). God's real voice is thus not, in Spinoza's language, miraculous, but perfectly ordinary. It signifies Moses' understanding that God's commands are those a friend commands.[53]

Moreover, just as Moses reveals the divine law of God to the Israelites, Christ does for humankind. Here Spinoza's distinction between – and connection of – natural and prophetic revelation returns. Even natural, universal knowledge is revealed; even prophetic, community-specific knowledge is true. As Spinoza puts it, "a man who can perceive by pure intuition that which is not contained in the basic principles of our cognition and cannot be deduced therefrom must needs possess a mind whose excellence far surpasses the human mind." This, he claims, only Christ achieved (TTP, 14). That is, Christ shows us that "the basic principles

---

[53] Donagan, by contrast, finds Spinoza's use of the distinction between the real and imaginary voice of God to imply only that Moses *thought* he heard a real voice, just as Christ's disciples *thought* the body of Jesus arose from the dead. In both cases, according to Donagan, it is not that Spinoza is denying these things were real. They were real for the people who believed them, and they are real in that the holding of these beliefs has real effects on the world – most of all, they are real in that Scripture credibly reports these accounts as the beliefs of trustworthy people. But otherwise, the notion of "God's real voice" can only be, in Spinoza's terms, a miracle, and thus, literally, untrue ("Spinoza's Theology," 361–364).

of our cognition" are bare and inadequate not only with respect to words and history; they cannot even produce the universal, the common, the rational, the true, the "natural light": even this, even natural knowledge, that which "contains the nature of God" in it, had to be revealed (TTP, 10).[54] What is common (human) is extraordinary (divine). Even God is not given but made. This was Christ's "intuition," the one that connects singular things to the eternal. This cannot be "found" in the mind alone but must be brought about, created, with great effort. Christ's uniqueness, like that of Moses and indeed of the Bible itself, is thus paradoxical. He is the only one to show us that, since what surpasses the human mind is the God present in the mind itself, he cannot be the only one who knows what he knows. Or rather, that God is present in the human mind in the beginning does not entail that we will have knowledge of God at the end. By the same logic, Moses is the only one who shows us that to speak with God face to face is the eternal inheritance of Israel. The Bible, we will see, is the only book to show us that chosenness (exclusivity) depends upon democracy (inclusivity) and democracy on chosenness.

This is not the familiar platitude that Christ is the figure of universality while Moses and the Jews are the figures of particularity. What Spinoza is saying is that *both* Moses and Christ are figures of universality; both hear God's real voice – the divine law – and communicate its universality to others, as opposed to the other prophets, whose vision is limited (though also augmented) by the sway of the "imaginary." While Moses communicates in "real" words to the people Israel, Christ does so in the mind. "Therefore," Spinoza says, "the Voice of Christ can . . . be called the Voice of God in the same way as that which Moses heard" (TTP, 14).

This is not to found Judaism on a more basic Christianity any more than it is simply to make the latter derivative of the former. Christ is mind, Moses is word, but there is no mind in itself; there is no mind that has not already "promised to obey God in all things" (TTP, 188). Christ is simply the natural law written (revealed) in the heart of humankind. As Spinoza makes clear in chapter 19, this law cannot substitute for any particular law, custom, and *natio*, and indeed it has no existence outside

---

[54] According to Donagan, what Spinoza must have meant by Christ's mind "far surpassing" the human mind (with its basic principles of cognition) is that Christ's knowledge was missing those basic principles, not that he knew something no one else could know. For Donagan, Christ possessed adequate knowledge, as the second kind of knowledge (*ratio*), unlike the other prophets (including Moses) who knew things only inadequately, through the imagination (the first kind of knowledge). But even "Jesus' adequate cognition, as Spinoza conceived it, was not accompanied by cognition of the principles determining its adequacy," i.e., the third and highest kind of knowledge, *scientia intuitiva* ("Spinoza's Theology," 372). This interpretation supports the view that for Spinoza, true religion, and especially its dogmas of faith, is rational but not blessed.

the particular laws whereby human beings construct social and political entities. Thus this is not an association of Moses with the "human" and Christ with the "divine." Both Christ and Moses are "divine," they both teach the divine law, and in so doing, both are only ever human, humanly conceived, humanly constructed, humanly known. To Spinoza, man is God to man. We know this, as Moses did speaking to God, at once in our "mouths" and in our minds.

The juxtaposition of these trajectories in Moses, Christ, and the prophets – on the one hand pointing away from the natural and on the other pointing back toward it – is a crucial dimension of Spinoza's endeavor in writing the TTP. He seems to be saying that, if it is true that with prophecy, words, histories, visions, we are speaking about something that transcends the natural, we are ultimately, by means of the imagination, directed back to the natural itself, than which there can be nothing greater, i.e., which ultimately nothing can transcend since nature, too, is revealed. It is as if he is suggesting that any notion of nature with which we might begin "in itself" is too bare, too void of substance and detail and life; as if the contrast itself between reason (with its clear and distinct concept of God or Nature) and revelation (scriptural narrative), while crucial, is ultimately in the service of enriching one thing: the life of the one who can learn how to interpret one as she interprets the other; as if this contrast itself must be transcended in order for nature in the widest sense to be constituted in the first (or perhaps last) place.

Revelation, then, is not supernatural, but, as theologico-political, it does transcend reason alone: it shows the very poverty of the notion of "reason alone." Thus the critique of reason here is both theological *and* philosophical. The critique, in other words, is in the service of a notion of reason that can include both philosophical (natural) and theological (cultural) notions of truth. What Spinoza's theory of reading forces us to do is to see the problematic of interpretation as pervading both these endeavors. In nature, the onus of interpretation is on the human mind and its relationship to other minds and to the natural order as whole. When we turn to a book, the rule of reading according to the standard of the text at hand is all the more crucial, because whereas in the case of natural knowledge, our failure to understand correctly will be accompanied by a correspondent diminution in the power to act in the world, a failure of understanding in the case of the words in a book is much less easy to catch: I can make it say whatever I want it to say, and I myself will not, or will not immediately, suffer the consequences of this. I can "fashion a new Scripture of [my] own devising" and the text will not itself protest (TTP, 113). As Spinoza puts it, "the essence of words and images is constituted only by corporeal motions" (E II p49sII), and therefore we can pronounce on things that we only dimly understand (TTP, 12). When Spinoza says, then, that we must seek to understand Scripture according to itself alone, he is reminding us that caring for its integrity, for what it actually says, is the sole avenue to appreciating what it conveys – its truth.

The special problems that attend discerning the meaning of the biblical text have formed the bulk of the secondary responses to the TTP. Taken in light of the problem of meaning, the TTP is construed above all as a text about historicizing the Bible and thus, whether a reader happens to think this is a good or a bad thing, the upshot is that Spinoza is either a Bible critic (agnostic with respect to its sacrality) or a critic of the Bible (hostile to its sacrality). But Spinoza does not distinguish between meaning and truth only in order properly to discern the Bible's meaning. As he notes,

when we possess this historical account of Scripture and are firmly resolved not to assert as the indubitable doctrine of the prophets anything that does not follow from this study or cannot be most clearly inferred from it, it will then be time to embark on the task of investigating the meaning [*mentem*, i.e., mind or spirit] of the prophets and of the Holy Spirit. (TTP, 93)[55]

As with the problem of meaning, here, too, there is a crucial connection to the interpretation of nature. Whereas in the case of meaning the analogy conveys the force of resisting the temptation to ascribe our particular interests and desires to the text, in the case of truth what reading the Bible shares with "reading" nature is a commitment to beginning with what the Bible most frequently or universally teaches, and using that as a standard against which to understand its wealth of particular details:

in examining natural phenomena we first of all try to discover those features that are most universal and common to the whole of Nature, to wit motion and rest . . . and then we gradually advance from these to other less universal features. In just the same way we must first seek from our study of Scripture that which is most universal and forms the basis and foundation of all Scripture; in short, that which is commended in Scripture by all the prophets as doctrine eternal and most profitable for all mankind. For example, that God exists . . . who loves above all others those who worship him and love their neighbors as themselves. (TTP, 93)

---

[55] Shirley unaccountably translates *mentem* here as "meaning." But two pages earlier, when Spinoza is discussing the importance of understanding Scripture historically via the distinction between meaning and truth, the word he uses for the former is *sensus*. In the passage here, he notes that now that he has shown how to discern the *sensus* he will now turn to the *mentem* of the prophets. *Mentem* here can be translated as meaning not in the sense of "what does the passage in the Bible mean" but what is the meaning (i.e. content or truth) of this meaning. In this light, it seems highly misleading to translate the *sensus* and *mentem* with the same word.

One proceeds, he continues, to "other matters which are of less universal import but affect our ordinary daily life, and which flow from the universal doctrine like rivulets from their source. Such are all the specific external actions of true virtue which need a particular occasion for their exercise" (TTP, 93). In the case of nature, the most "universal features" are those laws, like the laws of motion or the laws of cause and effect, which hold most generally throughout nature and on which all other laws and all human ends are dependent. In the case of Scripture, the notion of the most universal refers to those actions that are commended to all people universally, i.e., universal moral maxims, which Spinoza sums up here as the worship of God and the love of the neighbor. What Spinoza doesn't say here, but which enables us to see yet a further connection between Scripture and nature, is that motion and rest, cause and effect, are not, for human beings, the most universal feature of nature. For human beings, the most universal feature of nature – the feature that "is in almost everyone's mouth" – is man is God to man.

The Bible and the sacred

The employment of both philosophical and theological rhetoric in the interpretation, manipulation, and deployment of a text considered preeminently sacred has enormous social and political consequences. When Spinoza, in the preface to the TTP, identifies the separation of philosophy and theology with the creation of a polity founded on freedom, peace, and piety, he does so from the standpoint of asking: What is the sacred? What is its role in public and private life? How is it constructed, identified, disseminated? Where does it reside, and who has access to it? As questions, these are not all that different from what Spinoza is concerned with in the *Ethics*, where he begins defining God and ends with the way of life best suited to who and what God and human beings are. For the Spinoza of the TTP, the Bible is the natural starting place because the Bible is the putative repository of his society's conception of the sacred – that is, of religion, but more specifically, of religious authority and power. The difference between the two projects is not so much in the conception of religion they seek to propound (both are interested in the difference between true and false religion) but in the obstacles they each face. In the *Ethics*, the obstacles are above all the conceptions of God – both philosophical and theological – which locate the divine above and beyond human life. In this case the thrust is to bring God back into the world, so to speak. In the TTP, the obstacles are the conceptions of God and the sacred that place both *in* the midst of human social and political life, in a pivotal text and, more significantly, in the hands of a distinct and exclusive class of interpreters. Reading, or rereading, the Bible, then, is no ordinary endeavor, even if one decides in the end that the Bible is just an ordinary book – even if, as so many commentators on Spinoza have claimed, the point is to naturalize or secularize this book. For even in so doing, one is taking a stand on what religion is and isn't, what the sacred is and isn't, where it is and isn't, and so on.

The sacred, then, is what is crucially at issue (metaphysically, hermeneutically, politically), not only in how and why Spinoza reads the Bible, but also in how Spinoza understands reading per se, and thus in how we are supposed to read *his* texts. Spinoza introduces the point in chapter 12:

A thing is called sacred and divine when its purpose is to foster piety and religion, and it is sacred only for as long as men use it in a religious way. If men cease to be pious, the thing will likewise cease to be sacred; if it is devoted to impious uses, then that which before was sacred will become unclean and profane. (TTP, 150)

Spinoza is not saying here that there is nothing that is truly sacred, but that sacrality can never be singular. "A thing is called sacred when its purpose is to foster piety and religion." But those who "call" something sacred are often mistaken about what this sacrality consists of (or what the difference is between true and false religion), all too willing magically to displace the power of this ascription onto an object such as God or the Bible; all too reluctant to predicate this power of, say, Shakespeare, or one's kin. In fact, properly construed the sacred is not a "thing" at all, and wherever it is conceived in this way (and it usually is), there impiety inevitably arises. Sacrality is not a thing, for Spinoza, because it depends on and involves a relationship between (at least) two interlocutors: God and human beings, human beings and human beings, and, more specifically in the TTP, a text and a reader. Thus the Bible *is not sacred*, for Spinoza, even though we can discern that its purpose – its *meaning* – is indeed to foster piety and religion. But the Bible conjoined with a reader who understands it, that is, who lives piously, *is* sacred (true), and remains sacred only as long as it has such readers. This might sound like a perfectly orthodox Protestantism, and no doubt Spinoza identified with some readers of this description. But those readers, as well as most other theological and philosophical readers, would undoubtedly be unwilling to follow out the implications of Spinoza's conception of the sacred, which is that if the Bible must in some sense be interpreted like all other books, then all other books must be interpreted like the Bible.[56] Reading the Bible shows us what

---

[56] This felicitous expression is Brayton Polka's, "Spinoza and Biblical Interpretation: The Paradox of Modernity," *The European Legacy* 1.5 (1996): 1682.

reading any thing – text, person, God – involves. This, however, is not to secularize the Bible any more than it is to sacralize other texts. What is ordinary here is truly extraordinary, which is that reading and thinking are always relative to others.

The close relationship between the sacred (understood through the rubric of piety) and impiety is a major theme for the Spinoza of the TTP, the thinker for whom, in the *Ethics*, truth is the standard of itself and the false. Here, too, as with Spinoza's theory of religion, it is true sacrality, a conception involving both a text and a reader, self and other, that not only risks the possibility that it will become its opposite (that sacrality will become profanity): it positively ensures that this will occur, given Spinoza's understanding of the volatility and passions of human readers.[57] This is why Spinoza's theory of religion and the sacred is necessarily political: once the sacred explicitly involves not just identification and knowledge (of God, the Bible, and so on), but responses, actions, works; once sacrality itself is made dependent on a kind of practical reasoning – a reasoning that issues in moral acts (*pietas*); then the sacred is always at risk of being subverted; then the sacred itself is never protected from profanation, whether by its removal to a transcendent realm or its sequestration within institutions that guard its purity. Indeed, in this light these latter "protections" are themselves revealed as ultimately impious, for if, on the one hand, the risk of subjecting the sacred to the marketplace of humanity is high (given human nature), on the other hand, without this risk, there is no sacred to protect, and what is getting protected instead is simply an idol. Thus it is this very risk that is the defining mark of the sacred. More than the Christian insistence that faith without works is dead, what Spinoza is saying, more radically, is that without the democracy of inclusion, God is dead, the Bible is dead, the sacred in its heart is profane. The sacred is uniquely true only if it is available to all; it will be available to all only if it is uniquely true.

This notion of the sacred is grounded in Spinoza's reading of the Bible. That is, the Bible is the book that claims that sacrality is about piety above all. But for Spinoza, this connection of piety and interpretation is also true of other texts (and "things" like God, human beings, nations), most notably the one he has written here. Even though Spinoza claims he is secure in the knowledge that what he is saying does not undermine piety and true religion (but rather promotes them), there is also nothing that he says that could not be used utterly impiously: "nothing can be so

---

[57] There are echoes here of the biblical distinction between faith and idolatry, in particular the ways in which the Bible sees the constant possibility of the latter to be a condition of the former, though Spinoza himself does not use the language of idolatry.

accurately stated as to be incapable of distortion by misrepresentation" (TTP, 150). There is no guarantee against this since the point of what Spinoza is saying is that pious content is only guaranteed by the production of pious readers, and pious readers are hard to come by. The sacred does not prevent its own overturning – it can be falsified. Spinoza's book can be falsified, e.g., read as a destruction of the sacred and a promotion of social control and unfreedom. But impiety is fundamentally parasitic, which can be seen, Spinoza thinks, in the fact that impious people always cloak their actions in the mantle of piety. As he says,

although there is no crime so abominable as not to have been committed by someone, there is no one who, to excuse his crimes, would attempt to destroy the law or to introduce some impiety as eternal doctrine and the road to salvation. For we see that human nature is so constituted that any man (be he king or subject) who has committed a base action seeks to clad his deed with such outward show as to give the impression of having done nothing contrary to justice and decency. (TTP, 156)

It is important to see, therefore, that although we have no other authority than the words of the prophets to access what Spinoza thinks of as the truth of the Bible, this does not mean we have to accept everything they say as *dvar Hashem*, the word of God. To Spinoza, the biblical authors acknowledge that not everything the prophets say is identical to God's word in the very fact that there are multiple accounts of the same prophecy, as in Isaiah's and Ezekiel's differing accounts of "the Lord leaving the temple" (TTP, 26). More significantly, as in the case of the differing accounts of the revelation to Moses on Sinai in Exodus and Deuteronomy, Spinoza's claim is that the word of God is in a certain sense unrecoverable, even for Moses himself who heard God's real voice. Even Moses had to interpret the law when he wrote it on tablets, and therefore,

when Moses broke the first tablets, he certainly did not in his anger cast from his hands and shatter the Word of God – this would be inconceivable of Moses and of the Word of God – but merely stones which, although previously sacred because on them was inscribed the Covenant under which the Jews had bound themselves to obey God, were now without any sanctity whatever, the Jews having nullified that Covenant by worshiping the calf. And for the same reason the second tablets could not avoid destruction along with the Ark. (TTP, 151–152)

This is a crucial point. What Spinoza is claiming here is not that the word of God, while once written, now (post-Christianity) has been internalized in the heart. His point is rather that the word of God is always already internalized in the heart, not "by nature," but in a moment in time, the moment when Moses heard God's real voice. This hearing is the "original revelation" – the hearing is the pact with God, that which can never be fully recovered since it can only be known by its fruits. Spinoza does not make a difference here between speech and writing. His claim is that both writing and speech are corruptible, both writing and speech require interpretation, which means, to him, they require that we "lead a better life" in light of them (TTP, 70). The human heart is no more or less holy than the pen and ink of the biblical text. As Spinoza puts it, "men were no better in time gone by when they had the original writings, the Ark of the Covenant, and indeed the prophets and the Apostles in person, nor were they more obedient. All men, Jews and Gentiles alike, have always been the same, and in every age virtue has been exceedingly rare" (TTP, 150). For both text and heart equally, holiness is entirely dependent on what we do. "Therefore," Spinoza says,

> it is not surprising that the original of Moses' writing, too [in addition to the Ark of the Covenant], is no longer extant, and that the events we previously described have befallen the books which we do possess [i.e., their textual corruptions over the years], seeing that even the true original of God's Covenant, the most sacred of all things, could have completely perished. (TTP, 152)

The original of the covenant is unrecoverable, then, not because it is holy and esoteric. It is unrecoverable because it only ever existed as the words spoken between God and Moses "as a friend might do," and these words need *ruach* to live on. It is unrecoverable not because it is infinite and we are finite; not because it is eternal and we are historical. It is unrecoverable precisely because it is none of these things – it is nothing out of the ordinary – and therefore it is something utterly extraordinary, utterly rare, the "most sacred of all things," and "that which has come down to us uncorrupted." In the TTP, Spinoza identifies the word of God – that which *could not* have been corrupted, that which would be identical written in a different book in a different language – as the biblical maxim to "love God above all, and one's neighbor as oneself" (TTP, 155). But he also shows that this, too – perhaps this kind of maxim above all – can become simply another thing to worship like pen and ink (for, as he himself asks, who is God? And who are my neighbors?). Words rarely change their meaning *and* they mean what we do with them.

There is a notable quality of immanent demonstration here: the fact that Spinoza's book led to strife and impiety does not, by his criteria, prove that it is profane, though it does demand that one reread the book carefully. The same goes for the fact that, in our day, Spinoza still creates strife, whether read as a secularist critic of religion, a hater of Judaism, a despiser of the masses, or all of the above. Spinoza knows all too well that his theory of interpretation is extremely vulnerable to distortion, since it can easily be employed as a justification for the dissemination of genuinely destructive or pernicious ideas or conversely for the destruction and manipulation of what is genuinely sacred (corresponding respectively to the ways he has been read, then and now). This theme of the proximity of truth and falsity (perfection and imperfection, good and evil) pervades Spinoza's corpus, the danger of which accounts for why he includes the caveats at the beginning and the end of the book that he will take back (withdraw, revise) whatever therein proves repugnant to the public good. Spinoza's theory of interpretation is radical by any standard, and it is hence at odds with the conservative and prudent sides of Spinoza's public character. But he is deeply committed to it anyway, and the price of that commitment is his concomitant commitment to "testing" its adequacy in public. Indeed, he precisely defends his interpretation of the Bible by claiming that "I have said nothing unworthy of God's Word, for I have affirmed nothing that I have not proved to be true by the plainest of arguments" (TTP, 150). In other words, one surmises, those arguments are repeatable and verifiable by others in their own time.

This is a connection of truth with community, of truth with the "populace," that manages not to reduce the former simply to the reigning attitudes of the latter. Spinoza holds out hope for what he calls in the preface a "learned reader," a reader not all that different from the one who reads the Bible and strives to live better in light of it, without which his own text cannot be secure. Therefore, in these crucial caveats, he admits he might be wrong, either because his theses are incorrectly stated, or because he has misjudged his readership, or both. These caveats show Spinoza in his most pragmatic light, testing and revising his notion of truth with reference to a society he is also attempting to reform, as well as making truth itself relative to and productive of utility and actions. To employ a less anachronistic reference, they show him to be a Machiavellian in his philosophy as well as his politics. For, as Warren Montag elegantly puts it, "there is no higher court [for Spinoza], a Supreme Court of Reason to which one might appeal the verdicts of history, capable of 'overturning' one's failure in this world, or to 'vindicate' either the vanquished princes or misunderstood philosophers."[58] Indeed, it is such a "court" that his project critiques from beginning to end. The caveats also show him at his most politically optimistic, a materialist thinker committed to the possibility of transforming the conditions which prevented him from being properly read. Spinoza's basic interpretive commitment to clarity and reformability is simultaneously a commitment to the values of "peace, joy, and cheerfulness," which, as he insisted to Blyenbergh, he cares about beyond even the truth itself. This latter commitment is the source of the "democracy" of his hermeneutics above all:

---

[58] Montag, *Bodies, Masses, Power*, 3.

Thus we can conclude that, with the help of such a historical study of Scripture as is available to us, we can readily grasp the meaning of its moral doctrines and be certain of their true sense. For the teachings of true piety are expressed in quite ordinary language, and being directed to the generality of people they are therefore straightforward and easy to understand. And since true salvation and blessedness consist in true contentment of mind and we find our true peace only in what we clearly understand, it most evidently follows that we can understand the meaning of Scripture with confidence in matters relating to salvation and necessary to blessedness. Therefore we have no reason to be unduly anxious concerning the other contents of Scripture; for since for the most part they are beyond the grasp of reason and the intellect, they belong to the sphere of the curious rather than the profitable . . . and although we grant that our method does not suffice to explain with certainty everything that is found in the Bible, this is the consequence not of the defectiveness of the method but of the fact that the path which it tells us is the true and correct one has never been pursued nor trodden by men, and so with the passage of time has become exceedingly difficult and almost impassable. (TTP, 101–102)

By making the sacred about the teachings of true piety and ordinary understanding – by insisting that revelation signifies not what is "beyond the grasp of reason and the intellect" but precisely what is in its purview – Spinoza returns both reason and religion to the polis, to the community, to readers. His insistence that theology shares no basis with philosophy and therefore that the Bible "commands only obedience and neither seeks nor is able to oppose reason" (TTP, 174) is directed toward the standpoint (whether that of theology or that of philosophy) which is unable to keep both reason and religion (both truth and faith) sovereign. By "separating" theology and philosophy, by arguing that "this fundamental dogma of theology cannot be investigated by the natural light of reason," Spinoza paradoxically shows that reason itself no less than faith involves revelation, moral certainty (TTP, 175). It is Spinoza who demonstrates that the natural light of reason that seeks to subordinate the truth of religion (true religion, *vera religio*), to make religion over in its own image, to make what is only ever morally certain into a mathematical truth – this reason is itself inadequate. Since the difference between moral and mathematical truth (religion and reason) is not one of opposition – since certainty of either kind is always about some model we have put before ourselves, something we desire – for this reason "it was essential that there should be revelation," a revelation of theological and philosophical import: for although revelation was necessary, "nevertheless, we can use judgment before we accept with at least moral certainty that which has been revealed" (TTP, 175).

3   Politics, law, and the multitude

A man who is guided by reason is more free in a state, where he lives according to a common decision, than in solitude, where he obeys only himself.   (E IV p73)

The politics of the multitude

Spinoza's focus on the equality and sovereignty of philosophy and theology turns seamlessly into an account of equality and sovereignty in political life. What we have seen in the last two chapters is that both philosophy and theology are organically connected to certain kinds of political stances – that transcendence and immanence alike, taken in themselves, result in a confusion that fails to harness the human power that is actually available to us and turns human relationships into sites of conflict and strife. This confusion can be clearly seen, for Spinoza, in the ways the Bible has been read, and most especially in the assumption that it is either wholly true or wholly false. Texts, like all forms of human production, are works that express truth and falsity in close proximity to each other, and the task of reading is therefore always about establishing the principles that any given text itself enunciates.[1] In this chapter and the next one, I turn to Spinoza's political theory, or rather his theologico-politics – his treatment of the relationship between God, law, and the twin ideals of freedom and obedience. It is in these chapters that I will make explicit what has been only implicit in the argument so far, namely why the language of revelation is so important for Spinoza even as, in its narrowest reference to the prophetic imagination, it is a complex amalgam of truth and falsity. What I will show is that revelation is the best way of talking about what Spinoza does with human nature in the TTP, which is to make it creative, revelatory, in the most fundamental sense. This will ultimately be to connect this creativity with the dynamic of the *causa sui*

---

[1] Norris's *Spinoza and the Origins of Modern Critical Theory* deals brilliantly with Spinoza's treatment of "truth, error, and historical understanding" (98).

in the *Ethics*, but not before the uniqueness of the TTP in this regard is fully appreciated.

I begin here with the multitude (though the multitude has, of course, already been present from the beginning) because, like Spinoza's concept of religion, it is a place in his texts where it is too easy to accept his critique without following out his defense – to accept the multitude's ignorance and wretchedness without following out its power and force. What Spinoza argues is that this power is harnessed through the origination of divine and human laws alike, a dual origination that makes each (divine and human) the inexorable companion and critic of the other. The difficulties inherent in this relationship of the divine and the human manifest themselves in the structure of religion and politics in any given polity, and in the commands to obey that run in different directions. But the more fundamental difficulties emerge in the construction of origins, as thinking (theologically and politically) comes into conflict with its own limits. It is the multitude that bears the brunt of this conflict. But then, as always in Spinoza, the multitude is not "them" but "us."

In the *Ethics*, Spinoza explicitly denies that he has contempt for the multitude, distinguishing himself from those "who prefer to curse or laugh at the Affects and actions of men, rather than understand them." To such people, he observes, "it will doubtless seem strange that I should undertake to treat men's vices and absurdities in the Geometric style, and that I should wish to demonstrate by certain reasoning things which are contrary to reason, and which they proclaim to be empty, absurd, and horrible" (E III pref). It is all too easy, he seems to be saying, to condescend to the multitude; all too easy to see human weaknesses as contemptible; and just as easy to act like the multitude as it is to disdain it.

Nevertheless, throughout his work, Spinoza scatters contrary opinions, giving readers good reason for thinking that his is a project for elite ears only, one designed to ensure the obedience of the multitude. There are two texts that stand out in this regard: the preface to the TTP, which urges "the common people" not "to read this work," claiming that the "multitude remains ever at the same level of wretchedness" and thus "can no more be freed from their superstition than from their fear" (TTP, 8, 2), and the scholium to proposition 54 in Part IV of the *Ethics*, which states that "the mob is terrifying, if unafraid."[2] Both texts assert that the masses "are not guided by reason" (TTP, 8). In the TTP, Spinoza's

---

[2] See also TTP, 9, 18, 69, 72, 73, 83, 235, and E IV p58. In this passage in the *Ethics* (there are a few others), Spinoza refers to the "fickle and inconstant multitude" in an identical way to the language of the TTP. But by and large, the *Ethics* identifies all human beings

concern is with the turmoil created by "prejudices embraced under the guise of piety," prejudices, he says, that are as "deeply rooted in the mind" as the fear that gives rise to them (TTP, 8). The statement in the *Ethics*, however, appears to assert the opposite, that only without fear are the masses a threat to social stability:

Because men rarely live from the dictate of reason, th[e] two affects [of] Humility and Repentance, and in addition, Hope and Fear, bring more advantage than disadvantage . . . If weak-minded men were all equally proud, ashamed of nothing, and afraid of nothing, how could they be united or restrained by any bonds? (E IV p54s)

This contrast results in part from Spinoza's distinct projects in these works. Despite his pessimistic declarations in the preface, the TTP is devoted to the task of creating a social order that will minimize the conditions (internal and external) of fear, and thus reduce the hold that superstition has on the populace. As it stands, he seems to be saying, superstitious readers are a threat to this project, but it is on their behalf that he has taken up the theologico-political problem in the first place. "Only while fear persists," he writes, "do men fall prey to superstition" (TTP, 2), and while it is important to realize that fear, and the social instability that comes with it, can never be entirely extirpated, it is also material insecurity – finding oneself "reduced to such straits as to be without resources" – that exacerbates this natural human tendency (TTP, 1). In the *Ethics*, Spinoza's emphasis is on the ways in which fear and hope (and humility and repentance), more than other affects such as arrogance and pride, can be transformed into genuinely rational affects. As he puts it, "those who are subject to these affects can be guided far more easily than others, so that in the end they may live from the guidance of reason, i.e., may be free and enjoy the life of the blessed." Thus while in the *Ethics* the "guides" are portrayed as those who have the goal of transforming the multitude – for which task fear is somewhat more useful than other "weak-minded" affects – in the TTP the guides, such as they are, are the unscrupulous ministers of the Church, "none of them actuated by desire to instruct the people, but keen to attract admiration" (TTP, 4) and above all to connect servitude in a political sense with salvation (TTP, 3).

What is threatening in both cases is "the mob" – whether fearful, and thus "sustained . . . by emotion of the most powerful kind" (TTP, 2), or "unafraid," and thus insusceptible of being "restrained by any bonds"

in this way, without singling out any group in particular, e.g., "men are accustomed to call natural things perfect or imperfect more from prejudice than from true knowledge of those things," and "men are commonly ignorant of the causes of their appetite" (E IV pref).

(E IV p54s). In the *Ethics*, Spinoza simply cites without comment Tacitus' observation that the masses "terrorize unless they are afraid."[3] But invoking the identical observation again in the TP, Spinoza states his own premises in contrast to Tacitus, claiming that the latter's view is itself prejudicial: for "all men have one and the same nature: it is power and culture which mislead us" (TP VII: 27). The problem, Spinoza clarifies in the TP, is not the mob taken as a certain class of people. The problem is the *condition* of the mob ("all men"). In other words, the masses *are* terrifying if unafraid, but this is not only something wrong with the masses.

In the political works, Spinoza is interested in the "body" of the masses as a whole, in the multitude as a force possessing a logic of its own. The question as to whether the multitude functions identically to a Spinozian individual is a much debated one. What is at issue is whether the laws governing social bodies can be understood as analogous to physical laws or whether social entities are historical collectivities with no central unifying *conatus*. Both interpretations begin with Spinoza's conception of the hierarchy of individuation in Part II of the *Ethics*. Having defined an individual as a composite body differentiated from other bodies through the fixed motion and rest of its parts (E II p13L3def), and having argued that individuals so composed retain their nature as long as their parts "keep the same ratio of motion and rest to each other as before" (E II p13L5) and as long as "each part retains its motion, and communicates it, as before to the others . . . whether [the individual] as a whole, moves or is at rest, or whether it moves in this or that direction" (E II p13L7), Spinoza makes the following crucial observation:

By this, then, we see how a composite Individual can be affected in many ways, and still preserve its nature. So far we have conceived an Individual which is composed only of bodies which are distinguished from one another only by motion and rest, speed and slowness, i.e., which is composed of the simplest bodies. But if we should now conceive of another, composed of a number of Individuals of a different nature, we shall find that it can be affected in a great many other ways, and still preserve its nature . . . But if we should further conceive a third kind of Individual, composed . . . of this second kind, we shall find that it can be affected in many other ways, without any change of its form. And if we proceed in this way to infinity, we shall easily conceive that the whole of nature is one Individual, whose parts, i.e., all bodies, vary in infinite ways, without any change of the whole Individual. (E II L7s)[4]

---

[3] Tacitus, *Annales*, I. xxix. 3.

[4] Recall also, more concisely, E II d7: "By singular things I understand things that are finite and have a determinate existence. And if a number of Individuals so concur in one action that together they are all the cause of one effect, I consider them all, to that extent, as one singular thing."

The question, briefly, is whether, given Spinoza's physicalist conception of an individual, one can regard one of these movements upward
(say, from the second to the third kind of individual) as the constitution
of political society, and thus whether political existence has the same ontological import as human individuals and nature as a whole. Spinoza
clearly regards social bodies as natural entities to at least some degree.
But those who hold the view that the social body is "literally" an individual on a par with a human individual emphasize the extent to which
the state possesses interests independent of the individuals comprising it,
and thus that the state is not simply the necessary condition for individual
flourishing but is a primary, self-interested actor in its own right. By contrast, those who view Spinoza's physicalist description as "metaphoric"
contend that this latter interpretation cannot account adequately for "the
natural right or power of human persons within civil society" nor evade
"the twin difficulties of totalitarianism and the metaphysical reification
of social aggregates."[5] The issue is to some degree one of emphasis, for
in neither position are individuals simply "swallowed up in the whole,"
nor is the state simply the expression of a collectivity with no ontological
status at all.[6] The crucial difference between these positions concerns
the interpretation of Spinoza's concept of history, with the "literalists"
asserting (and the "metaphoricists" denying) that the laws of nature (human and otherwise) have just as much force and validity on the historical
as on the individual plane, and thus that history is simply the unfolding
of the laws of human nature seen from the perspective of the multitude,
the body social.[7]

---

[5] Lee C. Rice, "Individual and Community in Spinoza's Social Psychology," in *Spinoza:
Issues and Directions*, ed. Edwin Curley and Pierre-François Moreau (Leiden: E. J. Brill,
1990), 282. I borrow the distinction between literal and metaphoric interpretations of
Spinoza's theory of the individual and the social body from Rice's excellent discussion.
See also Rice, "Emotion, Appetition, and Conatus in Spinoza," *Revue internationale de
philosophie* 31 (1977): 101–116. For another interpretation of the metaphoric view, see
Douglas J. Den Uyl, *Power, State, and Freedom* (Assen: Van Gorcum, 1983), 66–96. For
the opposing view see Matheron, *Individu et communauté*, esp. ch. 8, 287–355; Sylvain Zac,
L'Idée de vie dans la philosophie de Spinoza (Paris: Presses Universitaires de France, 1963),
225ff.; W. Sacksteder, "Communal Orders in Spinoza," in *Spinoza's Political and Theological Thought*, ed. C. De Deugd (Amsterdam: North-Holland, 1984); W. Sacksteder,
"Spinoza on Part and Whole: The Worm's Eye View," *Southwest Journal of Philosophy* 11
(1980): 25–40; and Antonio Negri, "*Reliqua Desiderantur*: A Conjecture for a Definition
of the Concept of Democracy in the Final Spinoza," in *The New Spinoza*, ed. Warren
Montag and Ted Stolze (Minneapolis: University of Minnesota Press, 1997), 219–247.

[6] Rice, "Individual and Community," 278.

[7] Steven Barbone makes the issue one of power, noting that Spinoza uses *potentia* to refer primarily to individual power, whereas he uses the less frequent *potestas* when speaking about
sovereign power (there are no cases of Spinoza referring to the *potentia imperii*). Barbone
suggests we translate the former as "power" and the latter as "authority," and he makes

My approach is to follow Spinoza's distinction in chapter 3 of the TTP between laws that have individual blessedness as their end and laws that are directed solely towards the security and peace of political entities. I follow the metaphoricists in assuming that one can differentiate between the status of these two levels of law, for, as Spinoza says, "nature creates individuals not nations" (TTP, 207), while following the literalists in insisting that there is an essential continuity between them, and that the difference between these levels can be seen through the lens of the multitude. As Spinoza puts it, "it is clear that what is true of each man in the state of nature is true likewise of the body and the mind of the whole state – it has as much right as it has power and strength," that is, "the right of the state or of the sovereign is nothing but the right of nature itself, and as such is determined by power; not however by the power of a single individual, but by that of a people which is guided as if by one mind [*una veluti mente ducitur*]" (TP III: 2).[8] The difference is that the state retains this "state of nature," while the individual precisely gives it up in a state, i.e., a commonwealth is not itself bound by laws while an individual in a commonwealth is (see TP IV: 5).[9] The question for Spinoza is, what kind of laws – and what kind of political entity – can maximize the rationality (freedom) of the multitude as a whole without infringing on individual liberty? Unlike Machiavelli, who holds that every state can be divided into an elite and a populace, and that the freedom of the social order thus consists in allowing each to pursue their distinct ends, Spinoza's commitments, perhaps despite himself, are to a state that is democratic, not just in terms of representation but in terms of the ends of life themselves.[10] I say "despite himself" because it is not that Spinoza has any higher view of the populace than Machiavelli. It is rather that he thinks the populace is no less in pursuit of the ends of glory and ambition than the elites (according to Machiavelli, it is only the elites who pursue

---

a case for why the latter (*potestas*, authority) is the weaker term, which reflects, he holds, "Spinoza's conception that the political state [*imperium*] is not a *bona fide* metaphysical individual, but exists, perhaps, as a social construct": "Power in the *Tractatus theologico-Politicus*," in *Piety, Peace, and the Freedom to Philosophize*, ed. Paul Bagley [Dordrecht: Kluwer Academic Publishers, 1999], 102).

[8] Etienne Balibar goes so far as to assert that this conception of the multitude implies that "the political problem no longer has two terms but three. 'Individual' and 'State' are in fact abstractions, which only have meaning in relation to one another. In the final analysis, each of them serves merely to express one modality through which the *power of the multitude* can be realized as such": *Spinoza and Politics*, 69.

[9] Sylvain Zac puts it strongly when he argues that "La société est une association de *conatus*, dans ce qu'il y a en eux de positif et non en tant qu'ils sont contrariés les uns par les autres. Or, ce qu'il y a de positif dans les *conatus* malgré la diversité des natures individuelles, c'est la vie de Dieu qui reste toujours la même." Zac, *L'Idée de vie*, 225–226.

[10] See Niccolò Machiavelli, *Discourses* I: 4 in *Machiavelli: The Chief Works and Others*, trans. Allan Gilbert, vol. I (Durham, N.C.: Duke University Press, 1989), 202–204.

these things, while the populace more simply pursues security and self-preservation), and that this is the reason why (in the TP) democracy is a more prudent form of government than monarchy.[11]

While it is in the TP that Spinoza pursues the multitude as the distinguishing component of the state as such, the concept is present in the TTP in his discussion of superstition, as well as in that of the foundations of the state and the ancient Hebrews and their polity.[12] There are two principal differences between the political theory of the TTP and that of the TP, both of which have contributed to a great deal of scholarly commentary. The first is the abandonment by Spinoza in the TP of the TTP's model of the contractual basis of society in chapter 16, and the second (stemming from the first) is the transformation of Spinoza's concept of democracy from a mode of governing that is preferable (more stable and more natural) but not the only legitimate form (TTP), to the conception in the TP of democracy as the foundation of the state as such.

In the first case (TTP), the constitution of the state is seen as a transfer of right (power) to a sovereign, and this transfer works whether the sovereign is one person or the entire social body.[13] In the second case (TP), the power of the state is transferred not to a sovereign but to the multitude itself – in fact, the whole language of transfer is by this fact abandoned and sovereignty is conceived entirely according to the *potentia multitudinis* (TP II: 17), whose existence is itself foundational (TP 1: 7). In the TP, democracy is not only the ideal state, but the immanent condition of all other states, and thus the very existence of nondemocratic states is something that requires an explanation. Spinoza offers one by invoking his principle that "nobody rejects what he judges to be good except through hope of a greater good or fear of a greater loss . . . that is to

[11] See TP VII: 5: "it is certain that everyone would rather rule than be ruled."
[12] The key sections in the TP are II: 16 and 17: "Where men hold rights as a body, and are all guided as if by one mind, then, of course . . . each of them has the less right the more the rest together exceed him in power; that is, his only real right against other things in nature is what the corporate right allows him. In other matters he must carry out every command laid upon him by the common decision . . . or be compelled to do so by right. This corporate right which is defined by the power of a people [*multitudinis potentia*] is generally called sovereignty, and is entirely vested in those who by common consent manage the affairs of state, i.e., who make, interpret, and repeal laws, fortify cities, take decisions about war and peace, and so on." Like the TTP, Spinoza goes on to say that this corporate right can be held by all the people (democracy), a council only (aristocracy), or a single man (monarchy). But the language of *multitudinis potentia*, which constitutes sovereignty as such, has generally been given a reading according to which only democracy is fully sovereign, i.e., only democracy is truly a *multitudinis potentia*; the others are corruptions of this and are less likely to last, as Spinoza does indeed hold.
[13] Spinoza, however, only discusses democracy in the TTP, a fact which must, in my view, influence one's reading of the equivalence of these systems, leaving aside the question of which he found preferable, which is not in doubt.

say, everyone will choose of two goods that which he judges the greater, and of two evils that which seems to him the lesser" (TTP, 181). According to this principle, the multitude only abandons self-rule when it finds itself unable to rule by democracy, an obviously greater good: "[since] everyone would rather rule than be ruled . . . clearly, then, a whole people will never transfer its right to one man or a few if its members can agree among themselves and avoid falling into civil strife as a result of the controversies which often arise in large assemblies" (TP VII: 5). Both aristocracy and monarchy, on this model, are less absolute than democracy because they are derivative of a democratic multitude, whereas in the TTP Spinoza conceives the state as such as absolute, i.e., the transfer of power to the sovereign is always absolute, though at the same time utterly dependent on the de facto existence of this power, without which the state simply dissolves: "this right [of supreme power] he will retain only as long as he has this power of carrying into execution whatever he wills; otherwise his rule will be precarious, and nobody who is stronger than he will need to obey him unless he so wishes" (TTP, 183).

Spinoza has, then, two distinct concepts of the origin of the state, the first, we will see, intimately related to religion and the second requiring religion only in a politically instrumental sense. What is relevant in this chapter is that what Spinoza calls in the TP "the power of the multitude" is also operative in the TTP.[14] What I explore in the next chapter is the extent to which it is through the language of contract (*pactum*), however problematic (both for him, insofar as he abandons it in the TP, and for us, insofar as it has elements of incoherence) that Spinoza accounts for the relationship between the divine and human laws – in other words, the ways in which democracy (as a "merely" preferable form of governing in the TTP) is connected to theocracy.

What is important to see is that the TTP sheds light on problems in the *Ethics* that the TP does not. It is in the TTP that one can trace the relationship between religion and politics, and specifically the impact of superstition on the multitude's behavior and its manipulation by people who exploit these tendencies. This is far from simply a critique of the multitude, as I have already argued. "No one," Spinoza admits, "is so vigilant that he does not nod sometimes; even the most resolute and upright of men falter on occasion, and allow themselves to be overcome by their passions, especially when strength of mind is needed most" (TP VI: 3).

---

[14] Cf. Negri, "*Reliqua Desiderantur*," 231ff., and Alexandre Matheron, "The Theoretical Function of Democracy in Spinoza and Hobbes," in *The New Spinoza*, ed. Warren Montag and Ted Stolze (Minneapolis: University of Minnesota Press, 1997), 207–217.

What is interesting to Spinoza in his political works is that political communities are effective to some degree at alleviating the vulnerability that produces or exacerbates superstition, credulity, and tyranny. Indeed, the multitude owes its very existence to the constantly reevaluated judgment of individuals that they will have a better chance of self-preservation cooperatively than singly (TTP, 181). This is not to say that communities are literally formed or contracted on the basis of this recognition, for the natural state of human beings is a dependent one (in the TTP, there is a contract made anyway, with all the aporias this involves, as I will discuss; in the TP the multitude itself is natural).[15] This is what Spinoza means to draw attention to with his claim that human beings are born ignorant (not free or rational or some such thing) – that is, by virtue of birth alone, we are most dependent on others, less able to preserve ourselves by ourselves. Society's origin cannot be the decision of rational individuals to enter into agreement with one another since rationality is unthinkable outside the power to act on one's own counsel, and *this* is achievable only in cooperation with others:

a man in the state of nature is possessed of his own right, or free, only as long as he can protect himself from being subjugated by others; and his own unaided power is insufficient to protect him against all. Hence human natural right or freedom is a nonentity as long as it is an individual possession determined by individual power; it exists in imagination rather than fact, since there is no certainty of making it good. (TP II: 15)

To some degree, then, freedom (the power to preserve oneself) will involve creating the institutional mechanisms whereby we can reduce our dependence on others. It will not involve liberating ourselves from dependence as such since it is only in common that true independence (true individuality) can be achieved. As Spinoza puts it in the TP, "If two unite and join forces, then together they have more power, and consequently more right against other things in nature, than either alone; and the more there be that unite in this way, the more right will they collectively possess" (TP II: 13). Spinoza thinks that the notion of individual "rights" which preexist any particular social body is an absurdity (as are the notions of an "original" equality or freedom). The very notion of individual right is implicated in (and presupposes) the distribution of political power and the constitution of a state, and therefore it is only law (*lex*) and power (*potestas*) that can make sense of right (*ius*): "the right of nature peculiar

---

[15] "We desire political society by nature, and can never dissolve it entirely" (TP VI: 1). To some degree Spinoza's contractarian model similarly functions to naturalize the multitude. To the extent that these accounts can be harmonized, I suggest that what Spinoza says in TP VI: 1 is to at least some degree what he actually *meant* in TTP, ch. 16.

to human beings can scarcely be conceived save where men hold rights as a body, and thus have the power to defend their possession of territories which they can inhabit and cultivate, to protect themselves, to repel all force, and to live in accordance with the common judgement of all" (TP II: 15). This does not mean equality is a nonissue. "That citizens may enjoy as much equality as possible" is, according to Spinoza, a "prime necessity in a commonwealth" (TP VII: 20).

But the multitude, for Spinoza, is a contradictory power, internally divided against itself. As Spinoza puts it in the TP, "the main problem is to show how it can be done, i.e., how men, even when led by passion, may still have fixed and stable laws" (TP VII: 2). This is not so much resignation to the fact that these passions will always (despite the laws) be present, but the claim that law begins with the acknowledgment of these passions and the ways they have a hold on us, and seeks to ameliorate them as much as possible, for "just as the vices of subjects, and their excessive lawlessness and perversity, must be attributed to the faults of the commonwealth, so conversely their virtues and steadfast observance of the laws must be chiefly credited to its excellence and absolute right" (TP V: 3). This is a crucial statement, not least for Spinoza's connection of a state's absolute character to the virtue of its citizens.

While the multitude, then, provides individuals protection on one front against the winds of fortune, on the other front, it inflames the passions by the very proximity of individuals, one to the other. This lack of power, or dependence on others and on fortune, is the norm, not the exception. Only in certain respects and in certain contexts will human beings be able to be "the adequate cause" of something happening (in them or outside them), since "all men are not equally suited to all activities" and must therefore "afford one another mutual aid" (TTP, 64). Only God (or nature taken as a whole) is fully independent. Thus the way in which human beings are different from one another in useful ways – the ways in which their individual weaknesses issue in the division of labor, for example – is connected to the ways in which they clash with one another. The ways in which human beings are limited by what is "outside them" and thus are dependent on each other to be able to supply their own needs is intimately related to the ways in which human beings are limited by what is "inside them," that is, by their tendency to "need" things "determined only by fleshy desire," things that cannot be shared (TTP, 64). For this reason, they tend to "disagree in nature" (E IV p34s).[16]

---

[16] Spinoza puts this more bluntly in the TP: "[I have proved in my *Ethics*] that men are necessarily subject to passions [E IV p4c]; that by nature they pity the unfortunate, but envy the fortunate [E III p32s]; and incline more to vengeance than to compassion

Therefore the very facts that can serve to differentiate people and contribute to the diversity and richness of the social body (the more things a body can do, the more things the mind can think) can also tend to undermine it. As Spinoza notes, even "those who live in a barbarous way" do not acquire "their few poor and crude resources . . . without some degree of mutual help," not to mention those societies dedicated to more "civilising influences," which revolve not only around life support but "the arts and sciences which are also indispensable for the perfection of human nature and its blessedness," and without which we would "lead a wretched and almost brutish existence" (TTP, 64). This would all be for the good "if men lived according to the guidance of reason" (E IV p37s2), but of course, as individuals, they do not, and thus even less do they do so as a multitude. As Spinoza caustically observes, "those who believe that a people, or men divided over public business, can be induced to live by reason's dictates alone, are dreaming of the poets' golden age or of a fairy-tale" (TP I: 5).

The multitude as a whole, then, is more than the sum total of its diverse passions, possessing a kind of identity of its own. What is, on the one hand, a stabilizing force, namely a cooperative and rational "neighbor" with whom one has a better chance of advancing one's interests, is also, on the other hand, a profoundly destabilizing force insofar as human beings are naturally prone to envy, hatred, ambition, and so on: "all may know perfectly well that this is contrary to religion, which teaches that everyone should love his neighbor as himself, i.e., should defend the rights of another just as he does his own; but, as I have shown, this conviction is of little avail against the passions" (TP I: 5). When Spinoza speaks about the "the fickleness of the masses" and the fact that they are "governed solely by their emotions," he is speaking about the dynamics of a group, not a collection of irrational individuals. "Vanity," "envy of superior fame or fortune – which is never equal for all men," "hasty anger" – all of these (which are much more scrupulously dissected in Part IV of the *Ethics*) are the result of social proximity. The multitude's very coherence, as Balibar puts it, is a "power for discord as well as a power for harmony."[17] One could say that its coherence or identity just is this antagonism at its heart. Or again, in Negri's words, "the *multitudo* is a continuous and contradictory mixture of passions and situations," which doesn't mean it

---

[E IV app13]. I have also shown that each man strives to make others live as *he* pleases, approve what *he* approves, and reject what *he* rejects [E III p31c]. In consequence, since all are equally bent on supremacy, they start to quarrel, and do their utmost to enslave one another; and he who comes off victorious prides himself more on having harmed his opponent than on having benefited himself" (TP I: 5).

[17] Balibar, *Spinoza and Politics*, 69.

lacks "a certain rationality, and therefore a certain power. The *multitudo* is neither *vulgus* nor *plebs*." It simply means that "the 'will of all' . . . could never become a 'general will'" in Rousseau's sense.[18]

Thus the masses are superstitious because they are internally antagonistic: fighting among themselves for uncommon goods, they fail to connect their material dependence on one another with a rational dependence on goods that are common, leaving them vulnerable to credulity of all kinds as the goods themselves constantly change. And they are internally antagonistic because they are superstitious: convinced above all that the most uncommon (exclusive *and* extraordinary) of goods is God himself, they turn what would otherwise be manageable disagreement into a hatred that knows no bounds. Spinoza's point is that both are true, and each, clearly, exacerbates the other. But neither of these facts is in itself the principal cause for concern, or rather it is this very circularity that laws are intended to address. Indeed, as Negri points out, if one leaves aside the religious question, this plurality, and the conflicts it generates, is "the foundation of one of the highest values of the republican tradition: tolerance." It is the power of the internally diverse multitude that, in the TP especially, constitutively resists the rational uniformity that is the sign of absolutism.[19]

But clearly the religious question *is* his principal concern in the TTP, specifically the matter of those in power who exploit superstition for their own benefit.[20] As Spinoza notes, while "command cannot be exercised over minds in the same way as over tongues, yet minds are to some degree under the control of the sovereign power, who has many means of inducing the great majority to believe, love, hate etc. whatever he wills." Whether the sovereign, then, refers to a religious or a political authority, "there is no absurdity in conceiving men whose beliefs, love, hatred,

---

[18] Negri, "*Reliqua Desiderantur*," 233–234.

[19] Negri, "*Reliqua Desiderantur*," 235. For all of Spinoza's more Marxist readers, this dimension of conflict within the multitude is central to its liberatory power. But it is also true of the revised republican model of Machiavelli, that conflict (between the *grandi* and the *plebe*) is what safeguards (rather than threatens) public *virtù*, for this conflict rarely results simply in disorder (which stems from oppression) but rather in laws that are more and more representative of both viewpoints. See *Discourses*, I: 4, in *The Chief Works*, vol. I, 202–204.

[20] As Balibar astutely observes, Spinoza's project is not only to identify the force of religion in the foundations of the state (through his analysis of the Hebrew theocracy) but also to "detach" the "Calvinist mass (imbued with 'theocratic' conceptions) from its collusion with the monarchist party, in order to rally it in the name of patriotism to the republican camp, on the condition of finding a terrain common to the republic and the mass's religion, which would imply *also* that the republic be reformed in a 'democratic' sense." Etienne Balibar, "*Jus-Pactum-Lex*: On the Constitution of the Subject in the *Theologico-Political Treatise*," in *The New Spinoza*, ed. Warren Montag and Ted Stolze (Minneapolis: University of Minnesota Press, 1997), 203.

contempt and every single emotion are under the sole control of the governing power" (TTP, 192). Spinoza refuses to ridicule those features of human individuals and societies that are simply facts of nature. However, he spares no vitriol for "the prejudices of theologians," for those who unscrupulously advance their own social and political power through the manipulation of the multitude:

ambition and iniquity have reached such a pitch that religion takes the form not so much of obedience to the teachings of the Holy Spirit as of defending what men have invented. Indeed, religion is manifested not in charity but in spreading contention among men and in fostering the bitterest hatred, under the false guise of zeal in God's cause and a burning enthusiasm . . . They ascribe to the Holy Spirit whatever their wild fancies have invented, and devote their utmost strength and enthusiasm to defending it. (TTP, 88–89)

Like superstition, this "ambition and iniquity" has its foundation in the passions, and is therefore to some degree both predictable and even inevitable. But unlike the problem of superstition, the theologians to whom Spinoza refers in the above passage threaten the basis of sovereign power, which Spinoza considers the key to freedom:

it is the fundamental purpose of democracy to avoid the follies of appetite and to keep men within the bounds of reason, as far as possible, so that they may live in peace and harmony. If this basic principle is removed, the whole fabric soon collapses. It is for the sovereign power alone, then, to have regard to these considerations, while it is for the subjects . . . to carry out its orders and to acknowledge no other right but that which the sovereign power declares to be a right. (TTP, 184)

Insofar as theology directs people's attention to "extraordinary" and "wondrous" things, it acts to undermine the social and political amelioration of superstition, training the collective imagination toward the fear and uncertainty that inflames strife between individuals and away from the narratives by which a people defines itself and that serve a socially cohesive role (though, as we will see, at the cost of fomenting strife *between* nations). For Spinoza, true religion is that which "brings people together in love" (E IV appXV). But he stands out among philosophers of religion for holding few illusions about how complex a task this is. While he tells us repeatedly that true religion consists only in loving "justice and charity" (TTP, 166), we have the *Ethics* to teach us exactly what are the obstacles to this love between neighbor and neighbor, and we have the TTP to show us what the political stakes are in setting up a society along these lines.

Spinoza's conception of the multitude changes the question from whether it is, literally, "vulgar" (in contrast to some philosophical elite), to the question of the sources and effects of this conception of the ignorant majority. Hence Spinoza's powerful statement in the TP: "citizens are not born, but made" (V: 2). The lens of analysis is simply turned around. Those who attempt to set themselves or their class over against what they characterize as the terrifying immoderation of the "common people" thereby display only their own pride and ignorance:[21]

> Those who confine to the common people the vices which exist in all human beings will perhaps greet my contentions with ridicule, on the ground that "there is no moderation in the masses, they terrorize unless they are afraid," that "the common people are either an obsequious servant or a domineering master," that "they have no truth or judgement in them," and so on. But all men have one and the same nature: it is power and culture which mislead us. (TP VII: 27)

The point in both the TTP and the TP is that, if one keeps the masses in ignorance and without the possibility of being consulted concerning the common good, one cannot wonder why it is that they behave brutishly. For this reason, Spinoza is convinced that "it is much better for the honest policies of a state to be obvious to its enemies than for the guilty secrets of tyrants to be kept hidden from its citizens" (TP VII: 29). No one is denying, he continues, that "secrecy is often useful to a state." Nevertheless,

> no one will ever prove that the same state cannot maintain itself without it . . . Of course, it has always been the sole theme of would-be tyrants that secrecy in the conduct of affairs and the like are absolutely necessary in the interests of the commonwealth; but the better their proposals are disguised by a show of utility, the more swiftly do they issue in slavery and oppression. (TP VII: 29)

The point holds true for the ways in which religious authorities and institutions advance their interest through the exploitation of superstition. The difference, to Spinoza, is twofold. First, religion is far more potent than most other discourses or disagreements. Referring to the Reformation, Spinoza notes that "what no monarch could achieve by fire and sword, churchmen succeeded in doing by pen alone." Second, religious authority precisely sets itself up above political authority, as "the Pope of Rome" does (or as the Hebrew commonwealth eventually does with the division of power between kings and priests). At the very least, as in the case of Luther and Calvin, it foments "strife and dissension" to a very great degree by articulating a fundamental division between the kingdom

---

[21] Following Machiavelli, who notes that "anybody who accuses both the people and the princes surely tells the truth, but in excepting the princes he deceives himself, because a people that commands and is well organized will be just as stable, prudent, grateful as a prince, or will be more so than a prince, even though he is thought wise" (*Discourses* I: 58, in *The Chief Works*, vol. I, 315).

of heaven and the kingdom of earth (TTP, 225–226). All such a division does, Spinoza holds, is give us one more set of laws, and these not to ensure peace and stability, but precisely to control minds:

Laws of this kind, prescribing what everyone must believe and prohibiting the saying or writing of anything that opposes this or that opinion, have often been enacted to pander to, or rather surrender to, the anger of those who cannot endure enlightened minds, men who by the exercise of a stern authority can easily turn the devotion of the unruly masses into a rage, inciting them against whomsoever they will. Yet how much better it would be to curb the frenzied anger of the mob instead of passing useless laws which can be broken only by those who love the virtues and the arts, and reducing the state to such straits that it cannot endure men of noble character! (TTP, 235)

Spinoza can't resist drawing attention to his own plight at the end of this exhortation. But the point is not only a self-serving one. How can one, he wants to know, "curb the frenzied anger of the mob"? Certainly not through such laws (whether religiously or politically motivated) which serve only to set up a regime of terror: "What can be more calamitous than that men should be regarded as enemies and put to death, not for any crime or misdeed, but for being of independent mind? That the scaffold, the terror of evildoers, should become the glorious stage where is presented a supreme example of virtuous endurance, to the utter disgrace of the ruling power?" (TTP, 235–236).

In the case of both political and religious tyranny, the key is the manipulation of ignorance, not ignorance itself, a principle Spinoza finds in Scripture which, he notes, "condemns only obstinacy, not ignorance" (TTP, 166). More precisely, the manipulation of ignorance and the mystification of knowledge by the powerful are themselves ignorant, for they perpetuate the antagonisms that ultimately will turn against them:

that "there is no truth or judgement in the common people" is not surprising, when they are kept in ignorance of the main affairs of state, and merely guess at the facts from the little that cannot be concealed. For to suspend judgement is a rare virtue. Thus to keep all the work of government a secret from the citizens, and then to expect them not to misjudge it and put the worst construction on everything, is the height of folly. (TP VII: 27)

It is not that Spinoza doesn't make distinctions of power or ability between people. On the one hand, he frequently uses the locutions "most men," "all men," "everyone thinks," or "no one can have lived without knowing," and so on. This manner of speaking is almost always in comparison to those who hold themselves apart from what Spinoza considers our baser tendencies, from which no one is exempt. On the other hand, when speaking about positive human gifts he is not so wary of making comparisons between people, whether gifts of education, as when he claims that Scripture cannot have complicated metaphorical or allegorical meanings because it was written for "the uneducated masses," not for the generally "learned" and a fortiori not for "philosophers" (TTP, 161), or gifts of ability, as when he speaks of "sluggish minds" (TTP, 157) or people of "limited intelligence" (TTP, 69). This is a complicated point, though, because Spinoza clearly suggests in the *Ethics* that one and the same person can be rational and irrational at different times and because of different experiences. We can be "torn by affects which are passions" very easily, he shows, simply because of who and what we encounter in the world (E IV p34). To be sure, the point is to become "intelligent" enough not to be so torn. But we are inevitably torn. In one passage, Spinoza observes somewhat poignantly that "sometimes a man undergoes such changes that I should hardly have said he was the same man" (E IV p39s). Indeed, this is precisely what his political theory begins with and is designed to address, as opposed to beginning with a notion of equal "rights" and being unable to account for, much less address, the profound inequalities that actually exist (and the various reasons for them). Spinoza is realistic about the differences between "the fool and the man who understands," neither stressing such differences nor pretending they don't exist (E IV p17dem). He is also not above expressing dismay at the ways in which the "learned" are vilified by the "ignorant" and, more precisely, their spokespeople:

it [often] happens that one who seeks the true cause of miracles, and is eager, like an educated man, to understand natural things, not to wonder at them, like a fool, is generally considered and denounced as an impious heretic by those whom the people honor as interpreters of nature and the Gods. (E I app)

But he tends to come down on the side of the influence of culture and education, because he wants to reform "sluggish minds" – to extol the "temperament and manner of living" to which freedom (political, intellectual, psychical) gives rise (E IV p66s) – not abandon them to their sluggishness. For this reason Spinoza does not exempt himself, or anyone else, from the multitude's fate, and in fact makes this very exemption the guarantee of despotism:

if the common people could practise self-restraint, and suspend judgements about public affairs with little information to go on, they would certainly be more worthy to rule than to be ruled. However, as I have said, all men have the same nature; all are puffed up by rule, they terrorize when they are not afraid, and it is everywhere common for truth to be disregarded by bitter enemies or servile followers, especially when one man or a few have despotic power. (TP VII: 27)

One might see Spinoza's theory of religion as proto-Marxist in its focus on the material conditions of illusory ideas, in its insistence that changes in the social and political order will reduce the most pernicious effects of such ideas, and in its condemnation of the employment of religion by those who have an interest in keeping the masses docile.[22] As Spinoza puts it,

[the masses] are readily induced, under the guise of religion, now to worship its rulers as gods, and then again to curse and condemn them as mankind's common bane. To counteract this unfortunate tendency, immense efforts have been made to invest religion, true or false, with such pomp and ceremony that it can sustain any shock and constantly evoke the deepest reverence in all its worshipers. (TTP, 2–3)

Both Spinoza and Marx contend that the separation of religion from the state is ineffective at addressing the problems of superstition, though they proceed from this recognition in opposite directions. Spinoza's concern is the extent to which religious authority, thus separated, constitutes a dominion within the dominion of the political, and his solution is to subordinate religious to political authority; Marx's concern is the extent to which separation, which in the nineteenth century meant the relegation of religion to the private sphere (civil society), leaves in place the liberal (or what he calls "Christian") state.[23] However, unlike Marx, Spinoza does not think that "true religion" (*vera religio*) is *only* a "relic of man's ancient bondage" (TTP, 3), or only a function of the success or failure of particular human laws. He does not, in other words, identify religion with superstition, even though he does think that the divine law is intrinsically political, and therefore that it cannot be purified of its imaginative dimension. True religion is more than just a mirror image of the fortunes of social bodies, though it is crucially bound up with their historical constitution through the representation of divine discourse as law, and through the concept of election, by which Spinoza thinks all nations represent their particularity. Superstition, for all that we can understand and sympathize with its causes, is always a force for social ill. Religion, at its best, is not. What's more, the proper relationship between the divine

---

[22] On the relationship between Spinoza and Marx, see Alexandre Matheron, "Le *Traité théologique-politique* vu par le jeune Marx," *Cahiers Spinoza* 1 (1977): 159–212; Balibar, "Spinoza, the Anti-Orwell: The Fear of the Masses," trans. Ted Stolze, rev. J. Swenson and E. Balibar, in *Masses, Classes, Ideas: Studies on Politics and Philosophy Before and After Marx* (New York: Routledge, 1994); and Yovel, *Spinoza and Other Heretics, vol. II: The Adventures of Immanence* (Princeton, N.J.: Princeton University Press, 1989), 78–103.

[23] See Karl Marx, "On the Jewish Question," in *The Marx-Engels Reader*, ed. Robert Tucker, 2nd edn. (New York: W. W. Norton and Co., 1978), 26–53.

and human laws is the political key to the effort to reduce the inequality and material discomfort, which, as above, lead to resentment, envy, and fear, the cornerstones of superstition.

The problem with religion for Spinoza (as for Marx) is that, as a discourse about a putatively invisible realm, it not only all too easily tempts people with illusory consolations for what they do not have. It plays to the human tendency to want to empower oneself by disempowering others, i.e., the "monstrous lust of each to crush the other in any way possible" (E IV p58s). Those with some form of privilege can find nothing more amenable to their self-aggrandizing purposes than religion, and specifically, the dissemination of a mysterious and magical text which only a few can genuinely understand. This is Spinoza's ultimate problem with an anthropomorphic God, with a God who is at once conceived on the model of human power (and usually tyrannical power at that) and at the same time removed from the human, political domain where this power can be contested.

However, Spinoza opts for neither the eradication of religion as "false consciousness" nor for its exile *in toto* to the purely private realm. For while the problem of religion significantly recedes in the TP, in the TTP at least, Spinoza remains convinced that the only adequate response to religion, one that addresses both its implication in superstition and its abuse by religious authorities, is to harness it for society, not individuals – to make religion public, which is to say, to analyze and thematize the relationship between divine law and human laws. Whereas the liberal response to religion is to assign its ritual dimension very little, if any, public significance, Spinoza holds that there is a crucial relationship between religious expressions (including language, rituals, "promised lands," and conceptions of kinship or ethnicity) and national identity. It is "difference of language, of laws, and of established customs that divides individuals into nations. And only . . . laws and customs can be the source of the particular character, the particular mode of life, the particular set of attitudes that signalise each nation" (TTP, 207).[24] In other words, while he appears to be calling for the absolute reduction of the "outward forms of religion" to piety – conceived as acts of justice and charity in conformity with the peace of the commonwealth – he is at the same time claiming that the peace and well-being of polities has to do precisely with a sense

---

[24] "Natura . . . nationes non creat, sed individua, quae quidem in nationes non distinguntur nisi ex diversitate linguae, legum, & morum receptorum, & ex his duobus, legibus & moribus, tantum oriri potest, quod unaquaeque natio singularia praejudicia" (G III: 217).

of "nationality" and that "devotion to one's country is the highest form of devotion that can be shown" (TTP, 219, 222).

Thus the Mosaic law, like all human laws (regardless of its origin), refers to "temporal and material prosperity and peaceful government" and therefore, like all human laws, it "could have been of practical value only while [the Hebrew] state existed" (TTP, 60). Without occupying its land – that is, by occupying the land of another *natio* – it loses its connection to social well-being, to power, becoming, instead of a liberatory force (that by which a "free multitude" can achieve independence from other nations), an enslaving one (TP V: 6). It is only through the laws of the land that freedom is possible – competing laws serve simultaneously to distract attention from the channels of power and undermine them. Spinoza's concept of the multitude is thus intrinsically political.[25] It is not identical to the 'state' or even to the *civitas*, to the extent that one can distinguish these in Spinoza, but it is explicitly in and through the *potentia multitudinis* that a community's laws and customs have coherence for him (TP II: 17). This does not mean that Jewish law, to take the case that Spinoza repeatedly returns to, bears no intrinsic relationship to the divine law, or even that, outside of the literal occupation of its state, it has no force or import, but only that it itself, like any human law, is not identical with the divine law as such.

What is significant about divine law and its "dogmas of faith" is that they "strengthen the will to love one's neighbor" in the context of a particular polity, while resisting the rationale that the actions they command have a telos other than individual enlightenment (TTP, 166). Not only do these dogmas tend to promote social harmony, in the sense of encouraging the multitude to be obedient; they are also both democratic, in the sense of commanding behaviors founded on equality regardless of whatever human laws they happen to coexist with, and they are democratizing, that is, resistant to manipulation by priests, pontiffs, and rabbis who guard and authorize religious "externals" for their own purposes (and downplay the autonomy of the divine law). They are not intended to replace particular human laws, since in one sense they are more properly "principles" than they are literally laws. But, as principles, they have no force or reality outside of human civil institutions. Indeed, while

---

[25] The multitude does not, to be sure, play the kind of political role in the TTP that it does in the TP, where it is entirely unconnected to religion (a virtue for some readers). But it is misleading to say, as Negri does, that in the TTP it is a "sociological, nonpolitical concept" (*"Reliqua Desiderantur,"* 231). In the TTP it does not refer to a coherent political "subject," as Negri puts it, and is, as I have noted, a source of social malaise for Spinoza. But it is at the very least a political "object," and one whose proto-subjectivity, so to speak, is the focus of Spinoza's analysis of the Hebrew theocracy.

we are bound by God's command to practise piety towards all men without exception and harm to no man . . . So no one can exercise piety towards his neighbour in accordance with God's command unless piety and religion conform to the public good. But no private citizen can know what is good for the state except from the decrees of the sovereign. (TTP, 223)

As I will explore further below, one of the principal questions raised by the TTP is thus the question of whether the "neighbor" and the "citizen" are constitutively at odds with one another.

The problem with the solution of the separation of church and state is very simply that it doesn't solve the problem of religion for Spinoza, either its hold on credulity or its deployment by elites.[26] All it does is make religion an *imperium in imperio*, that is, it divides people's loyalties, focuses their attention on religion's apolitical features, and allows religious law to escape from the checks and balances and self-limitations that keep any social and political order always tending toward democracy. To Spinoza, there is a blatant contradiction between the biblical notion that "every man is in God, and God in every man" and the fanaticism, conflict, and esotericism of ostensibly private religion (TTP, 166). It is obvious, to him, that "divisions in the church do not arise from zeal for truth (which breeds only courtesy and tolerance) but from lust for supremacy" (TTP, 237). Out of the realm of public life where it can be measured by its fruits, religious law shares with human law the demonstrably ill effects of being relegated to behind closed doors. Thus for Spinoza the state ought to be "religious" to some degree, with the proviso that religion itself is always to some degree both true and false. In its true guise, religious ideas are in accord with both divine law (which has reference to individual flourishing) and the laws of society (which have reference to the security and peace of particular social bodies). They are not "oughts" that human beings can rationally take or leave, but are simply adequate descriptions of what works best at both levels.

Thus Spinoza, as we have seen, is a defender of true religion over against what he thinks of as false religion, not a critic of religion *tout court*. He is just as passionately interested in disentangling what is good and useful about it as he is in exposing what is pernicious and useless. Above all, it

---

[26] As Spinoza puts it, "as for the arguments by which my opponents seek to separate religious right from civil right, maintaining that only the latter is vested in the sovereign while the former is vested in the universal church, these are of no account, being so trivial as not even to merit refutation. But one thing I cannot pass over in silence, how lamentably deceived they are when, to support this seditious opinion (pardon the bluntness of this expression) they cite the example of the Hebrew high priest who once had control over matters of religion – as if the priests did not receive this right from Moses . . . and could not also have been deprived of it by his decree" (TTP, 224).

is human beings he is interested in: Why are they religious? Why be religious at all? Does it lead to flourishing? Does it lead to social harmony? Does it lead to enlightenment? Spinoza's answer is definitive: sometimes. The separation of philosophy and theology is about disabusing both of their pretensions to make complicated what is both very simple – obedience as love of neighbor – and extremely hard to achieve, since the obstacles to loving one's neighbor are pervasive and systemic. The fact that the precepts of true religion "can be readily grasped by everyone by the natural light of reason" does not mean they can so readily be enacted (TTP, 146). This is the play of the ordinary and the extraordinary that is so fascinating in Spinoza: the problem with the priests and pontiffs, whoever they are, is that they make what is ordinary (natural) and available to all, extraordinary (supernatural) and available only to the few. In so doing they unscrupulously obscure, under a mask of theological and philosophical speculations (and thus "disputes and schisms" [TTP, 148]), what is genuinely extraordinary, namely the simple moral truths of justice and charity that are so difficult to enact and to legislate.

To be sure, there is always more than one voice on the question of the utility of religion in the TTP. If religion is, on the one hand, a positive and useful solution to the healthy functioning of an antagonistic multitude, it is also part of the problem, part of what can reinforce these antagonisms. This is why it is not enough in reading the TTP simply to stress either the political utility of religion or its superstitious and inflammatory qualities, much less to claim that Spinoza conflates these (i.e., that he considers the utility to consist *precisely* in keeping the masses superstitious). Spinoza's claim is that without a political solution to the religious question, a solution that is addressed not only to the problem of superstition but also to the speculative and power-hungry machinations of the learned religious elite, there is no chance that what is positive in religion can outweigh what is negative, and we would in this case be better off entirely free of it. What is clear is that it is *despotism* that is at issue – it is despotism that perverts religion for its own ends. In other words, religion does not make us false as much as we make religion false:

> Granted, then, that the supreme mystery of despotism, its prop and stay, is to keep men in a state of deception, and with the specious title of religion to cloak the fear by which they must be held in check, so that they will fight for their servitude as if for salvation, and count it no shame, but the highest honor, to spend their blood and their lives for the glorification of one man. Yet no more disastrous policy can be devised or attempted in a free commonwealth. (TTP, 3)

The key connection in Spinoza between religion and politics is that the sign of illegitimacy in both is the attempt to render secret what ought to be public, the attempt, in other words, to remove and privilege knowledge from the public eye where it can both educate and be challenged. What makes true religion *true* for Spinoza is precisely that it is *law*, and not simply a set of rational ideas, and law for Spinoza can both restrain and reform. On one level, the conception that God reveals laws (as "instructions and precepts") is to mistake God's "eternal truth" for a contingent one and God himself for a political ruler (TTP, 55). It is to see law as the "enactment from which good or ill consequence would ensue not from the intrinsic nature of the deed performed but only from the will and absolute power of some ruler" (TTP, 54). In fact, though, this is no closer to the true understanding of *human* law than it is divine law; it is no closer to the understanding of human law as resistant to both secrecy and fiat, nor to understanding obedience (religious and political) as acting in conformity to one's own will. The problem for both human and divine law is this tendency to construe political or divine authority as external to one's own ends – in a sense to alienate oneself from one's own actions. For Spinoza this alienation is especially pronounced in the arrogation of the right to speak for God (something that can only occur if God is seen as judge and lawgiver), prompting "sycophants and traitors" to "usurp the government's authority and right, and . . . unashamedly [to] boast that they have been chosen directly by God and that their decrees are divinely inspired, whereas those of the sovereign are merely human and should therefore give way before divine decrees – that is, their own" (TTP, 238). It is the image of God as a judge that precisely casts the human as "mere." Yet on another level, then, God's "eternal truth" is nothing other than a "law for the wise" (TTP, 57), a law whose very clarity reforms and educates the human tendency to act from fear of (or the promotion of the fear of) punishment rather than with "loyalty and virtue" (TTP, 193). For Spinoza, the only ill consequence we ought to be concerned with is simply the "deprivation of these things, and bondage to the flesh, that is, an inconstant and irresolute spirit" (TTP, 53).

It is not correct, then, to say that Spinoza's religion is a "religion of reason," since what is usually meant by this is a notion of reason as ideational and apolitical.[27] But Spinoza rejects this notion just as much as he rejects a notion of faith as supernatural. His religion, however, *is* a religion of reason as long as reason is understood in a Spinozistic way, as concerning lawfulness, practice, and publicity. The perversity of Strauss's reading in

---

[27] See Yovel, *Spinoza and Other Heretics*, vol. I: *The Marrano of Reason*, ch. 6, 153–171. The classic statement in this regard is Wolfson's claim that "the religion of reason which Spinoza briefly outlines for us here [viz., the disinterested love of God] is nothing but a modified form of the philosophic conception of Judaism as described by Maimonides" (*The Philosophy of Spinoza*, vol. II, 328).

this light becomes all the more glaring, for he grounds the legitimacy of *his* reading in what he takes to be the signs of *Spinoza's* secrecy, when the TTP is a sustained critique of secrecy from beginning to end. Legitimacy in both the hermeneutical and the political realm, then, is tied up with clarity and democracy, a connection that can be seen most vividly in the case of religion and its principal text, the Bible. Removed to protective institutions, divided from the sovereign authority, the Bible becomes a source of strife and hatred, which eventually leads to its inefficacy even for those who have commandeered its power. As Spinoza puts it, even the prophets, as the interpreters of God's word, are not free from this problem of the "strength and power of religious authority" to divide and sow strife. For "although the prophets were endowed with a divine virtue, yet, being men of private station, in exercising their freedom to admonish, to rebuke and to denounce, they had the effect of provoking men rather than reforming them" (TTP, 226). Thus the crucial issue is that the separation of religious and political authority is in itself inefficacious, undermining both under the signs of mystery, uniqueness, and privilege. Democracy per se may not be a necessary condition for constructing religious and political authority in the proper ways, but its signatures – accessibility, publicity, clarity, and incompleteness – are, as well as being the hallmarks of a text's sacrality.

This is the point of the focus on hubris in the *Ethics*. The judgment that human beings form a unique dominion in nature is not only a false belief. In granting to themselves a special "supernatural" power which they do not intrinsically possess, human beings precisely exacerbate the ways in which they are wholly limited by nature. By understanding things incorrectly, Spinoza shows, we decrease rather than increase our power to act, thus bringing about the very limitation we claim to be beyond. This is the force of the ordinary in Spinoza. It is the attempt to escape from it into the extraordinary that effaces the (ordinary) power we do actually possess, and which Spinoza understands to be truly rare in its own way. The object, rather, is to *know* the ways in which we are limited in order precisely to become less limited, and this works in the political realm, too, where the supernatural inhibits the power not only of the superstitious masses, but of the priests and the pontiffs, whose dominance can only be temporary. What makes something extraordinary, for Spinoza, is the tremendous effort involved in simply understanding what it is to be a human being, what human beings are by "nature." To figure the extraordinary, instead, as mystery, and thus attainable only by way of authorities and precisely by circumventing the actual work involved in achieving the highest blessedness, is an outrage to him:

But what dogma! – degrading rational man to beast, completely inhibiting man's free judgement and his capacity to distinguish true from false, and apparently devised with the set purpose of utterly extinguishing the light of reason. Piety and religion – O everlasting God – take the form of ridiculous mysteries, and men who utterly despise reason, who reject and turn away from the intellect as naturally corrupt – these are the men (and this is of all things the most iniquitous) who are believed to possess the divine light! Surely, if they possessed but a spark of the divine light, they would not indulge in such arrogant ravings, but would study to worship God more wisely and to surpass their fellows in love, as they now do in hate. They would not persecute so bitterly those who do not share their views: rather would they show compassion, if their concern was for men's salvation, and not for their own standing. (TTP, 4–5)

Spinoza is outraged most of all because the deployment of the language of mystery doesn't just mask ugly power-mongering. It also corrupts the natural resources people possess to be able to contest it, for what the masses do not know they cannot be expected to know how to contest. What is ordinary and natural, then, is what is by definition democratic, available to all equally. It is only in grasping this thrust of the TTP that we can see the extent to which not only is Spinoza not propounding one "morality" for the masses and another for the philosophers, but this very notion itself is the source of both philosophical error and political self-destruction.

One could say that Spinoza's interest in keeping religion subject to the (ideally democratic) political sovereign is not just about keeping religion under control or, even more, using religion to control the masses. It is about keeping religion *true*, which is to say, keeping it mixed up with ordinary life, without simply reducing it to a particular polity's laws. The religious commandments of universal charity and justice, then, far from being irredeemably abstract, are only abstract if they are to refer to a realm other than the political one, whether conceived according to the model of an afterlife, or a separate spiritual realm in this life. One cannot be charitable and just without changing the political conditions that lead to injustice and hatred. The paradox is that only when religion is cast as unpolitical does it actually have politically negative effects, setting itself up as a spiritualist critique of the material realm – what Spinoza calls the "philosophic speculations" that were to produce endless schisms in Christendom (TTP, 148) – and at once dividing the devout masses from genuine power and counseling nonresistance. Spinoza spends little time struggling with Jesus' maxim that one should turn the other cheek. This is valid, he says, only in situations of extreme oppression, "in a corrupt commonwealth where justice is utterly disregarded." Otherwise we would do better to learn from Moses, who "please note, was concerned to found a good commonwealth," and ensure that "justice is upheld" (TTP, 94). Spinoza was no revolutionary.[28] But he was thoroughly committed to the historical and political instantiation of a more blessed world and thoroughly critical, metaphysically and politically, of the kind of dualistic thinking that threatened this instantiation or substituted false solutions to its challenges.

This may be to picture Spinoza in terms of an overly black-and-white world: impious theologians over against pious ordinary folk. But we are all, in theory, the unscrupulous theologians, feeding our own power through ambition and iniquity, for this need for power is itself as much a product of as a contributor to a specific social order. And we are all equally the masses, credulous, lazy, not wanting to put in the time to discover things for ourselves. Spinoza is ever the realist. He is not interested in idealizing *any* group of people, for human beings are everywhere and always the same and "those who wish to give rein to their desires can easily find any reason for so doing" (TTP, 150). He is, rather, trying to curb excesses and show the minimal amount of enlightenment that is socially possible. There are no guarantees whatsoever to prevent what Spinoza himself says from leading to impiety, since this itself is dependent on the mind of *his* reader. As he says,

I do admit that some ungodly men can assume from my views a license to sin and, without any justification and merely to gratify their desires, can conclude therefrom that Scripture is at all points faulty and contaminated, and therefore has no authority. But such people are beyond help; as the old saying goes, nothing can be so accurately stated as to be incapable of distortion by misrepresentation. (TTP, 150)

Spinoza's dilemma, however, in claiming that there is a difference between true and false religion, is that of verification or legitimacy. Specifically, if what makes religion true for Spinoza is that it is *law*, and not simply a rational idea, how do we know whether the laws that "command and restrain" us are divine laws? How do we know whether our human laws are good laws? To what end are the divine ordinances of justice and charity directed? To make human beings moral? To make them obedient (and to whom)? To make them holy? What's the difference between these? What relationship can obedience have to knowledge other than, at best, a useful stepping stone and at worst, a form of social control?

---

[28] Spinoza adamantly identifies the attempt to "seize for [oneself] the sovereign power's right or to transfer it to another" as treason, an act which is "rightly and properly condemned" (TTP, 187).

Law

Spinoza's treatment of law in the TTP is complex. "The word law [*lex*] taken in its absolute sense," he declares at the beginning of chapter 4 ("Of the Divine Law"), "means that according to which each individual thing – either all in general or those of the same kind – acts in one and the same fixed and determinate manner, this manner depending either on Nature's necessity or on human will." Law that "depends on Nature's necessity . . . which necessarily follows from the very nature of the thing" refers to the laws of the natural order, by which he means not just "nature" but all things taken together – things "in general," as he puts it. By contrast, "law which depends on human will, and which could more properly be called a statute" (*ius*) is directed more narrowly and contingently to things "of the same kind," and therefore makes reference to some kind of judgment (will) about a particular end (TTP, 49).

But this distinction is by no means clear cut. For "man, in so far as he is part of Nature, constitutes a part of the power of Nature" (TTP, 49). From one perspective, therefore, insofar as all (kinds of) things originate in God, they are necessary, appearing contingent only due to a defect in our knowledge, i.e., "because the order of causes is hidden from us" (E I p33s1). Still, Spinoza continues, "the enacting of these manmade laws [*legum ex hominem*] may quite legitimately be said to depend on human [as opposed to divine] will, for it depends especially on the power of the human mind," and the human mind can be conceived without these (manmade) laws though not without "Nature's necessary laws" (TTP, 49).

The key point for the TTP is not the distinction between necessary and contingent laws, but rather the stipulation that manmade laws are relative to the mind, relative to human interest.[29] While we do have access to the regularity and immutability of natural laws, e.g., the laws of the conservation of motion or the laws of memory and association, and, in the *Ethics* at least, must strive more and more to understand the necessary causes of what only appears contingent, Spinoza's claim in the TTP is that "generalisations about fate and the interconnection of causes can be of no service to us in forming and ordering our thoughts concerning particular things" (TTP, 49–50). What can Spinoza mean by this, in light of his repeated insistence that it is knowledge and understanding that free human beings from "bondage" to natural law? While it would

---

[29] As Spinoza says of Scripture, too, "Ex quo sequitur nihil extra mentem absolute, sed tantum respective ad ipsam, sacrum aut profanum aut impurum esse" (From this it follows that nothing is in an absolute sense sacred or profane or impure apart from the mind, but only relative to it) (G III: 146).

seem from his initial declaration that human law is a subspecies of natural law, a way of ordering groups of things from within a larger system in which their order is necessary or given, Spinoza seems here, somewhat obliquely, to be suggesting just the reverse, that it is only in "forming and ordering our thoughts concerning particular [kinds of] causes" that "generalisations about fate and the interconnection of things [in general]" have any purchase or foothold.

As I have emphasized, Spinoza considers the natural state of human beings to be one of relative powerlessness. It is clear that the knowledge of nature he is recommending in the *Ethics* is directed toward an understanding of how natural law affects human beings. This is not simply an empty truism, because Spinoza's notion that the mind does not constitute a separate *ingenium* in nature means that, in theory at least, what Spinoza's individual scientist can know of the world is significantly less than an individual whose mind is conceived to be independent of natural law (though, as I have shown, Spinoza thinks this other kind of individual is a fiction). Another way of putting this is that human beings can know *that* "all things have been determined from the necessity of the divine nature to exist and produce an effect in a certain and determinate way" (E I p29) – and indeed this knowledge is the condition of liberating ourselves from anthropomorphisms and theologies of providence – but we *experience* this necessity as a limitation. We know of the existence of other bodies in nature only insofar as they affect our bodies ("the human Mind does not perceive any external body as actually existing, except through the ideas of the affections of its own Body" [E II p26]), and this is reflected in the fact that the investigation of natural causes leads in itself to infinite regress (E I p28), a state of affairs only remedied through the third (most powerful) kind of knowledge, which is to understand the connection of singular things to God (E V p24).

Thus while knowledge of natural law is crucial, what concerns human beings, buffeted as they are by fortune, is what they can *do* with law to ensure their survival and flourishing. It is not simply that they must strive to act in accordance with nature (as the natural lawyers hold), for by nature human beings are very weak indeed. As singular entities whose understanding of other singular entities is relative to how the latter affect them, human beings are concerned with controlling their surroundings and creating the conditions for themselves that will maximize their own self-preservation. Thus, Spinoza says, "for practical purposes it is better, indeed it is essential, to consider things as contingent" (TTP, 50).

Spinoza's concept of understanding, then, is divided between this recognition that things are necessary and that they are changeable or perfectible. From the one perspective, all singular things are determined to "exist and to act in a definite way" and "the natural right of man is determined not by sound reason, but by his desire and his power." Therefore nothing that human beings are urged to do from their appetites, and which may appear inconvenient, "ridiculous, absurd, or evil," is in fact frowned on by nature, "which forbids only those things that no one desires and no one can do" (TTP, 180). From the other perspective, however, human beings must be self-legislating to at least some degree, for following one's appetites simply increases the ways in which we are dependent on the power of others, and thus there are natural "reasons," if one can put it that way, to attempt to determine one's own actions. As Spinoza puts it in the TP, "I call a man completely free in so far as he is guided by reason, for then he is determined to action by causes which can be understood adequately through his own nature alone. But he is necessarily determined to action by them; for freedom . . . does not remove the necessity of acting, but imposes it" (TP II: 11). From the perspective of human interest, even nature is seen as contingent in the sense that we can never have a full grasp of its scope – we "are born and for the most part live" according to "Nature's right and her established order," but this is something we ourselves can never see from the "outside," as it were (TTP, 180). This is one of the key dimensions of Spinoza's use of the concept of fortune: our partial perspective and our dependence on others ensure that, while things and events are not wholly controllable, they can sometimes seem (accidentally) beneficial or detrimental to human needs.

I have discussed Spinoza's conception of "bondage" and its role in his understanding of human power, distinguishing the latter both from the wisdom available to the intellect according to the model of the perfection of God and the resignation (stoicism) that results from seeing this "bondage" – and the inequalities it reflects and produces – as infused with moral content (sin). Here I am concerned especially with Spinoza's conception of knowledge as mediated by the rule of law – with the notion that the knowledge that enables human beings to attain independence is itself dependent upon "manmade" laws, whether construed as divine, that is, "of universal application, or common to all mankind" and directed toward "the supreme good," or human, that is, a "rule of conduct whose sole aim is to safeguard life and the commonwealth" (TTP, 50–52). In contrast to natural law, in the context of which "man is but a particle" (TTP, 180), both human and divine laws are entirely focused around the "rules for living a life," in the one case with the aim of constructing a particular polity and in the second case with the aim of achieving blessedness and enlightenment (TTP, 51). While Spinoza also considers natural law a law of God, this is not the only meaning that he gives to the divine law. The knowledge and love of God that concerns our highest good is not limited to the knowledge of natural laws, but includes the moral law of justice and charity that are not part of natural law.[30] In this light, Spinoza notes, it is really only by analogy that the word *law* is extended at all to the phenomena of nature, for "ordinarily 'law' is used to mean simply a command which men can either obey or disobey, inasmuch as it restricts the total range of human power within set limits and demands nothing that is beyond the capacity of that power" (TTP, 50).

Natural law is clearly not something that one can obey or disobey. As Spinoza puts it (quoting Paul in Rom. 9: 21), "we must always remember that we are in the power of God like clay in the power of the potter, who from the same lump makes some vessels for honourable, and others for dishonourable use" (TP II: 22). As opposed to the "decrees of God, as far as they have been written like laws in the minds of ourselves or the prophets," by which he means the *lex divina* and the *lex humana* (which one can indeed transgress), "against that eternal decree of God which is written in universal nature, and has regard to the course of nature as a whole, he can do nothing" (TP II: 22). But this notion of the voluntary nature of manmade laws is not the crux of the matter for Spinoza. Once established, they also command us in a "fixed and determinate" manner, and indeed as he says of divine law, "it must be considered as innate in the human mind and inscribed therein, as it were" (TTP, 60). The question is: What can it mean to establish something that has this kind of force? What is the origin of these laws, beyond simply the fact that, like everything else, they follow from the nature of God? More precisely, it is one thing to speak about the origin of human law in the foundation of society – in a version of a *pactum* – as Spinoza does in chapter 16 of the TTP, but quite another to speak of the divine law as having an origin in the same sense. Surely this is either a reinscription of a notion of innate morality, or alternatively a reduction of the divine law to a particular society's fiction. But if the latter, how can it be "common to all mankind" and of "universal application," as Spinoza insists that it is (TTP, 52)? And if the former, how is this different from an Aristotelian notion that the moral law is imprinted in the human essence, as it were, as its natural telos? How is it thus "manmade"?

What is at issue here are two claims that Spinoza is advancing. The first is that there is no such thing as justice or morality outside of the institution of human laws: "in the state of nature nothing is done which can be called just or unjust . . . [only] in the civil state . . . where it is decided by common consent what belongs to this man, what to that" (E IV p37s2).[31] As I have shown, the fact that Spinoza considers the

---

[30] Cf. Den Uyl, *Power, State, and Freedom*, 4. See also Gail Belaief, *Spinoza's Philosophy of Law* (The Hague: Mouton, 1971).

[31] See also TTP, 185–186.

values of good and evil and perfection and imperfection to be relative to human desire does not mean he thinks they are arbitrary or that they do not command us positively or negatively. What Spinoza is getting at is that, as values that refer to something that people have in common, they do not preexist "manmade" law, that is, law that takes human goods as its aim: "that which our reason declares to be evil is not evil in respect of the order and laws of universal Nature, but only in respect of the laws of our own nature" (TTP, 181). In this light, Spinoza's crucial claim is that "justice and, in sum, all the precepts of true reason, including charity towards one's neighbor, acquire the force of law and command only from the right of the state, that is . . . only from the decree of those who possess the right to command" (TTP, 220).

Justice, then, is not only relative to individual desire and conduct; it is relative to a particular social order. This claim is perfectly consistent with the republican tradition with which Spinoza clearly identifies, in which the *civitas* is organized according to a conception of a common purpose. For Spinoza, it is not only the case that a political community is formed to provide security in an instrumental sense; in addition, the *civitas* has as its *raison d'être* to "safeguard life," by which he means the creation of conditions adequate for citizens to live according to the precepts of reason. This the *civitas* provides through the rule of law, which both brings moral and humane values into existence and disciplines populace and ruler alike according to a shared ethos (in the case of a monarchy, "even the king himself cannot repeal" the laws [TP VII: 1]). This collective ethos – what Spinoza calls "a union or agreement of minds" (TP VI: 4) – need have no more content than simply the desire not to be determined or dominated by other states. The point is simply that this "desire" concerns law, not psychology – it concerns the creation of laws that do not need to depend on "man's good faith":

> If a state is to be capable of lasting, its administration must be so organized that it does not matter whether its rulers are led by reason or passion . . . In fact it makes no difference to the stability of the state what motive leads men to conduct its affairs properly, provided that they *are* conducted properly. (TP I: 5)

Yet, on the other hand, in order to achieve the goal of stability, which for Spinoza is not simply an absence of war but the very "virtue of a state" (TP I: 5), one needs "virtuous" laws, laws that, as Machiavelli would put it, *make* people more rational:[32]

---

[32] Machiavelli, *Discourses* I: 3, in *The Chief Works*, vol. I, 201. See also the third discourse where he discusses the means by which a state may fruitfully be renewed, that is, brought back to what was fruitful in its origins that has corrupted over time. This can result from either "internal prudence" or "external accident," and the former can take place "in republics either by virtue of a man of by virtue of a law" (III: 1, 419–420).

> Just as in the state of nature the man who is guided by reason is most powerful and most fully possessed of his own right . . . so also the commonwealth which is based on and directed by reason will be the most powerful and most fully possessed of its own right. For the right of a commonwealth is determined by the power of a people guided as if by one mind; but this union of minds is quite inconceivable unless the commonwealth does its best to achieve those conditions which sound reason declares to be for the good of all men. (TP III: 7)

Spinoza's claim is that a commonwealth guided by reason is better – more powerful – than one guided by force or the accidents of noble birth.[33] The power of Spinoza's state resides *not* in the existence of a rational elite but in the "union of minds" of "a people." This union of minds, he insists, "is quite inconceivable unless the commonwealth does its best to achieve those conditions which sound reason declares to be for the good of all men." Not only is Spinoza saying that the *civitas* is responsible for creating the conditions for its citizens to govern themselves ("the power of a people"), whether they are "led by reason or passion." He is also suggesting that in order for them to do so, a particular state must make it possible for citizens to live according to the good that is common to "all men," reason.

Thus, in addition to the claim that justice is relative to human law, the second crucial point that Spinoza is making is that justice is also a feature of the divine law, and not simply the creation of a particular social order. It is not simply, as Hobbes puts it, that "injustice against men presupposes Human Laws."[34] For Spinoza (contra Hobbes) sin, or rather the injustice against God, also presupposes such laws: "In order that the precepts of true reason – that is . . . the very precepts of God – might have the absolute force of law . . . every man must surrender his natural right to the whole community, or to a number of men, or to one man" (TTP, 220). Spinoza agrees, then, that justice is dependent upon a political sovereign. He thinks, in other words, that the sovereign determines what justice is (rather than subordinating itself to a preexisting standard), just as desire determines what the good is. But the "sovereign" *is* law – the literal "man," "number of men," or "whole community" is itself a function, or rather a creation, of "men surrendering their natural right." Spinoza's crucial addition to Hobbes is that, if no one has any natural duty whatsoever to obey human law, this is equally true of divine law: "if men were by nature bound by the divine law, or if the divine

---

[33] See Jonathan Israel, *The Dutch Republic: Its Rise, Greatness, and Fall 1477–1806* (New York: Clarendon Press, 1995), 762 ff.

[34] Thomas Hobbes, *On the Citizen*, ed. Richard Tuck and Michael Silverthorne (Cambridge: Cambridge University Press, 1998), I: 10. See also TP II: 19, 20, 21, 22.

law were a law by nature, there would have been no need for God to enter into a contract with men and to bind them by covenant and by oath" (TTP, 188). It is, then, a "contract" that originates justice, both human and divine; a contract that determines that the precepts of justice and charity (i.e., the idea of loving God and neighbor) command "all men without exception, whether or not they have the use of reason" and whatever *civitas* they happen to occupy (TTP, 187–188). "God has no kingdom over men save through the medium of those who hold sovereignty," but sovereignty itself is thus of both universal and particular significance.

We cannot *know* that we should obey God, just as we cannot *know* that we should "render every man what is his by civil right" since, prior to entering into a contract with him, we don't have to, or rather, we "should" do so only to the degree to which it is to our greater advantage (TTP, 186, 188). After entering into such a contract or covenant, however, God's law, *unlike* human laws, possesses the force whereby Spinoza can speak of it as being "innate in the human mind and inscribed therein, as it were" (*ipsa humanae menti innata, & quasi inscripta existimanda sit*) (TTP, 60, G III: 69). The difference between this law and human laws is thus its universal scope, commanding all human beings equally, commanding behaviors *toward* all human beings equally. But it does not preexist this covenant, and most importantly, while it does command all human beings as individuals (all individuals are sovereign with respect to the law), it is also paradoxically relative to a sovereign (all sovereigns are individuals), who can consult these precepts or not "without any violation of right, civil or natural" (TTP, 189).

The divine law thus shares a basis (*fundamentum*) with human law – the forfeiture of natural right – though this is rarely perceived by those who are invested in the autonomy and privacy of the religious realm. For Spinoza, the Hebrew commonwealth is the one polity that explicitly did not make this mistake, for "their church originated together with their state," unlike "the origins of the Christian religion," where "it was not kings" who were its first teachers "but men of private station" (TTP, 227). The consequence of this difference for Spinoza is tremendous.[35] The Hebrews, at least initially, held power in common, they rarely suffered civil strife, their laws were commonly known by all and, when it was a matter of interpretation, vouchsafed to those who had no political axe to grind: in short, "the practice of religion and the exercises of piety

---

[35] For readers of Spinoza's political theory for whom religion is only an instrumental political tool, this difference cannot be attributed to anything particular to religion itself but only to Moses' ability as a leader to channel the passions of the multitude. See Den Uyl, *Power, State, and Freedom*, 30–31.

[accorded] with the peace and welfare of the commonwealth," with the citizens striving both to obey God in all things and to defend the cause of their nation under threats from without (TTP, 219). As Spinoza avers, this commonwealth cannot, for all that, "be imitated in all respects," and this for the very reasons that it was initially successful, namely, that it achieved complete identification of divine and human laws – that it claimed, in other words, that what is true for "all men" was more true for Hebrews. This identification produced intense loyalty in its citizens, and thus stability for a time, but the price was the eventual dissolution of both loyalty and stability, i.e., internecine fighting within and threats (hatred) from without. The commonwealth nevertheless "possessed many features which are at least worthy of note," not least of which is the very tension between the divine and the human that Spinoza thinks is common to social orders as such (TTP, 212).

Thus the second claim that Spinoza is advancing with his conception of the establishment of divine and human laws is that while they share a basis or a foundation (an "origin"), they are not identical. The divine law is not simply the imagination of what one people's God considers true or virtuous but is rather something that is true and virtuous for all human beings. If Spinoza's divine law is *not* the natural law of either the ancients ("man is a rational animal") or the medievals (man insofar as he is man participates in the eternal law), it nevertheless cannot simply be reduced to the *civitas*.[36] *Vera religio* is not simply a useful social tool that keeps people united and republics strong, even purged of its superstitious accretions and "reduced" to the purified maxims of justice and charity. For this purging is simply to internalize (inscribe in the heart) what can be stipulated only by God, namely, that one obey the command to love one's neighbor (where the neighbor is construed universally). This is Spinoza's claim at the outset of chapter 12:

I am confident that reflection will at once put an end to their outcry [those who accuse him of maintaining the Word of God is faulty]; for not only reason itself, but the assertions of the prophets and the Apostles clearly proclaim that God's eternal Word and covenant and true religious faith are divinely inscribed in men's hearts – that is, men's minds – and that this is the true handwriting of God which he has sealed with his own seal, this seal being the idea of himself, the image of his own divinity, as it were. (TTP, 149)

---

[36] According to Thomas Aquinas, for example, the rational creature is "subject to divine providence in a more excellent way [than other natural beings], insofar as it partakes of a share of divine providence, by being provident both for itself and for others. Wherefore it has a share of the eternal reason, whereby it has a natural inclination to its proper act and end, and this participation of the eternal in the rational creature is called the natural law" (*Saint Thomas Aquinas on Law, Morality, and Politics*, 20).

While one might argue that Spinoza is simply "Christianizing" what he calls true religion, this statement must be understood alongside the claim that the divine law has no force outside political entities, and thus his insistence that the "handwriting of God" in the "mind" is not only a private or spiritual but also a social and political matter. This is precisely what he criticizes Christianity for failing to realize, instead setting itself up as a "religion" over against the law of the state, and thus corrupting both. The command to love the neighbor is one that no political order could come up with. Political orders are the source of local justice, not charity toward all others. No political order would have any *reason* to require this obedience, and yet, for Spinoza, every human law requiring obedience (to respect *some particular* neighbor) is also a sign of the validity – "the fixed and determinate nature" – of the divine law (to respect all others as neighbors).[37] It is by virtue of the imagination that the divine law is seen as something that is received from God for a particular people. In the case of the Hebrew commonwealth, the notion that the law was from God was the main reason the Hebrews obeyed it so fervently, and thus were able to survive for so long. But as Spinoza also says, "the mind, so far as it makes use of its reason, is dependent not on the supreme authorities, but on itself. And so the true knowledge of God cannot be subject to the dominion of any, nor yet can charity towards one's neighbour" (TP III: 10).

This is the TTP's critical tension. The knowledge of God is not pursued by philosophers in isolation, not simply because philosophers, like ordinary people, need security and material subsistence. More fundamentally, the knowledge of God is inaccessible outside of law, outside of "the rules for living a life" that concern both our material welfare and our highest blessedness. Thus the knowledge of God, for Spinoza, is always socially and historically specific. And yet God is the infinite, the eternal, the substantive union of all that is in all times and places.

What is at issue is that law as something one can obey or disobey is law that begins and ends with human beings as its sole subjects: law that takes human ends as its sole purpose, whether spiritual or material. It is therefore "fitting," Spinoza says, "that law should be defined in its narrower sense, that is, as a rule of life which man prescribes for himself or for others for some purpose" (TTP, 50). While natural law is decisively not teleological for Spinoza (E I app), the "laws of human reason" are, in the sense that they "aim only at man's true interest and his preservation" (TTP, 180). Both divine and human law, then, consist

---

[37] On this point it is proper to consider Spinoza a critic of Judaism, namely that the Mosaic law is like other human laws.

of the formulation of rules of conduct to bring about particular ends, the first taking human nature per se as its subject and the "supreme good" as its end, the second taking human beings in particular social and political contexts as its subject and the flourishing of a particular commonwealth as its end. One could see the second as a further specification of the first, the polity being a translation of the laws of human flourishing to the health of a social body. Alternatively (as I discussed in the case of superstition), the flourishing of a particular social body can be seen as the necessary, if not sufficient, condition for effecting what it is that is of supreme good for human beings per se.

An autocratic sovereign may well see these things as entirely independent of each other, advancing its political interests without in any way contributing to the good of its citizens. By the same token, philosophers and their followers can see their work as separate from the larger common good, or, even if they don't conceive it as separate, they can nevertheless guarantee that it will be through esoteric speech.[38] But Spinoza remains a classical republican thinker – a critic of autocracies both political and spiritual – in assuming that the societies most likely to preserve themselves in terms of peace and security over the long term are those that pay the most heed to the divine law and to human nature, and especially to the ways in which they conflict: in other words, to the tension between what *actually* enables human beings to flourish, which is to share the goods of blessedness and enlightenment in common, and what human beings often desire instead, namely goods each can only possess by disinheriting others (the origin of material inequality and social instability):

experience seems to teach that it makes for peace and harmony if all power is vested in one man. For no state has stood so long without any notable change as that of the Turks, and, conversely, none have proved so short-lived and so liable to constant civil strife as popular or democratic states. But if slavery, barbarism, and desolation [*servitium, barbaries, et solitudo*] are to be called peace, peace is the greatest misfortune that men can suffer. It is true that the quarrels which arise between parents and children are generally more frequent and much more bitter than quarrels between masters and slaves, yet it is not conducive to good family management to make the father a master, and to treat children as slaves. So it is slavery, not peace, that is furthered by the transfer of all power to one man; for peace, as I have said already, is not mere absence of war, but a union or agreement of minds. (TP VI: 4)[39]

[38] See TTP, preface – the articulation of Scripture's "profound mysteries" (5).
[39] Cf. Hobbes's "first law of nature," which is "to seek peace when it can be had; when it cannot, to look for aid in war" (*On the Citizen*, II: 2). Spinoza's language of agreement is much stronger than Hobbes's, even though they share the same basic view of the hostility of human being to human being. It was Rousseau who picked up this notion of agreement through his concept of the general will: "A Discourse on Political Economy," *The Social Contract and Discourses*, trans. G. D. H. Cole (London: J. M. Dent & Sons, 1973), 120–121.

This unequivocal defense of democracy, with its conception of peace as the flourishing of both individuals and their polities, also introduces one of the principal difficulties of Spinoza's political theory. For, while it is undoubtedly a good thing to distinguish citizens from slaves, what can Spinoza have in mind by associating the former with "children"? In the earlier TTP, Spinoza makes a threefold distinction, between "a slave, a son, and a subject" (*servum, filium, et subditum*), noting that

a slave is one who has to obey his master's commands which look only to the interests of him who commands; a son is one who by his father's command does what is to his own good; a subject is one who, by command of the sovereign power, acts for the common good, and therefore for his own good [*potestatis*] also. (TTP, 185)

But even here, he continues to speak of "obedience" to the "sovereign power," insisting that "it is for the sovereign power alone . . . to have regard to [curbing the follies of appetite] . . . while it is for the subjects . . . to carry out its orders and to acknowledge no other right but that which the sovereign power declares to be a right" (TTP, 184). "Similarly," Spinoza tells us once again, "although children are in duty bound to obey all the commands of their parents, they are not slaves; for the parents' commands have as their chief aim the good of the children" (TTP, 184–185). It would seem that, even in "a sovereign state where the welfare of the whole people, not the ruler, is the supreme law," the rule of law is to perform the function of both training the mind and constraining the body. And for this it requires obedience.

Obedience

Obedience occupies a central place in Spinoza's thought.[40] In brief, his claim is that, whether the sovereign (*summa potestas*) is God or the state (and whether the state is the people as a whole or a representative minority), sovereignty is constituted through the power to command obedience: "sovereign power is bound by no law, and all must obey it in all matters; for this is what all must have covenanted tacitly or expressly when they transferred to it all their power of self-defence, that is, their right" (TTP, 183). In practice, however, it is the political sovereign only whose power is absolute, for if it is indeed true that "we must obey God before all things when we have a sure and indubitable revelation, . . . in matters of

---

[40] The centrality of obedience in Spinoza's political thought is enunciated with force and clarity by Balibar in *Spinoza and Politics*. See also F. Haddad-Chamakh, "Liberté individuelle et paix civile d'après le *Traité théologico-politique* de Spinoza," and W. Bartuschat, "The Ontological Basis of Spinoza's Theory of Politics," both in *Spinoza's Political and Theological Thought*, ed. C. De Deugd (Amsterdam: North-Holland, 1984).

religion men are especially prone to go astray and contentiously advance many ideas of their own devising." If religion – understood as "judgments and feelings that vary with each individual" – were invested with an authority to compel obedience equal to human law, "nobody would be bound to [the state and its laws] if he considered [them] to be contrary to his own faith and superstitious belief, and so on this pretext everyone could assume unrestricted freedom to do as he pleases." In this way, Spinoza holds, "the right of state" would be "utterly destroyed" (TTP, 189). "Acts of piety," therefore, "and the outward forms of religion . . . must be determined only by [political] sovereigns," while "the inward worship of God and piety itself belong to the sphere of individual right" (TTP, 219).

Spinoza's preoccupation with obedience has been seen to go hand in hand with his promulgation of two truths throughout the TTP, for it is in the realm of obedience that he is especially thought to be speaking to the discrete problem of the multitude. It is the multitude above all that must be instructed in the value of obedience, for as Spinoza notoriously observes, if everyone were able to live solely according to the dictates of reason, there would no need for laws at all: "nothing would be required but to teach men true moral doctrine, and they would then act to their true advantage of their own accord, whole-heartedly and freely" (TTP, 64). The laws exist to control and educate those incapable of living according to the dictates of reason alone, and therefore the education of the multitude should be directed toward the inculcation of respect for the law and desire to conform to its norms.

Spinoza *is* convinced that opinions and beliefs cannot be forcefully codified, while actions can, and therefore a state ought to direct its attention to the latter and give up on policing the former. Spinoza's most explicit statement in this regard is that,

since the true purpose of law is usually apparent only to the few and is generally incomprehensible by the great majority in whose lives reason plays little part, in order to constrain all men alike legislators have wisely devised another motive for obedience, far different from that which is necessarily entailed by the nature of law. For those who uphold the law they promised what most appeals to the masses, while threatening transgressors with dire retribution, thus endeavoring to keep the multitude on a curb, as far as is practicable. (TTP, 50)

The "true purpose of the law" concerns the achievement of self-legislation, the formulation of "a rule of life" with the end in view to expand the range of human power (TTP, 50). But the masses are frequently confused about the causes of their lack of power, and seek in the law simply the furtherance of their own appetites. In this light, laws can only meet the needs of social stability if they construe obedience in terms of reward and punishment. From this standpoint, it is as if freedom itself (construed as freedom of belief, opinion, and expression) is yet one more reward for obeying the law, a concession to the limits of sovereign power and a consolation to the individual, whose "right to reason and judge" goes hand in hand with his or her right to engage in "dissipation, envy, avarice, drunkenness and the like" (TTP, 232, 234).

Even for the masses, however, obedience seems to refer to conduct alone, namely, to the surrender of the "right to act as [one sees] fit" (TTP, 232). For "not only sound reason but experience with its daily examples" shows that the attempt to crush freedom of belief and opinion results not in obedience but in "the disgusting arts of sycophancy and treachery," since "it would thus inevitably follow that in their daily lives men would be thinking one thing and saying another" (TTP, 234). From the standpoint of the state, "the disadvantages in allowing such freedoms" are far outweighed by the benefits, namely the flourishing of the "sciences and the arts" which are the mark of a healthy society (TTP, 234). Moreover, their suppression is not only tyrannical. It is ineffective, since "it would be vain to command a subject to hate one to whom he is indebted for some service, to love one who has done him harm, to refrain from taking offense at insults, from wanting to be free of fear, or from numerous other things that necessarily follow from the laws of human nature" (TTP, 191). And it is destabilizing, "For men in general are so constituted that their resentment is most aroused when beliefs which they think to be true are treated as criminal, and when that which motivates their pious conduct to God and man is accounted as wickedness" (TTP, 234).

Thus it is not incidental that Spinoza's discussion of "internal" freedom in chapter 20 of the TTP is entirely from the standpoint of the futility of the attempt to control people's inner life. The force of these passages is directed not only to the capabilities of the multitude but to the limits of tyranny, and the radically unhappy political consequences of laws designed to ensure conformity of opinion:

If no man . . . can give up his freedom to judge and think as he pleases, and everyone is by absolute natural right the master of his own thoughts, it follows that utter failure will attend any attempt in a commonwealth to force men to speak only as prescribed by the sovereign despite their different and opposing opinions. (TTP, 231)

Hence, "however much sovereigns are believed to possess unlimited right and to be the interpreters of law and piety, they will never succeed in preventing men from exercising their own particular judgments on any matters whatsoever and from being influenced by a variety of emotions." The enforcement of obedience in the realm of belief and ideas produces just the opposite of what obedience is intended to encourage, viz., peace, loyalty, and docility (TTP, 234).[41] In sum, he declares, "the most tyrannical government will be one where the individual is denied the freedom to express and communicate to others what he thinks, and a moderate government is one where this freedom is granted to every man" (TTP, 231).

Spinoza's concepts of obedience and "outer" conformity are, then, complemented by a conception of "inner" freedom, a carefully circumscribed domain that is directed toward providing the soil for legitimate intellectual achievements, as well as a constant outlet for all of the diverse and often irrational views of the populace. This works at the level of both political obedience and religious obedience. In the first case, the law is human political law, and conformity of behavior refers to obeying the laws of the state. In the second case, the law is the divine law of God, and conformity of behavior refers to obeying the maxims of justice and charity. In both cases, the point seems the same: the law is a constraint, even a restraint, for those whose actions would otherwise be a threat to stability and peace, and has nothing really to do with enlightened existence. For "if men were so constituted by nature as to desire nothing but what is prescribed by true reason, society would stand in no need of any laws" (TTP, 64). Thus this notion of law leads to the view that even the divine law, which Spinoza calls the "highest blessedness," is itself nothing but a prolegomenon to philosophical blessedness (the love of God as the "supreme good," beyond law) and thus that religious and political obedience are ultimately the same thing, the first simply the handmaid and guarantor of the second (TTP, 51).

Obedience, however, is not simply about a useful or even semi-rational conformity, but is the key to Spinoza's notion of independence, *libertas*. For obedience (both political and religious) has two senses for Spinoza, and the difference between enlightened and unenlightened existence does not involve transcending obedience to the law, but rather resisting this very notion of purely external lawfulness – obedience as what he calls "obsequiousness" (*assentatio*) as opposed to honesty (*fides*) (TTP, 236). What obeying the state and obeying God share is the fact that both can either be true or false; both depend on a distinction between an obedience that is (merely) constraining, in which freedom and law are opposed (law

---

[41] Citing Seneca, but equally echoing Machiavelli, Spinoza's more immediate interlocutor here, the point is that "'violenta imperia nemo continuit diu'–tyrannical governments never last long" (TTP, 184).

as the enunciation of rewards and punishments and freedom as the power to disobey the law), and an obedience that is (also) liberating, in which freedom and law are at best congruent and mutually sustaining (freedom *as* obedience to the law). What Spinoza shows is that, if both the divine and human laws are manmade, revealed, created (from nothing), to obey these laws is ultimately to obey one's very self (the law one gives to oneself; the sovereignty that is the self).

In this light, religious obedience can be interpreted as a form of political crowd management only if religion is conflated with superstition – in other words, if religion is regarded simply as a useful political tool to achieve the docility of the masses.[42] But this is precisely, I showed, what Spinoza thinks only the self-aggrandizing theologians do. It is not simply that religion is an equivocal force in this respect for Spinoza. It is that obedience is itself equally and distinctly a problem in its own right, not only as that which is connected to social stability but also that which bears a crucial relationship to blessedness.

Freedom

While freedom of expression is indeed a major concern of Spinoza's in the TTP, as well as, of course, in his own life, this is not the only notion of freedom he is operating with. As he states in the preface, his concern is not only to show that "freedom [can] be granted without endangering piety and the peace of the commonwealth, but also that the peace of the commonwealth and piety depend on this freedom" (TTP, 3). The question is, what exactly is the nature of this "dependence"? If the first clause, as a point addressed to the nature and causes of social instability, can be seen as pragmatically true of all political regimes, the second is a different kind of claim, for it is not a matter simply of "granting" freedom but about freedom being built into the very nature of a commonwealth. This is surely specific to what Spinoza thinks of as the "best" kind of political regime – a notion not only of the extension and limits of popular speech, but a conception of liberty that a social order positively enhances and a conception of a common good where peace is not only about the absence of strife (e.g., the elimination of superstition) but about something

---

[42] See Den Uyl, who argues that "for Spinoza religion has no supernatural character and thus possesses no 'higher' claim on the behavior of men than any other device that might be used to move them. Indeed, Spinoza is quite clear that religious rituals have nothing to do with salvation, but are rather merely useful devices in obtaining obedience" (*Power, State, and Freedom*, 29). The fact that religion is not supernatural, however, does not imply for Spinoza that it has only an instrumental claim on human beings.

more concretely "in common" than simply the freedom to express one-self, however precious this also is. Indeed, as Spinoza frames the issue,

[The state's] ultimate purpose is not to exercise dominion nor to restrain men by fear and deprive them of independence, but on the contrary to free every man from fear so that he may live in security as far as is possible, that is, so that he may best preserve his own natural right to exist and to act, without harm to himself and to others. It is not, I repeat, the purpose of the state to transform men from rational beings into beasts or puppets, but rather to enable them to develop their mental and physical faculties in safety, to use their reason without restraint and to refrain from the strife and the vicious mutual abuse that are prompted by hatred, anger, or deceit. Thus the purpose of the state is, in reality, freedom. (TTP, 231–232)

In most of its essential points, this paragraph could have been written by Hobbes: security, the elimination of strife, the ability to use reason without restraint, the cultivation of autonomy – none of these are any different from Hobbes's conception of political existence and so-called negative liberty. However, for Spinoza, unlike Hobbes, security is achieved by "preserving" natural right (even as it is transferred to the sovereign), not by forfeiting it. As he says in laying out the basis of the state, "actions under orders – that is, obedience – is indeed to some extent an infringement of freedom" (TTP, 184). But the question is, in what sense? What is the difference between the freedom that individuals possess by natural right (*de iure naturali*) and the freedom that is granted to them by a sovereign (*de iure civili*)?

Spinoza's political theory, while sharing some fundamental features in common with that of Hobbes, is distinguished most basically by Spinoza's identification of natural right with power. While both thinkers hold that human beings have a natural right to try to preserve themselves as far as they can, and the right "to use any means and to do any action" to achieve this end, Hobbes's conception is of a right granted to all men equally, and therefore it is a right that is essentially (naturally) limited.[43] For while I have the right to do anything it is in my power to do to preserve myself, I nevertheless do not possess the right to deprive someone else of her right to preserve herself unless she directly threatens me (or seems to do so). As Hobbes puts it, "things are done *by right of nature*, and are held to be so done, if they necessarily contribute to the protection of life and limb."[44] While "the natural tendency of men [is] to exasperate each other, the source of which is the passions and especially an empty self-esteem," right is something entirely different, namely "the liberty each

---

[43] Hobbes, *On the Citizen*, I: 7 and 8, 27.   [44] *On the Citizen*, I: 10, 28.

man has of using his natural faculties *in accordance with right reason.*"[45]
It is not contrary to reason that human beings do everything they can
do to preserve themselves, but their power extends more widely than
this, including being aggressive toward others simply for the purpose of
domination. Thus "a person may sin against the Natural Laws . . . if
he claims that something contributes to his self-preservation, but does
not believe that it does so."[46] It is precisely because we have a natural
tendency to do so – to dominate others simply for reasons of glory – that
Hobbes conceives the original social contract (which presumes natural
right) to be constructed on the basis of fear. Rejecting the notion that
human beings seek society out of a desire for friendship or love of one's
neighbor, Hobbes's view is that it is a law of nature itself "to seek peace
when some hope of having peace exists, and to seek aid for war when
peace cannot be had," to which end human beings consent together to
transfer their natural right to a sovereign who can guarantee the security
of all.[47]

Spinoza agrees that it makes no sense to speak of some original fellow
feeling. But in contrast to Hobbes, he rejects both the notion of equality
in the state of nature (on which Hobbes founds his notion of right) and
the notion that the origin of social existence involves rational deliberation
(consent). From the perspective of nature alone, according to Spinoza,
the "right of every man is determined not by sound reason, but by his
desire and power." Every individual's freedom in this sense extends precisely as far as his or her power, and is limited only by his or her weakness.
Natural freedom is therefore theoretically absolute: it is absolute in the
sense that it is not guided by anything other than pure self-interest (it is
devoid of notions of duty as much as notions of reason or even common
sense), and it is absolute in the sense that it is unlimited by anything other
than what the power of the individual can bring about:

Thus whatever every man, when he is considered as solely under the dominion
of Nature, believes to be to his advantage, whether under the guidance of sound
reason or under passion's sway, he may by sovereign natural right seek and get
for himself by any means, by force, deceit, entreaty, or in any other way he best
can, and he may consequently regard as his enemy anyone who tries to hinder
him from getting what he wants. (TTP, 180)

As Spinoza vividly puts it, the identification of power and right in nature
implies that men are "no more in duty bound to live according to the
laws of a sound mind than a cat to live according to the laws of a lion's
nature" (TTP, 180).

---

[45] *On the Citizen*, I: 12 and 7 (emphasis added), 29, 27.
[46] *On the Citizen*, I: 10, III: 27, 28, 53.   [47] *On the Citizen*, I: 15, 31.

Nevertheless, Spinoza continues,

> if we also reflect that the life of men without mutual assistance must necessarily be most wretched and must lack the cultivation of reason . . . for there is no one whose life is free from anxiety in the midst of feuds, hatred, anger and deceit . . . it will become quite clear to us that, in order to achieve a secure and good life, men had necessarily to unite in one body. (TTP, 181)

This is not the view that individuals agree to forfeit the immediate good of their natural freedom for the larger good of security. Rather, while natural freedom ("the unrestricted right naturally possessed by each individual" [TTP, 181]) is boundless, it is also constitutively unrealizable, not because, as Hobbes claimed, all have equal power and therefore none are truly safe from being accosted by their neighbor. Rather, for Spinoza, *none* has any power. In the context of nature as whole, natural right is minuscule and irrelevant, and therefore natural freedom, while theoretically absolute, is in fact precisely illusory: "human natural right or freedom is a nonentity as long as it is an individual possession determined by individual power; it exists in imagination rather than in fact" (TP II: 15). Thus Spinoza's point is not that natural freedom (the power to act on one's own counsel) is pragmatically forfeited for a greater good, since what is merely illusory cannot be given up. Rather, the sovereign takes over this theoretical power to act and puts it into "common ownership," thus transferring "the strength and appetite of the individual" to "the power and will of all together" (TTP, 181).

The stronger reason, then, why Spinoza thinks that sovereigns cannot control minds is that the forfeiture of right to the sovereign is a forfeiture of power, and this can never be complete. Even if a sovereign were heedless of the disruptive consequences of suppressing freedom of opinion and expression, and even if it were able to become (however temporarily) the "master" of minds (through terror, for example), its power is necessarily limited by the fact that "nobody can so completely transfer to another all his right, and consequently his power, as to cease to be a human being, nor will there ever be a sovereign power that can do all it pleases" (TTP, 191). The *transfer* is absolute, since human beings possess no power "by nature," but it is constitutively incomplete, because to Spinoza a human being just is a certain quantity of power (*conatus*) relative to other things, and this quantity, while it can be radically reduced, cannot be eliminated (without eliminating the person). In the hypothetical case of a complete transfer of power, it is not simply that a person would no longer possess some feature we consider essential to what a human being is. Spinoza means literally there would be no person left, since it would be the person that was transferred. Nature, in this sense, is itself culture, creation, *factum*. Nature is reserved over against society (the transfer is incomplete) as that which had to become society over against nature (without the transfer, there is no natural power at all).

What is constant is that individuals are directed to pursue what they think is in their own best interests, for "nobody rejects what he judges to be good except through hope of a greater good or fear of greater loss," and further "no one endures any evil except to avoid a greater evil or to gain a greater good." For Spinoza, this is a law that is "so deeply inscribed in human nature that it should be counted among the eternal truths universally known" (TTP, 181). The force of it here is that a society that does not continually satisfy these judgments, whether the "facts necessarily correspond" to them or not – that is, whether or not these judgments are themselves rational – thereby forfeits its "right" (that is, power) to exist at all. The social compact is utterly dependent upon its utility for individuals as they themselves understand this, "without which the agreement automatically becomes null and void" (TTP, 182). In short, a state is legitimate only insofar as it does continue to persuade individuals that it is a greater good than the goods they could have without it, or in some other state.

Another way of seeing Spinoza's point here is to observe that he considers the power of sovereigns along a model similar to that of individuals in the state of nature. The position articulated in TTP, chapter 16 is that the sovereignty of the state, whether it is a theocracy, a monarchy, or a democracy, is always *absolute*.[48] Since a social compact consists of individuals who have surrendered to a sovereign their natural power, this sovereign then assumes the power of the entire collectivity to "compel all by force and coerce them by threat of the supreme penalty, universally feared by all." Like individuals, a sovereign only retains this right "as long as he has this power of carrying into execution whatever he wills; otherwise his rule will be precarious, and nobody who is stronger than he will need to obey him unless he so wishes" (TTP, 183). But also like individuals, sovereigns needn't consult anyone's standard of "right" or "good" except their own:

in a state of nature everyone is bound to live by God's revealed law from the same motive as he is bound to live according to the dictates of sound reason, namely, that to do so is to his greater advantage and necessary for his salvation. He may refuse to do so, but at his own peril. He is thus bound to live according as he himself wills, and no other, and to acknowledge no man as judge or as

---

[48] Cf. TP III: 11: "the right of the state or of the sovereign is nothing but the right of nature itself, and as such determined by power; not however by the power of a single individual, but by that of a people [*multitudinis*] which is guided as if by one mind."

rightful arbitrator over religion. This is the right, I say, that has been retained by the sovereign, who can indeed consult others but is not bound to acknowledge anyone as judge or any person but himself as claiming any right, except a prophet expressly sent by God and proving his mission by indisputable signs. (TTP, 188–189)

This latter proviso once again reiterates Spinoza's point that individuals must obey God above all in all things, but only when they have a "sure and indubitable revelation" that it is in fact God whom they are obeying. Here it proves the rule that the political sovereign has, *mutatis mutandis*, right over all. By the same token, however, the complete and single-minded pursuit of their own self-interest will inevitably lead sovereigns not only to consult but even to pander to the interests of those who are governed. "It should be observed that the government's power is not strictly confined to its power of coercion by fear, but rests on all the possible means by which it can induce men to obey its commands" (TTP, 191–192). As Spinoza says of monarchs, "his main endeavor [is] to win everyone's support" and "to prove his value to his subjects in peace as well as in war. He will thus be most fully possessed of his own right and most firmly seated on his throne, when he gives most heed to the general welfare of his people" (TP VII: 345). On the one hand, "the sovereign power is bound by no law, and all must obey it in all matters . . . even if those orders are quite irrational." On the other hand, no one really needs to worry that much about this absolute submission to another, for sovereigns have an equally absolute incentive to grant freedom and to avoid "unreasonable commands" (TTP, 183–184). Sovereignty is as much about individuals as it is about the state – each is sovereign only in and through the other. Both find that they must seek the inclusion of the other in order to achieve their own ends.

In this light, Spinoza proffers two reasons for preferring democracy to other forms of government. The first is that it is the form of governing that legally grants the point that no one can (by nature) wholly alienate their right/power, and thus it is the form of governing that most satisfies the purpose of entering into common agreement in the first place. Democracy, for Spinoza, is that society – that sovereign – that is formed "without any infringement of natural right" because "in a democratic state nobody transfers his natural right to another so completely that thereafter he is not to be consulted; he transfers it to the majority of the entire community of which he is a part" (TTP, 183, 185). All societies are rooted in their citizens' conviction that the existent social compact constitutes a greater good or provides protection against a greater evil than alternative societies. Monarchies, however, are more likely to become tyrannical, since "a man in whom the whole right of the state has been vested will always be more afraid of his citizens than of external enemies."[49] As Spinoza continues, "he will therefore try to protect himself from them; instead of furthering their interests he will plot against them; and especially against those who have a reputation for wisdom or are too powerful because of their wealth" (TP VI: 6). Such a sovereign is faced with very particular challenges in this light, needing either to provide greater security for its citizens than they could get in a freer state, or at least to *persuade* them that they are more secure than elsewhere: "if sovereignty is invested in a few men or in one alone, he should be endowed with some extraordinary quality, or must at least make every effort to convince the masses of this" (TTP, 65).

Because sovereignty is absolute, for Spinoza, "all men are bound to keep faith even with a tyrant" (TTP, 224).[50] But tyrants have a difficult time holding onto their power:

It is true that sovereigns can by their right treat as enemies all who do not absolutely agree with them on all matters, but the point at issue is not what is their right, but what is to their interest. I grant that by this right they can govern in the most oppressive way and execute citizens on the most trivial pretexts, but no one can imagine that by so doing they are acting in accordance with the judgment of sound reason. Indeed, since they cannot so act without endangering the whole fabric of the state, we can even argue that they do not have the absolute power to do so, and consequently that they do not have the absolute right to do so. (TTP, 231)

It is not that tyrannical regimes do not survive in a limited way and even appear to flourish. Spinoza considers it an established fact that it is rare indeed that tyranny is succeeded by anything but new tyrants. We know from Machiavelli, Spinoza says, "the folly of attempting – as many do – to remove a tyrant when the causes which make a prince a tyrant cannot be removed, but become rooted more firmly as the prince is given more reason to be afraid" (TP V: 7). But the effort and resources that they require to succeed are vastly greater than in a democracy, in which security is attained more naturally and economically, because, as he puts it, "men are impatient above all at being subject to their equals and under their rule . . . Indeed they inevitably rejoice at misfortune or injury to their [violent] ruler even when this involves their own considerable misfortune, and they wish every ill on him, and bring this about when they can"

---

[49] Spinoza gives a much fuller discussion of monarchies in the TP, but the argument is the same in both political works, namely, that the concentration of power in the hands of one man is corrupting. See TTP, 216–217.

[50] Once again, though, the exception "is made in the case of one to whom God, by sure revelation, has promised special help against the tyrant, or has given specific exemption" (TTP, 189–190).

(TTP, 64–65). Acts like treason, for example, involve the usurpation of the "sovereign power's right," but the sovereign power in a democracy is broadly shared, minimizing the risk that one person will either desire or be able to usurp it (TTP, 187). In a more general sense, since right is determined by power alone, a single sovereign never in fact *does* possess the supreme right of the commonwealth, for "the power of one man is far too small to bear so great a burden. The result," according to Spinoza, "is that the man whom the people has chosen as king looks for generals or counsellors or friends to help him, and entrusts them with his own safety and the safety of all; so that the state which is believed to be a pure monarchy is really an aristocracy in practice, but a concealed and not an open one, and therefore of the very worst type" (TP, VI: 5).

The second reason that democracy is preferable, then, is that because of the number of voices admitted into the sovereign power, "there is less danger of a government behaving unreasonably." Spinoza's quite brilliant, if now commonplace, observation is that while states, like individuals, act purely on the basis of self-interest, their "sovereign" (i.e., themselves, taken as a governing body) will be rational at least to some degree, even if the individuals that comprise a democracy are utterly ignorant and thoroughly selfish, "for it is practically impossible for the majority of a single assembly, if it is of some size, to agree on the same piece of folly" (TTP, 184). For this reason, aristocracies are preferable to monarchies in that "the will of so large a council must be determined by reason rather than caprice; since evil passions draw men in different directions, and they can be guided as if by one mind only in so far as they aim at ends which are honourable, or at any rate appear to be so" (TP VIII: 6). But aristocracies are also problematic on this score. Since it is simply "human nature" that everyone "pursues his private advantage with the greatest eagerness . . . and defends another's cause if – but only if – he believes that by doing so he is strengthening his own position," Spinoza recommends that members of an aristocratic council should be chosen with an eye to representing "each class or group of citizens," even if in so doing one does not end up with the most "cultivated" minds. Indeed, those who attempt to fill a council only with the elites of the mind do not avoid "uneducated men," "for every member does his best to secure the appointment of slow-witted colleagues who will hang upon his lips. In large councils there is no opportunity for this" (TP VII: 4).

This is a point of some significance. For while multitudes possess relatively equal dimensions of harmony and strife – while the fact of organizing into a society does little to diminish individual passions and even augments them ("for men, I said, are enemies by nature" [TP VIII: 12]) – and while, further, a democratic state is simply the transference of these passions to an organized social body, it is nevertheless the case that this transference is rational (i.e., it satisfies the conditions of greatest advantage for the multitude itself).[51] To be more precise, whereas for individuals (whether ignorant or enlightened), this transference is reasonable regardless of the kind of polity (given natural disempowerment), democracy is the only form of government that is itself rational, taken as a social body, a kind of singular thing.[52] Only a democracy is by definition (for reasons of survival) actually committed to addressing the problems of strife that plague any social order. Thus only in a democracy can the multitude *become* rational, since it is only if human law is vested in the entire community that the multitude's obedience can be of itself alone rather than of "one to his equal," just as the most free individual is one who is able to act from his or her nature alone (TTP, 65).

It is only in a democracy, then, that real security can be achieved. For a democracy, of all forms of government, has an interest not in *persuading* its citizens that their interests coincide with its interests, but in precisely generating common interests, in devising laws so that "men may be influenced not so much by fear as by hope of some good that they urgently desire; for in this way each will be eager to do his duty" (TTP, 65). Only in a democracy will the self-interest of the state precisely consist in refining and educating individual self-interest to minimize the conflictual passions and to encourage "sound reason" and diversity in a positive sense (TTP, 184). A king or an aristocracy, by contrast, is not invested in the amelioration of these passions to the same degree, and may even strive to keep the multitude as irrational (fearful) as possible in the hopes of better controlling it (though thereby greatly amplifying its own instability).

What characterizes all states, for Spinoza, is a kind of negotiated balance between autonomy and conformity. Since "opinions vary as much as tastes," they should be free to flourish in every way (TTP, 230). But since human beings "for the most part . . . are determined [to act] only by fleshy desire . . . which take[s] no account of the future or of other considerations . . . no society can subsist without government and coercion, and consequently without laws to control and restrain men's lusts and their unbridled urges" (TTP, 64).

[51] See also TP III: 6: "the political order is naturally established to remove general fear and to dispel general suffering, and thus its chief aim is one which every rational man would try to promote in the state of nature; though his efforts in that state would be useless."

[52] Cf. Hobbes's argument that "whether a Common-wealth be Monarchicall, or Popular, the Freedome is still the same": *Leviathan*, 149. (I am indebted to Quentin Skinner for this reference: "The Idea of Negative Liberty," in *Philosophy and History*, ed. Richard Rorty, J. B. Schneewind, and Quentin Skinner [Cambridge: Cambridge University Press, 1984], 208.) On the difference for Hobbes between the kinds of commonwealths, see *Leviathan*, ch. 19, 129–138.

The problem with this notion of freedom, however, and the reason it has led to the view that Spinoza is mainly interested in controlling the behavior of the multitude, is that prima facie it is not very Spinozistic: "in a democracy (which comes closest to the natural state) all the citizens undertake to act, but not to reason and to judge, by decision made in common" (TTP, 236). Construed as a divorce between the inside and the outside of a person, the right "to reason and to judge" seems pretty trivial if this right doesn't extend beyond the boundaries of the individual, and conversely, the right to command conformity of actions seems equally trivial if it stops at this boundary. The issue is not even that this picture of the individual and the polity is un-Spinozistic with respect to works other than the TTP, e.g., the identity of mind and body from the *Ethics*. The point is that it does not accord with other things Spinoza says in the TTP, i.e., it does not accord with Spinoza's conception of democratic sovereignty whereby an individual's obedience is essentially to be commanded by him- or herself (TTP, 65). It does not even accord with his notion of absolute sovereignty in general, whether democratic or not, for Spinoza says very clearly that "obedience is not so much a matter of outward act as internal act of mind. Therefore he who whole-heartedly resolves to obey another in all his commands is fully under another's dominion, and consequently he who reigns over his subjects' minds holds the most powerful dominion" (TTP, 192). By the same token, Spinoza insists that "words can be treasonable as well as deeds; and so, while it is impossible to deprive subjects completely of this freedom, to grant it unreservedly could have the most disastrous consequences" (TTP, 231).[53]

It is not that Spinoza has no notion of private life or a private sphere of decision-making or private beliefs. On the contrary, he is a vigorous defender not only of "the freedom to philosophise" but also simply of the right of "every man [to] think as he pleases, and say what he thinks" (TTP, 234, 230). The point is that the extent to which this realm is completely divorced from public life depends on the nature of the state – the sovereign – itself. If it is true that a state has the absolute right to determine how far freedom of political beliefs can extend, this extension is not separate from the health of the polity as such – the stronger and more plural it is, the more difference it can tolerate in the public and not just the private sphere:

---

[53] Balibar's account of obedience in the TTP and the *Ethics* takes up in detail the fruitful contradictions inherent in Spinoza's theologico-political project overall: *Spinoza and Politics*, esp. ch. 2 and 4.

What greater misfortune can be imagined for a state than that honourable men should be exiled as miscreants because their opinions are at variance with authority and they cannot disguise the facts? What can be more calamitous than that men should be regarded as enemies and put to death, not for any crime or misdeed, but for being independent of mind? (TTP, 235)

Spinoza's concern is not only to defend the right of "independent" minds to say what they like. He defends just as strongly (albeit with considerably less passion) those whose minds are dependent and weak, i.e., those who are subject to "dissipation, envy, avarice, drunkenness, and the like" (TTP, 234). The point is very simply that "the less freedom of judgment is conceded to men, the further their distance from the most natural state, and consequently the more oppressive the regime" (TTP, 236).

But therefore Spinoza's interest is not only in freedom of belief, regardless of what beliefs they may happen to be. He thinks it is absurd and harmful to legislate in the area of belief (TTP, 234–235), but this does not mean he doesn't hold out the possibility that beliefs can be reformed, i.e., made into "rational convictions" (TTP, 232). The point for Spinoza is not to turn everyone into a philosopher. But it is only insofar as beliefs are reformed – made free in a constructive sense – that societies can benefit along with their members. Beliefs are *also* free, but they are not the locus of true freedom, the freedom that it is the state's "ultimate purpose" to enact, the freedom, in other words, that *is* of actual and measurable utility to the state. The freedom to "reason and to judge," for Spinoza, means precisely the freedom to call existing laws into question, "provided one does no more than express or communicate one's opinion, defending it through rational conviction alone." The only body that actually makes and repeals laws, of course, is the sovereign body. But "if a man maintains that a certain law is against sound reason," he may "therefore "advocate its repeal," at the same time "submit[ing] his opinion to the judgement of the sovereign power." In so doing, as long as "meanwhile [he] does nothing contrary to what is commanded by that law, he deserves well of the state, acting as a good citizen should do" (TTP, 232). This is not as conservative as it sounds. Spinoza is claiming that "judgments" – rational ones – are efficacious with respect to social change. This is to say nothing less than that the more rational judgments there are in a given society – and the more "good citizens" take it upon themselves to challenge laws as they see fit – the better. A state, then, has to insist on the one hand on lawful behavior, without which it would instantly disintegrate. But it must also ensure that the greatest possible number of "rational convictions" expressed by the populace are enshrined in these laws. There is a tendency, in other words, in the very notion of the state itself, whether democratic or not, to attempt to include as many voices in the law as possible, purely for self-interested reasons.

The key to Spinoza's notion of freedom – and its relationship to good government – is that he considers obedience structural not volitional. It is not about the individual acting in accordance with the sovereign *as an individual*, i.e., as someone who could choose to act otherwise, but rather about someone who has already granted to the sovereign the right to determine through law the direction of action itself:

It is not the motive for obedience, but the fact of obedience, that constitutes a subject. Whatever be the motives that prompt a man to obey the commands of the sovereign power, whether it be fear of punishment, hope of reward, love of country or any other emotion, while it is he who makes the decision, he is nevertheless acting under the control of the sovereign power. From the fact, then, that a man acts from his own decision, we should not forthwith conclude that his action proceeds from his own right, and not from the right of the government. For whether a man is urged by love or driven by fear of a threatened evil, since in both cases his action always proceeds from his own intention and decision, either there can be no such thing as sovereignty and right over subjects or else it must include all the means that contribute to men's willingness to obey. Consequently, whenever a subject acts in accordance with the commands of the sovereign power . . . he acts from the ruler's right, not from his own. (TTP, 192)

This crucial passage addresses two of the questions that have been alive thus far. First, it makes clear why individual enlightenment is tied to the quality and nature of the sovereign; why, for example, the achievement of understanding in a tyranny is so difficult. One can come at this question from the metaphysical side by recalling Spinoza's connection of understanding and the power (independence) of the body. But here he takes the opposite route, ironically emphasizing freedom of mind in the TTP and freedom of body in the *Ethics*. For Spinoza is saying here that minds cannot be free unless the sovereign is free, because sovereigns control minds; or at least, as he further nuances it, although "command cannot be exercised over minds in the same way as over tongues," still "experience abundantly testifies [that affects of love, hate, belief, and so on] often proceed from the authoritative nature of the sovereign power and from his guidance, that is, from his right" (TTP, 192). A democratic sovereign, on this model, is not simply a sovereign that allows freedom of belief and expression, or even freedom of action within the bounds of the law. It is, rather, a sovereign that "guides," a sovereign that understands its own "mind" to be enlarged by the minds of its members.

The second thing that this passage makes clear is that the relationship between what Spinoza calls a "son" and a "subject" is one of

continuity. Spinoza tells us here that regardless of one's motives for obedience, sovereignty just is the fact of obedience. But we will always, he
also implies, have some motive or other for doing so, both depending on
who the sovereign is and depending on our own experiences. Obedience
itself, then, can either be free or unfree. In other words, the second claim
about obedience is that, while it does indeed depend on the state, it also
depends on the individual. It is more than possible to be unfree in a free
state. While a democracy, as above, may have an interest in my freedom
(for its own ends, if not for mine also), I am perfectly free not to take advantage of alleviating my own wretchedness and superstition. What this
means is that the difference between unenlightenment and enlightenment
is one of degree. Passions we never get rid of. But we can strive to act less
and less from disabling motives – we can strive, therefore, not to become
less obedient, but to transform our obedience into something that is also
freedom; to transform *servitus* into *libertas*.

Obedience, then, is not about "outward behavior" alone. "Indeed,"
Spinoza says, "as long as a man is acting in accordance with the sovereign's
decrees, he cannot be acting against the decree and dictates of his own
reason; for it was with the full approval of reason that he resolved to
transfer to the sovereign his right to live by his own judgment" (TTP,
233). This is not to say that every citizen will agree with all the sovereign's
laws, for not all people at all times will be convinced that they constitute a
greater good, which is why it is in the interests of the state to educate (or
coercively persuade) the populace. Democracy is always Spinoza's ideal
here, for only in a democracy will education be about the revelation of the
actual connection of individual goods with social goods, as opposed to
simply persuading individuals that this is so. But the language of "ideal"
here is very intentional, because Spinoza thinks it is neither desirable nor
possible to eradicate differences at the level of belief.

What he means to describe is a state that is inherently, though fruitfully,
unstable; a state that is constantly being adjusted in order to protect itself;
a state whose very stability depends on its mutability (from a lesser to a
greater perfection, the Spinoza of the *Ethics* might say); a state that is continually demanding obedience to a law that is continually being remade,
and in the context of which freedom is an expression of a commitment
to obey the law while obedience is itself a form of freedom (increasingly
coming to act, as the *Ethics* says, from our selves alone). When Spinoza
says that the "purpose of the state is, in reality, freedom," he means much
more than that no one can be made to think according to the authorities. He means in fact that the democratic state is actively and positively
dependent upon the cultivation of free and diverse judgments, and that
these, far from being "private," are the very foundation of law.

It is only in a repressive regime that the "good of the state" and the "good of the individual" will contradict one another. It is only in a repressive state that thought and action will be divorced such that obedience is something merely external, "for as long as men act only from fear, they are doing what they are most opposed to doing, taking no account of the usefulness and the necessity of the action to be done, concerned only not to incur capital or other punishment" (TTP, 64). Conversely it is only in a democracy where these can overlap, however incompletely. The instability of the state is not due to the incongruity between individual freedom and social security, but to their congruity. The interests of individuals overlap with (or are taken over by) those of the state, but only ever incompletely, even or especially in a democracy where the interest of the state is to maximize individuality, for there can never be a power so sovereign "that it can do all it pleases" (TTP, 191). Sovereignty, then, is absolute, but it is most fully enacted in an incomplete and changeable form. As with the physical body, viz., "Whatever so disposes the human Body that it can be affected in a great many ways, or renders it capable of affecting external Bodies in a great many ways, is useful to man" (E IV p38), so the social body: "the right of a commonwealth is determined by the power of a people guided as if by one mind; but this union of minds is quite inconceivable unless the commonwealth does its best to achieve those conditions which sound reason declares to be for the good of all men," among which the "power of judgement" is the first (TP III: 7–8). The inward is outward, for Spinoza, and the outward is inward. No state is permanent, but a repressive one much less so than a democratic one. As with the portrait of the individual in the *Ethics*, political enlightenment is not about the achievement of some rational moment of stasis or balance. It is just the opposite. The perfection of the state implies that it is a breathing entity, one that, like any organism, naturally and inevitably comes to an end and one whose endurance is therefore an *achievement*, a function of effort.

4 Reason, revelation, and the case of the Hebrews

> [W]hether we consider religion to be revealed by the natural light or by prophecy; the proof applies in all cases, since religion is the same and equally revealed by God in whatever way we suppose men have come to know it.
> (TTP, 220)

> [W]e must concede without qualification that the divine law began from the time when men by express covenant promised to obey God in all things, thereby surrendering, as it were, their natural freedom and transferring their right to God in the manner we described in speaking of the civil state.
> (TTP, 188)

The pacts

Despite Spinoza's rigorous argument for the rational ends of the democratic state, there are at least two conceptual dilemmas in his notion of its origins that have bothered most recent readers of the TTP, especially those reading it with the TP in mind.[1] First, if human beings are so powerless individually, if in fact, as Spinoza seems to suggest, power itself (and thus natural right) does not preexist some form of sociality, what sense can a conception of a contract (*pactum*) have? This is not the question of whether the state of nature could actually have existed (historically), but simply a problem with the explanatory power of the model, its ability, in other words, to account for the rights that people possess in the social body, as it does in Hobbes. For Hobbes, to say that human beings possess rights in the state of nature is to say that these rights are more fundamental than – and should not be transgressed by – the state. If for Spinoza there are no rights to speak of in nature, and thus no rights the state should not transgress, what is the logic of the language of a transfer? How is the power that people possess in a social body understood through the power that they possess – or don't possess – in nature? Second, if there

---

[1] See especially Den Uyl, *Power, State, and Freedom*, 20–65; Balibar, "*Jus-Pactum-Lex*"; Matheron, "The Theoretical Function of Democracy in Spinoza and Hobbes"; and Haddad-Chamakh, "Liberté individuelle."

is some kind of recognition in the state of nature that things could be better, i.e., more amenable to self-preservation, what can such recognition consist in? If, unlike Hobbes, it is not a rational deliberation about the best means to secure self-preservation (again, implying that rationality is more fundamental than other socially specific faculties), what kind of a deliberation, or decision, is it? While it may be the case that if *we* reflect on the life of human beings in the state of nature, it will be clear to *us* that it was better, indeed essential, to have banded together into "one body," it is much less clear how this could have motivated such human beings themselves. If by definition human beings in the state of nature are ruled almost entirely by appetite, on what basis do they band together in this way?

Both dilemmas begin with what Spinoza says immediately following his claim that, due to the wretchedness of life "without mutual assistance," "[human beings] therefore arranged that the unrestricted right naturally possessed by each individual should be put into common ownership":

Yet in this they would have failed, had appetite been their only guide (for by the laws of appetite all men are drawn in different directions), and so they had to bind themselves by the most stringent pledges to be guided in all matters only by the dictates of reason (which nobody ventures openly to oppose, lest he should appear to be without capacity to reason) and to keep appetite in check in so far as it tends to another's hurt, to do to no one what they would not want done to themselves, and to uphold another's right as they would their own. (TTP, 181)

According to this passage, the state of nature is not entirely bereft of reason (or at least the desire to appear rational, which itself seems incommensurate with the urging of appetite alone), and thus we may surmise that, like Hobbes, Spinoza considers human beings in this state to be capable of some kind of calculation of what is in their best interests. The palpable experience of being unable to live on their own, i.e., wretchedness, simply drove human beings to band together in a more organized way than they naturally found themselves. Having done so, it was obvious to them that in order for this banding together to be permanently obligatory (*debeat ut ratum fixumque*), they had to "bind themselves by the most stringent pledges" (*firmissime statuere et pacisci*) to keep their appetites in check (G III: 191). If appetite had, in a sense, gotten them there in the first place, it is possible to regard it as recommending its own self-limitation, for although individuals may not see the advantage in suppressing their own appetites, they can want others to by the "logic" of appetite alone, and can therefore want to devise some way of ensuring and regulating this suppression. Such a contract, and the submission to a sovereign – whether one man, a group of men, or the community as a whole – need not, then, make reference to something other than appetite itself; or, rather, appetite itself contains a rational dimension. As Spinoza notes, this submission "to the will of the sovereign" is made both "by force of necessity and by the persuasion of reason itself" (TTP, 183).

This notion that appetite, conceived as the pursuit of advantage, is itself rational squares with Spinoza's claim that "we may therefore conclude that no one [ever] does anything contrary to the precept of his reason" (TP III: 6). But then, it becomes difficult to know how to interpret Spinoza's insistence that nature gives human beings *nothing else* but "the urging of appetite alone," and indeed denies them "the actualised power to live according to sound reason" (TTP, 180).[2] It seems either that what Spinoza means by reason in the above passage is an attenuated version of what he elsewhere considers rational, attenuated precisely by appetites that don't always judge advantage correctly, or he means that this pursuit of social existence is fully rational because it *is* correctly in our best interests, and this we cannot avoid perceiving, even in a state of nature. It is, therefore, like all rational judgments, something that is common to all and may properly, if only in hindsight, be considered rational in the highest sense.

This quandary appears to illuminate the crux of the difference between the TTP and the TP, for in the TP Spinoza seems to give up the attempt to account for the origin of the social body altogether, noting that:

Since men . . . are led more by passion than by reason, their natural motive for uniting and being guided as if by one mind is not reason but some common passion; common hope, or common fear, or a common desire to avenge some common injury . . . But since all men fear isolation, because no isolated individual has enough power to defend himself and procure the necessaries of life, they desire political society by nature, and can never dissolve it entirely. (TP VI: 1)

Spinoza's claim in the TP, in other words, is that we needn't account for the origins of society by way of a pact at all. Political society is itself a fact of nature – desired by nature and indeed irreducible. Thus the fact that men are powerless by nature and totally led by passion shouldn't concern us, since they are always already, by these very facts, in some form of mutual dependence. As I quoted in the Introduction, "since all men, savage and civilized alike, everywhere enter into social relations and form some sort of civil order, the causes and natural foundations of the

---

[2] Den Uyl points out that the locution "his reason" "seems to imply that reason may vary from individual to individual," even though "Spinoza himself will usually regard reason as something that is conceptually common to all men" (as in E IV p35: "only insofar as men live according to the guidance of reason, must they always agree in nature") (*Power, State, and Freedom*, 59 ff.).

state are not to be sought in the precepts of reason, but must be deduced from the common nature or constitution of men" (TP I: 7). According to some commentators, this passage makes clear that the challenge is not to account for the origins of sociality per se, but to account for the movement from one form of dependence, which remains uncertain and relatively chaotic, to a form of dependence that is regular and stable.[3]

Is the problem, then, precisely the very model of the pact, a problem that Spinoza solves, by simply abandoning it, in the TP? This has been the response taken by some of the readers of Spinoza's political theory.[4] But the TTP itself contains apparently conflicting notions of the state of nature, and thus conflicting notions both of whether a pact is possible, and, if possible, what it consists in.[5] The TTP, in other words, reveals just as clearly as the TP that in some basic sense the model of the state of nature (and thus the contract) is deeply problematic given the notion of individual powerlessness, and therefore given some sense of a primitive and irreducible dependence. If one is going to claim that Spinoza simply changed his mind about the existence or nonexistence of an original pact, one still has to grapple with what clearly is a tension internal to the TTP.[6] More strongly, the contention that the pact is unnecessary because human beings are always already in some kind of social relationship fails to address the fundamental issue. For the issue is not how society came about, to which one can simply respond that, on Spinoza terms, it didn't and couldn't have. This, after all, is just as true of Hobbes and Rousseau – it is true of the state of nature theories in general. The issue is, what is society? Asking about its origins is the same thing as asking about its meaning; asking where it "came from" is the same as asking what it requires of us; what is changeable and not changeable; what is natural and what unnatural.

The apparent inconsistencies concerning the role of rationality in the creation of the pact are less revealing on their own than the fact that the

---

[3] See especially Matheron, *Individu et communauté chez Spinoza*, 318 ff., and "Le Problème de l'évolution de Spinoza du *Traité théologico-politique* au *Traité politique*," in *Spinoza: Issues and Directions*, ed. Edwin Curley and Pierre-François Moreau (Leiden: E. J. Brill, 1990), 258–270.

[4] To some degree this is a position advanced by Matheron and Balibar. For its sharpest articulation (that Spinoza is simply in contradiction), see A. G. Wernham in his introduction to *The Political Works*, 26.

[5] On the ways in which the TTP and the TP contain similar problems, and can be harmonized in most important respects, see Den Uyl, *Power, State, and Freedom*, 38–65.

[6] Balibar's position is that the TTP presents us with explicit contradictions ("*Jus-Pactum-Lex*," 176). His point is a different one than Den Uyl's, because while Den Uyl seeks to harmonize the two treatises by harmonizing the claims internal to the TTP, for Balibar the TTP's contradictions are both intentional and productive, illustrating Spinoza's insistence that the state of nature is not, once and for all, overcome or escaped in civil society, even as it still does make sense to speak of some kind of difference between the two realms.

pact functions in the TTP not only to account for the origins of civil society, but also to account for the origins of the divine law, i.e., for the obedience that human beings owe to God. We saw in the last chapter that Spinoza thinks that even the divine law, which is of "universal application," is "manmade." In chapter 16, this notion receives a more explicit explanation: "the divine law began from the time when men by express covenant promised to obey God in all things, thereby surrendering, as it were, their natural freedom and transferring their right to God in the manner we described in speaking of the civil state" (TTP, 188). In this passage, Spinoza conceives the pact with God to be something all human beings make, a kind of transfer that speaks, as does the pact between human and human, to something functional and not historical. He notes that he "shall later treat of these matters at greater length." However, when he turns to do so, in chapter 17, he changes the narrative, making the pact with God something one particular nation makes in a certain time and place. This key passage is worth quoting in its entirety:

after their departure from Egypt, the Hebrews were no longer bound by the laws of any other nation, but were free to establish new laws as they pleased, and to occupy whatever lands they wished. For after their liberation from the intolerable oppression of the Egyptians, being bound by no covenant to any mortal man they regained their natural right over everything that lay within their power, and every man could decide afresh whether to regain it or to surrender it and transfer it to another. Finding themselves thus placed in a state of nature, they hearkened to Moses, in whom they placed the greatest confidence, and resolved to transfer their right not to any mortal man but to God. Without much hesitation they all promised, equally and with one voice, to obey God absolutely in all his commands and to acknowledge no other law but that which he should proclaim as such by prophetic revelation. Now this promise, or transference of right to God was made in the same way as we have previously conceived it to be made in the case of an ordinary community when men decide to surrender their natural right. For it was by express covenant and oath (Exod. 24: 7) that they surrendered their natural right and transferred it to God, which they did freely, not by forcible coercion or fear of threats. Furthermore, to ensure that the covenant should be fixed and binding with no suspicion of deceit, God made no covenant with them until they had experienced his wonderful power which alone had saved them, and which alone might save them in time to come (Exod. 19: 4, 5). For it was through this very belief, that God's power alone could save them, that they transferred to God all their natural power of self-preservation – which they probably thought they themselves had hitherto possessed – and consequently all their right." (TTP, 195)

There are two crucial questions that emerge from looking at this passage together with the one from chapter 16. First, there is the question of the relationship between the pact that all human beings make with God and the pact the Hebrews make with God. Is the latter an illustration of the

former, or is it a different kind of pact? Second, there is the question
of the relationship between the pact with God (in either case) and the
civil pact among humankind. Spinoza says in the passages from both
chapter 16 and chapter 17 that the pact with God is made in the same
manner – in the same way – as in the case of civil society. This means, he
tells us, that in the pact with God, as in the civil pact, individuals surrender
their natural right/power. The question then is, what is the order of the
two pacts? On this question, the chapters differ from each other.

In chapter 16, on the origins of the state, Spinoza does not relate which
pact is prior (either in time or value). They are both unnatural in the
sense that no one knows "by nature that he has any duty to obey" either
God or a political sovereign (TTP, 188). Sovereignty just is the ability
to command obedience, and in both cases, Spinoza says emphatically,
this is made (created), not found (given naturally). But he does not tell
us which pact comes first, and in fact, the pact with God is intended
precisely to deny at least one way of constructing the priority of divine to
human law, namely the notion that God's laws are known to the mind by
nature; the notion that natural (moral) law is something extracovenantal.[7]
On the contrary, says Spinoza, the idea that "we cannot [in nature] inflict
injury on another and live solely by the laws of appetite . . . without doing
wrong" (i.e., sin) is not a maxim we can find in nature itself. It has an
origin, before which the maxim is simply not binding (though it may be
prudent). Only law creates justice, as above, and even with a contract,
it is binding only insofar as a sovereign "has this power of carrying into
execution whatever he wills; otherwise his rule will be precarious, and
nobody who is stronger than he will need to obey him" (TTP, 183). But
while it is unclear which pact comes first – or implied that they come into
existence together – it *is* clear that God alone never possesses the power to
command obedience to his own law. Rather, it is political sovereigns who
are charged with commanding obedience (TTP, 226–227). Conversely,
political sovereigns possess the power to command obedience to *their*
laws only insofar as those laws are moral: inclusive, democratic, just – in
Spinoza's terms, divine. Without the other, each would fail to command
anything.

In chapter 17, on the Hebrew commonwealth, the pact with God *is*
figured as prior to the pact with a political leader, though prior in what
Spinoza calls a suppositional or theoretical (*opinione*) sense (TTP, 196).
Having left Egypt and the state of slavery, the Hebrews "regained their

---

[7] This goes, too, for Spinoza's statement in the *Ethics* that "the human Mind has an adequate knowledge of God's eternal and infinite essence" (E II p47). In other words, this
knowledge the mind possesses "by nature" is so only by virtue of the pact that Spinoza
describes in the TTP; that is, by virtue of the *causa sui*.

natural right," i.e., they found themselves "thus placed in [a] state of nature," and transferred this right/power to God, approaching "God on equal terms to hear what he wished to command" (TTP, 195, 196). The caveat is that this pact with God, according to which God was the sole sovereign over the Hebrews and "civil law and religion . . . were one and the same thing," was instantly abrogated. For, "on this first appearance before God they were so terrified and so thunderstruck at hearing God speak that they thought their last hour had come. So, overwhelmed with fear they went to Moses," and, as Deuteronomy relates, they asked Moses to act in their place. As Spinoza puts it, "by this they clearly abrogated [*aboleverunt*] the first covenant [*primum pactum*], making an absolute transfer [*absolute transtulerunt*] to Moses of their right to consult God and to interpret his decrees . . . Therefore Moses was left as the sole lawgiver," that is, the "supreme sovereign" (*supremam majestatem*) of the Hebrews (TTP, 197, G III: 207). While on the one hand, "this form of government could be called a theocracy, its citizens being bound only by such law as was revealed by God," it was Moses who held the sole power to interpret those laws and to act on God's behalf. Therefore, Spinoza says, this theocracy "was a matter of theory [*opinione*] rather than fact" (TTP, 196).[8]

The Hebrews, then, in *fact* (*verum*), as opposed to supposition (*opinio*), made their covenant with Moses in the same way as all human beings make a civil pact out of the state of nature. But why does Spinoza go out of his way to say that they first make a pact with God? It would be one thing if he only depicted the pact with God in chapter 16 on the origin of the state in general. One could then interpret 17, as I note above, as the illustration of a theoretical principle, i.e., the Hebrews (like all humans) didn't *in reality* contract with God but with a human leader, Moses. Indeed, Spinoza begins chapter 17 by claiming that "the picture presented in the last chapter [16] . . . although it comes quite close to actual practice and can increasingly be realised in reality, must nevertheless remain in many respects no more than a theory [*theoretica*]" (TTP, 191). Yet this is not the route Spinoza takes with the pact with God. In other words, it doesn't disappear once he turns to "actual practice." Rather, he introduces a new pact with God in 17 – the very chapter in which

---

[8] Shirley's translation of *opinio* as theory is somewhat misleading. It is not as misleading as it might be, because, as I argue, Spinoza connects the pact with God in 17 to the pact with God in 16, and the latter chapter is described *tout court* as *theoretica*. However, Spinoza does use a different word in 17 – and in fact, once one enters into the historical, he shows, theory itself is transformed. I shall flag this along the way, translating *opinio* as supposition unless directly quoting from Shirley (in which case I will indicate the Latin in brackets).

he is illustrating "in reality" the theory of the state from chapter 16 – and calls this new pact between God and the Hebrews *opinio* (TTP, 191, 196). The illustration, one could say, itself seems to theorize in addition to illustrating.

If the point in chapter 17 on the Hebrews is the same as that in chapter 16 on humankind, namely that neither pact has priority – that, in some sense, civil law and divine law come into existence together – one is still left with the question of why he emphasizes in 17 (and not in 16) that *first* a pact is made with God. One response to this question is to point to Spinoza's virtually identical discussion of the Hebrews in chapter 5, where he does seem to claim that the Hebrews really only contracted with Moses. He notes (as in 17) that "when they first went out from Egypt, being no longer bound by the laws of any other nation, [the Hebrews] were at liberty to sanction any new laws they pleased or to establish new ordinances, to maintain a state wherever they wished and to occupy any lands they wished" (TTP, 65). But in this chapter, there is no mention of a pact with God at all. Spinoza simply says that "the task of establishing a wise system of laws and of keeping the government in the hands of the whole community was quite beyond them; for they were in general inexperienced in such matters and exhausted by the wretched conditions of slavery." Therefore, he notes, they could not govern themselves – they could not function as a democracy – and so "government had to remain in the hands of one man who would issue commands and enforce them," and this man was Moses. The only reason Moses is special in chapter 5 is because "he surpassed all others in divine power which he convinced the people that he possessed, providing many proofs thereof" (TTP, 65). Thus the point seems to be that while the Hebrews *thought* they were making a pact with God (because of what Moses was able to convince them of), they were *in fact* only ever making a pact with Moses. Using 5 as the key to 17, the statement that the pact with God was *opinio* (supposition or theory) is identical to the statement that it is merely the opinion of the multitude. It is introduced again in 17 because it is important to see that religion can be valuable as a social tool. Moses uses religion, in chapter 5, as an instrument to make a state – to command obedience and loyalty among an exhausted populace – but religion is not prior to such a state and is in fact, if not entirely detachable therefrom, then simply a means to achieve rational ends.

This is certainly one way of understanding what Spinoza is getting at in chapter 17, namely, that Moses is a powerful leader who claims the authority of God for his own laws. But it doesn't account for the relationship between the pact with God in chapter 17, and that of chapter 16, where there is no question of manipulating, or if one prefers, guiding a multitude. In chapter 5, the Hebrews in the wilderness are depicted as traveling between the government of the Egyptians, under which they were slaves, and that of Moses, under which they were as if "children." As Spinoza puts it, "in order that a people incapable of self-rule should be utterly subservient to its ruler, [Moses] did not allow these men, habituated as they were to slavery, to perform any action at their own discretion" (TTP, 66). Recalling Spinoza's distinction from chapter 16 between a slave, a son, and a subject (TTP, 185), the situation of the Hebrews as described in chapter 5 is of a people having moved from slavery to "sonhood": "they could not even eat, dress, cut their hair, shave, make merry or do anything whatsoever except in accordance with commands and instructions laid down by the law" (TTP, 66). In this way, Spinoza accounts for the origin of the "ceremonial law" (Jewish law, *halakhah*), which he conceives as formulated to guide a people infantilized by slavery toward the freedom they couldn't yet possess.

In chapter 17, however, it is not simply that the Hebrews were between governments; not simply that they had been weakened as a result of their experience of slavery. "Being bound by no covenant . . . they found themselves placed in the state of nature" (TTP, 195), exactly as Spinoza describes the situation of human beings in general making a pact with God in 16. In 17, then, this interstitial "period" between Egypt and Moses is not at all about being "incapable of self-rule," nor is it about weakness or fear, at least until the Hebrews get too close to God. Rather, Spinoza tells us, "they surrendered their natural right and transferred it to God . . . freely, not by forcible coercion or fear of threats" (TTP, 195). This, Spinoza tells us in chapter 16, is an act not by "sons," "who by [their] father's command do what is to [their] own good," but by subjects, "who, by command of the sovereign power, act for the common good, and therefore for [their] own good also" (TTP, 185). For, according to 17 (*unlike* the covenant with Moses in 5), "this covenant left them all completely equal, and they all had an equal right to consult God, to receive and interpret his laws; in short, they all shared equally in the government of the state" (TTP, 196). Whereas chapter 5 resembles the argument of the TP that the state of nature is already social – "being no longer bound by the laws of any other nation, they were at liberty to sanction any new laws they pleased," i.e., they simply regained control of their own laws – chapter 17 resembles the argument from chapter 16 in the TTP that we begin in a state of nature, which is itself likened to a state of slavery, a "life most wretched and . . . lack[ing] the cultivation of reason" (TTP, 181). According to this model, the pacts with God and man are about freedom; but therefore equally, for Spinoza, about *servitus*: "by this they clearly abrogated the first covenant" (TTP, 196).

Facing these various complexities, a reader has two basic choices. The first is to make the account of the Hebrews in chapter 5 Spinoza's official account of religion in the TTP, and then to read the accounts in 16 and 17 through this lens. According to this interpretation, there is no real pact with God, as chapter 5 would seem to suggest. This tack, adopted and vigorously argued by Douglas Den Uyl, holds that the key to understanding the nature of the civil pact as it is conceived in 16 – as a contract among equals, all of whom are driven by appetite – and the pact as Spinoza envisions it in 17 between the Hebrews and Moses, is to posit two different (and ultimately harmonious) versions of the civil pact. In 16, Spinoza is operating with a notion of the pact as an "absolute moment," a purely theoretical construct which functions to highlight a dividing line, on the near side of which are the conditions of minimal sociality and mutual dependence without which it is impossible to conceive of individual existence, and on the far side of which is a strictly hypothetical account of "pure passionate behavior," which always does in some sense threaten any particular social order.[9] The state of nature according to this notion of the pact is nonexistent (or always already concluded), but the features of human nature isolable in the absolute moment "persist" in having an impact on social existence.[10]

The pact in the state of nature, however, is not only a model or an absolute limit. In the Hebrew case, it is possible to see it functioning as a historical reality. This accords well with the fact that the state of nature for Spinoza is never abandoned in a Hobbesian sense. One moves out of a state of nature, but nature is somehow conserved, especially in a democracy, which, again, Spinoza calls "the most natural form of state" (TTP, 185). Thus according to this interpretation, Spinoza has a second notion of the pact which is contracted not in a state of absolute irrationality and powerlessness but in the context of the loose and informal social dependence that is basic and irreducible. What Den Uyl calls the "'intermediary moment' in Spinoza's theory of the state of nature refers to a situation where there is at least minimal sociality, but either a) there is no definitive authoritative structure, or b) those lines of authority which do exist are on the verge of collapse and a transition to another order is taking place."[11] In this intermediary state, individuals do possess a measure of rationality (though Den Uyl rightly assumes that the force of

---

[9] Den Uyl, *Power, State, and Freedom*, 45.

[10] Balibar agrees, contending that "what the pact institutes is a collective power that assumes *after the fact* the form of a relation between wills . . . Theoretically speaking, individual or collective *wills* do not exist before the pact but are constituted under its effect" ("*Jus-Pactum-Lex*," 187).

[11] Den Uyl, *Power, State, and Freedom*, 46.

Spinoza's argument is the association of rationality with the *civitas* itself), but what accounts for the construction of a more organized and formal social entity is not rational deliberation and consent but the existence of a powerful and domineering leader, like the Moses of chapter 5, around whom collective passions coalesce.

These two moments (absolute and intermediary) solve the problem of the role of rationality in the founding of society, since they don't assume the social pact is a rational act – it is a limit concept (absolute moment). In the case of Spinoza's "historical" example, Moses also needn't be especially rational, but must only surpass the others in the passion to rule (intermediate moment).[12] This dual model also solves the problem of an original powerlessness, since it assumes only that the initial social collectivity was less powerful (more chaotic and undependable) than it might have been, or would become, when properly led. What Den Uyl identifies as the "evolutionary interpretation" of the origin of the state – which focuses on the TP, denies the role of reason in founding the state, and stresses the motivation of fear and other passions, especially the desire to "join a large number of individuals" in order to seek relief from the fluctuating and often hostile patterns inherent in nature – can then easily be reconciled with the "hero-founder" interpretation, based on the social impact of a leader such as Moses.[13] One is then not troubled by a rift between the TP and the TTP, since it is both true that we begin always already socialized and also that socialization has a beginning – or rather two beginnings, one theoretical, one historical.

This model has some explanatory power. Social existence has no literal origin (TTP and TP agree). But it is possible to speak of a limit concept in order to account for the natural tensions inherent in any social body, and it is possible also to speak of an apolitical state of sociality out of which particular states construct themselves by virtue of charismatic leaders (TTP is internally consistent).[14] However, while this interpretation correctly places the dynamics of the Hebrew theocracy at the heart of Spinoza's political theory, it does so paradoxically by voiding it of religious significance, making it a question of the nature of Moses' leadership and not a question of a pact with God (indeed, God is utterly irrelevant on this view). The theory of the intermediate stage, focused on TTP chapter 5,

---

[12] Den Uyl, *Power, State, and Freedom*, 27–28.
[13] Den Uyl, *Power, State, and Freedom*, 35–36.
[14] It is debatable, however, whether the commentators whom Den Uyl thus harmonizes would agree with his reading. Matheron's "evolutionist" account, for example, is intended to show precisely how political societies can form *without* the intervention of so-called "hero-founders." See Matheron, "Le problème de l'évolution de Spinoza," 258–270.

in common with the evolutionary model, focused on the TP, completely bypasses any question that Spinoza meant to account for the origin of religion in the TTP, much less to connect the origin of religion with the origin of politics. For Den Uyl, what is originated in the intermediary pact is a social and political body, *any* and *every* social and political body. The Jews are a single example of the (intermediate) transition out of the state of apolitical sociality, but the religious dimension of the Jewish state is marginal, if not totally insignificant. It is specific to the Jews themselves because the dissemination of religion (the rhetoric of divine law and divine authority) was the particular way in which Moses secured obedience to his social order. But it is not the only or even the best way to secure this obedience. From the perspective of Spinoza's political thought as a whole, then, one can just, in a sense, factor out religion and focus on the dynamics of group passions and the laws and personalities that control and channel them.[15]

What this first solution proposes in light of the difficulties of the pacts in the TTP is to read chapters 16 and 17 through the lens of chapter 5 (making the pact with God solely about a pact with Moses). The alternative is to do just the opposite, namely, to read chapter 5 through the lens of chapters 16 and 17. The alternative, in other words, is to seek to understand the four pacts (two with God, two between human and human) in the chapters (16 and 17) in which they are introduced and discussed – in the chapters where the TTP as a whole moves from the interpretation of the Bible to political theory. This would still be to recognize that Spinoza gives us two notions of the pact in the TTP, one of which is "absolute," i.e., a limit concept, and one of which is historical, or "real." The pact introduced in the first few pages of chapter 16, according to which human beings "arranged that the unrestricted right naturally possessed by each individual should be put into common ownership" (TTP, 181), functions for Spinoza to account for the actual challenges that sovereigns face – in other words, for the contradictions and conflicts that exist in any kind of minimal social arrangement.[16] The pact is a limit concept in that it is something we posit from the standpoint of finding ourselves already socialized. Thus when Spinoza notes that in a democratic state "all men remain equal, as they were before in a state of nature," this statement, and the state of nature itself, is comprehensible only in light of the recognition of its impossibility (TTP, 185). Our "recovered" equality in a democracy is obtainable on the basis of what human beings have in common with one another, which is that, without one another, we are powerless. Since

---

[15] See Den Uyl, *Power, State, and Freedom*, 29, 50–51.
[16] Den Uyl, *Power, State, and Freedom*, 45.

power and rationality are the same thing for Spinoza, this amounts to the claim that there is no rational way to narrate a transition between "before" and "after" sociality without ending up in contradiction.[17]

The civil state, then, does not abrogate the state of nature in the way that it does for Hobbes: "the fact is that man acts in accordance with the laws of his own nature and pursues his own advantage in both the natural and the political order" (*homo namque tam in statu naturali quam civili ex legibus suae naturae agit suaeque utilitati consulit*) (TP III: 3). What is theoretical is not the state of nature per se, but the state of nature conceived starkly as the individual pursuit of appetite. The "moment" of the pact signifies the moment when the conflictual nature of human society in a more primitive form "begins" to be focused around common goals and aims:

the chief difference between the two [nature and polis] is that in the political order all fear the same things, and all have one and the same source of security, one and the same mode of life; but this, of course, does not deprive the individual of his power of judgement. For the man who decides to obey all the commands of the commonwealth, whether through fear of its power, or because he loves tranquillity, is certainly pursuing his own security and advantage in accordance with his own judgement. (TP III: 3)

In this way, civil society contains within itself the contradictions that are articulated through the aporia of a first founding.

But the pact made with God in chapter 16, rather than being on the "civil" side of this aporia (rather than being about enforcing sociality among an exhausted populace), in fact expresses it in the very same way – it is "absolute" in the same way. For here it is not an actual historical people making a pact but, as with the *civitas*, it is human beings in general who are doing so. "Since all men without exception," Spinoza writes, "whether or not they have the use of reason, are equally required by God's command to love their neighbour as themselves," this command must be accounted for by way of a covenant. For, again, "nobody knows by nature that he has any duty to obey God" (TTP, 188). Yet "this commandment is the one and only guiding principle for the entire common faith of mankind, and through this commandment alone should be determined all the tenets of faith that every man is in duty bound to accept" (TTP, 164). In this light, civil society contains within itself *not only* the contradictions that are articulated through the narrative of a first founding. Civil society – as the only context for "acts of piety," i.e., the outward forms of religion – *also* contains within itself the aporias of the origins of religion.

---

[17] This is the problem with the fall of Adam and Eve, as Spinoza sees it.

Both the civil pact and the pact with God involve a "passage" out of nature. Both, as I showed in last chapter, are relative to the mind – they are manmade – and the mind itself is something both natural, i.e., essentially *conatus*, like all other singular things, and creative. For the mind can understand the extent to which it is connected to the whole of nature ("the human mind has an adequate knowledge of God's eternal and infinite essence" [E II p47]), which to Spinoza means that the mind, the human being, rather than simply being subject to universal nature, can formulate laws that enable her to become *like* nature, or God (free). Understanding is freedom if and only if understanding itself is *conatus* – the striving to bring it about that we are more and more empowered, and more and more empower others. Divine and human laws, then, are connected through the mind, and they come into existence together.

Election, divine and human

It is the Hebrew commonwealth that illustrates this connection between religion and the state in their origins – that vividly shows the conflicts and aporias of both in action. It is not that the Hebrews exemplify humankind, for Spinoza. But their state – founded as it was on an actual pact with God (i.e., God was to be the head of state and God's laws were to be identical to civil laws) – perfectly illustrates the tensions that result from the intrinsic (absolute) pull between the commands of God (the divine law of justice and charity) and the commands of (any and every historical) state. The Hebrews are paradigmatic for Spinoza – they are not simply examples of the role of "hero-founders" in the creation of the civil order – because, once again, it is not Moses with whom the Jews enter into a pact, but God. To be sure the Jews do "make an absolute transfer to Moses of their right to consult God and to interpret his decrees." The Jews were, he observes, "terrified" and "thunderstruck at hearing God speak:"

So, "overwhelmed with fear they went to Moses again, saying 'Behold, we have heard God speaking in the midst of the fire; now therefore why should we die? For this great fire will surely consume us; if again we are to hear the voice of God, we shall surely die. Go thou near, therefore, and hear all that our God shall say. And speak thou (not God) to us.'" (TTP, 196)

But it was "*again*" that they went to Moses. The first time, they simply "hearkened" to him, placed "the greatest confidence" in him, transferring their right "not to any mortal man, but to God alone" (TTP, 195). It was "our God" (*Adonai Eloheinu*) that they subsequently begged Moses to interpret for them, the one with whom they had first covenanted.[18] And, in so begging, it was this "first covenant" that they "abrogated" (TTP, 196).[19]

What, then, of the claim that the Hebrews' pact with God is merely supposition: "to be sure this is more supposition than truth" (*verum en-imvero haec omnia opinionis magis*) (G III: 206)? It is not simply that Spinoza uses *opinio* here to mean false or imaginary.[20] He says very plainly that the covenant with God was abrogated (i.e., ephemeral), and what is abrogated must, in some sense, exist. But in what sense? At the beginning of chapter 17 on the Hebrews, Spinoza tells us that what is theoretical about chapter 16 on the origins of the state is its depiction of "the overriding right of sovereign powers and the transference to them of the individual's natural right." This, as I quoted above, "must nevertheless remain in many respects no more than a theory." For according to the logic of Spinoza's identification of right and power, I showed, the notion that sovereignty is absolute does not have to do with the fact that individuals transfer all of their right, but that the sovereign has the absolute power to command obedience. What is absolute is the sovereign insofar as it has this power, but the power itself cannot be total, and it can also be abrogated (TTP, 183).

The notion that chapter 16 is theory, then, qualifies the notion of an absolute transfer. Human beings cannot be "deprived of their natural right as thereafter to be powerless to do anything except by the will of those who hold the supreme right." If this were possible, "the subjects of the most violent tyranny would be without resource, a condition," Spinoza insists, "no one can possibly envisage." Therefore "it must be

[18] Deut. 5: 22–23. Spinoza is in accordance with the Talmud on this point, which implies that Israel is able to say "our God" here because it hears the first two commandments "directly from the mouth of the almighty," before asking Moses to intercede. Harris begins *How Do We Know This?* with this passage (from Bavli, Makkot 23b–24a), which asks the question "what is the biblical source" for the communication to Moses of 613 commandments? The Talmud responds, "Moses charged us with Torah, an inheritance etc. (Deut. 33: 4). The numerical value of 'Torah' is six hundred and eleven. [To this we add] 'I am' and 'You shall have no other Gods' (Exodus 20: 2–7), which were heard directly from the mouth of the Almighty" (quoted in Harris, 1).

[19] Cf. Novak, who claims that Spinoza "rejects the primary biblical sense of 'covenant' precisely because it designates a divinely elected and structured relationship with a particular people," but he "skillfully appropriated the secondary biblical sense of the word. 'Covenant' in this sense is an agreement initiated by humans among themselves and placed within the context of the primary covenant between God and his people." Spinoza, according to Novak, gets rid of this primary covenant altogether, but retains the second, that between human and human. David Novak, *The Election of Israel: The Idea of the Chosen People* (Cambridge: Cambridge University Press, 1995), 32 ff.

[20] Spinoza uses the word *opinio* (lit. opinion, supposition, conjecture, belief, expectation, report, estimation) to describe knowledge of the first kind, which he calls "opinion or imagination" (E II p40s2).

granted . . . that the individual reserves to himself a considerable part of his right, which therefore depends on nobody's decision but his own" (TTP, 191).

If the political pact in chapter 16 is "in many respects no more than theory," is this true of the pact with God? Can human beings – do they need to – reserve their rights over against God in the same way they do with a political sovereign? We might recall that to Spinoza, God cannot command any amount of obedience on his own, much less a degree that might threaten human rights. It should therefore be clear that while Spinoza clearly means to leave indeterminate the order and priority of the divine and civil laws in the nature of their origins, they are not in every way identical. To say that God cannot command obedience to his law in the same way as a political sovereign, and indeed that "God has no special kingdom over men save through the medium of those who hold sovereignty," is not simply to say that God needs human mediators (TTP, 220). It is to say that, unlike the case of human law, God's law with humankind, once made, *is* total, it *cannot* be abrogated. Like human laws, God's law has a beginning – a cause, a *pactum*. But unlike human laws (though like their original pact), it is irreversible (universal). As the first quotation at the start of this chapter succinctly relates, "whether we consider religion to be revealed by the natural light or by prophecy; the proof applies in all cases, since religion is the same and equally revealed by God in whatever way we suppose men have come to know it" (TTP, 220).

Thus in one sense, God's law *is* prior to civil law. For as we can see in the case of the Hebrews, "before [religion] could have the force of law with [them] it was necessary that every one of them should first surrender their natural right, and that all should by common consent resolve to obey only what was revealed to them by God through prophecy." This, Spinoza tells us, "is an exact parallel to what we have shown to be the development of a democracy, where all by common consent resolve to live only by the dictates of reason." The Hebrews "went further," he continues, "by transferring their right to God" *as if* he were a political sovereign; but this "transference was notional rather than practical" (*hoc magis mente, quam opera facere*), for God is not a political ruler, and therefore this transference cannot in fact occur (TTP, 221, G III: 230). What is "notional" (or better, a matter of only the mind) in the case of the pact the Hebrews made with God is the idea of God as a lawgiver. Therefore what is also notional in this pact is the idea that God's law – the law that God made with humankind – can ever belong to only one people.

But the Hebrews, Spinoza insists in 17, nevertheless surrendered their right to God. And this, I submit, points to a third kind of theory or supposition that is in play here. The first sense, *theoretica*, refers to the ways in which human beings retain their rights/powers over against political sovereigns. The second, *opinio*, refers to the ways in which God retains his rights/powers over against human beings, as that "sovereign" whose law is "innate" in our *mens* (*lex necessarius*) and not only "man-made" (*lex ex hominum*) (G III: 58). One could say that human beings retain a "considerable part of [their] right" over against human sovereigns because they have already – first – transferred everything to God: not God as a competing sovereign who could command (this right as) obedience to himself, but God as the one (sovereign) who commands (this right as) obedience to oneself.[21] Therefore God is that sovereign who is/which is the immanent critique of all tyranny. Of *course*, one might protest to Spinoza, one can "envisage" a situation wherein the subjects of the most violent tyranny would be "without resource." One can, unfortunately, envisage this all too well. What Spinoza is saying, however, is that we can never be "without resource" and still be a human being, since, once again, a human being just is a certain quantity of power. This power can be reduced to a speck – one can be tortured in all manner of terrifying ways so as to be utterly deprived of everything that feels human. But one will still, he holds, be in possession of the one, single, inalienable resource, *conatus*, which is, seen from a "theoretical" angle, our connection to *Deus sive Natura*.[22]

God is, on this reading, the principle of human rights, so to speak, which at the beginning of 17 makes 16 "in many respects no more than a theory." What cannot be transferred to a human sovereign is the divine covenant that all human beings have already made with God. It is *opinio*

---

[21] Here, then, is the convergence of the two "obediences" whereby the "son" becomes "subject," and it is also, for Spinoza, the key to the connection between individual goods and the common social good, viz., a "subject is one who, by command of the sovereign power, acts for the common good, and therefore for his own good also" (TTP, 243).

[22] Spinoza clearly does not intend this as a consolation to the tyrannized. It is a structural point, which is why "we cannot envisage it," i.e., we can imagine it, but we wouldn't be right, strictly speaking. It is also, of course, to locate a place of resistance, though again, one can be theoretically able to resist but in practice totally unable. In the *Ethics*, Spinoza notes that "it should be noted that I understand the Body to die when its parts are so disposed that they acquire a different proportion of motion and rest to one another. For I dare not deny that – even though the circulation of the blood is maintained, as well as the other [signs] on account of which the Body is thought to be alive – the human Body can nevertheless be changed into another nature entirely different from its own. For no reason compels me to maintain that the Body does not die unless it is changed into a corpse" (E IV p39s). Spinoza seems not to have torture in mind here. He refers to the difference between an infant's body and that of an old man, and alludes to "a Spanish Poet who suffered an illness" which left him "oblivious of his past life." But it seems clear that this notion of a body's death in life is sympathetic to the kinds of suffering we can undergo and feel no ability to resist whatsoever.

for the Hebrews because it is abrogated; it is absolute for humankind because it cannot be. This is why, without making clear the relationship of the divine and civil laws, it is totally unclear what Spinoza is getting at by casting the origins of the *civitas* as a pact. Human beings are not, he shows, rational enough in nature to do such a thing. Yet from another angle ("by necessity and by the sound counsel of reason"), a human being just is a being who is rational enough to do such a thing, or in other words, a human being just is a being who, like God, can cause herself (*causa suae*) – whose existence implies this power. The problem for the civil state, then, is equally "freedom," and "piety," and "peace," for what God establishes is the *fundamentum* on the basis of which human beings can pursue blessedness. In this sense, it both antedates and inherently troubles the civil contract, with the latter's focus on its own particular flourishing. It was the *civitas* that enslaved the Hebrews in Egypt. It was God's law that brought them out.

But the pact with God is not only a critique of tyranny. Spinoza focuses on the Hebrew commonwealth because he wants to show that this critique is of any and every political order, including the Hebrew one itself. The pact with God, in the third sense of theory (as notional, or relative to the mind), is a critique of tyranny only insofar as it is unconditional, absolute, and abrogated. The moment this pact is seen to command on its own – as theocracy – its power as a critique is weakened. Failing to abrogate the pact (failing to see that it comes into history *as* abrogated) will in principle ultimately produce the very opposite of freedom – a society that is an example of tyranny rather than a critique of it. This is not initially what happened in the case of the Hebrews, whose political life "possessed many features which are at least worthy of note, and which it may perhaps be quite profitable to imitate" (TTP, 212). In the segment of Hebrew common life that Spinoza surveys, their attempt to live under God's laws exemplifies the permanent instability of divine and human laws. For, as chapter 5 shows, human beings are indeed affected, both positively and negatively, by religious narratives, by narratives of chosenness, and by laws that "fix and determine" our lives. While 17 shows that freedom concerns not overcoming obedience but transfiguring our motives for obeying the law, these motives nevertheless can never be pure. Religion is equivocal, both true and false. On the one hand, the Hebrews could not make a pact (covenant) with God because they had already, like every people, made an eternal pact with God. Yet on the other hand, because this latter is only ever theoretical (it requires human rulers), the Hebrews, like every people, sought rightly ("reserving to themselves a considerable part of their rights") to make it again, to choose and be chosen. They found they could not make such a pact without immediately – in the same moment – abrogating it. But the paradox is that without do-ing so, without choosing and being chosen by one's political community on the basis of the divine law of justice and charity (the eternal pact with God), political existence itself would have been impossible. For the *civitas* is a pact that recognizes, as much as it creates, the divine natural equality between human and human. The eternal pact between God and humankind cannot be abrogated; the historical pact between God and the Hebrews must be. Another way of putting this is that the eternal pact *is not* eternal in the sense of having always been in the world. It is revealed, created, made. Like God himself, the pact (and in this sense all four are identical) comes into existence (*causa sui*) as *conatus*, as history.

To be sure, it is illegitimate to claim, as the Hebrews claimed, that God made a pact *only* with them. To Spinoza, chosenness refers to the ability of a polity to live in "security and good health," not to some superior quality one people possesses over another, such as "knowing things through their primary causes" or "acquiring the habit of virtue" (TTP, 38). What is denied here is crucial. It is not that the Hebrews in particular were of unexceptional intelligence or only moderately virtuous. Rather, the gifts of intelligence and virtue "are not peculiar to any nation but have always been commanded to all mankind – unless we entertain the delusion that Nature at some time created different species of men" (TTP, 38). In every nation, "few [are] chosen" in respect of their wisdom and virtue, and the Hebrews are no exception to this rule (TTP, 39), though he also points out that neither are they especially "stubborn," as it sometimes claimed. Again, the principle is that "if it has to be allowed that the Hebrews were stubborn beyond other mortals, this would have to be attributed to defectiveness of their laws or of their customs" (TTP, 207).

But further, the point Spinoza is making is not to distinguish "individ-ual" traits from "collective" traits. What he is denying in the case of the *natio* is exactly the same thing that he denies in the case of individuals, namely that, qua human, they possess any "essence" except *conatus*. In the case of individuals, we *can* point to those who are wiser or more virtu-ous than others, but these "attributes" are expressed entirely in the power an individual in fact possesses to live "securely" and in "good health," to be, in other words, less buffeted by fortune. This is clearly not an attribute one possesses once and for all, but something that continually needs to be remade. So, too, in the case of a nation: its "wisdom" is equivalent to its ability to achieve and sustain "material prosperity and freedom, i.e., political independence" (TTP, 41).

The difference between nations and individuals concerns the role of "external causes" in the achievement of the ends of independence and peace. Spinoza thinks that nations have less control over fate than individuals. For an individual, the achievement of wisdom and virtue (freedom) "lies within the bounds of human nature itself, so that their acquisition must depend on human power alone; i.e., solely on the laws of human nature" (TTP, 38). Now, among those "laws of human nature" Spinoza includes the fact of *servitus* – to nature and to others. He is not saying human beings can achieve wisdom by themselves, but that, insofar as they *can* become wise, they do so without needing to rely on (to hope for) *bona fortunae*. Of course, it is precisely a nation that is the condition for this achievement, according to Spinoza, i.e.,

> much can be effected by human contrivance and vigilance to achieve security and to avoid injuries from other men and from beasts. To this end, reason and experience have taught us no surer means than to organise a society under fixed laws, to occupy a fixed territory and to concentrate the strength of all its members into one body, as it were, a social body. (TTP, 38)

It is otherwise with nations themselves, Spinoza claims. The social body, he holds, is beholden to "external circumstances" and the "gifts of fortune" to a much greater degree than individuals (TTP, 38). A social body, unlike an individual, is (relatively speaking) alone. There are other nations, of course, but Spinoza thinks of a nation as an entity that by definition pursues its own ends, and not those of other nations (there is no common good among nations). Unlike individuals, nations *can* do so, and this may be the only difference. But again, "a quite considerable degree of ability and vigilance is needed to organise and preserve a society," and all societies are intrinsically unstable, if only because of this basic dependence on fortune (TTP, 38). If they "overcome great perils and enjoy prosperity" for "some considerable time, this is to be attributed to some other guidance, not its own" (TTP, 38–39). Nevertheless, like individuals, "that society will be more secure, more stable and less exposed to fortune, which is founded and governed mainly by men of wisdom and vigilance, while a society composed of men who lack these qualities is largely dependent on fortune." Thus Spinoza holds both that wisely governed societies are more likely to flourish than unwisely governed societies and that the "wisdom" of a social body is always also going to involve luck.

Since it makes little sense to compare societies on the basis of luck, Spinoza focuses on the ways in which "nations differ from one another in respect of the kind of society and laws under which they live and are governed" (TTP, 39). In this respect, the Hebrews are an interesting case. For they were able to prosper and to "surpass other nations in achieving security for themselves" for a time (TTP, 39). Spinoza identifies two reasons for this achievement. The first, shared by other successful nations, is simply that the Hebrews had good laws. They were not a representative democracy, because, in the context of the abrogation of the covenant with God, Moses became the ruler of the commonwealth. But it was not a monarchy either, Spinoza points out, because Moses appointed "no successor" to rule after him, "but left the state to be so governed by those who came after him that it could be called neither a democracy nor an aristocracy nor a monarchy, but a theocracy." By this he means in one sense that (to employ an anachronistic reference), God retained the status of the head of state as in a parliamentary system, the official rulers being the governing party, with a prime minister at the head. God, in other words, had a role in the polity even though the covenant with him was – had to be – abrogated (God is not a ruler). But it also means, Spinoza tells us, that "the right to interpret the laws and to promulgate God's answers was vested in one man, [while] the right and power to govern the state in accordance with laws thus expounded and answers thus made known was vested in another" (TTP, 197–198). It was still God the Hebrews saw themselves as interpreting, but they had the wisdom to insist that the judicial branch be separated from the legislative branch, and this is something that all nations would do well to ensure.[23]

There was a second reason they were able to prosper, Spinoza observes, "peculiar to [this state] and of indisputable weight," and it has to do with the fact that God did, after all, remain the head of state. We know, he tells us, that "the motive of self-interest [is] the strength and life of all human action" (TTP, 205). And we know, from his discussion in chapter 16, that democracy is the most natural state, the one that most satisfies the self-interest of its citizens (TTP, 185). In the case of the Hebrew commonwealth, their first pact, again, was with God, "equally and with one voice," in freedom, "not by forcible coercion," and this equality and freedom continued to bear fruit even after (precisely because) the pact was abrogated (TTP, 195):

Nowhere else did citizens have stronger right to their possessions than did the subjects of this state, who had an equal share with the captain in lands and fields, and were each the owners of their share in perpetuity. For if any man was compelled by poverty to sell his farm or field, it had to be restored to him when the jubilee came round, and there were other similar enactments to prevent the alienation of real estate. Then again, nowhere could poverty have been lighter to endure than there, where charity to one's neighbour, that is, to one's fellow-citizen, was a duty to be practised with the utmost piety so as to gain the favour of God, their king. Thus the Hebrew citizen could enjoy a good life only in their own country; abroad they could expect only hurt and humiliation. (TTP, 205)

---

[23] Spinoza describes the checks and balances in the Hebrew commonwealth in some detail. See TTP, 261–266.

In the Hebrew commonwealth, he tell us here, there was a distinctive motive that enabled solidarity among self-interested human beings above and beyond that of simple survival and accommodation. Justice and charity were imbued with feelings of devotion, and the natural tendency of human beings to fight among themselves was thereby mitigated. For here, "no man served his equal, but only God" (TTP, 206). Here no one's basic needs were left to the vagaries of human law, but rather God's law – the law of justice and charity – ensured that "charity and love towards one's fellow-citizens was . . . a supreme religious duty," and thus a political duty as well (TTP, 206). In the Hebrew polity, in other words, poverty, wretchedness, material suffering, were against the law. This entirely praiseworthy state of affairs was possible, however, only by virtue of magnifying precisely the religious hopes and fears that are the flipside of material uncertainty in the opening pages of the preface. For if "no more effective means can be devised to influence men's minds [than] joy springing from devotion, that is, love mingled with awe," this devotion has the consequence of producing an equal measure of hate for outsiders – God's kingdom was their kingdom, "while all other nations were God's enemies" (TTP, 206, 204).

Thus what enabled the Hebrews to experience an incredibly intense cohesiveness and stability was coupled with "a lasting hatred of a most deep-rooted kind," for "their daily worship was not merely quite different, making them altogether unique and completely distinct from other peoples," it was also "utterly opposed to others." Hatred itself, in addition to charity toward one's Hebrew neighbor, "was believed to be a religious duty." To Spinoza, this kind of hatred is "of the bitterest and most persistent of all kinds" (TTP, 204–205). It is not only destabilizing for those who experience it; it is also, he holds, utterly infectious, leading other nations to hate the Hebrews in turn (TTP, 206).[24]

All of these things taken together, "their freedom from human rule, their devotion to their country, their absolute right against all others and a hatred that was not only permissible but a religious duty, the hostility of all around them, their distinctive customs and rites," these "combined to fortify the hearts of the Hebrews to endure all things for their country with unexampled steadfastness and valour." What is "confirmed by reason" is also "attested by experience," namely that this enabled this small nation to endure many assaults from without (TTP, 205). But what it did not do was enable them to survive the internal stresses that excessive amounts of hate inevitably produced. Because the Hebrew nation was otherwise so profoundly successful, the causes of its destruction are of

[24] According to Spinoza's maxim that "hate is increased by being returned" (E III p43).

enormous significance to Spinoza. Since what makes a state successful in the first place is its laws and customs, it is there that he looks to find the source of its destruction. Given that the Hebrews initially had good laws, Spinoza's question is: How did their laws become bad? Why did the Hebrews "so frequently forsake the Law [so that] it came about in the end that their state was utterly destroyed" (TTP, 207)? Since according to Spinoza we cannot express this falling away from the law in terms of "the stubbornness of the race," he says that it must be that "God was angry with them" (TTP, 207). What Spinoza means by God's anger is that God himself became a subject of dispute. The Hebrew commonwealth began to become undone, he notes, when religious authority passed from the "firstborn" of all the tribes to an autonomous body, the Levites. The problem was that the Levites were distinguished purely by the fact that, while all the rest of their nation turned to idolatry during the episode of the golden calf, they alone kept faith in God (Exod. 32). They thus were a constant reminder to the people of their own "defilement and rejection." To Spinoza, this first separation between church and state was the beginning of the end for the commonwealth, because very quickly the people resented this authority and began to rebel against it, leading to all manner of sedition, political upheaval, and ultimately the demise of the state (TTP, 207–208).

The lesson to be learned from this is not that the Levites' latter-day ancestors (priests) are worthy and blameless victims of mob unruliness. It is rather the principle that violence, disorder, and unscrupulous power-mongering are inflamed by the separation of religious and political orders – the creation of two sovereigns with their own laws. In the name of establishing a realm above politics, this succeeds only in producing factionalism and hatred (TTP, 213). It is not that secular rulers are any more virtuous than religious ones, and in fact Spinoza thinks that the case of the virtuous Levites and the disasters of the Hebrew monarchy are instructive here. "We see how fatal it is," he notes, "for a people unaccustomed to the rule of kings, and already possessing established laws, to set up a monarchy." The Hebrews had such established laws, ones that were inherently democratic, and their polity was thus ill used by the kings they chose for themselves when it began to degenerate. As Spinoza puts it, "the newly established monarch will make every effort to introduce new laws and to reconstitute the state's legal code to his own advantage, reducing the people to a point where it will find it not so easy to abolish monarchy as to set it up" (TTP, 216–217). The point is that, if democracy and the rule of law are one's political goals – if one desires to be the victim neither of religious nor secular despotism – the only possible condition for this is at least some kind of concerted and systematic coordination between religious and secular power. For Spinoza, this has to be under the aegis of the state, for God must remain invisible (abrogated, if not irrelevant) in political life:

everyone knows how much importance the people attach to the right and authority over religion . . . so that one might even go so far as to say that he to whom this authority belongs has the most effective control over minds. Therefore anyone who seeks to deprive the sovereign of this authority is attempting to divide the sovereignty; and as a result, as happened long ago in the case of the kings and priests of the Hebrews, there will inevitably arise strife and dissensions that can never be allayed. Indeed, he who seeks to deprive the sovereign of this authority is paving the way to his own ascendency. (TTP, 225)

For all of Spinoza's critique of religious authority, he never trivializes its power over people, which returns him to what is admirable about the Hebrew commonwealth, namely, its respect for democracy, including its recognition of the relationship between material prosperity and virtue (TTP, 205). "It is noteworthy," he says, "that as long as the people was sovereign there was only one civil war, and even that ended with peace completely restored, the victors showing such compassion to the conquered that they sought every means to restore them to their former dignity and power" (TTP, 214).

For Spinoza, there is a basic recognition in the Hebrew polity that real holiness consists ultimately in what a society does and how it treats its members, however much it tends to attribute this flourishing to some divine privilege. One could say that they *did* possess divine privilege insofar as they remained democratic, and in this sense alone Spinoza's distinction between nations and individuals cannot be sustained. What Spinoza implies through the case of the Hebrews is that if a state were to be truly and fully democratic it would be just as powerful as an individual who had achieved independence. Thus the Hebrews were right, Spinoza thinks, in understanding the divine law as political and particular from the start. To get beyond this particularity, or rather to avoid invidious comparison while also maintaining a sense of distinctiveness, requires an appreciation for the full implications of the democracy they never fully instantiated. It requires a sense of law that is both particular – relative to a particular time and place – and universal: not a law of universal application, but a law that is universally accessible to all to whom it applies. As Spinoza observes,

Those who govern the state or hold the reins of power always strive to cloak with a show of legality whatever wrong they commit, persuading the people that this action was right and proper; and this they can easily achieve when the interpretation of the law is entirely in their hands. For this in itself undoubtedly affords them the greatest latitude in doing whatever they want and whatever their appetite suggests, whereas they are largely deprived of this freedom if the right to interpret the laws is vested in somebody else, and likewise if the true interpretation of the laws is so obvious that it is not open to doubt. (TTP, 202)

Now laws, like texts, are never simply self-evident. They always do require interpreters, and thus the Hebrews initially dealt with this fact through the appointment of the Levites, "who had no share either in the administration of the state or in its territory, and who saw their entire welfare and prestige dependent on a true interpretation of the law" (TTP, 202). This proved disastrous, Spinoza shows, not because of the unscrupulousness of the Levites themselves but because they held themselves apart from the multitude over whom they had power. In fact, he continues, this appointment was unnecessary, not because the laws needed no interpreters but because the Hebrew laws were disseminated clearly to all: "the entire populace was required to assemble at an appointed place every seventh year to learn the laws from the priest, and in addition everyone was expected to read and re-read the book of the Law on his own, constantly and with utmost concentration" (TTP, 202). The self-evidence of the law, then, did not consist in its transparency but in the fact that it was available to all who were willing to put it in the time to understand it. As long as the point of human laws is to educate and reform human desire – as long as the only guarantee that one's laws are holy is if they produce a more pious and wise multitude – their legitimacy can only consist in their clarity and accessibility. It is clarity and accessibility, for Spinoza, that function both as the critique of pernicious power-mongering (election as invidious comparison) and as the condition of both political and individual enlightenment.

Thus Spinoza tells us that, "although [the commonwealth of the Hebrews] cannot be imitated in all respects, it possessed many features which are at least worthy of note, and which it may perhaps be quite profitable to imitate" (TTP, 212). This claim is crucial. Spinoza does not say we "should not" imitate the Hebrews in all respects, implying in other words that we should learn from their mistakes and emulate their virtues. He says we "cannot" imitate them in all respects. The reason he gives is because "if any people should resolve to transfer their right to God, they would have to make a covenant expressly with God, as did the Hebrews, and so it would be necessary to have not only the consent of those transferring their right but also the consent of God to whom the right was to be transferred." Why, one asks, can one not procure God's consent in the way that the Hebrews did? Because, Spinoza says, "God . . . has revealed through his Apostles that his covenant is no longer written in ink or engraved on tablets of stone, but is inscribed by God's spirit in men's hearts" (TTP, 212). In the other place in the TTP where Spinoza uses this language of inscription in the heart, he cites Moses (Deut. 30: 6): "Then the Lord your God will open up your heart and the hearts of your offspring to love the Lord your God with all your heart and soul, in order that you may live," and Jeremiah (31: 33): "But such is the covenant I will make with the House of Israel after these days – declares the Lord: I will put My Teaching into their inmost being and inscribe it upon their hearts. Then I will be their God, and they shall be my people" (TTP, 149).

Spinoza did not think the Christian spiritualization of the law overcomes the problem of law in Judaism. As he says, "Christ was sent not to preserve a state and to institute laws, but only to teach the universal law. Hence we can readily understand that Christ by no means abrogated the law of Moses, for it was not Christ's purpose to introduce new laws into the commonwealth" (TTP, 61). More importantly, both statements claiming the law is inscribed in the heart express Spinoza's claim in chapter 17 that even the pact the Hebrews made with God ("the written law") was a "matter of theory [*opinio*] rather than fact" (TTP, 196). Even the Hebrews did not procure God's consent, for God's consent cannot be procured "in fact."[25]

The Hebrews themselves learn this through the fate of their own polity. That is, they perforce come to see that the issue is not *where* or from *whom* a law or a polity (or a text or a people) comes from, but whether it enables a people to govern wisely. There are differences between nations in this regard, to be sure. But insofar as one turns backward to find some source of the difference, one will find only God, in whom all polities originate. The problem with looking backward is that, unlike ends, which are concrete and measurable, origins are concretely unidentifiable and undifferentiating, and thus precisely ripe for manipulation, precisely the site of the confusion of the human with the divine. Origins of the kind that would differentiate *natio* from *natio* or person from person are dead ends for Spinoza, because, as above, they are only and always theoretical:

I acknowledge no distinction whether it is by the natural light of reason or by revelation that God teaches and commands the true practice of justice and charity, for it matters not how the practice of these virtues is revealed to us as long as it holds the place of supreme authority and is the supreme law for men. So that if

---

[25] This would transform the prospective quality of the statements of Moses and Jeremiah into something always already concluded, which is precisely how Spinoza understands moral ends (and origins). In saying that the "covenant is no longer written in ink," Spinoza is saying the same thing as he says when he insists the first covenant was immediately abrogated.

I now show that justice and charity can acquire the force of law and command only through the right of the state, I can readily draw the conclusion – since the state's right is vested in the sovereign alone – that religion can acquire the force of law only from the decree of those who have the right to command, and that God has no special sovereignty over men save through the medium of those who hold sovereignty. (TTP, 219–220)

Justice and charity cannot be separated from how particular political entities define and enact them, but neither can they be wholly reduced to one particular polity's version of them.

The notion of chosenness that is grounded in a holy (esoteric or mysterious) origin is, if not radically pernicious in the sense of giving rise to all manner of theological and philosophical arrogance, simply vapid. The test, rather, for both individuals and states is their ends, what they produce, what they amount to. What is crucial for individuals to recognize is that the more they seek their own advantage, the more useful they are to one another, and conversely, the more they conflict with one another, the less they will be able to seek their individual advantage. Spinoza's view, as we have seen, is that

there is no singular thing in Nature that is more useful to man than a man who lives according to the guidance of reason . . . for the more each one seeks his own advantage, and strives to preserve himself, the more he is endowed with virtue . . . or what is the same . . . the greater is his power of acting according to the laws of his own nature, i.e., of living from the guidance of reason. (E IV p35c1)

This is to say, then, that the more powerful (independent) individuals become, the more they will see themselves as dependent on others. Thus, paradoxically, what is most common or universal is also at the same time what is most individual or particular, for what human beings most profoundly share is the desire for power (autonomy), and this power is most fully realized in concert with others.

By the same logic, a nation's pursuit of its own distinctive ends is greatly enhanced by its conception of the commonality or universality of the divine law. The divine law needn't be conceived as an independently existing abstraction of which all particular polities are simply manifestations. This in itself is antithetical to Spinoza's notion of valuation, which is rooted in human desire. Rather, the desire for peace and security themselves gives rise to a model of the divine law that particular polities can put before themselves. As with individuals, their success or failure will be dependent on the extent to which they can live up to these ideals, but the ideals themselves will be more or less useful (vis à vis fortune) depending on their inclusivity, depending, in other words, on the imagination of the content of the divine law.

The divine law of the Hebrews, then, is inscribed not in their laws but in their hearts, for the demolition of their polity was not the demolition of God's pact, the one that commands justice and charity absolutely, the one that they strove to make historical. The case of the Hebrews reminds us, on the one hand, that justice and charity survive the fate of particular nations, for "the natural Divine Law does not enjoin ceremonial rites, that is, actions which in themselves are of no significance and are termed good merely by tradition" (TTP, 53). Spinoza stresses here that ceremonies "in themselves are of no significance" except a traditional one, while insisting in chapter 5 that "the observance of ceremonies has regard only to the temporal prosperity of the state," as other human laws do (TTP, 61). The difference is simply that, with respect to religious ceremonies, Spinoza feels an especial need to divest them of a direct relationship to blessedness since, unlike most human laws, this is what they precisely claim to lead to. A ceremony is usually something that gains its rationale simply from its source – simply from tradition or from God. This is the problem, for Spinoza – for all laws originate in God. They can be differentiated only by their ends. And this is the virtue of the Mosaic Law for him, namely that it was directed toward the creation of a "good commonwealth" (TTP, 94). Yet on the other hand, we learn at the same time that justice and charity do not exist outside some nation or other, and thus one or another nation's customs. (The "making historical," the abrogated pact, has weight.) What the Hebrews show us, through the intensity of the emotions that kept them together for a time, is that emotions like hope and fear, while they play a role in any nation, can be excessive. In the case of the Hebrews, the force of their distinctiveness vis à vis others, coupled with the devotional significance of hatred, allowed them to survive even though "scattered and stateless" (TTP, 47) – it allowed them to cling, in other words, to the divine law unmoored from its polis, which is paradoxically to make what is truly divine law into what is not even truly human law. For Spinoza, this "hatred" is not simply an emotion; it is functional, "fostered and nourished by their daily ritual" which keeps them not only distinct from others but opposed to them (TTP, 204). Whether any given person experienced this hatred is less the point than that it followed simply from the radical separation of Jew and Gentile. Spinoza can be accused of overemphasizing the "hate" involved in this separation. But his point is not only a psychological one; his argument is not undermined by the claim that separation does not *really* produce this in people. To Spinoza, it functionally does. What disturbs Spinoza about this is not Jewish distinctiveness per se, i.e., the constitution of a *natio* with its own laws and customs. It is not even the fact of hatred for outsiders, for this, he claims, is inevitable in any nation, regardless of religion, simply according to the law of human nature that,

> If someone has been affected with Joy or Sadness by someone of a class, or nation, different from his own, and this Joy or Sadness is accompanied by the idea of that person as its cause, under the universal name of the class or nation [*classis vel nationis*], he will love or hate, not only that person, but everyone of the same class or nation. (E III p46)

What Spinoza laments is that an unequivocal good – the "organis[ation of] a society under fixed laws, [the] occup[ation of] a fixed territory, and [the] concentrat[ation of] the strength of all its members into one body, as it were, a social body," is entirely substituted with what is only ever a necessary evil – the piety that engenders hate as well as loyalty (TTP, 38). With nothing to be loyal *to*, he seems to be suggesting, the only thing left is hate itself.

To be sure, Spinoza failed to investigate the ways in which a people could constitute a multitude in some kind of quasi-political sense (at least involving *potentia*) without literally occupying its land. What he was clearly worried about were the ways in which the preservation of law and custom *without* political power posed as much threat to political authority as the utter subordination of political to religious authority, represented by the Calvinist elites of his day. For him it was crucial that Moses was a *political*, as well as a religious, leader (unlike, say, Abraham). Clearly, Spinoza was not overly concerned about the survival of the Jews as a people because their survival, as he saw it close up in the Jewish communities of Holland, was purchased at too high a price, namely their depoliticization. There is, though, a simpler way of putting this. In contemporary terms, Spinoza could never have understood the lure of Judaism as essentially diasporic, for rituals and customs that do not enhance, connote, or make some reference to power (construed as the ability of a social body to act on its own counsel) could have no rationale for him.[26] More strongly, rituals and customs that do not admit and take responsibility for the power they have by definition are all the more likely to use that power in ways we can only lament.

---

[26] See Daniel Boyarin, *A Radical Jew: Paul and the Politics of Identity* (Berkeley: University of California Press, 1994), 242–246, 258–259. Boyarin's claim is that "Jewishness disrupts the very categories of identity, because it is not national, not genealogical, not religious, but all of these, in dialectical tension with one another" (244). What this means is that the Jew is actually a critic of "cultural nativisms and integrisms" (243). This is a claim that clearly does not ignore power. On the contrary, Boyarin claims that the Jew deploys the power of her laws by withholding them from an association with a particular polis. This is, like hatred for and of Jews for Spinoza, a structural point (indeed Boyarin follows Spinoza in allowing as to how it has exacerbated anti-Semitism [243]).

There is a final thing that we can learn from the "peculiar" case of the Hebrew commonwealth, and this is something Spinoza never makes entirely explicit. What he seems to be suggesting is that theocracy – however "theoretical," however temporary and unworkable, however false – is also the most perfect democracy. We cannot imitate it (there is nothing original to imitate), but every democracy in its own imperfect way testifies to the pact humankind made with God "as equals," and the Hebrews understood this correctly in seeking to make it present for themselves, even if they saw themselves (incorrectly) above all nations. This move the Hebrews made is illegitimate, but it is not wholly false. What Spinoza seems to be suggesting is that, in their own way, all peoples make this "mistake," that is, make historical what is (also thereby) eternal, and therefore all peoples have to struggle with the fact that they are commanded by two laws: one to make all human beings their neighbor, and one, just as valid, just as commanded, to value a set of particular human beings *more* – one's family, friends, cohort, *natio*. As Spinoza shows in the case of the Hebrew commonwealth, this double command was a source of strength as well, ultimately, as a source of weakness. We should not imitate them in all respects, for they took what was unique to each nation to be something unique only to them. But it is not that no nations are chosen before others. It is that each nation is chosen before others – i.e., a *natio* just is this choice, and therefore hope and fear are inevitable.

What we nevertheless learn from them is the power of dual commandedness, and thus the instability of all polities. In the Hebrew polity we vividly see the connection between the divine and the human laws – the ways in which the former only has force in the context of the latter, but then inexorably always troubles it and its finite borders. And we therefore learn something about religion – we learn *why* it cannot be set up as an *ingenium ingenio*, namely, because it is Moses with whom the Hebrews are left once the first (historical) pact with God is abrogated. It is Moses alone who bears responsibility for the interpretation of the word of God – not Moses as opposed to other human beings (with whom he must, Spinoza shows, share this power),[27] but Moses as opposed to God. It is human rulers with whom we have to deal in making religion true. The priests and pontiffs get religion wrong, to Spinoza, not simply because they lust for tyranny and secrecy over clarity, democracy, and accessibility (we all have "monstrous lusts"). They get religion wrong because they fail to learn from Moses and the Hebrews – to make explicit what is always implicit – that whatever power they possess is political in addition to religious. The political is the condition for religion to be true; and it is

---

[27] See Spinoza's discussion of Moses' successors, TTP, 258 ff.

also, then, the condition for religion to be false – in other words, tyranny is exactly the same whether in the *ecclesia* or in the *civitas*.

There is a messiness to all of this that Spinoza wants us to see. By calling religion "true" in some cases and "false" or superstitious in others, he is pointing not to instances of getting religion right, but to contexts like that of the Hebrew commonwealth which, for all its weaknesses, embodied a real adequacy, i.e., it was a context in which human beings could flourish, could move from a lesser to a greater perfection. What chapter 5 makes clear is that the laws of the Hebrews were Moses' laws; what chapter 17 makes clear is that Moses was interpreting God.[28] It was Moses who, faced with a people "exhausted by the wretched conditions of slavery," promulgated laws that "did not allow these men . . . to perform any action at their own discretion" (TTP, 66). It was God who, faced with this same exhausted multitude, commanded them to be subjects and not slaves (TTP, 195). Unlike Kant, Spinoza does not think Jewish law is necessarily heteronomous.[29] As with all human laws, the question for Spinoza is whether one is a subject, obeying the law "for the common good, and therefore for one's own good," or whether one is a son, who "by his father's command does what is to his own good also" (TTP, 185). The most important point is that the passage from one to the other, like the movement from a lesser to a greater perfection, is not a change of essence. One can begin a "son" and nevertheless become a "subject."[30] All the more did the Hebrews begin as "sons," coming out of slavery in Egypt:

---

[28] On the Bible's "recognition" of a distinction between the word of God and the word of Moses, see Tikvah Frymer-Kensy, "Revelation Revealed: The Doubt of Torah," in *Textual Reasonings: Jewish Philosophy and Text Study at the End of the Twentieth Century*, ed. Peter Ochs and Nancy Levene (Grand Rapids, Mich.: Eerdman's, 2002).

[29] Spinoza often gets lumped in with Kant and other modern figures for whom Jewish law is a mere "legalism." See most recently Novak, *Natural Law in Judaism*, 27. The claim is based on Spinoza's association of the Mosaic law with the Hebrew polity and his claim that the law itself has political and not moral significance. But this comparison is extremely misleading. For Kant, Judaism "in its original form" was "a collection of mere statutory laws" whose moral dimension was "later appended" and in no way "belongs to Judaism as such": *Religion Within the Limits of Reason Alone*, trans. Theodore M. Greene and Hoyt H. Hudson (New York: Harper Torchbooks, 1960), 116–118. For Spinoza, by contrast, the Mosaic Law is founded on the divine (moral) law and only "subsequently" became adapted to political existence. More significantly, for Kant, the particularism of Jewish "legislation" implies that its foundation is entirely different from the universal moral law, whereas for Spinoza, civil and religious laws have different "ends" but they "originate" in the same way. The issue then is not to separate out what is moral (universal) from what is legal (historical) but rather to account for the tensions and paradoxes that inhere in the very connections between these.

[30] Spinoza's language is: "we therefore recognize a great difference between a slave, a son, and a subject" (TTP, 243).

The Israelites knew scarcely anything of God, although he was revealed to them. This they made abundantly clear when a few days later they transferred to a calf the honour and worship due to him, believing the calf to be the Deity who had led them out of Egypt. Indeed, it would be hardly likely that men addicted to Egyptian superstition, uncultured and sunk in degrading slavery [*miserrima servitute*], should have had any sound understanding of God, or that Moses could have taught them anything more than a moral code [*modum vivendi*] – not, indeed, as a philosopher might inculcate the morality that is engendered by freedom of spirit, but as a lawgiver, compelling people to live good lives by command of law. Therefore the right way of life [*ratio bene vivendi*], or true living [*vera vita*], and the worship and love of God was for them bondage [*servitus*] rather than true freedom [*libertas*], the grace and gift of God. (TTP, 32)

Of course, it is possible to see Moses as overinterpreting – overdoing – his role as a "father" to the Jews. One gets a sense in the description in chapter 5 that this is Spinoza's view, though no less is it his view that the Jews themselves were (understandably) childlike as a consequence of their experiences. Nevertheless, Moses established a system of laws by which the Hebrews could recover some kind of national coherence. The strictures and minutiae, the "ceremonial observances," of Jewish law are simply a vivid example of what is true for all communities, namely, that laws are essential for the provision of life. This is so not only because "each would find strength and time fail him if he alone had to plough, sow, reap, grind, cook, weave, stitch, and perform numerous tasks to support life," but also simply because without "government and coercion" human beings could not live together at all given their "lusts and their unbridled urges" (TTP, 64). Ceremonial observances are not merely rituals: they are directed toward "temporal prosperity," and thus even though Jewish law is structured so as to insist that "men should never act of their own volition but always at another's behest," it is clearly, for Spinoza, of a piece with human law in general in its intention to aid in the flourishing of material life and in its power to transform *servitus* into *libertas* (TTP, 66).

But within the messiness there is also a point of utter clarity. Just as the pact with God is contained (as the condition) in the civil pact – both simultaneous with and prior to it – so the reverse is also true, that the pact with God contains the civil pact within it. For even in the case of the pact with God in 16 – the most theoretical of the two theoretical pacts, the one most shrouded from plain view (i.e., most erroneous if brought into plain view) – even this pact is neither abstract nor indefinite. For God does not make a pact with humankind cum every possible man, woman, and child in this world or the next – an abstract and meaningless universal. Rather, God makes a pact – and this is the very force of *pactum* – with humankind, as if it, taken together, were a *natio*. God enters into a covenant "with men," who, together and with one voice, "promised to obey God in all things." This is *not*, for Spinoza, a mythos containing a rational kernel – an imperative binding on the human condition per se or on all rational animals. The mythos *is* the imperative: the universal binding law, the one law to which all humankind is "subject," is, functionally, the law of one chosen people. It is indeed unrecoverable but it is not thereby abstract. Nature, the "divine intellect," is infinite (abstract); humankind is singular (concrete). God has infinite attributes; but an attribute just is what an intellect knows of substance as constituting its essence, and by this logic there are only two. In other words, there is no universal; there are no "men in general"; there is not even a "God in general" – God is always someone's God, always mine and not yours, as the Hebrews show us. When human beings banded together en masse in this way, with one voice, they, like Israel, were beloved of God. But therefore, when the *civitas* goes awry and needs to be reformed (or ditched), there is no recourse to the universal – to the divine law taken in itself, to "religion" in general – because the universal is just another *civitas*, and the problems there are the same.

The argument here is so delicate, yet so simple. Although the divine and human laws – reason and revelation – are eternally in conflict, one is never, except in theory, faced with a choice between the "neighbor" – the universal other – and one's clan, family, lover, friend. Choice is of particular others, desire of particular things (E II a3). It is all revelation, all theologico-political, including reason and the universal themselves. In choosing others, one learns what choice is, and what it is to be chosen, whether by family, tribe, *natio*, or *humanitas*. One is only ever striving to love chosen others – friend, lover, parent, sister, brother, tribe, *natio* – *sub specie aeternitatis*, i.e., through the lens of eternity. Man is God to man.

Hominibus apprime utile est, consuetudines iungere, seseque iis vinculis astringere, quibus aptius de se omnibus unum efficiant, & absolute ea agere, quae firmandis amicitiis inserviunt. (G II: 269)

It is especially useful to men to form associations, to bind themselves by those bonds most apt to make [from all of them] one people of them, and absolutely, to do those things which serve to strengthen friendships. (E IV appXII)[31]

The love of God

Spinoza begins chapter 5 ("Of the Reason for the Institution of the Ceremonial Observances") with the claim that what he has shown in

[31] I am grateful to Brayton Polka for making explicit the phrase that I indicate in square brackets.

chapter 4 ("Of the Divine Law") is that the divine law is "of universal application to all men." Indeed, he says, "our method of deducing it from human nature shows that it must be considered as innate in the human mind and inscribed therein, as it were" (TTP, 60). This "as it were" (*quasi*) cannot pass by unnoticed, I have argued, for Spinoza thinks that the only law that is truly innate is "Nature's necessary law," a law, namely, that "necessarily follows from the very nature of the thing, that is, its definition" (TTP, 49). As Spinoza puts it in chapter 16, "a state of nature must not be confused with a state of religion; we must conceive it as being without religion and without law, and consequently without sin and without wrong" (TTP, 188). Thus, the divine law, while innate in some (quasi) sense, follows from "human power," even as it can equally legitimately be expressed as the necessity of Nature *insofar* "as we conceive her to be determinately expressed in man's nature" (TTP, 49). Because Spinoza claims that the divine law, or the "natural Divine Law," as he sometimes calls it (TTP, 52), is innate in human nature, and expresses something eternal and necessary, it is easy simply to assume that the divine law is itself one of the laws of nature. The question has been, what does Spinoza mean by a law that, apparently unlike human laws, has the force of "eternal necessity or truth" (TTP, 54), and yet that, in its theological maxim, is accessible only via something called "moral certainty"?

Spinoza is usually careful to distinguish between the conception of God as he is popularly (theologically or imaginatively) depicted and God as that infinite substance without which nothing can be or be conceived. Insofar as God is understood in this latter sense, the "rules for living a life" that concern "our supreme good and blessedness" can be summed up in the simple precept that one should know and love God (TTP, 51). Knowledge and love, Spinoza tells us, have nothing to do with obedience, or rather, are entirely opposed to the morally certain notion that one can become blessed by obedience alone, for they concern "the knowledge and the certainty that banishes every possible doubt," namely, the knowledge of "natural phenomena" through which we can gain an ever-increasingly sure knowledge of God (TTP, 51). Put differently, the perfection of a human being is greater "according to the nature and perfection of the thing that he loves above all others. So he who loves above all the intellectual cognition of God, the most perfect Being, and takes especial delight therein, is necessarily most perfect, and partakes most in the highest blessedness" (TTP, 51).

But these two formulations seem quite different. The first (that we know God through natural phenomena) expresses Spinoza's conviction that the knowledge of the natural order is the truest path to the knowledge of God. The second articulates the path toward blessedness from the standpoint of love – she who loves what is most perfect herself becomes perfect, and presumably the discernment of what is most perfect is not limited to a knowledge of nature's laws alone (one cannot "love" a natural law). Both are true, for Spinoza, because God is not only an infinite substance, not only the totality of all that is, without which nothing can be or be conceived. God is also *our* "supreme good" (TTP, 51), and therefore knowledge of God must in some way involve a knowledge of human beings and what is perfect for them. Another way to put this is to observe that all singular things (including human beings) are dependent on God – "everything in Nature involves and expresses the conception of God in proportion to its essence and perfection" – and therefore the knowledge of God involves the knowledge of singular things. But the knowledge of these things is not simply quantitative – if it were, we would have no way in fact to know God, since a knowledge of the totality of things is utterly out of reach (by E I d6, God consists of an infinity of attributes, of which we can only know two). Spinoza's point is not that the more singular things we understand the more we will know God, but rather "the more we understand singular things, the more we understand God" (E V p24). To understand singular things in the right way (i.e., by the third kind of knowledge, *scientia intuitiva*), then, is to understand God in the right way, and this, for Spinoza, is an activity that is essentially dynamic, involving both cognition and desire: "the more the Mind is capable of understanding things by the third kind of knowledge, the more it desires to understand them by this kind of knowledge" (E V p26). It is not, then, simply that "since our intellect forms the better part of us, it is evident that we should endeavour above all to perfect it as far as we can" (TTP, 51); it is also that this perfection is affective and progressive – the more we know, the more we desire to know, and the more knowledge will be accompanied by love, "for the love of God arises from the knowledge of God" (TTP, 52).

The problem that the TTP most vividly brings to life is that love is an equivocal emotion, especially where God is concerned. While the *Ethics* makes very clear that love is an affect that can be "excessive" when it is solely focused (or fixated) on an object of pleasure that "prevents the Body from being capable of being affected in a great many other ways" (E IV p43), the TTP traces the ways in which God can in fact function as such an object. This is a very different problem from the one Spinoza in the main faces in the *Ethics*, because there the issue is simply (though of course it is by no means simple) to show the ways in which love, as a derivative of the primary affect of joy, can be both an action (that whereby the body's power of acting is increased) and a passion (that whereby the body's power of acting is diminished) (E II d3). It is not until Part V that the emotion of love is directed towards God, and by then, Spinoza has laid out what he means by "intellectual love," namely, "a desire that arises from reason [which] cannot be excessive" (E IV p61). But this rational desire for, or love of, God is not purged of its affective content; first, because insofar as the mind "considers itself and its power of acting, it rejoices, and does so the more, the more distinctly it imagines itself and its power of acting" (E III p53), and second, because the love that one possesses toward a thing we imagine to be free is "greater than if we imagine it to be necessary" (E III p49), that is, "determined by another to exist," and God in this sense is the only thing that is truly free (E I d7, p17). The intellectual love of God, it would follow, is therefore the strongest possible love (given the nature of God) and the one that enables us most to rejoice in our power, that is, our understanding (E II p58, 59).

Both of these features of the love of God involve the imagination, in the first instance directed toward ourselves and in the second instance directed toward God. Indeed, it is precisely the imagination that gives love its powerful affective force. As Spinoza says, "the mind strives to imagine only those things that posit its power of acting" (E II p54), which, when properly imagined, precisely augment that power. Love is, in other words, neither simply a synonym for understanding nor an emotion that results in equanimity. As a species of joy, it has tremendous effects in the world, most notably in Spinoza's insistence that it can "conquer hate." The way in which love conquers hate is entirely mediated through the imagination, for it is only insofar as we "imagine that the one [we] hate is affected with love towards [us]" that we will regard ourselves with joy and will strive, therefore, to "please" this other, experiencing in our own being thereby an augmentation of power in the face of which the initial hate is overcome (E III p43). Even further, according to Spinoza, this love is "greater than if Hate had not preceded it . . . for he who begins to love a thing he has hated, *or* used to regard with Sadness, rejoices because he loves, and to this Joy which Love involves . . . there is also added a Joy arising from this," namely the removal of the hate (E III p44 and dem).

Thus, while the more perfect the thing that we love is, the more perfect we will be, it is also the case that the more we love *in general* the more perfect we become, the more desire, the more *conatus* we will possess. In other words, if it is on the one hand God (as a certain kind of object) that determines whether our love is adequate or not, it is equally our love that enables us to know what God is or, in theological language, it is through love that we become (more) like God. As Spinoza puts it, no deity, not anyone else, unless he is envious, takes pleasure in my lack of power and my misfortune nor does he ascribe to virtue our tears, sighs, fears, and other things of that kind, which are signs of a weak mind. On the contrary, the greater Joy with which we are affected, the greater perfection to which we pass, i.e., the more we must participate in the divine nature. (E IV p45s)

This is not to suggest that Spinoza's concept of love is undifferentiated. Love itself can be a form of sadness insofar as it is excessive; love can actually cause us to pass to a lesser perfection (inhibit our power to act, i.e., understand, and so on). But it is to observe that love for Spinoza is double-edged, and more importantly, to see that loving the right object in the right way does not involve transforming love itself into something that is devoid of what Spinoza calls *affectus* (affect).

The problem that the TTP faces, then, is how to explain the "essential nature of the Divine Law" in such a way that it avoids the shoals of superstition while still being something that pertains solely to the human desire to increase power. Spinoza tends to articulate the "commands" of the divine law in the starkest terms, referring them, as he puts it, "only to philosophic thinking and pure activity of mind" and eschewing all "fleshly appetites which are [most people's] chief delight" (TTP, 52). But this not a distinction that works very well (to say the least) in Spinoza's metaphysics, where not only is the mind the idea of the body, but appetite "is nothing but the very essence of man [where this essence is related to the mind and body together], from whose nature there necessarily follow those things that promote his preservation" (E III p9s). What is Spinoza's point, then? Why does he use this language here, opposing love and "carnality," "the [mind's] knowledge of God" and the body's obedience to God, if elsewhere these distinctions serve him so poorly?

The answer to this has to do with the nature of love much more than with Spinoza's putatively ignorant readers. While the *Ethics* can wait until Part V to introduce the love of God, the TTP begins with a kind of love of God that is wholly problematic – that reduces God to an object among other objects, rather than seeing God as that object on which all objects depend. One way of seeing the relationship between these two texts is in terms of Spinoza's sense that, if one cannot begin the path toward knowledge of God *with* love – for this will only result in superstition – one cannot begin without it either, because love, or desire toward something that we imagine will increase our power of acting, is the very motor, so to speak, of knowledge itself. Human beings at their best do not simply seek to "know God" – why bother, we might ask? Rather, this knowledge is driven entirely by the sense that this knowledge is instrumental to our desire to preserve ourselves, and is inconceivable without this desire. Thus the knowledge of God that involves love is "innate" in the human mind, not because it concerns the apprehension of God's infinite substance, but because we imagine God as our "highest happiness and blessedness" (TTP, 51). We can therefore imagine God incorrectly, that is, we can love God in the wrong ways, precisely for the same reason that we can love God in the right ways, for we ourselves can misapprehend the actual causes of our unhappiness. "Carnal man cannot understand" that "the knowledge and love of God is the final end to which all our actions should be directed" because carnal man loves God "excessively," i.e., loves God as a thing that can increase his power over nature rather than "rejoicing" in what power he has (and thus increasing it). His knowledge of God, as Spinoza puts it, is "stunted" by desire for "fleshly" things (TTP, 52). The catch is that there is no desire (for happiness and blessedness) without some affect (of joy or sadness), and there is no affect without inadequacy, for affects are simply the "affections of the Body by which the Body's power of acting is increased or diminished," and, as a part of nature, these powers are never absolute one way or the other (E III d3).

It is in this light that Spinoza's opposition between what the Bible teaches or commands (morality) and what is innate in the mind (namely, "God in so far as his idea exists in us" [TTP, 51]) must be seen. He clearly thinks that it is essential to separate these two (kinds of) things, not because the knowledge of God has nothing to do with morality, or, for that matter, "historical narratives" or "ceremonial rites," the two other principal things that have, as he says, nothing to do with the divine law (TTP, 52–53). If on the one hand the divine law involves a consideration of the nature of the human mind apart from these things – apart from re-vealed or historical knowledge, which is always relative to communities – the mind in itself is nothing other than the desire to preserve itself, and this preservation is unthinkable outside of the *causa sui* – the ontological argument that brings desire into existence. The Bible is not *mistaken* that the love of God, embodied in the maxims of justice and charity, is our highest good. But Spinoza's point in the TTP is that if *we* take the Bible's exhortation to love God as identical to the knowledge of God, we (not it) will be incapable of stepping outside of our more primitive and self-serving notions of love – the imagination, namely, that what increases our power of acting is God himself, conceived as a being like us, a conception which is in reality a source of sadness (impotence). This "image" of God – a God who commands us "through fear of punishment [or] love of some other thing such as sensual pleasure, fame, and so forth" – is not the knowledge of God that the divine law recommends (TTP, 52).

But without some kind of image, God will not command us (because he will not affect us) at all. For Spinoza, "the Mind, as far as it can, strives to imagine those things that increase or aid the Body's power of acting" (E III p12), for the imagination is what registers this power. As long as there is nothing to exclude the present existence of a thing, our imagination of it will be more intense: "the Mind will continue to imagine this thing until it imagines something else that excludes the thing's present existence," and all the more so if the thing affects us with the joy that comes from the experience of empowerment (E III p13dem and s). God, then, while not strictly speaking a thing, will presumably give rise to the most intense imaginations possible, since there is nothing that can exclude his "present existence." Indeed, as Spinoza says, "this Love toward God must engage the Mind most . . . for this Love is joined to all the affections of the Body, which all encourage it" (E V p16).

This fact that God cannot be "excluded" clearly works both ways, for if this means that the idea of God as something present affects us intensely, there is nothing to prevent this idea from being simply false, except of course if it does in fact "encourage," or empower, the body to act. "So," Spinoza says, "the means required to achieve this end of all human action [the knowledge and love of God] – that is, God in so far as his idea exists in us – may be termed God's commands, for they are ordained for us by God himself, as it were, in so far as he exists in our minds" (TTP, 51). Since the commands of morality are "innate" only with respect to human (manmade) ends, the particular content of which each human being must choose for him or herself, morality begins with something (love) that can be both devoid of understanding (disempowering) and a signature of understanding truly. What it means to be devoid of understanding is to be torn by contrary affects, to love too many things at once or to love something that is itself uncertain – in effect, this is to be prevented from acting because of "an inconstant and irresolute spirit," which is exactly how he describes the "penalty" for not obeying the divine law (TTP, 53). But obeying the law, then, is a sign, not of a lack of understanding (ability to act) but precisely of its presence – "so long as we are not torn by affects contrary to our nature, we have the power of ordering and connecting the affections of the Body according to the order of the intellect" (E V p10).

In a fundamental sense, then, the distinction between knowledge (blessedness) and morality (salvation) does not work in Spinoza. His conception of reason is inseparable from his conception of virtue, which itself is inseparable from his conception of acquiring a disposition powerful enough to act in accord with our own natures, namely, to bring about as much of our individual flourishing as possible. The ideal philosopher of the *Ethics* is not the person most able to contemplate God's attributes, but rather the person who is able to bring about more virtue than he or she natively finds in the world. What Part V of the *Ethics* finally shows us is that the complex metaphysical account of God's nature and attributes is only in the most limited sense directed toward the understanding of "nature" as it actually is. Rather, the point above all is to know what nature *isn't*, that it isn't a teleological force directed by a providential ruler, for only in knowing and understanding this – and that therefore the real difference between good and evil depends on human desire and *conatus*, not divine fiat – that human beings can choose the good as their own end in a way that is life-affirming (that enhances desire, power to act, and so on). The ultimate point of an understanding of God's attributes is an understanding of God's *affections*, namely, the ways in which human beings, as part of the nature of God, are affected and affect other human beings and the world around them.

Thus when Spinoza says in the TTP that the masses do not have the leisure to understand God correctly or truly, he doesn't mean they do not have the intellectual ability requisite to contemplate God or that they are, any more than anyone else, subject to "monstrous lusts." He means precisely that they have not understood that valuation and teleology are relative to *them*, not to some political or religious potentate dispensing reward and punishment. Virtue is something, therefore, that they have to enact themselves – it is something whose only measure is an actual augmentation of (intellectual and moral) ability. They have not understood that "blessedness is not the reward of virtue, but virtue itself," nor that "we [do not] enjoy it because we restrain our lusts; on the contrary, because we enjoy it, we are able to restrain them" (E V p42). To Spinoza, most do not understand "why [God] is the exemplar of true life, whether this is because he has a just and merciful disposition, or because all things exist and act through him and consequently we, too, understand through him, and through him . . . see what is true, just and good" (TTP, 168).

But if the measure of virtue is an actual augmentation of ability, power, intellection, and so on, then the masses' intellectual mistake, which as always for Spinoza can equally be stated as a disempowerment, presumably can be remedied in two distinct ways, either through further understanding or through virtuous conduct. In fact, by this logic, the very notion that one can only arrive at an understanding of God through intellection has precisely mistaken what Spinoza means by God (or intellection). Thus when Spinoza refers in the TTP to "the intellectual knowledge of God which contemplates his nature as it really is in itself – a nature which men cannot imitate by a set rule of conduct nor take as their example," and claims that this knowledge "has no bearing on the practice of a true way of life, on faith, and on revealed religion," he is *not* referring to the knowledge of God with which *he* is concerned (TTP, 161). He is referring, pointedly, to the God of traditional theology, equally the God of the philosophers. It is *this* concept of a transcendent God, or rather as Spinoza would say, these "speculations" about God (TTP, 148) – the ultimate tool of interested religious authorities – which have no bearing on a true way of life. It is this notion of God which utterly divorces "mere" morality from true knowledge, and which mistakes expert speculations about God's nature for the divine law that is binding on all equally. It is this concept of God that people are perfectly free not to understand, or to have "false" views about (TTP, 162).

This is not to suggest that Spinoza thinks all truth is inherently about practical reasoning. He does have a conception of natural or scientific truth that he thinks the Bible mostly does not contain. But this scientific conception of truth, i.e., the laws of nature, is not the principal measure of philosophical enlightenment to which Spinoza is committed in the *Ethics*, and it is not, more importantly, the prerequisite of genuine piety. In failing to separate philosophy from faith, the problem is not that philosophy gets mixed up with practice, virtue, morality. The problem is primarily that faith becomes "philosophical," or speculative, thus losing its own particular force as well as extending reason where it has no business going:

Now if anyone says that, while there is no need to understand God's attributes, there is a duty to believe them straightforwardly without proof, he is plainly talking nonsense. In the case of things invisible which are objects only of the mind, proofs are the only eyes by which they can be seen; therefore those who do not have such proofs can see nothing at all of these things. So when they merely repeat what they have heard of such matters, this is no more relevant to or indicative of their mind than the words of a parrot or a puppet speaking without meaning or sense. (TTP, 160)

To be sure, the notions of justice and charity with which Spinoza operates in the TTP are not in every way identical to the virtue of the *Ethics* because, for the TTP, the point is to construct a polity in such a way that virtue is maximized even if most individuals fall short of this. The point, in other words, is to create and educate through the social conditions – the laws – in which the possibility of becoming virtuous in the sense understood by the *Ethics* can be realized. As I have shown, Spinoza does not have an especially exalted anthropology to go along with this desire, which is precisely why he focuses on maximizing the conditions for this achievement and not on the dissemination of knowledge per se. What Spinoza is getting at with the notions of justice and charity, however, is *not* some kind of "external resemblance" to actual virtue, good for the control of the masses, but insignificant philosophically.[32] Rather, as Spinoza shows throughout Part IV of the *Ethics*, it is in associations based on "justice, fairness, and being honorable" with one another that all human beings are most able to flourish as individuals, and most able to live in rational ways (E IV appXV).

In both cases, Spinoza's anthropology is a profoundly democratic one: we are all, as he says in the TTP, born "in a state of complete ignorance" and our differences can be turned toward cooperation only with great effort (TTP, 180). If anything, the *Ethics* is, even more than the TTP, directed toward the problem of ignorance and the TTP is, at least as much as the *Ethics*, convinced that difference can be a source of peace and harmony. For when one turns to the anthropology of the *Ethics*, a text dedicated to describing "how [God] comes to be the Exemplar of the true life," one finds nothing less than an account of the attributes of the multitude: one finds, in other words, nothing but the most searing portrayal of *servitus*, as well as the power of desires and passions to create both inner and outer turbulence (along with the hope and fear that are the soil of superstition). One finds, in other words, nothing other than a philosophy of *ordinary life*, not an account of some privileged and rarefied truth. Or at the very least, the "privileged truth" of Part V is only accessible by way of thickly and doggedly passing through the ordinary toils of human life.

Thus no one segment of society has a special claim on either ignorance or virtue. Spinoza's elitist rhetoric is therefore better understood as pragmatic and descriptive, not speculative and prescriptive. The multitude, to be sure, do not have the leisure or the patience to work through the arguments of a book like the *Ethics*, though in actuality, as Spinoza seems to recognize, most philosophers do not either. But the religious vision articulated there is not a speculative one in the sense of being removed from the practical cultivation of moral conduct, and this, in turn, leads us back to the language of morality and the practical in the TTP. If the *Ethics* and the TTP are textual interlocutors, each shedding light on confusing or complex claims in the other, the notion that "obedience alone can lead to salvation" is overwhelmingly the main contribution of the TTP to the argument at the end of the *Ethics*. Though it is clear from the latter that understanding and virtue (practice) are identical, the first being the condition of the second no more than the second is the condition of the first, Spinoza's brilliant move in the TTP is explicitly to show that "faith must be defined as the holding of certain beliefs about God such that, without these beliefs, there cannot be obedience to God, and if this obedience is

[32] Yovel, *Spinoza and Other Heretics*, vol. I: *The Marrano of Reason*, 145.

posited, these beliefs are necessarily posited" (TTP, 165). From reason alone, we would likely not come to the conclusion that obedience by itself could lead to true "beliefs" about God (so intoxicated is reason with its own autonomy and absolute sovereignty). But this claim is simply the claim that the only measure of understanding is virtue. The fact that this truth is "revealed" is not at all what guarantees its extraordinariness. It is extraordinary, extrarational, revealed, precisely because its truth is that truth itself, whatever its origin, is practical.

For Spinoza, then, the Bible's conception of piety is the key to its democratic character, which itself is connected to a critique of philosophy and theology as esoteric and elite. Far from the cynical concession to the masses this notion is often taken to be, Spinoza's notion of obedience encompasses everything he understands by the word *piety*, in its political character. Like the language that he uses to describe the sacred in his theory of interpretation, the term *obedience* is characterized above all by its simplicity, its clarity, its accessibility. Like moral truths, obedience refers to our conduct with others, for "Scripture itself tells us quite clearly over and over again what every man should do in order to serve God, declaring that the entire Law consists in this alone, to love to one's neighbor" (TTP, 164). But unlike morality arrived at by way of reason alone, the Bible's revelation is that by this conduct one may be "saved."

Spinoza does not *really* mean by this that as long as the masses internalize the value of obedience, the *philosophers* can be saved. He is perfectly aware that the notion of obedience can be abused, which is why he goes out of his way to root it in faith and piety. Referring to his derivation of the contents and meaning of faith from the principle of what is most general and common in Scripture, he writes, "unless I can achieve this . . . it will rightly be held that I have so far accomplished nothing. For anyone will still be able to foist on religion whatever doctrine he pleases under this same pretext, that it is a means for inculcating obedience. This is especially so," Spinoza continues, "when it is the divine attributes that are at issue," for the manipulation of divine mysteries are the dominant ways both theologians and philosophers have assured an obedient multitude, a multitude deluded into "fighting for their servitude as if for their salvation" (TTP, 3). It is a very specific notion of obedience with which Spinoza is working here, one focused on moral actions to be sure, but set apart through the notion of salvation. For the Spinoza of the *Ethics*, salvation is about the attainment of the intellectual love of God, a life's work, as Parts III, IV, and V make clear. The practice of obedience, the Spinoza of the TTP is suggesting, is its own work toward this goal: "for there is nothing to prevent God from communicating by other means to man that which we can know by the natural light" (TTP, 10):

The best thing, then, that we can do, so long as we do not have perfect knowledge of our affects, is to conceive a correct principle of living, or sure maxims of life, to commit them to memory, and to apply them constantly to the particular cases frequently encountered in life. In this way our imagination will be extensively affected by them, and we shall always have them ready. For example we have laid it down as a maxim of life . . . that Hate is to be conquered by Love, *or* Nobility, not by repaying it with Hate in return. But in order that we may always have this rule of reason ready when it is needed, we ought to think about and meditate frequently on the common wrongs of men, and how they may best be warded off by Nobility. For if we join the image of a wrong to the imagination of this maxim, it will always be ready for us . . . when a wrong is done to us. If we have ready also the principle of our own true advantage, and also of the good which follows from mutual friendship and common society, and keep in mind, moreover, that the highest satisfaction of mind stems from the right principle of living . . . and that men, like other things, act from the necessity of nature, then the wrong, or the Hate usually arising from it, will occupy a very small part of the imagination, and will easily be overcome . . .

One, therefore, who is anxious to moderate his affects and appetites from the love of Freedom alone will strive, as far as he can, to come to know the virtues and their causes, and to fill his mind with the gladness which arises from the true knowledge of them, but not at all to consider men's vices, or to disparage men, or to enjoy a false appearance of freedom. And he who will observe these [rules] carefully – for they are not difficult – and practice them, will soon be able to direct most of his actions according to the command of reason. (E V p10s)

It is possible, then, to comprehend Spinoza's claim that the maxim "man is God to man" is "confirmed by daily experience" as the claim that true knowledge must be so confirmed; it must pay attention to what experience shows us, or it will not be true. That "man is God to man" is confirmed by daily experience is at once ordinary and extraordinary. It is ordinary in that it can easily be confirmed: if one goes through life able to love singular things *sub specie aeternitatis*, this will mean a more profound immersion in their singularity, and a more profound immersion in the lessons of experience, which, to Spinoza, will always amount to the commonplace that "there is no singular thing in Nature that is more useful to man than a man who lives according to the guidance of reason" (E IV p35c1). There is no "confirmation" of this fact other than the experience of it. But this is also, then, something extraordinary, for if one ends in ordinary experience, one begins there as well. As Spinoza describes the beginning of his philosophical journey in the well-known opening paragraph of the TdIE:

After experience had taught me that all the things which regularly occur in ordinary life are empty and futile, and I saw that all the things which were the cause or object of my fear had nothing of good or bad in themselves, except insofar as my mind was moved by them, I resolved at last to try to find out whether there was anything which would be the true good, capable of communicating itself, and which alone would affect the mind, all others being rejected – whether there was something which, once found and acquired, would continuously give me the greatest joy, to eternity. (TdIE, §1)[33]

The labor that is involved in moving from this comment in TdIE to Part V of the *Ethics* is nothing short of monumental. One *experiences* this in reading it alone, never mind living it out, as Spinoza well knew: "if the way I have shown to lead to [blessedness] now seems very hard, still, it can be found. And of course, what is found so rarely must be hard" (E V p42s).

---

[33] Pierre-François Moreau's monumental *L'Expérience et l'éternité* (Paris: Presses Universitaires de France, 1994), devoted to an exploration of the centrality of the concept of experience in Spinoza's thought, takes off from this comment in the TdIE, as well as a comment Spinoza makes to Simon de Vries (Ep 10) concerning the role of experience in comprehending eternal truths.

Conclusion

Spinoza has always been hard to place in the history of philosophy, religion, and politics. Unlike many of Spinoza's medieval precursors, for whom reason and revelation were hierarchically related, and unlike many of his contemporaries, for whom reason and revelation agreed in all important respects except for the supernatural claims of the latter (to which reason gives informed but deferential assent), Spinoza attempted to put this perennial question on a footing which leaves both sovereign. In so doing, he developed a way of thinking not simply about the relationship (epistemological and ontological) between God and human beings, but about the relationship between thinking, interpretation, and political life whose conceptual riches were in many respects misunderstood or misplaced by later thinkers.[1]

This book has shown that the difficulty of placing Spinoza – and the tendency to see his authorship divided against itself – has its source at the very heart of his project. For Spinoza's critique is, above all, a double-edged one. His critique of religion is also a defense of religion; his critique of reason is also a defense of reason; his critique of law is also a defense of law. What Spinoza critiques above all is the attempt to attain salvation or blessedness, whether philosophical, theological, or political – the attempt to attain *libertas* – by escaping the struggle, labor, work of transforming bondage, slowly and with great effort, into freedom. His critique, therefore, is equally of origins and ends insofar as they are figured as pristine loci of everything which human beings are not: pure divinity, pure reason, pure freedom. This figuration, this temptation, is not only found in theological depictions of a paradise lost and ultimately to be regained, though this depiction is an important target in his work. It is also found

---

[1] The most impressive recent rethinking of Spinoza's influence is Jonathan Israel's *Radical Enlightenment: Philosophy and the Making of Modernity 1650–1750* (New York: Oxford University Press, 2001). Israel challenges the assumption that Spinoza's thought was obscure or marginal in the European Enlightenment, showing that Spinoza was central to what is called the Radical Enlightenment, and that this latter was itself central to the Enlightenment *tout court*.

in philosophical conceptions of truth as eternal (everlasting), of liberty as contemplative of one's ends, of reason as a connection to things or ideas as they are in themselves. Spinoza's formidable insight is that the alternative to eternity is not temporality, not the claim that truth is simply finite, corruptible, relative, (thus) nonexistent. Indeed, this "alternative" is nothing of the kind, for holding that truth is eternal, found not made, pursued not created, is to admit that it does not exist, for, to Spinoza, what we do not take part in making, in interpreting, we are forever ignorant of. What Spinoza shows is that the alternative to the eternal as what has always been is the eternal as what originates, creates, makes: reveals. Only what has not always existed can exist (eternally). Only what is eternal has a beginning. Only what begins is eternal, sacred, fruitful.

For Spinoza, then, what is at stake is not (necessarily) God any more than it is (necessarily) reason or religion or politics. God, reason, and law can be equally wrongheaded or equally liberating, and it is a thoroughgoing waste of time to parse the difference between them while ignoring the difference they, together, inaugurate. What is at stake for Spinoza is, precisely, inauguration, beginning: again, revelation. What matters, for Spinoza, is that what will move human beings from bondage to freedom – *conatus* – is always already in the world because – as the *causa sui* – it has come into the world. Insofar as origins originate, they cannot exist in themselves (cannot be recovered, are not original). Religion, democracy, and reason, then, can be the substance of *libertas*, can be true eternally, because they are what we strive to originate. They are eternally true only as long we continue to do so.

Despite his vaunted conservatism, Spinoza was a revolutionary thinker in explicitly turning most of the major intellectual and political commonplaces of his day (and ours) on their head. Among the many paradoxes of this endeavor is the extent to which perhaps the most uncommonplace thing to hold in the early years of the Enlightenment (as in the late) is that the truth, the one truth to which we need to be committed, is itself a commonplace – not just that it is known by the authority of reason alone, but that it is socially commonplace, i.e., available to the masses, experienced by everyone. This one truth of Spinoza's, namely that religion, reason, and politics all come to the same recognition that "man is God to man," is rooted in what he shows is the complexity of the ordinary – its hold on us and its burden for us. For Spinoza, what matters are habits of thinking – whether religious or secular – that posit salvation or blessedness as transcendent of where one happens to be. Although he focused primarily on the tendency of religious thinking to create transcendent ideals (in the form of God), no ideal – or in theologico-political terms, no "pontiff", no "despot" – was immune for him. His point is that if God is conceived as transcendent of the world, then a whole assortment of other ideals get dragged along with this one, most importantly the ideals of intellection that human beings then set themselves, according to which reason is cast as something transcendent of the body or nature. To be in a state of blessedness, on this view, is to be in contradiction with oneself, an ideal that can only have lamentable political consequences.

It is this line of thinking that I have followed out in Spinoza, namely, his transfiguration of both transcendence and immanence – his conception of both transcendence and immanence as containing their own critique. This is a critique not simply of religion or reason moving beyond their proper bounds, but a critique of the inexorable human tendency to seek to think beyond our proper bounds, and therefore an account of the continual need to recover (and recover from) the relationship between *servitus* and *libertas*, which is therefore (for good and for ill) in some sense a permanent, if ever unstable, dimension of human life. To focus solely on Spinoza's views on God is to mistake his investment in the difference between truth and illusion with some theological claim about God's whereabouts, in which he had little invested in itself. As he puts it in the brief introduction to the second part of the *Ethics* (after having focused on God in Part I),

> I pass now to explaining those things which must necessarily follow from the essence of God, or the infinite and eternal Being – not, indeed, all of them, for we have demonstrated (E I p16) that infinitely many things must follow from it in infinitely many modes, but only those that can lead us, by the hand, as it were, to the knowledge of the human Mind and its highest blessedness.

Spinoza's unorthodoxy lies in the claim that what revelation shows that we wouldn't otherwise have "known" is not a set of metaphysical beliefs but a practice, a "rule of life," a law. What revelation shows that we wouldn't otherwise have "believed" is that this law is the law of reason itself. Revelation is the principle of interpretation, the principle that shows us that reason itself is not self-evident and therefore always requires faith. It shows, as with Bible and reader, that reason is the standard of itself and faith is the standard of itself, and each are rational if and only if they are neither confused for nor divorced from one another. If only human beings could act rationally, Spinoza always speculates, there would be no need for (human) law. Everyone would simply act in conformity with her true interests and this would provide the unproblematic condition for social harmony. But human beings never simply act rationally; or rather, rationality is not simple. Like the divine law, it is only quasi-innate – binding, true, universal – requiring something from us to make it fully so. Human laws are those laws that connect us to history, narrative, prophecy, revelation – that enable all to attain the divine law of reason.

Spinoza's own rhetoric in the TTP sometimes belies this point, opposing mathematical truths to moral ones, what is universally true to what is merely historically, theologically, or politically contingent, what is true for the few (achieving blessedness through reason alone) to what is true for the many (achieving salvation through obedience). But it is not necessary to have recourse to the *Ethics* to see that Spinoza's metaphysics does not bear these oppositions out. His scalding critique of this kind of oppositional thinking is the substance of the TTP from beginning to end. That he is less careful in the TTP than in the *Ethics* not to fall into using this language himself is doubtless connected to the fact that, in his day, the opponents were primarily theological and he must have felt the need to counter them – to criticize theology – with especial fervor (all the more surprising, though, that he does not leave philosophical opponents out of his critique). In our day, it is, if anything, just the opposite. It has been almost impossible to see his defense of theology – his critique of philosophy – with anything other than a cynically jaundiced eye. But Spinoza is, ultimately, consistent and rhetorically clear that both critiques, both defenses, are his.

Mindful of the many controversies which Spinoza's work has perennially stimulated, one might ask: Whose Spinoza is this? What has *he* originated? What can we still learn from him? In this book, I have sought to position Spinoza as a thinker whose most fundamental insight is that the human project to attain freedom, morality, and peace is at once a philosophical, a theological, and a political endeavor – more precisely that the theologico-political task of forming just human societies is the condition of the philosophical task of understanding (and vice versa) – that both presuppose the labor of *conatus* and *causa sui*. While there is no more sober critique of the foibles and errors of humankind, Spinoza's dialectics of divine and human, elite and vulgar, sacred and profane, freedom and obedience, knowledge and love ultimately constitute a defense of the power of the human being in solidarity with others: man is God to man. The issue is not only that Spinoza's metaphysical and political thought is unified. The issue is the complex negotiation of human inadequacy, both metaphysical and political, that Spinoza makes dependent upon a critique of metaphysics (theology and philosophy) and politics from the standpoint of revelation, a term I have used throughout to connect *causa sui* (the cause of itself) with *conatus* (effort, striving).

Spinoza's revelation that revelation itself is *causa sui* has generated a certain discomfort especially among readers in modern Jewish thought, who have otherwise cause to want to celebrate Spinoza's contribution to the field. I have argued that, in making the *causa sui* about the most valuable and most difficult human project, which, as the Bible would have it, is to become holy as God is holy – to become, in the words of Genesis, "like God" – Spinoza does defend a biblical concept of creation. Part of what Spinoza is always asking is the very elemental question: Why have a notion of God at all? Or revelation? Or eternity? What is the allure of these concepts? What exactly would one be giving up if one abandoned them, or more positively, what does one gain by holding them to be true?

Biblically speaking, the concept of God contains two principal dimensions. God is separate from the world as its creator (as God famously says to Job, "where were you when I laid the foundations of the earth?" [Job 38: 4]) and God is connected to the world as its center ("I the Lord am your God who brought you out of the land of Egypt, the house of bondage: You shall have no other gods besides Me" [Exod. 20: 2]). Both are needed theologically in order to depict what the Bible seeks to depict: the struggles of human beings to become holy; moral; truthful; righteous. God's separateness is his power to create from nothing; his connection is his determination to share that power – covenantally – with his people. In the Bible, human beings know what righteousness is. Unlike, say, Socrates, they know *what* they don't know (not just *that* they don't know) – they know what error is, what immorality is, what weakness is; they know what the standard is even if they don't attain it. They are not *on the way* to knowledge but to understanding and freedom, for "as the light makes both itself and the darkness plain, so truth is the standard of itself and the false" (E II p41s). In Spinoza's language, they do not desire the good, but the good is what they desire – they desire "what [they] certainly know to be useful to [them]" (E IV d1), even if it proves less useful than anticipated. In the Bible, God is not blacked out, as he is quite literally at the end of the *Republic* or in book 10 of Aristotle's *Metaphysics*. He may be hidden in the sense that we don't see clearly; but it is God that is before us, and whether we see clearly or fully is up to us.

Both features of God are present in Spinoza. God is separate from the world in the sense that, in the beginning, nothing in the world does what God does: *causa sui*. Spinoza doesn't need God to be a separate being in order to assert that God is separate. In nature, there are two kinds of thing: those that cause themselves and those that are caused by another. Human beings (and all natural beings) begin Part I as the latter. God begins Part I as the former. In Spinoza's terms, this means simply that a human being is, in the beginning, a being who experiences the power of the standard, the power of freedom, independence, eternity, and equally experiences her inadequacy in all respects. Freedom is, for the human being of Part I, separate from where she is. She is unfree. But God is also, in Spinoza, connected to the world. And this is the crux of Spinoza's God from a biblical standpoint. For Spinoza, what the *causa sui* enables is the recognition both of radical otherness and of radical intimacy – of inexorable inadequacy and adequacy nonetheless.

Where human beings are concerned, then, what matters are two things: first, that they are not *causa sui*, not free, not eternal. And second, that they can become so. This is the only sense in which Spinoza can be called a monist: namely, that there are two things (freedom and unfreedom), but that, as he says of truth and falsity, one is the standard of itself and the other. God causes himself and his other. Unlike in Aristotle/Maimonides, where, for all the rhetoric of *imitatio dei* or the contemplation of God, it is ruled out in principle, in Spinoza this imitation or becoming like God is the very meaning of the ontological argument (which is the holding together of the divine and the human, God and mind, the infinite and the finite). For Spinoza, holding a concept of God is only meaningful if it makes sense to speak of human beings as achieving something that transcends them (goodness, holiness, righteousness). Or more positively, if one does speak of human beings achieving something transcendent in this sense, one is employing a concept of God. What one might seem to give up with his concept – a sense of reverence, perhaps, for something greater than ourselves – is hardly lost, and indeed it is augmented. As anyone who has tried to read Spinoza's books knows, the obstacles to becoming free, independent, eternal (in Spinoza's sense of self-caused) are far more monumental and awesome precisely because we see the fruits of what might be if they are overcome. As Kant would later insist, the fact that there are no examples of a good will should not incline us to resignation, but to effort. That the good is hidden from us is not something about it, but something about us. The *causa sui* in Spinoza is just as stark and "impossible" as the notion of freedom in Kant. Or rather, one could say that if one wants to understand just how difficult Kant's project is, one can look at E I d1. Or Leviticus 9: 2 ("you shall be holy for I, your God, am holy"). We are accustomed to think that mere human freedom, even human holiness, is a great deal easier to enact than the creation of the world. Spinoza enables us to see, perhaps unfortunately, why this is not true.

Spinoza truly forces us to think at our limits. What he is saying is that the old frameworks for God fail to produce a viable theology on their own grounds. His work is directly about this failure – about the untenable consequences that follow from being beholden to a transcendent God, and the virtues of being beholden to the proposition that man is God to man: that God is man to man (E IV p35s). But his work is also, primarily, about human beings and why they think what they do and what difference it makes. What he shows is that our love for a so-called personal God can be just as neurotic as our love for other human beings can be; but *amor Dei* is enlightenment itself – our love of God is the greatest engine, realized only in becoming like God. If this were to happen, God would then disappear only from his perch as master of the world (which perch he has only by virtue of our inadequate understanding); he would reappear in the intimacy of between "man and man," where Spinoza finds him in the first and last place.

It is in this light that it is possible to say that not only is Spinoza's a biblical God, with a biblical concept of creation; Spinoza's God is in fact far closer to biblical theology and philosophy than many, perhaps most, Jewish theological positions through the ages, and not simply because he avoids the rabbinic readings that transform the Bible. His ultimate debate is with philosophy, not the rabbis. The Bible's "meaning," its *sensus*, is that God created the heavens and the earth. Its philosophical truth is usually rendered as that the one created the many. Spinoza renders it as that the one created the one and the many. God created God and human beings. It is a bizarre notion only for eyes that are trained to look for the ultimately finite difference between the one and the many, eternity and time, infinite and finite; for eyes trained to see contradiction where there is in fact paradox.

The *causa sui*, Spinoza shows, is what preserves the difference between God and human beings without using finitude to do so. The *causa sui*, Spinoza shows, infinitely shows us what are our origins, and ultimately, with great effort, our end. Of course there is a disanalogy between God and human beings; this he acknowledges from the beginning. There are no examples of a person causing herself, i.e., becoming perfectly independent. What Spinoza shows is what it *means* to speak of God doing so. So instead of saying gnomic things about God and then requiring that one either believe or disbelieve them depending on previous spiritual commitments, Spinoza shows us what it would mean *to us* to assert something like creation *of God*. What it shows is that *if* we assert this of God, we must be prepared to assert something *like* this of human beings, too. In other words, we must be prepared to bring it about that we are capable of what we attribute to God, however difficult and rare. The theological claim, then, is that God only exists if we (strive to) become like God; if we don't (strive to) become like God, God doesn't exist. God only exists if she can, in fact, disappear. God disappears only if her existence can be proven.

It is not enough to say that Spinoza bridges the contradiction between immanence and transcendence. Spinoza's God is transcendent horizontally – we are not there yet, if we ever will be, depending on our own effort.

This is no less transcendent than the vertical kind, because what matters in transcendence is difference. God is immanent, too, of course, not because the world is God but because in our aspiration to become *causa sui*, we do not have to become something other than what we are. Thus God's disappearance is obviously only apparent; since to disappear in this sense is to become, in fact, utterly present *as* the human essence. The supposed piety of considering it impossible to imagine how God could have created the world has nothing on trying to imagine how God could have brought himself into being as the call that demands we all, philosophically, theologically, politically, do the same. The greatest challenge of freedom is to hold together the fact that it is both perfectly ordinary (i.e., lawful, available to all) and yet never free from interpretation, which in Spinoza's case always involves the difficult task of aligning one's life with what one knows, reads, hears. If ultimately the most common, and the most elevated, notion is that man is God to man, this must be the beginning, and not only the end, of a life's work.

Bibliography

WORKS BY SPINOZA

Spinoza, Benedictus de. *The Collected Works of Spinoza*. Ed. and trans. Edwin
   Curley. Vol. I. Princeton, N.J.: Princeton University Press, 1985.
The Letters. Trans. Samuel Shirley. Indianapolis: Hackett, 1995.
The Political Works. Ed. and trans. A. G. Wernham. Oxford: Clarendon Press,
   1958.
Theological-Political Treatise. Trans. Samuel Shirley. Indianapolis: Hackett,
   1998.
Spinoza Opera. Ed. Carl Gebhardt. 4 vols. Heidelberg: Carl Winter, 1925.

OTHER WORKS

Anselm, *Proslogion*. Trans. M. J. Charlesworth. Notre Dame, Ind.: University of
   Notre Dame Press, 1965.
Aquinas, St. Thomas. *Saint Thomas Aquinas on Law, Morality, and Politics*. Ed.
   William P. Baumgarth and Richard J. Regan, SJ. Indianapolis: Hackett,
   1988.
Aristotle. *The Complete Works of Aristotle*. Ed. Jonathan Barnes. 2 vols. Princeton,
   N.J.: Princeton University Press, 1984.
Balibar, Etienne. *Spinoza: From Individuality to Transindividuality*. Delft: Eduron
   1997.
   "*Jus-Pactum-Lex*: On the Constitution of the Subject in the *Theologico-
   Political Treatise*." In *The New Spinoza*. Ed. Warren Montag and Ted Stolze.
   Minneapolis: University of Minnesota Press, 1997.
Spinoza and Politics. Trans. Peter Snowdon. London: Verso, 1998.
   "Spinoza, the Anti-Orwell: The Fear of the Masses." Trans. Ted Stolze, rev.
   J. Swenson and E. Balibar. In *Masses, Classes, Ideas: Studies on Politics and
   Philosophy Before and After Marx*. New York: Routledge, 1994.
Barbone, Steven. "Power in the *Tractatus Theologico-Politicus*." In *Piety, Peace, and
   the Freedom to Philosophize*. Ed. Paul Bagley. Dordrecht: Kluwer Academic
   Publishers, 1999.
Bartuschat, W. "The Ontological Basis of Spinoza's Theory of Politics." In
   Spinoza's Political and Theological Thought. Ed. C. De Deugd. Amsterdam:
   North-Holland, 1984.
Bayle, Pierre. *Historical and Critical Dictionary* [1697]. Indianapolis: Hackett,
   1991.

Belaief, Gail. *Spinoza's Philosophy of Law*. The Hague: Mouton, 1971.

Bennett, Jonathan. "Eight Questions about Spinoza." In *Spinoza On Knowledge and the Human Mind*. Ed. Yirmiyahu Yovel. Leiden: E. J. Brill, 1994.

A Study of Spinoza's "Ethics." Indianapolis: Hackett, 1984.

Berman, Lawrence V. "Maimonides on the Fall of Man." *AJS Review* 5 (1980): 1–15.

Boyarin, Daniel. *A Radical Jew: Paul and the Politics of Identity*. Berkeley: University of California Press, 1994.

Buber, Martin. *Between Man and Man*. Trans. Ronald Gregor Smith. New York: Collier Books, 1965.

Curley, Edwin. *Behind the Geometrical Method*. Princeton, N.J.: Princeton University Press, 1988.

"Notes on a Neglected Masterpiece: Spinoza and the Science of Hermeneutics." In *Spinoza: The Enduring Questions*. Ed. Graeme Hunter. Toronto: University of Toronto Press, 1994, 64–99.

Davidson, Herbert. "Maimonides' Secret Position on Creation." In *Studies in Medieval Jewish History and Literature*. Ed. Isadore Twersky. Cambridge, Mass.: Harvard University Press, 1979.

De Deugd, C., ed. *Spinoza's Political and Theological Thought*. Amsterdam: North-Holland, 1984.

Den Uyl, Douglas J. *Power, State, and Freedom*. Assen: Van Gorcum, 1983.

"Power, Politics, and Religion in Spinoza's Political Thought." In *Piety, Peace, and the Freedom to Philosophize*. Ed. Paul Bagley. Dordrecht: Kluwer Academic Publishers, 1999, 133–158.

Descartes, René. *The Philosophical Writings of Descartes*. Ed. and trans. John Cottingham, Robert Stoothoff, and Dugald Murdoch. 3 vols. Cambridge: Cambridge University Press, 1985.

Donagan, Alan. *Spinoza*. Chicago: University of Chicago Press, 1988.

"Spinoza's Theology." In *The Cambridge Companion to Spinoza*. Ed. Don Garrett. Cambridge: Cambridge University Press, 1996.

Fix, Andrew C. *Prophecy and Reason: The Dutch Collegiants in the Early Enlightenment*. Princeton, N.J.: Princeton University Press, 1991.

Freudenthal, J. *Spinoza: Sein Leben und seine Lehre*. Vol. I: *Das Lebens Spinozas*. Stuttgart: Frommann, 1904. Vol. II: *Die Lehre Spinozas auf Grund des Nachlasses*. Heidelberg: Carl Winter, 1927.

Frymer-Kensy, Tikvah. "Revelation Revealed: The Doubt of Torah." In *Textual Reasonings: Jewish Philosophy and Text Study at the End of the Twentieth Century*. Ed. Peter Ochs and Nancy Levene. Grand Rapids, Mich.: Eerdman's, 2002.

Haddad-Chamakh, F. "Liberté individuelle et paix civile d'après le *Traité théologico-politique* de Spinoza." In *Spinoza's Political and Theological Thought*. Ed. C. De Deugd. Amsterdam: North-Holland, 1984.

Harris, Jay M. *How Do We Know This? Midrash and the Fragmentation of Modern Judaism*. Albany: State University of New York Press, 1995.

Harvey, Warren Zev. "A Portrait of Spinoza as a Maimonidean." *Journal of the History of Philosophy* 19 (1981): 151–72.

"Maimonides' Commentary on Genesis 3: 22." *Daat* 12 (1984): 15–22.

Hazard, Paul. *The European Mind 1680–1715.* Trans. J. Lewis May. New York: Meridian, 1963.

Hegel, Georg Wilhelm Friedrich. *Lectures on the Philosophy of Religion.* Vol. I. Ed. Peter C. Hodgson, trans. R. F. Brown, P. C. Hodgson, and J. M. Stewart. Berkeley: University of California Press, 1984.

Hobbes, Thomas. *Leviathan.* Ed. Richard Tuck. Cambridge: Cambridge University Press, 1996.

On the Citizen. Ed. Richard Tuck and Michael Silverthorne. Cambridge: Cambridge University Press, 1998.

Israel, Jonathan. "The Banning of Spinoza's Works in the Dutch Republic (1670–1678)." In *Disguised and Overt Spinozism around 1700.* Ed. Wiep van Bunge and Wim Klever. Leiden: E. J. Brill, 1996, 3–14.

The Dutch Republic: Its Rise, Greatness, and Fall 1477–1806. New York: Clarendon Press, 1995.

Radical Enlightenment: Philosophy and the Making of Modernity 1650–1750. New York: Oxford University Press, 2001.

Israel, Menasseh ben. *The Conciliator: Reconcilement of the Apparent Contradictions in Holy Scripture.* London, 1842.

Ivry, Alfred. "Maimonides on Possibility." In *Mystics, Philosophers, and Politicians: Essays in Jewish Intellectual History in Honor of Alexander Altmann.* Ed. Judah Reinharz and Daniel Swetschinski. Durham, N.C.: Duke University Press, 1982.

Kant, Immanuel. *Critique of Pure Reason.* Trans. Norman Kemp Smith. New York: Macmillan, 1929.

Religion Within the Limits of Reason Alone. Trans. Theodore M. Greene and Hoyt H. Hudson. New York: Harper Torchbooks, 1960.

Kaplan, Yosef. *From Christianity to Judaism: The Story of Isaac Orobio de Castro.* Oxford: Oxford University Press, 1989.

Katz, D. S. and J. Israel, eds. *Sceptics, Millenarians, and Jews.* Leiden: E. J. Brill, 1990.

Kellner, Menachem Marc. *Maimonides on Human Perfection.* Atlanta, Ga.: Scholars Press, 1990.

Kierkegaard, Søren. *Philosophical Fragments.* Trans. Howard V. Hong and Edna H. Hong. Princeton, N.J.: Princeton University Press, 1985.

Klein-Braslavy, Sara. "The Creation of the World and Maimonides' Interpretation of Genesis I–V." In *Maimonides and Philosophy.* Ed. Shlomo Pines and Yirmiyahu Yovel. Dordrecht: M. Nijhoff, 1986.

Levene, Nancy. "Ethics and Interpretation, or How to Study Spinoza's *Tractatus Theologico-Politicus* without Strauss." *Journal of Jewish Thought and Philosophy* 10 (2000): 57–110.

Levene, Nancy and Peter Ochs, eds. *Textual Reasonings: Jewish Philosophy and Text Study at the End of the Twentieth Century.* Grand Rapids, Mich.: Eerdmans, 2002.

Levy, Ze'ev. *Baruch or Benedict: On Some Jewish Aspects of Spinoza's Philosophy.* New York: Peter Lang, 1989.

Locke, John. *An Essay Concerning Human Understanding.* Ed. Peter Nidditch. Oxford: Clarendon Press, 1975.

Macherey, Pierre. *Hegel ou Spinoza*. Paris: François Maspero, 1979.

Machiavelli, Niccolò. *The Chief Works and Others*. Trans. Allan Gilbert. Vol. I. Durham, N.C.: Duke University Press, 1989.

Maimonides, Moses. *Guide of the Perplexed*. Ed. and trans. Shlomo Pines. 2 vols. Chicago: University of Chicago Press, 1963.

A Maimonides Reader. Ed. Isadore Twersky. West Orange, N.J.: Behrman House, 1972.

Mark, Thomas Carson. *Spinoza's Theory of Truth*. New York: Columbia University Press, 1972.

Marx, Karl. "On the Jewish Question." In *The Marx-Engels Reader*. Ed. Robert Tucker. 2nd edn. New York: W. W. Norton and Co., 1978, 26–53.

Mason, Richard. "Faith Set Apart from Philosophy? Spinoza and Pascal." In *Piety, Peace, and the Freedom to Philosophize*. Ed. Paul Bagley. Dordrecht: Kluwer Academic Publishers, 1999.

The God of Spinoza: A Philosophical Study. New York: Cambridge University Press, 1997.

Matheron, Alexandre. *Le Christ et le salut des ignorants chez Spinoza*. Paris: Aubier, 1971.

Individu et communauté chez Spinoza. Paris: Editions de Minuit, 1969.

"Le Problème de l'évolution de Spinoza du *Traité théologico-politique* au *Traité politique*." In *Spinoza: Issues and Directions*. Ed. Edwin Curley and Pierre-François Moreau. Leiden: E. J. Brill, 1990.

"The Theoretical Function of Democracy in Spinoza and Hobbes." In *The New Spinoza*. Ed. Warren Montag and Ted Stolze. Minneapolis: University of Minnesota Press, 1997.

"Le *Traité théologique-politique* vu par le jeune Marx." *Cahiers Spinoza* 1 (1977): 159–212.

Meinsma, K. O. *Spinoza et son cercle* [1896]. Ed. Henri Méchoulan and Pierre-François Moreau. Paris: Vrin, 1980.

Mignini, F. "Theology as the Work and Instrument of Fortune." In *Spinoza's Political and Theological Thought*. Ed. C. De Deugd. Amsterdam: North-Holland, 1984.

Montag, Warren. *Bodies, Masses, Power: Spinoza and his Contemporaries*. London: Verso, 1999.

Montag, Warren and Ted Stolze, eds. *The New Spinoza: Theory out of Bounds*. Minneapolis: University of Minnesota Press, 1997.

Moreau, Pierre-François. "Fortune and the Theory of History." In *The New Spinoza: Theory Out of Bounds*. Ed. Warren Montag and Ted Stolze. Minneapolis: University of Minnesota Press, 1997.

Spinoza: L'Expérience et l'éternité. Paris: Presses Universitaires de France, 1994.

Nadler, Steven. *Spinoza: A Life*. Cambridge: Cambridge University Press, 1999.

Negri, Antonio. "*Reliqua Desiderantur*: A Conjecture for a Definition of the Concept of Democracy in the Final Spinoza." In *The New Spinoza*. Ed. Warren Montag and Ted Stolze. Minneapolis: University of Minnesota Press, 1997.

The Savage Anomaly: The Power of Spinoza's Metaphysics and Politics. Trans. Michael Hardt. Minneapolis: University of Minnesota Press, 1991.

Nesher, Dan. "Spinoza's Theory of Truth." In *Spinoza: The Enduring Questions*. Ed. Graeme Hunter. Toronto: University of Toronto Press, 1994, 140–177.

Niermeyer, J. F. *Mediae Latinitatis Lexicon Minus*. Leiden: E. J. Brill, 1984.

Norris, Christopher. *Spinoza and the Origins of Modern Critical Theory*. Oxford: Blackwell, 1991.

Novak, David. *The Election of Israel: The Idea of the Chosen People*. Cambridge: Cambridge University Press, 1995.

  Natural Law in Judaism. Cambridge: Cambridge University Press, 1998.

Novak, David, ed. *Leo Strauss and Judaism: Athens and Jerusalem Critically Revisited*. Lanham, Md.: Rowman & Littlefield, 1996.

Otten, Willemien. "Nature and Scripture: Demise of a Medieval Analogy." *Harvard Theological Review* 88.2 (1995): 257–84.

Pascal, Blaise. *Pensées*. Trans. A. J. Krailsheimer. New York: Penguin Books, 1966.

Pines, Shlomo. "The Limitations of Human Knowledge According to Al Farabi, Ibn Bajja, and Maimonides." In *Studies in Medieval Jewish History and Literature*. Ed. Isadore Twersky. Cambridge, Mass.: Harvard University Press, 1979.

  "Spinoza's *Tractatus Theologico-Politicus*, Maimonides, and Kant." In *Further Studies in Philosophy*. Ed. Ora Segal. Scripta Hierosolymitana, vol. XX. Jerusalem: Magnes Press, 1968.

Plato. *Euthyphro* and *Phaedo*. In *Five Dialogues*. Trans. G. M. A. Grube. Indianapolis: Hackett, 1981.

  Republic. Trans. G. M. A. Grube. Indianapolis: Hackett, 1981.

Polka, Brayton. "Spinoza and Biblical Interpretation: The Paradox of Modernity." *The European Legacy* 1.5 (1996): 1673–1682.

  "Spinoza and the Separation between Philosophy and Theology." *Journal of Religious Studies* 16.1–2 (1990): 91–119.

  "Spinoza's Concept of Biblical Interpretation." *Journal of Jewish Thought and Philosophy* 2 (1992): 19–44.

Popkin, Richard H. *Isaac La Peyrère (1596–1676): His Life, Work, and Influence*. Leiden: E. J. Brill, 1987.

  "The Religious Background of Seventeenth-Century Philosophy." *Journal of the History of Philosophy* 25 (1987): 35–50.

  "Spinoza and Bible Scholarship." In *The Cambridge Companion to Spinoza*. Ed. Don Garrett. Cambridge: Cambridge University Press, 1996.

Preus, J. Samuel. "The Bible and Religion in the Century of Genius." Part I: "Religion on the Margins." Part II: "The Rise and Fall of the Bible." Part III: "The Hidden Dialogue in Spinoza's *Tractatus*." Part IV: "Prophecy, Knowledge, and Study of Religion." *Religion* 28 (1998): 3–27, 111–138.

  Spinoza and the Irrelevance of Biblical Authority. Cambridge: Cambridge University Press, 2001.

Ravven, Heidi M. "The Garden of Eden: Spinoza's Maimonidean Account of the Genealogy of Morals and the Origin of Society." *Philosophy and Theology* 13.1 (2001): 3–51.

  "Spinoza's Rupture with Tradition: His Hints of a Jewish Modernity." In *Jewish Themes in Spinoza's Philosphy*. Ed. Heidi M. Ravven and Lenn E. Goodman. Albany: State University of New York Press, 2002, 187–223.

Rice, Lee C. "Emotion, Appetition, and *Conatus* in Spinoza." *Revue internationale de philosophie* 31 (1977): 101–116.

"Faith, Obedience, and Salvation." *Lyceum* 6 (1994): 1–20.

"Individual and Community in Spinoza's Social Psychology." In *Spinoza: Issues and Directions*. Ed. Edwin Curley and Pierre-François Moreau. Leiden: E. J. Brill, 1990.

"Meyer as Precursor to Spinoza on the Interpretation of Scripture." *Philosphy and Theology* 13.1 (2001): 159–180.

Rosenthal, Michael. "Why Spinoza Chose the Hebrews: The Exemplary Function of Prophecy in the *Theological-Political Treatise*." In *Jewish Themes in Spinoza's Philosphy*. Ed. Heidi M. Ravven and Lenn E. Goodman. Albany: State University of New York Press, 2002, 225–260.

Rousseau, Jean-Jacques. *The Social Contract and Discourses*. Trans. G. D. H. Cole. London: J. M. Dent & Sons, 1973.

Sacksteder, W. "Communal Orders in Spinoza." In *Spinoza's Political and Theological Thought*. Ed. C. De Deugd. Amsterdam: North-Holland, 1984.

"Spinoza on Part and Whole: The Worm's Eye View." *Southwest Journal of Philosphy* II (1980): 25–40.

Seeskin, Kenneth. "Maimonides, Spinoza, and the Problem of Creation." In *Jewish Themes in Spinoza's Philosophy*. Ed. Heidi M. Ravven and Lenn E. Goodman. Albany: State University of New York Press, 2002.

Shahan, Robert and J. I. Biro, eds. *Spinoza: New Perspectives*. Norman: University of Oklahoma Press, 1978.

Shapin, Steven. *A Social History of Truth: Civility and Science in Seventeenth-Century England*. Chicago: University of Chicago Press, 1994.

Siebrand, H. J. *Spinoza and the Netherlanders: An Inquiry into the Early Reception of his Philosophy of Religion*. Assen: Van Gorcum, 1988.

Simon, Richard. *Histoire critique du Vieux Testament* [1678]. Geneva: Slatkin Reprints, 1971.

Skinner, Quentin. "The Idea of Negative Liberty." In *Philosophy and History*. Ed. Richard Rorty, J. B. Schneewind, and Quentin Skinner. Cambridge: Cambridge University Press, 1984.

Smith, Steven B. *Spinoza, Liberalism, and the Question of Jewish Identity*. New Haven, Conn.: Yale University Press, 1997.

Steinmann, Jean, *Richard Simon et les origines de l'exégèse biblique*. Paris: Desclée de Brouwer, 1960.

Strauss, Leo. *Persecution and the Art of Writing*. Chicago: University of Chicago Press, 1952.

Tosel, André. *Spinoza ou le crépuscule de la servitude: Essai sur le* Traité Théologico-Politique. Paris: Aubier Montaigne, 1984.

Twersky, Isadore, ed. *A Maimonides Reader*. West Orange, N.J.: Behrman House, 1972.

Studies in Medieval Jewish History and Literature. 2 vols. Cambridge, Mass.: Harvard University Press, 1979.

Van Bunge, Wiep and Wim Klever, eds. *Disguised and Overt Spinozism Around 1700*. Leiden: E. J. Brill, 1996.

Walther, Manfred. "Spinoza's Critique of Miracles: A Miracle of Criticism?" In *Spinoza: The Enduring Questions*. Ed. Graeme Hunter. Toronto: University of Toronto Press, 1994, 100–112.

Wolfson, Harry Austryn. *The Philosophy of Spinoza*. 2 vols. Cambridge, Mass.: Harvard University Press, 1934.

"The Platonic, Aristotelian, and Stoic Theories of Creation in Halevi and Maimonides." In *Studies in the History of Philosophy and Religion*. Vol. I. Ed. Isadore Twersky and George H. Williams. Cambridge, Mass.: Harvard University Press, 1973.

Yovel, Yirmiyahu. "Bible Interpretation as Philosophical Praxis: A Study of Spinoza and Kant." *Journal of the History of Philosophy* 11 (1973): 189–212.

"Spinoza: The Psychology of the Multitude and the Uses of Language." *Studia Spinozana* 1 (1985): 305–333.

Spinoza and Other Heretics. Vol. I: *The Marrano of Reason*. Vol. II: *The Adventures of Immanence*. Princeton, N.J.: Princeton University Press, 1989.

Yovel, Yirmiyahu, ed. *Spinoza on Knowledge and the Human Mind*. Leiden: E. J. Brill, 1994.

Zac, Sylvain. *L'Idée de vie dans la philosophie de Spinoza*. Paris: Presses Universitaires de France, 1963.

"On the Idea of Creation in Spinoza's Philosophy." In *God and Nature: Spinoza's Metaphysics*. Ed. Yirmiyahu Yovel. Leiden: E. J. Brill, 1991.

Index